THE UNSTOPPABLE HUMAN SPECIES

In *The Unstoppable Human Species*, John J. Shea explains how the earliest humans achieved mastery over all but the most severe, biosphere-level, extinction threats. He explores how and why we humans owe our survival skills to our global geographic range, a diaspora that was achieved during prehistoric times. By developing and integrating a suite of ancestral survival skills, humans overcame survival challenges better than other hominins, and settled in previously unoccupied habitats. But how did they do it? How did early humans endure long enough to become our ancestors? Shea places "how did they survive?" questions front and center in prehistory. Using an explicitly scientific, comparative, and hypothesis-testing approach, *The Unstoppable Human Species* critically examines much "archaeological mythology" about prehistoric humans. Written in clear and engaging language, Shea's volume offers an original and thought-provoking perspective on human evolution. Moving beyond unproductive archaeological debates about prehistoric population movements, *The Unstoppable Human Species* generates new and interesting questions about human evolution.

John J. Shea is Professor of Anthropology at Stony Brook University, New York. He is the author of *Stone Tools in the Paleolithic and Neolithic Near East: A Guide* (Cambridge University Press, 2013), *Stone Tools in Human Evolution: Behavioral Differences among Technological Primates* (Cambridge University Press, 2017), and *Prehistoric Stone Tools of Eastern Africa: A Guide* (Cambridge University Press, 2021). A paleoanthropologist, archaeologist, and experienced practitioner of ancestral survival skills, Shea's demonstrations of stoneworking have appeared in numerous television documentaries and at the United States National Museum of Natural History in Washington, DC.

THE UNSTOPPABLE HUMAN SPECIES

The Emergence of *Homo sapiens* in Prehistory

JOHN J. SHEA

Stony Brook University

CAMBRIDGE UNIVERSITY PRESS

CAMBRIDGE UNIVERSITY PRESS

Shaftesbury Road, Cambridge CB2 8EA, United Kingdom

One Liberty Plaza, 20th Floor, New York, NY 10006, USA

477 Williamstown Road, Port Melbourne, VIC 3207, Australia

314–321, 3rd Floor, Plot 3, Splendor Forum, Jasola District Centre, New Delhi – 110025, India

103 Penang Road, #05–06/07, Visioncrest Commercial, Singapore 238467

Cambridge University Press is part of Cambridge University Press & Assessment, a department of the University of Cambridge.

We share the University's mission to contribute to society through the pursuit of education, learning and research at the highest international levels of excellence.

www.cambridge.org
Information on this title: www.cambridge.org/9781108429085

DOI: 10.1017/9781108554060

© Cambridge University Press & Assessment 2023

This publication is in copyright. Subject to statutory exception and to the provisions of relevant collective licensing agreements, no reproduction of any part may take place without the written permission of Cambridge University Press & Assessment.

First published 2023

A catalogue record for this publication is available from the British Library.

Library of Congress Cataloging-in-Publication Data
NAMES: Shea, John J. (John Joseph), author.
TITLE: The unstoppable human species : the emergence of homo sapiens in prehistory / John J. Shea.
DESCRIPTION: Cambridge, United Kingdom ; New York, NY : Cambridge University Press, 2023. | Includes bibliographical references and index.
IDENTIFIERS: LCCN 2022050766 (print) | LCCN 2022050767 (ebook) | ISBN 9781108429085 (hardback) | ISBN 9781108452984 (paperback) | ISBN 9781108554060 (epub)
SUBJECTS: LCSH: Human beings–Origin. | Human evolution. | Prehistoric peoples. | Survival.
CLASSIFICATION: LCC GN281 .S424 2023 (print) | LCC GN281 (ebook) | DDC 599.93/8–dc23/eng/20221208
LC record available at https://lccn.loc.gov/2022050766
LC ebook record available at https://lccn.loc.gov/2022050767

ISBN 978-1-108-42908-5 Hardback
ISBN 978-1-108-45298-4 Paperback

Cambridge University Press & Assessment has no responsibility for the persistence or accuracy of URLs for external or third-party internet websites referred to in this publication and does not guarantee that any content on such websites is, or will remain, accurate or appropriate.

For Ofer Bar-Yosef (1937–2020)

CONTENTS

List of Figures	*page* x
List of Tables	xii
List of Boxes	xiii
Preface	xv
Acknowledgments	xviii

1 Introduction 1
    An Unstoppable Species?   1
    Population Movements   5
    Questions about Human Evolution: Who, How, and Why   8
    Explaining the Past   14
    How This Book Is Organized   16

2 Hard Evidence 22
    Time: Geochronology   22
    Fossils: Paleontology and Zooarchaeology   31
    Artifacts: Archaeology   35
    Genes: Molecular Anthropology   46
    Summary   48

3 Who Are These People? 50
    Humans as Primates   50
    How Do Humans Differ from Other Animals?   52
    How Do Humans Differ from One Another?   55
    Summary   62

4 How Did They Get Here? 64
    Arrows on Maps   64
    Survival Archaeology   66
    The Big Six Survival Challenges   71
    Ancestral Survival Skills   74
    An Integrative Ancestral Survival Skills Hypothesis   80

	Reasonable Assumptions?	82
	Summary	85
5	**Ancient Africans**	87
	Geography: The "Four Africas"	87
	Important Ancient African Paleoanthropological Sites	90
	Ancient African Hominin Fossils	92
	Ancient African Archaeology	96
	Ancient Africans' Survival Strategies	100
	Interpretive Issues about Ancient Africans	105
	Summary	112
6	**Going East: First Asians**	116
	Geography: The Levant, Arabia, and India	116
	Important First Asian Paleoanthropological Sites	119
	First Asian Hominin Fossils	119
	First Asian Archaeology	122
	First Asians' Survival Strategies	124
	Interpretive Issues about First Asians	127
	Summary	132
7	**Down Under: Early Southeast Asians and Sahulians**	137
	Geography: Sunda, Sahul, and Wallacea	137
	Important Southeast Asian and Sahulian Paleoanthropological Sites	139
	Southeast Asian and Sahulian Hominin Fossils	140
	Pleistocene Archaeology of Southeast Asia and Sahul	142
	Southeast Asians' and Sahulians' Survival Strategies	144
	Interpretive Issues about Southeast Asians and Sahulians	148
	Summary	152
8	**Neanderthal Country**	155
	Geography: Northwestern Eurasia before 45 Ka	155
	Important Neanderthal Paleoanthropological Sites	158
	Neanderthal Fossils	158
	Neanderthal Archaeology	161
	Neanderthals' Survival Strategies	166
	Interpretive Issues about Neanderthals	171
	Summary	176
9	**Going North: Early Eurasians**	180
	Geography: Northern Eurasia after 45 Ka	180
	Important Early Eurasian Paleoanthropological Sites	183
	Early Eurasian Fossils	183
	Early Eurasian Archaeology	187
	Early Eurasians' Survival Strategies	192
	Interpretive Issues about Early Eurasians	199
	Summary	203

10 A Brave New World: Pleistocene Americans 207
  Geography: Pleistocene Beringia and the Americas 207
  Important Pleistocene American Sites 211
  Pleistocene American Fossils 215
  Pleistocene American Archaeology 216
  Pleistocene Americans' Survival Strategies 219
  Interpretive Issues about Pleistocene Americans 222
  Summary 228

11 Movable Feasts: Food Producers and Migrations 230
  Food Production 230
  A Survival Archaeology Perspective on Food Production 239
  Detecting Food Production 242
  Migrations by Food Producers 244
  Detecting Migrations by Food Producers 246
  Migrations by Hunter-Gatherers 253
  Summary 253

12 Distant Horizons and Stars Beckon: Oceanic Islands and Beyond 256
  Oceanic Migrations 256
  Pacific Ocean Migrations: The Road of the Winds 259
  Pacific Ocean Migrations: A Survival Archaeology Perspective 267
  Future Human Migrations: The Road of the Stars 269
  Summary 273

13. Unstoppable? Human Extinction 276
  Unlikely Extinction Threats 276
  Likely Extinction Threats 283
  Pseudo-Extinction? 286

14. Conclusion 290
  How Did They Do It? 290
  Differences between Early Humans and Living Humans 296
  Why Us? 297
  What Must We Do? 299

Appendix A: Traditional Archaeological Age-Stages 303
Appendix B: Survival Archaeology Recommended Readings 305
Appendix C: Further Reading 307
Glossary 311
Bibliography 320
Index 337

FIGURES

1.1	Where apes live	page 2
1.2	Human population movements	6
2.1	Marine oxygen-isotope record of temperature variation since 300,000 years ago	28
2.2	Basic stone tool categories	37
2.3	Major stone artifact-types discussed in the text	38
2.4	Major stone artifact-types discussed in the text (continued)	39
2.5	Ceramic plates, bowls, jars, and jugs	44
5.1	The "four Africas"	88
5.2	Map of Africa showing sites discussed in the text	93
5.3	*Homo heidelbergensis* versus *H. sapiens* skulls compared	95
5.4	Artifacts associated with *Homo heidelbergensis*	97
5.5	Artifacts associated with Ancient Africans	98
6.1	Map of Southern Asia showing sites discussed in the text	117
6.2	Artifacts associated with First Asians	122
6.3	Nubian cores and microliths	130
7.1	Map of Sunda, Wallacea, and Sahul showing locations of important sites	138
7.2	Artifacts associated with early Sahulians	143
8.1	Map showing important Neanderthal sites	156
8.2	Neanderthal and Early Eurasian human skulls compared	160
8.3	Neanderthal stone tools	163
9.1	Map of Europe showing Early Eurasian sites	181
9.2	Map of Northern Eurasia showing Early Eurasian sites	181
9.3	Early Eurasian and recent human skulls	186
9.4	Early Eurasian stone tools and other artifacts	188
9.5	Early Eurasian "Venus" figurines	198
10.1	Important Beringian and Pleistocene American fossil sites	208
10.2	Important Pre-Clovis and "Clovis" Pleistocene American sites	209
10.3	Later Pleistocene and early Holocene American artifacts	217
11.1	Hot spots for the origins of food production	235
11.2	Map showing distribution of Bantu languages	249

List of Figures

11.3 Urëwe pottery	250
11.4 Map showing hypothetical Bantu expansion routes in sub-Saharan Africa	251
12.1 Map showing major human population movements to Pacific Ocean islands	261
12.2 Lapita ceramic vessels	264
12.3 Innovations associated with Pacific Oceanic island voyaging	269
12.4 Traditional Marshall Islander navigation chart	270
13.1 Human population growth models	279
13.2 Atmospheric and lithospheric extinction threats	284

TABLES

1.1	Dispersals, migrations, and transhumance	page 7
1.2	Anthropogenic narratives and hero's journey narratives	15
2.1	Radiometric dating techniques compared	24
2.2	Geological time periods	27
2.3	Major diaspora-related events during Marine Isotopic Stages (MIS) 1–7	30
2.4	First appearance dates for important lithic artifact-types	42
4.1	Strengths and weaknesses among sources of hypotheses for survival archaeology	68
4.2	First appearance dates for ancestral survival skills	74
5.1	Important African paleoanthropological sites	91
6.1	Important Southern Asian paleoanthropological sites	120
6.2	Cultural stratigraphy of the Valley of the Caves	133
7.1	Important Southeast Asian and Australasian paleoanthropological sites	140
8.1	Important Neanderthal paleoanthropological sites	159
8.2	Behavioral differences between Neanderthals and early humans	172
9.1	Important Early Eurasian paleoanthropological sites	184
10.1	Important Pleistocene American sites	212
10.2	Pleistocene American versus Sahulian large terrestrial carnivores arranged by greatest adult mass	228
11.1	Domesticated plants and animals from food production hot spots	234
12.1	First appearance dates for human activity on Pacific Ocean islands	262
13.1	Mass extinctions and extraterrestrial impacts	285
14.1	Differences between early and living *Homo sapiens*	296
A.1	Archaeological age-stages (based on Eurasian and African evidence)	303

BOXES

1.1	Human morphological and behavioral modernity: Their discontents	page 18
2.1	Teleoliths, Child's play	48
3.1	What's in a name? Hominin alpha taxonomy	62
4.1	Prehistory's "Atlantis problem"	85
5.1	Boats, bows, and beads	113
6.1	The rise and fall of Mount Carmel Man	132
7.1	Ghost marriages: Fossils and stone tool industries	152
8.1	Imagining Neanderthals	177
9.1	The mystery of Mediterranean Europe	204
11.1	The need for speed: How fast and far can people migrate?	254
12.1	Peopling the Arctic	274

PREFACE

This book began with a college course I taught that at first I enjoyed, grew to despise, and finally learned to love again. That course, "The Archaeology of Human Dispersal," reconstructed humanity's wanderings over "deep-time" prehistory by pulling together fossil, archaeological, and genetic evidence. Teaching about fossils and archaeology posed few difficulties, for I know both subjects well. Also, frankly, the "hard evidence" does not really change all that much from year to year. As fortune would have it, though, I began offering this class just as advances in studies of both modern and ancient DNA exploded onto the paleoanthropological scene. This created a problem.

One welcomes new evidence that can settle long-standing debates about human evolution, as genetic evidence manifestly can, but it proved difficult to accommodate this evidence. Claims of "game-changing" genetic studies overturning all previous knowledge seemed to appear every week. Competing claims contradicted one another over laboratory procedures or interpretive issues, matters all but impenetrable to non-geneticists. My Internet-savvy students arrived in class armed with the latest claims from "press-release science." I tried to assimilate these findings and to answer students' questions about them, but by semester's end my lecture notes were full of cross-outs, updates, and updates on updates about, well frankly, who had sexual intercourse with whom during the Ice Age. The class had changed from one I loved to one I loathed.

Still, I did not want to stop teaching the course. Prehistoric population movements show humanity at its best: setting forth, surviving by our wits, and never, ever quitting. Our prehistoric past offers up an optimistic vision for our future, one I think the wider public and especially younger people need to understand. Reflecting, I realized I had spent too much time on "who questions" and not enough time on "how questions." "Who questions" ask about identity: Who were these people? Who moved from this place to that place? Who interbred with whom? Archaeologists struggle with "who questions," but they are molecular anthropologists' bread and butter. Your genes have ancestors, but fossils do not necessarily have descendants. "How questions" ask about activities. How did people get from one place to another? How did they overcome that challenge? How did they survive long enough to become our ancestors? Genetics brings little to the table about "how questions." There are no genes for kindling fire, for finding or making potable water, or for making clothing and constructing shelter. We endure because our ancestors did these things. Our genes are but passengers, not pilots.

A lifelong interest in bushcraft and "primitive" (ancestral) technology positioned me well to answer such "how questions." Long before I thought to become a paleoanthropologist, I nurtured an interest in primitive technology. Growing up in rural New England in what seemed endless tracts of woods and fields encouraged an early interest in bushcraft ("Native American lore," as the Boy Scouts put it). I discovered stoneworking and expanded my expertise to other ancestral skills, such as making fire, cordage, and mastics (glues). Teaching college classes, I recounted bushcraft experiences to enliven my lectures about human evolution and prehistoric archaeology. My students enjoyed these digressions, for they had a practical side to them. When I talked about how prehistoric humans avoided hypothermia (freezing to death) or other hazards, they asked me what gear they should keep in their cars during long winter commutes. When I lectured about "curated personal gear," we compared the things commuters versus residential students carried daily. (We found that commuters carried more and heavier things to class than their dorm-dwelling classmates.)

In overhauling "The Archaeology of Human Dispersal," I cut all but the minimum necessary discussion about "who questions," replacing it with discussions about "how questions." I also excised much of what archaeologists had written in service of answering "who questions," such as named prehistoric cultures and stone tool industries. Doing this conserved class time for the things which the students actually wanted to learn about and things which I wanted to teach them. How many different kinds of "Mousterian" industries occurred in southern France? Nobody cares. How to not freeze or starve to death? Everybody cares.

When I resumed teaching the course, renamed "The Unstoppable Species," discussions became livelier, and enrollments increased. (I deeply regretted that I had not made these changes earlier.) Any good undergraduate course can also be turned into a good book. This work covers the basics, the fundamental assumptions paleoanthropologists make in reconstructing the past. One does not need prior knowledge of anthropology or archaeology to read, understand, and, one hopes, enjoy *The Unstoppable Species*.

Finally, a note about citations. When the book lists "important paleoanthropological sites," it does not cite references for individual sites. Instead, it directs readers to paleoanthropological and archaeological syntheses in books or scientific journals. I have done this for several reasons. First, few of these "important sites" enjoy monographic publication, that is, a single book, special issue of a journal, or a long stand-alone paper synthesizing researchers' findings. Second, many remain the subjects of active research projects whose findings appear in multiple journal papers spread out over many years. Third, "authorship bloat" (listing as so-called authors technicians and others who have not written a word) takes up space better devoted to arguments about the evidence. Citing even a fraction of these references would unnecessarily lengthen the book's bibliography at the expense of the main text, and the "snapshot" of research in early 2022 would accelerate this book's inevitable slide toward being outdated. Nearly every important paleoanthropological site listed in this book (and many more not listed) boasts a frequently updated Internet webpage devoted to it listing relevant publications. Interested readers can find these webpages and the most up-to-date information about these sites with a couple of keystrokes and mouse clicks. One recognizes this citation strategy as unusual, but it is practical. You're welcome.

ACKNOWLEDGMENTS

I thank my wife, Patricia L. Crawford, for her forbearance during the long hours I spent writing this book in the "professorial man-caves" in Stony Brook, New York, and in Santa Fe, New Mexico. I thank Cody Lundin, Mark Dorsten, and the staff of the Aboriginal Living Skills School in Prescott, Arizona, for insights gained from their classes. I thank Beatrice Rehl of Cambridge University Press for encouraging me to develop "The Unstoppable Species" course into this book. I am grateful to the anonymous reviewers of the book proposal and of the book's final version. I thank Stephanie Sakson for her skilled copyediting. For generously allowing me to use artwork from their published works, I thank Daniel Lieberman and Christophe Sande. I drafted Figures 9.1, 9.2, 10.1, 10.2, 11.1, and 12.1 using templates from Free Vector Maps (http://freevectormaps.com). Above all, I thank my "Unstoppables," Stony Brook University students who attended my course ANT 273, "The Unstoppable Species," between 2020 and 2022. Always work as hard as you can and never quit.

CHAPTER 1

INTRODUCTION

AN UNSTOPPABLE SPECIES?

We are Earth's unstoppable species. Today humans live in a global diaspora within which we move about with ease. At just over 8 billion individuals, we outnumber all other primates combined. If some disaster depopulated an entire continent, enough humans would survive elsewhere to eventually repopulate that "lost continent." As long as the biosphere persists, so do we. Our global diaspora confers on us an "extinction immunity" without evolutionary precedent among creatures larger than microorganisms. Our extinction immunity contrasts starkly with that of other primates, past and present. The African apes (gorillas, chimpanzees, and bonobos), our nearest primate relatives, inhabit a narrow range of tropical habitats (Figure 1.1). Surrounded by skyrocketing human populations, extinction stalks apes as their own shadows do. Humans (*Homo sapiens*) are the opposite of endangered. For apes and countless other species, we are the danger.

Why us? Might trilobites, cephalopods, and other creatures whose remains crowd sediments from Earth's earliest ages have thought themselves unstoppable? We will never know. We, alone, among all life in Earth's history, can actually answer the challenge with which Carolus Linnaeus (1707–1778) defined *Homo sapiens*: "*Homo, nosce te ipsum*" (Latin for "Man, know yourself"). Why humans, rather than any other animal, became the unstoppable species is anthropology's ultimate and most consequential "big question," for how we choose to answer it and what we do with that answer will affect humanity's long-term survival.

What Is This Book About?

Asserting that our unstoppability results from our diaspora, this book explains how we achieved that diaspora. *The Unstoppable Human Species* describes *Homo sapiens*' origin and global dispersal after 300,000 years ago. It chronicles how

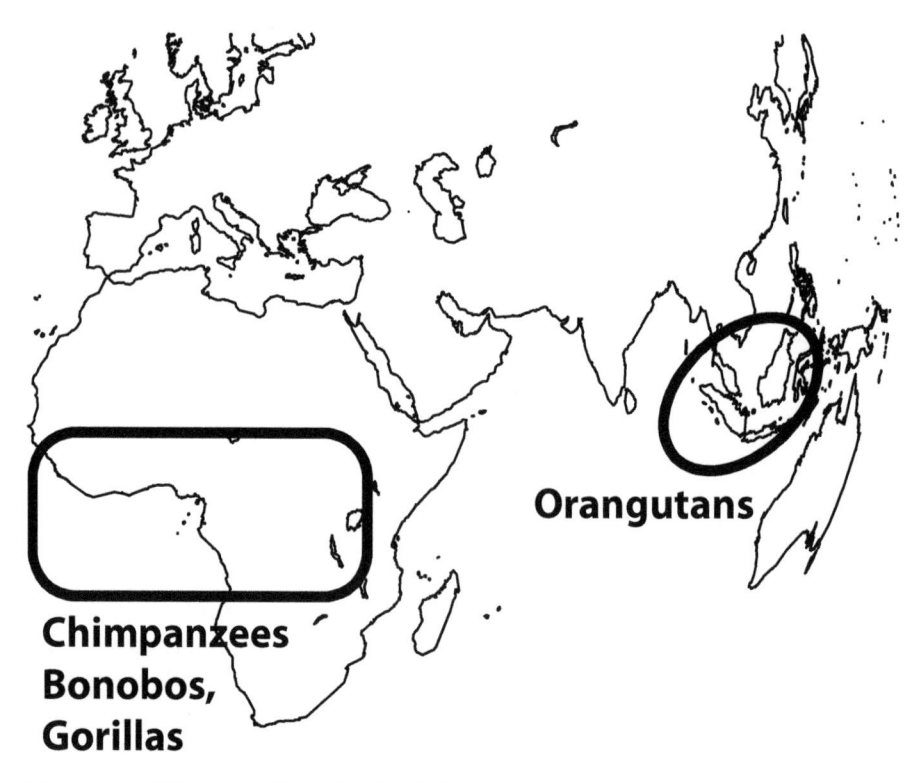

Figure 1.1 Where apes live. © John J. Shea.

mobile hunter-gatherers ("bows, boats, and beads" people) became sedentary food producers ("houses, herds, and hoes" people). Along the way, *The Unstoppable Human Species* overturns several long-standing conventions in archaeological research about prehistory.

First, this work challenges archaeology's use of migration as an explanation for past human population movements. For more than a century, archaeologists have sought and failed to find evidence for migrations in "deep-time prehistory" (before 10,000 years ago)(Clark 1994). Migration enjoys a recent renaissance, as archaeologists increasingly seek to correlate their findings with those from historical genetics and molecular anthropology (Lewis-Kraus 2019). One thinks this interdisciplinary flirtation misguided. Migrations require storable and transportable food surpluses of the sort that plant and animal husbandry (agriculture and pastoralism) or their functional equivalents create. Most if not all evidence for such "food production" dates to less than 10,000 years ago, long after humans settled most of the world except Antarctica and the most remote oceanic islands.

Second, *The Unstoppable Human Species* challenges archaeologists' long-standing obsession with questions about prehistoric humans' social identities – with who moved where and when and with who mated with whom.

Molecular anthropologists reserve special enthusiasm for such questions because they can provide conclusive answers in ways that traditional archaeological approaches cannot (Higham 2021). This work views these so-called hypotheses about such identities linking genes to fossils and fossils to archaeological remains as the unfalsifiable arguments they really are. We cannot call them hypotheses, because we cannot prove them wrong using evidence. Much like Medieval theologians' debates about how many angels could stand on the head of pin, they distract us from actual hypotheses, arguments that evidence can prove wrong. This work focuses on questions about prehistoric human behavior, on what our ancestors did. We are not the unstoppable species because of who our ancestors were. We are the unstoppable species because they solved survival challenges differently from other hominins (bipedal primates) that are now extinct.

Third, this work focuses on *Homo sapiens* and to a lesser degree on our immediate ancestor, *Homo heidelbergensis*, and on the Neanderthals (*Homo neanderthalensis*) with whom early humans were rough contemporaries. While there are certainly merits to placing *Homo sapiens*' origins and diaspora in the larger narrative of primate and hominin evolution (Stringer 2012; Gamble 2013; Hoffecker 2017), doing so requires one to sacrifice details about post-Pleistocene human migrations, migrations that shaped our world today, as well as to curtail discussions about extinction threats and what prehistory can tell us about humanity's future – the very things students and others so often ask paleoanthropologists about! Why else study the remote past than in search of lessons for our remote future?

Finally, *The Unstoppable Human Species* challenges archaeologists' conviction that we owe our evolutionary success to some specific quality that evolved since *Homo sapiens* fossils first appear in the fossil record around 200,000–300,000 years ago. Many recent works on this subject emphasize evolutionary changes in cognition, overlooking the difficulties in measuring cognitive differences among living humans, much less among extinct ones. Others attribute our success to "modernity," a metaphor pulling together a wide range of activities only tangentially connected to one another. *The Unstoppable Human Species* argues that we owe our evolved unstoppability to an integrated suite of "ancestral survival skills." These skills include powerful precision grasping, endurance bipedalism, predictive hallucination, spoken language, and hyper-prosociality. Other hominins possessed these ancestral survival skills, too, but our ancestors used them differently and better than other hominins did.

Why Is This Subject Important?

The Earth is by no means full, but we can no longer move away from our problems, as ancestral humans did. Nowadays, when rising waters flood coastal communities and drown towns located on floodplains, when fires burn rural communities to ashes, and when wars and earthquakes reduce cities to rubble, people rebuild in the same places. Strategies for a sustainable future? One thinks not. Calling *Homo sapiens* "unstoppable" expresses not a fact but a "hopepothesis" (a hypothesis one hopes is true but one cannot prove wrong). Future environmental and planetary catastrophes will put us in their crosshairs, too. The overwhelming majority of climate science suggests our current global heating trend will continue into the near future, afflicting us with increasingly severe storms, droughts, wildfires, crop failures, mass extinctions, epidemics, and pandemics (Bostrum and Cirkovic 2011). How will we overcome such challenges? Learning how early humans overcame past difficulties will enlighten, inspire, and guide us and our descendants about how to anticipate and overcome whatever difficulties the future throws at us, for difficulties it will assuredly throw. Like those ancestors, we must never, ever quit. As Antarctic explorer Sir Ernest Shackleton (1874–1922), put it, "Difficulties are just things to overcome, after all."

For Whom Is This Book Intended?

I wrote *The Unstoppable Human Species* mainly for college students and others interested in human evolution. This work seeks a larger audience and brings to the table different perspectives on prehistory than one finds in recent works professional anthropologists have written for other professional anthropologists (e.g., Bellwood 2013; Gamble 2013; Hoffecker 2017). I hope my colleagues and graduate students will enjoy *The Unstoppable Human Species* and find it thought-provoking. To aid nonprofessional readers, the book reviews basic terms and concepts in paleoanthropology (scientific research about human origins and evolution) and includes a Glossary at the back of the book. Professional paleoanthropologists may find these reviews unnecessary, even tedious, but one would rather inflict tedium on them than leave the greater number of other readers behind.

One also hopes colleagues in molecular anthropology will read this book. All too often, hypotheses about human evolution based on genetics simply use the archaeological record as "window dressing." That is, they assert evolutionary relationships among extinct humans and then rummage about for archaeological evidence that supports their claims about those relationships. Confirmation bias is a powerful thing: it encourages one to accept facts that agree with one's previously held beliefs and to ignore facts that do not. Archaeologists' views about prehistoric human population relationships vary so widely that, properly motivated, any molecular anthropologist can find an archaeologist or paleontologist whose previously published views on any issue support theirs.

How Does This Book Differ from Others?

One rarely sees the words "practical" and "archaeology" in the same sentence, but this is a work of practical archaeology. Other recent works about prehistoric human population movements concern themselves with prehistory, with who moved where and when. This work tacks differently. It focuses on how our ancestors survived long enough to become our ancestors. To do this, it delves into sources of hypotheses that other works largely neglect, namely the literature of bushcraft and wilderness survival. These two sources intersect in complex ways, but they share a core concern: how to not die before one's time in the great outdoors. We know little for certain about what early humans and other hominins did, but we can be confident that those who became our ancestors did not do the things bushcraft and wilderness survival works warn against doing.

POPULATION MOVEMENTS

Historically, humans cope with rapid climate change or other adverse circumstances either by intensification (working harder to remain in place) or by residential movement ("voting with your feet"). Political debates about modern-day population movements, as well as many scholarly works, often conflate migration, transhumance, and dispersal (Bellwood 2013; Shah 2020). Migrations, transhumance, and dispersals differ from one another (Figure 1.2 and Table 1.1).

Dispersal

In a dispersal, individuals or small numbers of people move over short distances. Small numbers allow them to feed as they go and to assimilate as they wish to or as necessary in their destinations. As a result, dispersing humans can rapidly change their culture, their social relations, and their archaeological "footprint" at their destinations. For example, the author's father's ancestors relocated from Ireland to Massachusetts, individually, decades apart, and from different parts of Ireland. On arrival, and as swiftly as they could, all became American citizens. They were dispersing. None of their descendants speaks Gaelic or self-identifies as Irish American, much less as Irish.

Migration

In a migration, large numbers of people (hundreds or more) move together over long distances (hundreds of kilometers). Because they carry food stored in bulk with them, they need not assimilate into other groups through whose

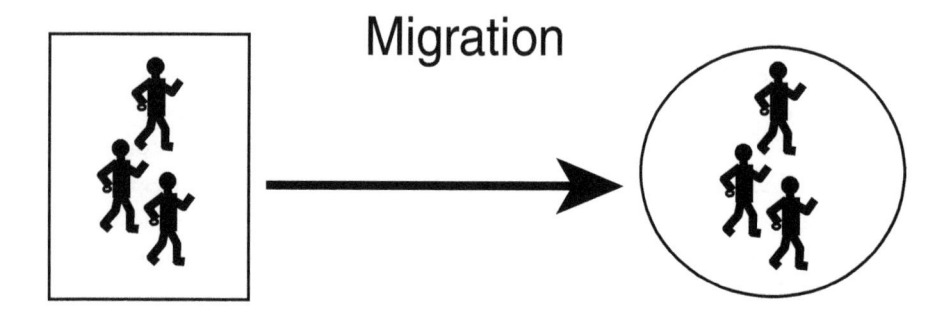

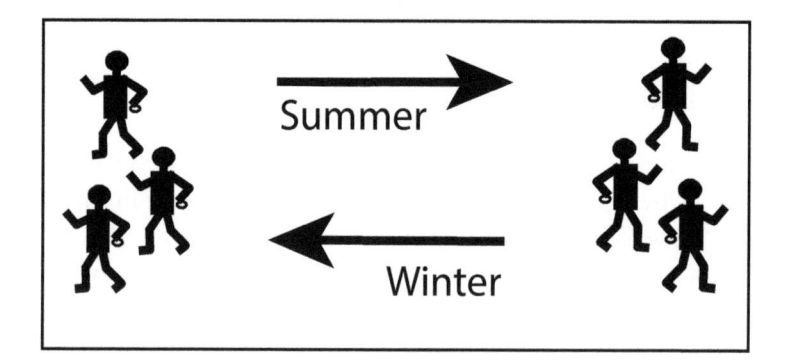

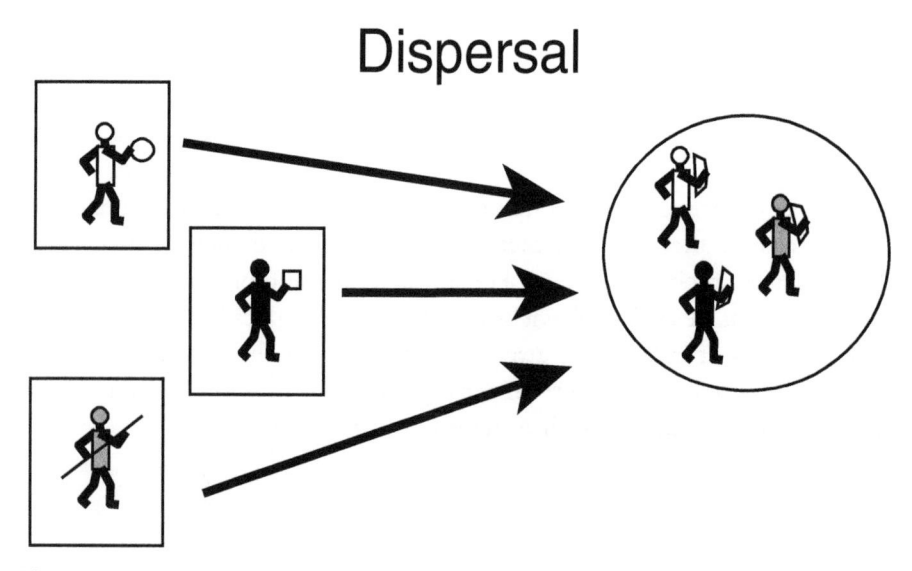

Figure 1.2 Human population movements: Migration, transhumance, dispersal. © John J. Shea.

TABLE 1.1 *Dispersals, migrations, and transhumance*

	Dispersals	Migrations	Transhumance
Who moves?	Individuals or small groups (low dozens or fewer)	Large groups (hundreds or more)	Variable
How far?	Tens of kilometers	Hundreds of kilometers	Tens of kilometers
Food sources?	Feed as you go	Stored in bulk and transported	Gathered in bulk at source and destination
Social relations?	Reconfigured in destinations	Remain intact	Remain intact
Archaeological signature?	Difficult to recognize due to rapid changes over time and distance	Recognizably the same or similar for long periods and over great distances	Varies depending on activities

territories they pass. For a time, migrating groups retain their culture and social relations at their destinations. Migrations leave a detectable archaeological "signature," of artifacts, food waste, and other things that remain recognizably the same or at least similar over vast distances and long time periods. For example, during the 17th century the author's maternal ancestors moved en masse from Brittany in northwestern France, to what is now Nova Scotia in Canada. They migrated. To this day, their descendants in northernmost Maine still speak French and self-identify as "Acadian" to distinguish themselves from their French-speaking Québécois neighbors in Canada and English-speaking American neighbors.

Migrations conjure up drama and conflict far more so than dispersal. Calling something a migration versus an invasion, after all, is a matter of perspective. European Americans' migrations were for Native Americans an invasion. Unsurprisingly, migrations command more popular attention than dispersals. Migrations figure more prominently in works written about prehistory for similar reasons (drama), but using them in prehistory has led to an imbalance in the sorts of questions paleoanthropologists ask about deep-time prehistory.

Transhumance

Transhumance describes cyclical and temporary shifts of habitation sites within a larger geographic range, such as between winter and summer camps or highland or lowland residences. Either the entire community moves or some specific subset of that larger group does. Pastoralists often practice transhumance so that their livestock can take advantage of plant foods that become available in different places at different times. Ethnographic and historic hunter-gatherers often did this to take advantage of migrating fish, such as salmon, or large mammals, such as reindeer. If the activities carried out at seasonal sites differed widely, then archaeologists could have trouble telling whether they were seeing the remains of the same group or different groups (Thomson 1939).

Mixed Dispersals and Migrations

Dispersals and migrations are not mutually exclusive of one another, but rather end points on a continuum. Both can occur simultaneously. The 17th-century English Pilgrims who settled Plymouth, Massachusetts (formerly Wampanoag Patuxet), included both members of a dissident Protestant religious sect as well as individual nonmembers ("strangers") traveling to the New World to seek their fortunes there (Bradford and Morrison 1651 (1952)). Therefore, in thinking about prehistoric human population movements, this work does not argue whether a particular prehistoric or historic population movement was either wholly a dispersal or a migration (a categorical distinction). Instead, it evaluates whether the evidence for the movements in question more closely matches our expectations about migrations versus dispersals.

QUESTIONS ABOUT HUMAN EVOLUTION: WHO, HOW, AND WHY

As innovations in 16th- to 18th-century maritime technology brought European explorers to ever more distant lands, different groups of people gazed at one another across beaches and rivers asking, "Who are these people, and how did they get here?" Anthropology developed out of European explorers' and scholars' efforts to find scientific answers to this question (Wolf 1982; Kuper 1988). But the question actually asks two very different things. "Who questions" ask about prehistoric humans' identities, their relationships to one another and to us. "How questions" ask about prehistoric humans' activities and how they solved problems.

"Who Questions"

Scientists recognized "prehistory," the time before written records, during the late 18th to early 19th centuries (Daniel and Renfrew 1988). Seeking scientific answers to historical linguists' and historians' questions about the origins of living human groups, 19th- and early 20th-century paleoanthropologists thought and wrote about prehistoric human population movements as migrations, and as a result, they devoted vastly more effort to answering "who questions" than "how questions." From the mid-19th century onward, archaeologists and other scholars populated deep-time prehistory with "cultures," "races," and stone tool "industries" and more recent prehistoric periods with groups defined in terms of variation among ceramic artifacts. Twentieth-century prehistorians treated these cultures, races, and industries as the equivalents of ethnographic (living human) cultures and races, and they wrote many journal papers and books speculating about their origins, migrations, mutual influences, and historical relations to living humans (Sackett 1991). Historians of archaeology call this approach to prehistory "culture history." Some archaeologists recognized such "prehistory" was not quite history, as historians understood their field, nor quite science as scientists understood theirs, but these remained minority positions (Taylor 1948; Binford 1962).

Signs of trouble with this culture-history approach appeared during the 1960s. By that point, race was on its way out as a serious research focus in evolutionary biology (Wolpoff and Caspari 1997). Radiocarbon and other geophysical dating methods demonstrated that many archaeological industries and cultures lasted far longer and exhibited far less variation than any historical human culture. A "culture" that lasts 100,000 years or more essentially unchanged is the *opposite* of culture as anthropologists define the term (Kroeber and Kluckhohn 1952). Second, archaeologists found traces of the same cultures spread out over entire continents (Bordes 1968), far more widely than any preindustrial ethnographic culture (Clark and Riel-Salvatore 2006). Finally, 20th-century cultural anthropologists showed that living humans maintain complex and multilayered social identities that we easily change as the need to do so arises (Boas 1940). Archaeologists' use of the culture concept denied these complex social identities to prehistoric *Homo sapiens* and to other hominins.

Today, the notion that one can meaningfully divide prehistoric human societies into anything like actual human cultures seems no more plausible than dividing living humans into named, meaningfully different groups based on the kinds of pens and pencils in their trash cans (Shea 2014). Culture-historical approaches to "who questions" equated trivial differences among stone tools and other evidence with evolutionarily important differences among prehistoric people.

Archaeologists' efforts to solve these problems with culture-history largely break up archaeological cultures into component parts. One currently popular approach focuses on reconstructing "operational chains,"[1] different strategies for making pottery, houses, or stone tools (or for doing anything, really), and archaeologists' reconstructions of those strategies. Patterned variation in the occurrences of different operational chains in the archaeological record then guide archaeologists in identifying prehistoric "communities of practice," conjectural groups of prehistoric people who did things the same way. The

---

[1] From the French *chaînes opératoires*.

procedures for recognizing communities of practice differ from those earlier archaeologists used for identifying prehistoric cultures, but the results are fundamentally the same: named groups of prehistoric humans defined in terms of the artifacts. Old wine in new bottles.

Contemporary "genetic history" perspectives on prehistory people the past with named "haplogroups" (DNA samples with similar and distinctive combinations of genes). Some such works treat haplogroups as specific human populations (Sykes 2001; Oppenheimer 2004; Wells 2009). And yet analyses of ancient DNA provide no support whatsoever for the notion that genetically "pure" haplogroups ever existed (Reich 2018). There were no "Haplogroup M people," merely human populations among whom some had Haplogroup M's distinctive genetic signature.

(The recent advent of "personal genetics" offers up a brand-new horror show of answers to "who questions." These tests promise to identify the percentage of different named "ethnicities" that make up one's genetic heritage. The ethnicities in question range from entire regions (sub-Saharan Africa), nations no more than a few centuries old (Germany), religious groups (Ashkenazi Jews), and so on. All these tests actually do is identify where in the world people live whose DNA most resembles yours. DNA-based claims of membership in one or another named human ethnic or national group are not the same things as 19th-century ethnology's "pure races," but they don't differ from them all that much either.[2])

A second sort of error occurs when "molecular" answers to "who questions" equate the inferred dates of divergences among haplogroups with momentous events in human evolution. Whatever events led to the Haplogroup L-M split 70,000 years ago could have been something that ancestral humans discussed around their campfires for centuries afterward. Alternatively, one person or family might have moved across a river because somebody else snored too loudly or failed to share food adequately. When paleoanthropologists equate haplogroup/gene histories with population histories, they make precisely the same mistake culture-historical archaeologists made, namely, equating potentially trivial differences among their observations with evolutionarily important differences among prehistoric people. Scientists

---

[2] Colleagues and students have encouraged me to take a "personal genetics" test to learn what if any percentage of Neanderthal DNA lurks in my genome. I have not done so and never will. After all, finding such Neanderthal DNA would not (and should not) change what I think about myself or (I hope) what my colleagues think about me. A DNA test would almost certainly trace "genetic heritage" back to the early humans who lived in Africa. Would that make me African? Suppose such a test revealed a trace of Native American ancestry. Should I start wearing "leathers and feathers" to work at the university? Some might do so, but I would not. No federally recognized Native American tribe or nation accepts DNA tests as evidence of membership. More importantly, I value the respect that my actual Native American students and colleagues have for me. Tellingly, no personal genetics test could reveal my actual American ethnicity.

call this error "assuming the consequent," or accepting hypotheses they ought to be trying to prove wrong.

If one thinks about it, proving paleoanthropologists' answers to "who questions" wrong would require interviewing and observing extinct humans. A device of the sort H. G. Wells envisioned in his 1888 novel, *The Time Machine*, would solve this problem (and put most archaeologists out of work), but our current understanding of physics holds such backward-and-forward time travel impossible. Prehistoric humans' social identities might have been less complex, less variable, and more tightly tethered to variation in their artifact designs than recent humans' social identities are, but neither anthropological nor evolutionary theory supports this assumption to the exclusion of competing hypotheses (i.e., that they were not). That none of the world's 8 billion humans lives in a society with innate (biologically based) "cultural conservatism" suggests such "cultures" are evolutionary non sequiturs. They do not exist either because they are structurally impossible or because past peoples whose cultures lacked such innate cultural conservatism replaced them.

None of the foregoing should be read as either condemning or disparaging research on "who questions." "Who questions" are important ones, and they deserve scientifically valid answers. However, answering "who questions" turns out to be a lot more complicated and difficult than the scientists engaged in this research and the general public who pays for it appreciate.

"How Questions"

Early archaeologists tried to answer "how questions," but they worked with limited resources. Like their counterparts today, most early archaeologists lived in urban centers of industrial states far away from where nonindustrialized peoples still hunted, gathered, fished, and made stone tools in ways that were plausibly analogous to how prehistoric humans did. A few early anthropologists conducted experiments making and using stone tools and other "primitive" (ancestral) technology, and a tradition of "experimental archaeology" persists (Leakey 1954; Schick and Toth 1993; Eren et al. 2016). Still, even today, few prehistoric archaeologists hunt, much less hunt and gather. Other early archaeologists relied on cultural anthropologists' and others' notes about preindustrial activities in remote parts of Africa, Asia, Australia, and the Americas. At the time anthropologists observed them, however, many of these preindustrial societies were becoming increasingly assimilated into global industrial economies.[3]

---

[3] Also, at the time, cultural anthropologists were more interested in ethnographic humans' kinship systems, social customs, and supernatural beliefs, things they thought guided "primitive" humans' behavior, than they were about their economic activities and material culture (artifacts).

Accounts of ethnographic humans' ecology, technology, subsistence, and settlement patterns often lacked the sorts of details archaeologists needed to develop hypotheses about prehistoric human activities. Recognizing these gaps in the ethnographic record, from the 1970s onward, archaeologists developed "ethnoarchaeology," research documenting how living humans create an archaeological record.

There is certainly nothing wrong with using observations of recent human activities as sources of hypotheses about the past. Basing one's theories about the past on observations of present-day phenomena is uniformitarianism (Lyell 1830–1833), the common theoretical touchstone of all natural history. Nevertheless, when archaeologists pose answers to "how questions" about prehistory, they face a problem. Projecting recent preindustrial human activities unaltered back into prehistory, especially "deep-time" prehistory, contradicts fundamental evolutionary principles. It conflates analogy and homology. Prehistoric human activities might have resembled recent human activities (analogy), but they were not identical (homology), because evolution never, ever stops.

Consider dogs. Nearly all recent hunter-gatherers keep and use dogs as hunting aids, as do many farmers, herders, and city-dwellers. Dogs allow hunters to pursue prey animals they might otherwise bypass, such as small and nocturnally active creatures and waterfowl. Anthropologists base theories about how prehistoric humans hunted on ethnographic observations of dog-using hunter-gatherers. And yet domesticated dogs appear in the fossil record less than 12,000–30,000 years ago (Shipman 2021), hundreds of thousands of years after humans do. "How did early humans hunt without dogs?" is an anthropologically important question with significant implications for what we think happened in human prehistory. "Who first domesticated dogs?" is far less consequential.[4]

Differences between Who and How Questions

"Who questions" and "how questions" differ from each other. Answers to "who questions" narrow. Much as family genealogies do, they connect a living person or people to a specific dead person or extinct groups of people to serve the living's social game: to assert authority about some matter, to claim exemptions, or to justify privileges (Jasanoff 2022). In the same sort of way

---

[4] Even assuming that one can identify a specific region or time period in the "big picture" of human evolution, it simply does not matter whether dogs first appeared in the Czech Republic, Israel, China, or elsewhere. After all, it is not as though modern-day residents of these countries can claim credit for their predecessors' having domesticated wolves without suffering the ridicule such a claim deserves.

that everyone cares deeply about their genealogy but nobody else does,[5] answers to "who questions" about one part of the world decline with distance and with time. That is, answers to questions about who made which sort of Middle Bronze Age pottery in central Europe might interest prehistorians working on the central European Early and Later Bronze age, or the Bronze Age in adjacent parts of Europe. They would probably not interest colleagues working further afield and in different time periods, such as the Bronze Age in China or the Iron Age in Africa. These problems with "who questions" are not exactly secrets.

Answers to "how questions" widen. They enlarge the range of people connected to one another. So, why are paleoanthropologists so less engaged with "how questions" than with "who questions"? "How questions" are tough questions. They require one to ask questions to which much current scholarship answers, "Nobody knows." On the other hand, learning how earlier humans solved a problem provides insights into the lives of *all* humans, past and present. For example, during the early 20th century in California, one Native American man, Ishi (Yahi, 1861–1916), "the last of his tribe," demonstrated to interested anthropologists how he and his people made stone tools (Nelson 1916). Today, thousands of craft/hobby "flintknappers" shape stone tools using the same or similar techniques to those Ishi used. They and others have learned what Ishi taught, and these insights have been deployed in archaeological research on the earliest prehistory onward (Whittaker 2004; Shea 2017b). Answers to "how questions" evoke the common heritage of all humanity.

Chronologically, "who" and "how questions" also look in different directions. Answers to "who questions" look backward. Learning that the indigenous inhabitants of Vanuatu (a group of Pacific Islands) came from the Philippines rather than New Guinea might be interesting, but this information does not affect Vanuatans' present or their future (Lewis-Kraus 2019). Neither the Philippines nor New Guinea can credibly claim these islands based on hypotheses about prehistoric migrations. Answers to "how questions" look forward. Learning how prehistoric Vanuatans overcame such survival challenges as rapidly rising sea levels, wildfires, food insecurity, and pandemic diseases suggest ways they can overcome similar challenges or, even better, avoid them entirely. For living Vanuatans and scientists (and those who are both), "who questions" are not irrelevant, but are vastly less interesting than "why questions," such as why their ancestors came to Vanuatu in the first place.

---

[5] Unless, of course, one cites such genealogy as conferring authority to speak on a matter of consequence or to receive benefits (e.g., reparations, preferences in hiring or college admissions) not available to others, or some other advantage in one's "social game," in which case, everybody cares.

"Why Questions"

Both "who" and "how questions" have something to offer in helping us answer questions about causes – or "why questions," such as why we rather than some other primate became the unstoppable species. Knowing "who" can help one identify chronologically and geographically unique combinations of natural selection pressures. Knowing "how" can winnow down hypotheses about mechanisms to a plausible core of multiple working hypotheses. The problem paleoanthropologists face in explaining the past is that assertions about "how" are falsifiable (capable of being proven wrong using evidence) in ways that assertions about "who" are not. This makes explanations of the past focusing on "who they were" vulnerable, indeed fragile, in the face of new evidence in ways that explanations focusing on "how they did it" are not.

EXPLAINING THE PAST

Why are we, rather than some other creature, Earth's unstoppable species? Scholars of human evolution have used both narrative and comparative approaches to answer this question. Narrative approaches are as old as the oldest written records, and probably much, much older. Comparative approaches are almost certainly deeply ancestral, too, but they play a smaller and more recent role in prehistoric research.

Narrative Approaches

Historically, paleoanthropologists have framed theories about the origins of human uniqueness using a narrative approach to explanations. These explanations share two important characteristics. First, they arrange observations into linear sequences of causes and effects. Second, they invoke single causes for major changes.

The focus on single causes is both an artifact of history and a result of academic specialization. Early evolutionists, including paleoanthropologists, expressed theories about human prehistory in "anthropogenic narratives," recruiting conventions from traditional folktales, most notably, the "hero's journey" (Landau 1991). Table 1.2 shows the anthropogenic narrative's basic elements by comparing a conjectural evolutionary narrative with the plot of a *Popeye the Sailor* cartoon[6].

Modern-day paleoanthropologists continue to use anthropogenic narratives, probably unconsciously and sometimes invoking more than one donor acting in sequence (as do some hero's journey folktales). Anthropogenic

---

[6] Originally an American comic strip, *Popeye the Sailor* cartoons debuted in 1933 and endure to this day in syndication on television and in a variety of other popular media.

Explaining the Past

TABLE 1.2 *Anthropogenic narratives and hero's journey narratives*

Stage in anthropogenic narrative	Evolutionary narrative	*Popeye the Sailor*
1. Initial situation: Things are stable, unchanging.	Miocene to Pliocene	A boat is at sea.
2. The hero is introduced.	Ape-like ancestors	Popeye appears.
3. Change.	Increasing aridity	Popeye sights land.
4. Departure: The hero's journey begins.	Ancestors leave woodlands for savannas.	On shore leave, Popeye sees Olive Oyl and falls in love.
5. Failed challenge: The hero survives but fails to overcome a challenge.	Carnivores prey on ancestors.	Olive's suitor, Bluto, beats up Popeye.
6. Donor: Something new appears that can change the hero.	Ancestors develop fire, tools, large-scale cooperation, or some other thing.	Popeye eats a can of spinach.
7. Transformation: The hero changes in some important way.	Ancestors become hominins.	Popeye becomes stronger.
8. Challenge again: The same or worse challenge emerges.	Carnivores try to prey on hominins.	Popeye defeats Bluto.
9. Triumph: The hero overcomes the second challenge.	Hominins defeat carnivores.	Popeye and Olive are united in a happy ending.
10. Apocalyptic coda: Something the hero does creates problems.	Hominins turn their antipredator defenses on one another.	Popeye returns to the sea, but Bluto survives.

narrative explanations offer satisfying explanations, but they share the same fragility. New observations can shatter linear chains of causes and effects. Inasmuch as we have the least evidence about the earliest phases of hominin and human evolution, in which anthropogenic narratives root themselves, narrative explanations of events on evolutionary timescales are intrinsically likely to be wrong.[7]

Comparative Approach

This book employs a different, comparative approach. A comparative approach involves the following five steps:

---

[7] Surprising discoveries overturning all previous knowledge sometimes happen in human origins research, as in science in general, but these are exceptions, among which few live up to the hype initially attached to them. The most useful scientific discoveries arise from prior theory – from patient efforts to test predictions scientists make based on previous knowledge. "Look what I found!" is not prior theory.

1. Arranging evidence into contrasting pairs of samples, such as evidence from different time periods, different regions, or some combination of time and geography:
2. Identifying the differences between those samples
3. Developing the minimum number of hypotheses necessary to explain those differences
4. Falsifying as many of those hypotheses as one can using available evidence
5. Accepting hypotheses that survive attempts to prove them wrong pending the discovery of new evidence.

Comparative approaches to human evolution are not immune to revision or refutation, but, because they do not propose simple and easily overturned cause-and-effect relationships over time, but rather claims about differences, they are less volatile than narrative explanations. In short, they endure.

The comparative approach this work uses shows that we owe neither our diaspora nor our uniquely evolved unstoppability to any one thing, but instead to how our ancestors employed a suite of survival skills they inherited from earlier hominin ancestors. They had the same skills; they just used them better.

HOW THIS BOOK IS ORGANIZED

If it achieves its best-hoped-for purpose, *The Unstoppable Human Species* will spur its readers to ask different sorts of questions and to think differently about human evolution and prehistory.

Chapter 2 introduces this "hard evidence" for prehistoric movements, dates, fossils, artifacts, and genes. It also discusses the limits of what paleoanthropologists can infer from such evidence. (One thinks of this chapter as an inoculation against the "press-release science" that so afflicts paleoanthropology.)

Chapter 3 reviews *Homo sapiens*' place in primate evolution, the differences between us and other animals, and the nature of differences among living humans. (Spoiler alert: most human-vs.-human differences are evolutionarily trivial.)

Chapter 4 introduces "survival archaeology," a new approach to investigating the "how questions" about prehistoric human population movements (Shea 2020b). It also identifies the suite of ancestral survival skills earlier humans used, illustrating them with examples from contemporary times.

Chapter 5 reviews evidence for behavioral differences between Ancient Africans (*Homo sapiens*) and their immediate evolutionary precursor, *Homo heidelbergensis*. The crucial behavioral innovations that accompany our species beyond Africa include watercraft, complex projectile weapons, and symbolic artifacts ("boats, bows, and beads").

Humans first appear outside Africa in Southwest Asia before 80,000 years ago. Settling the East Mediterranean Levant, the Arabian Peninsula, and the Indian subcontinent appears to have required few major changes to human survival strategies. Indeed, parts of South and Southwest Asia might have been part of the larger Afro-Asiatic region in which early *Homo sapiens* originated.

Chapter 7 focuses on human settlement in Sunda (a peninsula formed when low sea levels conjoined mainland Southeast Asia to the islands that make up the Indo-Malaysian archipelago) and Sahul (New Guinea, Australia, and Tasmania, also joined by low sea levels). The chapter considers what effect, if any, the eruption of the Mount Toba (Indonesia) supervolcano around 75,000 years ago had on humans living in these regions. The answer, it turns out, is surprisingly little.

Beginning around 45,000 years ago, humans moved northward over the Alpine and Himalayan mountain ranges into Northern Eurasia. This region's cold "Mammoth Steppe" habitats posed novel survival challenges. So that we can better understand how these "Early Eurasian" humans dealt with these cold habitats (Chapter 9), the preceding Chapter 8 reviews the earlier Neanderthal adaptations to them.

Chapter 10 examines the evidence for the peopling of the Americas. During the peak of the last glaciation around 20,000 years ago (or possibly slightly earlier), humans crossed into the Americas, moving southward and eastward with breathtaking speed. This chapter also considers the "mass extinctions" that swept the Americas around this time and their possible link to a distinctive set of stoneworking traditions, the Clovis phenomenon, for which evidence appears over much of North America.

With Chapter 11, *The Unstoppable Human Species* turns from recent prehistory to migrations. Archaeological evidence for population movements older than 10,000 years ago is consistent with dispersals, but after 10,000 years ago one finds increasingly convincing evidence for migrations. Chapter 11 explains this shift as the result of food production (plant and animal husbandry) and of correlated human population growth. These two changes provided both the incentive for migrations and the means by which to accomplish them. One thinks of those involved in these migrations as "houses, herds, and hoes" people.

Many prehistoric migrations after 10,000 years ago merely rearranged humans on those continents we already occupied. Chapter 12 discusses the migrations to far oceanic islands that were the final step in humanity's global diaspora. It considers evidence for Pleistocene seafaring, but it focuses especially on the peopling of the Pacific Ocean. Beginning around 20,000 years ago, humanity's greatest explorers extended our diaspora to fully one-third of the Earth's surface.

Are we truly unstoppable? An appropriately numbered Chapter 13 considers what could stop us. These include unlikely extinction threats that commonly appear in popular media as well as ones, chillingly real, that do not receive as much attention as they should and, ultimately, must.

A concluding Chapter 14 looks both backward at "how we did it" and forward to what we must do to remain the unstoppable species.

Readers already familiar with the broad outlines of human deep-time prehistory will note that this work uses neither traditional archaeological age-stages (e.g., Lower, Middle, Upper Paleolithic) nor named stone tool industries, other than in passing reference to the history of research. This is not an accidental omission. These terms and concepts add a superfluous level of description to archeologists' observations.[8] They create more problems than they solve, and as this work will show, human origins research is better off without them (see Shea 2017b). Nevertheless, archaeological age-stages are familiar touchstones. Appendix A reviews them very briefly so that readers unfamiliar with these terms will know what they mean if and when they encounter them in the references this work cites.

For readers unfamiliar with the bushcraft/wilderness survival literature survival archaeology uses as a source of hypotheses, Appendix B presents a select list of published introductory works.

Appendix C, "Further Reading," lists selected popular-science books, as well as a few technical works that present up-to-date syntheses of the archaeological and paleontological evidence that individual chapters discuss.

Box 1.1: *Human Morphological and Behavioral Modernity: Their Discontents*

Since the 1980s debates about human distinctiveness have focused on differences between "modern" versus "archaic" humans and "modern" versus "archaic" human behavior. Professional colleagues reading this work may note that, other than in this box, the book does not even mention these terms. This is not an accidental omission. Categorical distinctions such as "archaic" and "modern" needlessly clutter up human origins research. We are better off without them.

Paleontologists involved in "modern human origins" research disagree over just which individual fossils belong to "modern" versus "archaic" humans. Such disagreement is entirely expected. Paleontologists describe hominin fossils using discrete categories ("species" or taxa), but evolution varies continuously. That an unambiguously "archaic" human mother gave birth to an equally unambiguously "modern" human child sometime around 200,000–300,000 years ago seems a scientifically improbable scenario for our species' beginning. Most paleontologists recognize this, and so the controversy about which specific fossil or fossils are "modern" or not really involves little more than "moving the goalposts to improve the

---

[8] One thinks of archaeologists' complex systematics (frameworks for describing their evidence) as the "archaeology tax," the cost of including them in books for popular audiences or in classes for any but doctoral students.

Box 1.1: *(cont.)*

score." That is, paleontologists push the limits of what the field considers *Homo sapiens* in order to move said fossil or fossils into prominence as the "oldest modern human." This might seem a cynical view, but one finds it telling that few such "oldest modern human" claims bother to explain why one would expect a new hominin species to arise near wherever the fossil in question was found, and only in that place to the exclusion of others. A tough challenge? Not really. As the astronomer Carl Sagan (1936–1996) put it, "Extraordinary claims require extraordinary evidence." As this work will argue, the difficulty of pinpointing our species' metaphorical "Garden of Eden" may actually provide clues about the more complex processes underlying our evolutionary origins.

Archaeologists' misadventures with "behavioral modernity" are a bit more complicated. Paleoanthropology began in Europe. Most of the behaviors to which behavioral modernity refers are things that distinguish the European archaeological record associated with European humans after 45,000 years ago from that subcontinent's earlier prehistory (Mellars 1989a; Bar-Yosef 2002; Nowell 2010). Lists of "modern human behavior" based on that evidence usually include the following:

- Long-distance (>100 km) movements of stone and other materials
- Labor-intensive stone and bone tool production (prismatic blades, microlithic tools, carved bone implements)
- Specialized big-game hunting
- Complex projectile weapon use (bow and arrow, spear-thrower and dart)
- Systematic use of marine and aquatic resources
- Constructing freestanding architecture
- Use of fire as an engineering tool (ceramics, mastics [glues])
- Symbolic artifact use (mineral pigments, beads, and other personal adornments).

This list includes some clearly problematical behaviors. Using marine resources, for example, presumes the nearby presence of an ocean. Specialized big-game hunting is far more likely to occur in regions with large migrating herds of steppe-dwelling mammals than in, say, an equatorial rain forest. Of the behaviors on these behavioral modernity checklists, many paleoanthropologists agree that symbolic artifact use is the most important (Mellars 1996b; Henshilwood and Marean 2003).

Archaeologists began using this "modernity" metaphor in earnest during the 1980s as fossil discoveries in Africa and Asia increasingly showed first appearance dates for *H. sapiens* much earlier than 45,000 years ago. As an

Box 1.1: *(cont.)*

analytical construct, behavioral modernity turned out to be very useful. It allowed European paleoanthropologists – the overwhelming majority of whom focused their careers on the European evidence – to retain a central place in human origins research even though it grew increasingly clear that for much of the Pleistocene, Europe was a peripheral backwater. Paleoanthropologists working in Asia and Africa cited evidence of "behavioral modernity" outside Europe to attract attention to their findings abroad (McBrearty and Brooks 2000; Mellars 2007; Stern 2009; Zilhao 2011; Bae et al. 2017).

Current archaeological views about these issues converge on the following four arguments.

1. The suite of behaviors that made humans distinctively "modern" appeared late in human evolution and only among *Homo sapiens*. Historically the older position, it reflects the strong influence early research in Europe had on thought about human evolution more generally (Mellars 1989b; Klein 1992). In Europe, *H. sapiens* fossils appear around 45,000 years ago together with evidence for complex tools, artworks, and activities for which conclusive evidence rarely occurs together with fossils of other hominins. Specifically, it argues that the evidence for human evolution in Europe results from universal patterns in human evolution.
2. The suite of behaviors that made humans distinctively "modern" evolved at or around the time *H. sapiens* fossils first appeared in Africa (McBrearty and Brooks 2000; Willoughby 2007).[9] This position developed around the turn of the 20th to 21st century and reflected growing evidence from Africa and Asia. Those supporting this argument have no problem with "modernity" per se; they simply argue that Africans became "modern" earlier than humans elsewhere.
3. Some among the suite of "modern human behaviors" are more important than others. Specific claims focus on symbolic artifact use (Henshilwood and Marean 2003), complex projectile technology (Shea and Sisk 2010), or a division of labor in subsistence (Stiner 1993; Kuhn and Stiner 2006). Perhaps unsurprisingly, those making these claims emphasize behaviors on which their own research focuses.
4. Because it oversimplifies complex patterns in prehistoric human behavioral variability, the "modern humans/modern human behavior" concept lacks scientific value (Habgood and Franklin 2008; Shea

---

[9] This first appearance date has been migrating steadily earlier in time over the last decades. It currently hovers around 200,000–300,000 years ago.

Box 1.1: *(cont.)*

2011a, 2011b; Bae et al. 2017). Currently a minority position in paleoanthropology, this "a plague on all your houses" perspective is gaining traction in the scientific literature.

A simple thought experiment with "alternative history" shows how definitions of behavioral modernity reflect paleoanthropology's European origins. What if prehistoric archaeology arose among 19th-century Polynesians rather than among 19th-century Europeans? Our Polynesian paleoanthropologists' criteria for modern human behavior would almost certainly have included their civilizational high points, such as making ocean-going watercraft; celestial navigation; monumental architecture; domesticating root crops, chicken, and pigs; making feather cloaks; and creating complex tattoos. They might also, understandably, regard prismatic blades, finger-painted cave walls, and specialized big-game harassment as Afro-Eurasian eccentricities of no great evolutionary consequence.

Rather than arguing about who "modern humans" were and what made them modern, this work focuses instead on the behaviors responsible for our living in our global diaspora, the root cause of our evolved unstoppability. It argues that those behaviors arose from our ancestral survival skills.[10] As the name implies, these skills are evolutionarily primitive (ancestral) among hominins in the genus *Homo*. Other now-extinct hominins had these ancestral survival skills, too, but our ancestors used them differently than other hominins did. In evolution, only differences matter.

For thought and discussion: Using the checklist by which European archaeologists identify "modern human behavior," are you a modern human? Are they? Can you devise a list of such behaviors that include all living humans and that exclude evidence associated with all fossils other than those paleontologists assign to *H. sapiens*?

---

[10] And, no, we shall not be using an acronym for ancestral survival skills.

CHAPTER 2

HARD EVIDENCE

This chapter reviews the hard evidence, the dates, fossils, artifacts, and genes that paleoanthropologists use in developing hypotheses about prehistoric human population movements. It also touches briefly on the principles that guide interpretations of this evidence. Each of these topics is the subject of entire scientific disciplines, and so, this chapter focuses on the basics: key terms and concepts that recur in this book's later chapters. Note: From this chapter onward, this work abbreviates dates in the thousands of years ago as "Ka" (12,700 years ago = 12.7 Ka) and dates in the millions of years ago as "Ma" (1,800,000 years ago = 1.8 Ma).

TIME: GEOCHRONOLOGY

Geochronology refers to efforts to arrange fossils, artifacts, and other evidence in order of greater or lesser antiquity using methods from geology. Paleoanthropologists work with two kinds of geological dating methods: stratigraphic dating and geochronometric dating. Stratigraphic dating establishes the chronological order of events (i.e., younger vs. older), while geochronometric dating measures the amount of time between events, usually expressed in years before the present. Paleoanthropologists also divide time using geological epochs, marine isotope stages, and archaeological age-stages (aka "cultural periods").

Stratigraphic Dating

Centuries-old fundamental principles of stratigraphy (Lyell 1830–1833) still guide our interpretation of the paleoanthropological record. The most important of these "core principles" include the principles of association, superposition, and facies.

The *principle of association* holds that objects enclosed in the same sedimentary deposit were deposited at the same time. "At the same time" does not necessarily mean at the same instant; by the same persons, animals, or geological processes; or for reasons related to one another. Erosion routinely exposes older objects on the surface, where sediment deposition can bury them together with younger artifacts. Archaeologists and paleontologists use the term *assemblage* for things found in the same sedimentary deposit.

"In the same deposit" can mean different things. Modern-day paleoanthropological excavations employ individuals with geological training using precise tools. Excavations of the 19th and early 20th century often employed laborers with no geological training who worked using picks, shovels, and other heavy-duty tools. Understandably, they missed much. The thick sedimentary deposits of older excavations sample a longer time span than the thinner layers from recent excavations. This is important because comparing the assemblages older excavations gathered with those from recent excavations without keeping in mind the differences in the amount of time sampled can create the illusion of behavioral differences from differences in the amount of time sampled. Archaeologists and paleontologists use the term *time averaging* for the error of equating stratigraphic association with literal contemporaneity.

The *principle of superposition* holds that in an undisturbed sequence of sedimentary deposits, younger layers cover older ones. This principle seems refreshingly straightforward, and intuitively obvious, but erosion, burrowing animals, and human excavations can reposition older sediments on top of younger ones. One can detect such "reversed stratigraphy" easily if the sediments involved differ in structure and content. But if the sediments differ little from one another, reversed stratigraphy can elude detection. Undetected, reversed stratigraphy can create spurious associations among finds from the same deposit. This is important because reversed stratigraphy can create the illusion of gradual change over time rather than abrupt contrasts between assemblages.

The *principle of facies* argues that sediments from the same depositional event differ over the landscapes onto which they were deposited. Few perfectly level surfaces exist anywhere on Earth, and so, when wind or flowing water move sediment in bulk, heavier particles drop out and come to rest sooner than lighter ones. The same depositional event can have different geological, paleontological, or archaeological "signatures" in different places. This is important because differences in contents of sediments deposited at different places can frustrate paleoanthropologists' efforts to correlate them, or to establish chronological equivalences among different deposits. Paleoanthropologists nearly always try to test hypotheses about stratigraphic correlations by using geochronometric dating.

Geochronometric Dating

Geologists and physicists continue to work together to improve geochronometric techniques. For this reason, paleoanthropologists treat dates from newly devised and experimental techniques with caution. The most well-established and widely used geochronometric techniques include radiocarbon, radiopotassium, uranium-series dating, and various "trapped electron" dating methods.

Radiocarbon Dating Radiocarbon dating measures the amount of unstable carbon-14 (^{14}C) in preserved plant or animal remains (see Table 2.1). When exposed to cosmic radiation, the stable isotope nitrogen-14 (^{14}N) transforms into unstable ^{14}C, which all plants and animals absorb during their lifetimes and maintain until they die, at which point ^{14}C uptake ceases. ^{14}C decays into stable ^{13}C and ^{12}C at a known rate, or half-life (50% of a sample each 5,730 years). Geophysicists use a mass spectrometer to measure these various carbon isotopes in a sample and then calculate the age by comparing ^{14}C in the sample with atmospheric ^{14}C. Early research assumed atmospheric ^{14}C production was stable, but later research showed it varied over time, requiring radiocarbon dates be calibrated against known geological records of ^{14}C variation preserved in annual growth rings in long-lived trees and corals. One expresses radiocarbon dates in years "before the present" (AD 1950, the International Radiocarbon Year), distinguishing uncalibrated dates in lower case (bp) and calibrated ones in upper case (BP). Radiocarbon works on samples dating to 40–50 Ka or younger. The best such samples are charcoal, but even charcoal requires chemical pretreatment to remove recent contaminants.

TABLE 2.1 *Radiometric dating techniques compared*

Dating technique	Samples	Effective range	Comment
Radiocarbon	Carbonate fossils (e.g., charcoal, bone)	< 45–50 Ka	Accelerator mass-spectroscopy (AMS) dates are considered most accurate. Dates more than 45 Ka are generally considered infinite ages (>45 Ka).
Radiopotassium	Volcanic tuff, igneous rocks (e.g., basalt, obsidian)	10 Ka to > 4300 Ma.	Dates younger than 300 Ka usually involve single-crystal argon dating.
Uranium-series	Carbonate rock precipitates (travertine, flowstone), corals, teeth, bones, shells	0.01 Ka–1 Ma	Dating shells and bones can be problematic.
Trapped-electron	TL: Burnt flint, other silicate rocks ESR: Dental enamel OSL: Quartz sand grains	< 1 Ma	Dates are often presented as "early uptake" (EU) vs. "linear uptake" (LU), referring to different models of sample deposition and cosmic ray exposure.

TL, thermoluminescence; ESR, electron-spin resonance; OSL, optically stimulated luminescence.

Radiopotassium Dating The most commonly used form of radiopotassium dating, potassium-argon (K-Ar) dating, measures the amount of argon-40 (^{40}Ar) in volcanic rocks. Radioactive potassium (^{40}K) decays into the inert gas ^{40}Ar at a known rate. When in a liquid state, volcanic rocks vent their stores of ^{40}Ar. Potassium in those rocks continues to decay into ^{40}Ar, and so the amount of ^{40}Ar in a rock sample provides an estimate of that rock's age. Paleoanthropologists use potassium-argon dating to date volcanic tuffs and other igneous rock deposits interstratified with sediments containing fossils or archaeological sites. Like radiocarbon dating, K-Ar dating has been in wide use for nearly 60 years. Newer dates increasingly use a more precise method, argon-argon (^{39}Ar/^{40}Ar) dating, which produces valid dates for much younger rocks than traditional potassium-argon dating.

Uranium-Series Dating Uranium is radioactive and soluble in water, but its decay products, thorium and protactinium, are not. This means that sedimentary rocks often enclose minute quantities of uranium, especially water-deposited rocks, such as flowstones, speleothems, and stalagmites, that form in caves. Enclosure traps uranium together with such thorium and protactinium. Geologists measure these elements and their isotopes, and work with known rates of uranium radioactive decay to calculate sample ages. Uranium-series dating works over a very wide range of time, from around a century ago to a million years ago.

Trapped Electron Dating Methods (TL, ESR, OSL) The most commonly used trapped electron dating methods include thermoluminescence, electron-spin resonance, and optically stimulated luminescence dating. All three estimate a sample's age by measuring the electrons an object has absorbed over time during exposure to cosmic radiation. Heating samples releases electrons trapped in them, and the amount of light emitted at the time provides an estimate of sample age. All three methods require one to estimate "uptake," the rate at which the sample absorbed electrons in the past. One can obtain different ages for the same measurement depending on whether one assumes early uptake or linear uptake. Thermoluminescence (TL) dating measures electrons accumulated as a quartz or feldspar crystal is heated above 750–850°F (400–450°C). Electron-spin resonance (ESR) dating measures electrons that accumulate in fossil bones and dental enamel. Optically stimulated luminescence (OSL) dating works on a principle similar to TL, but in this case exposure to sunlight restarts electron accumulation.

Geochronology and "Who Questions"

Geochronometric dating techniques return statistical estimates of age rather than specific calendar dates. A radiometric date of "20,125 ± 200 years ago" looks precise, but standard error (the "plus or minus" figure) means there is only a 67 percent chance that the sample's actual age lies between 20,325 and 19,925 years ago.[1] Doubling the standard error to ± 400 increases the chances the actual age falls between 21,425 and 19,725 years ago up to a little more than 90 percent, but now one is dealing with a span of 800 years during which those the fossils and artifacts might have become buried in the same sediment. This is important because it suggests that we can never be certain that artifacts and fossils occurring in the same deposits were actually contemporary with one another, a crucial assumption underpinning most answers to "who questions" about prehistory.

Chronostratigraphy: Dividing Time

Time unfolds continuously, but all human societies divide it, often using several methods simultaneously (e.g., 4:00 p.m., 1600 hours, afternoon). Chronostratigraphy references the ways in which geologists and others divide up time into distinct periods. Paleoanthropologists use several such forms of periodization, primarily geological epochs, marine isotope stages, and archaeological age-stages. (Appendix A discusses traditional archaeological age-stages in detail.)

Geological Epochs Geologists define epochs in terms of global-scale changes in rock composition, usually either changes in the geochemistry of marine sediments or changes in earth's magnetic field polarity recorded in volcanic rocks. Table 2.2 describes the principal geological epochs this work discusses.

The Pliocene Epoch (5.3–2.6 Ma) was generally warm and humid with minor climatic oscillations. Hominins (bipedal primates) evolved during the Pliocene.

The Pleistocene Epoch (2.6 Ma–12 Ka) saw a cooling trend, increased aridity, and ever wider climatic variability than during the Pliocene. Around 0.9 Ma, 40,000–50,000-year-long cycles changed from moderately cooler and warmer periods to longer (100,000–120,000-year-long) cycles between extremely cold (glacial) and warm (interglacial) cycles. Some paleoanthropologists use the informal term "Plio-Pleistocene" for the later Pliocene and early Pleistocene, roughly 1.6–3.5 Ma. Geologists divide the Pleistocene into Early (2.6–0.7 Ma), Middle (728–128 Ka), and Later (128–11.7 Ka) Pleistocene periods. Fossils of the genus *Homo* appear near the beginning of the Early Pleistocene. *Homo sapiens* first appears in the later Middle Pleistocene. Most of our major dispersals took place during the Later Pleistocene.

The most recent interglacial period, the Holocene Epoch (< 11.7 Ka) has been generally warmer and more humid than the Later Pleistocene, and also

---

[1] Assuming the standard error is normally distributed around the given mean. This is often, but not always, the case.

Time: Geochronology

TABLE 2.2 *Geological time periods*

Epoch	Start date, in years ago	Notes
Anthropocene	0.5 Ka	Increasing evidence for climate change due to human activity
Holocene	11.7 Ka (boundary between Marine Isotope Stages 1 and 2)	Rapid global heating Origins of agriculture, migrations
Later Pleistocene	128 Ka (boundary between Marine Isotope Stages 5 and 6)	Rapid global warming, wide variation in temperatures, with overall cooling trend lasting to about 20 Ka *H. sapiens* disperses globally; extinctions of other hominins, megafauna
Middle Pleistocene	0.7 Ma (shift from reversed to normal magnetic polarity)	Colder, longer glacial periods Origin of *H. sapiens* and Neanderthals
Early Pleistocene	2.6 Ma (change from normal to reversed magnetic polarity)	Cooler conditions; many brief low-magnitude climate shifts Origin of the genus *Homo*, extinction of other hominin genera
Pliocene	5.3 Ma (criteria for start date vary between regions)	Overall cooling and increased aridity Northern hemisphere glaciations Evolutionary diversification of hominins

Note: For the Pleistocene, some sources use Lower, Middle, and Upper in place of Early, Middle, and Later.

(thus far) more stable than any Middle to Late Pleistocene time period of equivalent duration.[2]

The Anthropocene is a recently proposed geological epoch marked by global-scale human impacts on the environment. As of this writing, it enjoys no formal definition, but the term appears in some recent popular and scientific works. Most such works identify its start date as between 0.5 and 1.0 Ka.

Marine Isotope Stages Until the 1980s, 20th-century paleoanthropological discussions referenced glacial periods based on Alpine Ice Ages (Günz, Mindel, Riss, Würm) and or other regional sequences (Flint 1971). Difficulties correlating these Alpine sequences between regions led to the widespread use of a global marine oxygen-isotope sequence (Shackleton 1987; Burroughs 2005). This record is continuous, but geologists divide it into numbered Marine Isotope Stages (MISs) based on major changes in stable isotopes of oxygen, ^{16}O and ^{18}O, measured in sediment cores drilled in the ocean floor (see Figure 2.1). During colder periods, glaciers remove disproportionately large

---

[2] A growing movement among geologists calls for resetting the start date for the Holocene at around 14 Ka, the point at which deglaciation accelerates. As of early 2022, however, the most widely accepted date remains 11,650 calibrated years before the present.

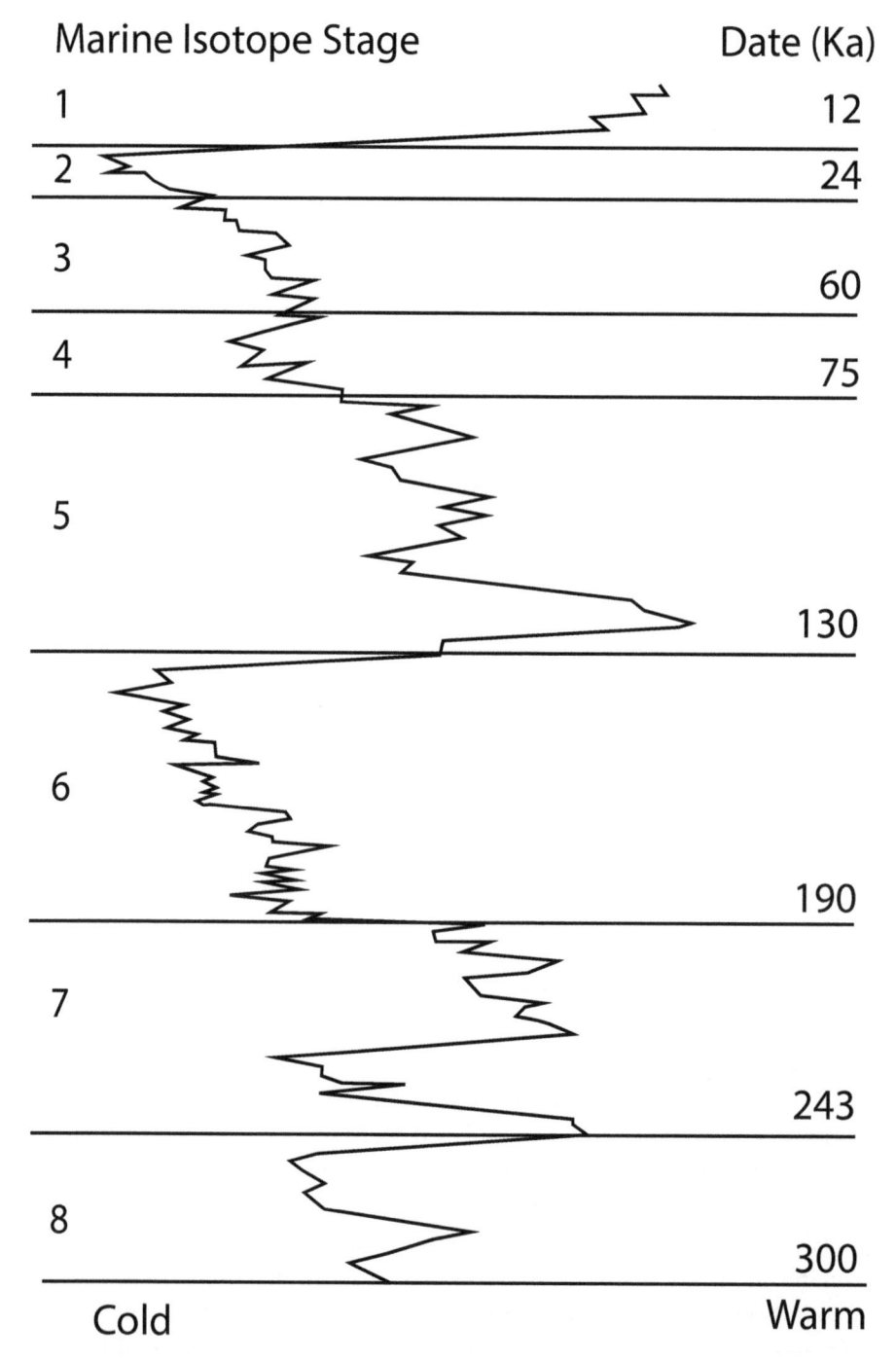

Figure 2.1 Marine oxygen-isotope record of temperature variation since 300,000 years ago. © John J. Shea.

quantities of ^{16}O from circulation, leaving the Earth's oceans correspondingly enriched in ^{18}O. Small marine invertebrates called foraminifera take up ^{16}O and ^{18}O into their shells in more or less the proportion in which they occur in the sea around them. When foraminifera die, their shells settle on the ocean floor, where over long periods they build up a continuous record of ocean chemistry, glacial ice volume, and thus sea level. Geologists date the MIS record using radiocarbon, potassium-argon, uranium-series, and other techniques. Deep sequences of ice deposits in Greenland and Antarctica preserve a mirror image of the marine oxygen-isotope record. Geologists number MISs from the present backward. Odd-numbered stages were relatively warm periods with high sea levels, small polar ice sheets, and small montane glaciers, conditions like those that have prevailed since around 12,000 years ago. (We live today in MIS 1.) Even-numbered stages correspond to colder periods with lower sea levels and extensive polar ice sheets and montane glaciers.

The principal forces driving marine isotope cycles appear to be variation in Earth's orbit around the Sun, namely, how round versus elliptical the Earth's orbit is (eccentricity), Earth's tilt with respect to the plane of orbit (obliquity), and variation in polar rotation (precession). Since 0.9 Ma, the marine isotopic record tracks warming/cooling cycles lasting a little over 100,000 years. They typically begin with rapid warming, a short "interglacial" period of around 10,000–20,000 years, followed by 90,000–100,000 years of gradual cooling and the onset of peak "glacial" conditions. Orbital forces predict these MIS cycles reasonably well, but changes in ocean circulation patterns and large-scale volcanism can affect them as well.

The human diaspora unfolded over the last 300,000 years. Table 2.3 summarizes major diaspora-related events during MISs 1–8. The paleoanthropological literature often uses the term "Last Glacial Maximum" (LGM) for MIS 2 and "Last Interglacial" for a period during MIS 5 lasting from around 115–130 Ka (MIS 5e). The Last Interglacial (MIS 5e) was the last time the Earth was as warm as it has been during Holocene times for an equivalently long period. European prehistorians often use the term "Interpleniglacial" for MIS 3, a period of cold but hypervariable conditions between the peak cold periods MIS 2 and MIS 4.

Biostratigraphy and Cultural Periodization *Biostratigraphy* refers to paleontological research seeking patterns of change and variability in long-term occurrences of fossils. Animal and plant communities evolve constantly. Forms previously unknown or uncommon appear and become common. For example, evolutionary changes in the teeth of pigs, elephants, and water shrews occur regularly enough across wide regions that paleontologists can infer chronological equivalences in the ages of sedimentary deposits in which these fossils occur. Geochronometric dating can verify, refute, or refine these age estimates. This is important because far more sedimentary deposits contain fossils than contain rock samples amenable to conventional methods of

TABLE 2.3 *Major diaspora-related events during Marine Isotopic Stages (MISs) 1–7*

MIS	Start date (Ka)	Global climate	Important events
1	12	Warm, and getting warmer	Agriculture, pastoralism, continental and oceanic migrations, first cities, industry based on fossil fuels, first movements to extraterrestrial space
2	24	Cold	Humans settled the Americas.
3	60	Cool, but widely variable	Humans moved into Northern Eurasia, near oceanic islands in Australasia. Last appearance dates for hominins other than *H. sapiens*.
4	75	Abruptly cold	First appearances of humans in Southeastern Asia and in Australasia
5	130	Warm, but widely variable	Humans present in Southwest Asia. Increased evidence for use of symbolic artifacts, complex projectile weaponry, and coastal resources.
6	190	Cold	Possible early human movements from Africa to southern Europe and Southwestern Asia
7	243	Warm	*H. sapiens* evolves from African *H. heidelbergensis*.
8	300	Cold	*H. heidelbergensis* fossils exhibit features later seen only in *H. sapiens*.

geochronometric dating. Paleontologists divide time based on changes in (usually marine invertebrate) fossil assemblages.

Archaeologists maintain a variety of chronostratigraphic frameworks, or *cultural periodization*, based on the presence or absence of various kinds of artifacts in archaeological collections. As these "cultural periods" and "age-stage" frameworks vary from region to region, and because different archaeological research traditions differ over how to recognize them, this work does not use them (see Appendix A).

Proposed Dates Are Hypotheses Why is it important to understand geochronology? Proposed dates are hypotheses. They can be proven wrong and are proven wrong at least as often as otherwise. Popular-science discussions about fossils and archaeology often fail to discuss chronological issues adequately. This leads to several sorts of mistakes.

Reports of geochronometric dates often fail to discuss the uncertainties around those dates. (A date of 37.5 ± 1000 Ka is a very different and far less precise a date than one of 37.5 ± 200 Ka.)

Different dating methods can produce different dates for rock samples and fossils of equal ages, and vice versa. Unethical paleoanthropologists sometimes shop around for methods that give older dates, selectively accept older dates, and reject younger ones.

Minor increases in age estimates for a fossil or other evidence are sometimes hailed as "game changers" when, in fact, many such changes occur within the standard errors of previous dates. Decreases in age estimates rarely attract much attention unless they concern chronological outliers, such as the oldest claimed evidence of something or another. Dates are not really game changers unless they differ from previous estimates in ways that require one to revise previously held hypotheses about matters other than dating.

Claims that different sets of fossils and archaeological remains date to the "same time" (or even the same stratigraphic levels of a site) can fail to recognize that such periods span thousands of years.

FOSSILS: PALEONTOLOGY AND ZOOARCHAEOLOGY

Paleontologists study fossils, the mineralized remains of organisms whose organic components have largely been replaced. Fossils vary widely. Vertebrate fossils consist mainly of teeth and bone, but also antler and horn in which inorganic minerals have replaced organic compounds. Invertebrate fossils include mainly mollusk shells and chitinous insect tissues. Plant macrofossils comprise chiefly seeds and other woody plant parts that have either been carbonized due to exposure to fire or preserved by waterlogging. Plant microfossils include pollen and phytoliths (opal silica secretions that form in woody plant parts). Recent years have seen these paleontological mainstays augmented by studies of ancient DNA (aDNA) and proteomics, or analyses of proteins preserved in fossils and sediments.

In describing paleontology's contribution to paleoanthropology, one distinguishes two major kinds of research: paleontology and zooarchaeology. Paleontologists investigate morphological and evolutionary variation among fossils. Hominin paleontologists (physical anthropologists) focus their energies on the remains of hominins and earlier primates. Zooarchaeologists analyze and interpret the nonhominin fossils found together with other traces of human activity. These fields overlap in complex ways, but their practitioners have somewhat different objectives. Hominin paleontologists differ from other paleontologists mainly in their greater concern for phylogeny, for the evolutionary relationships among extinct and living hominins, and for functional morphology, or for how activities shape bone. Zooarchaeologists differ from other paleontologists mainly in their concern for reconstruction of how human activities influenced the nonhuman fossil record. Zooarchaeology and hominin paleontology differ in that in hominin paleontology many different individual researchers measure the same fossil again and again. In zooarchaeology, multiple researchers rarely examine the same fossil. This is important because measurement errors on hominin fossils stand a higher chance of discovery than measurement errors in zooarchaeology.[3]

---

[3] Archaeological lithic (stone tool) analysis suffers the same problem. Once a stone tool assemblage has been "formally described," one struggles to secure permission and funding for a reanalysis unless one proposes truly revolutionary new analytical methods and techniques.

Describing Fossils

Regardless of their ultimate research questions, all paleontologists first try to identify the part of the fossil animal or plant they have before them by using general anatomical principles and by comparing the fossil with reference collections and published guides to teeth, bones, seeds, wood, pollen, and other tissues from recently living animals and plants. Next, they work to winnow down hypotheses about which specific animal or plant species a sample represents. Zooarchaeologists usually express their findings about vertebrate fossils in terms of number of identified specimens and/or minimum number of individuals.

The number of identified specimens (NISP) reports the number of specimens in a given collection that have been identified to a species or some other taxon. (Bones of some species, such as goats and sheep and different kinds of deer, are so similar that one cannot easily distinguish them, especially when they are mere bone fragments.) NISP is relatively simple to tabulate and to use for comparative purposes, and nearly all paleontologists and zooarchaeologists express their observations using NISP. But NISP has limited interpretive value. Mechanical damage before, during, or after archaeological excavation can fragment bones into small, unidentifiable pieces, thereby reducing NISP values for a given set of fossils.

The minimum number of individuals (MNI) is the smallest number of individuals necessary to account for the fossil species or another taxon in an archaeological assemblage. For example, a fossil collection with ten right mandibular fragments (jawbones) of a deer has an MNI of 10 for that deer species. MNI offers more analytical potential than NISP, but it has a few blind spots. The most useful bones for making taxonomic identifications include crania and mandibles (skulls, jaws, and teeth) and the ends of limb bones. Recent hunter-gatherers often discard such remains at kill/butchery sites in order to lighten the amount of bone they have to transport back to residential sites. This practice varies, depending on the size of the animal. Hunters will often carry an entire antelope back to their residential site but obviously cannot do so with a large animal, such as a bison or elephant.

Describing approaches to quantifying plant fossils poses special difficulties. For some research questions, such as whether or not people cultivated one plant or another, one or a few well-described and convincingly identified fossils may be sufficient. Questions about prehistoric climates based on pollen or about local habitats based on phytoliths typically require comparisons of relative frequencies of diagnostic remains among fossil samples.

Animals build their bones, and plants their woody tissues, from organic compounds consumed in their immediate habitats. As a result, fossils' isotopic geochemistry can provide further insights into prehistoric habitats and diets. For example, nitrogen-15 (^{15}N) becomes more concentrated in animal collagen up the food chain (i.e., more concentrated in carnivores than in herbivores). Measuring ^{15}N in collagen preserved in hominin fossils can shed light on variation in how much they meat they ate. Similarly, carbon-13 (^{13}C), commonly found in grasses, becomes more concentrated in the bones of animals that eat grasses as well as in the bones of carnivores that eat grass-eaters. Increases in ^{13}C can signal shifts to cereal grass consumption during transitions to food production.

Few animals are truly inedible before decomposition progresses, but plants' biochemical and structural defenses limit what humans select among them for food sources. Studies of recent human behavior provide some expectations about past subsistence strategies. In seeking food, humans cast the net broadly. Few animals are either too big or too small to escape hungry humans' attention. "Big game hunting" captures foragers' and anthropologists' attention (Speth 2010), but nearly all human societies consume small mammals, fish, and invertebrates in their diets. That large vertebrate remains dominate fossil collections from most archaeological sites may reflect preservation biases favoring their large, dense bones. Costs, benefits, risk, social factors, and even supernatural beliefs guide human food choices (Twiss 2019). Relying as they do on agricultural crops and herds raised and harvested in bulk, agrarian and industrial societies' diets can prove remarkably difficult to change.[4] Lacking such constraints, hunter-gatherer diets can change rapidly and vary widely in the short term (Kelly 2013).

Taphonomy

Taphonomy refers to systematic investigations into how the fossil record formed based on observations of modern-day animal death sites (Brain 1981; Shipman 1981; Lyman 1994). Taphonomy was one of the most important developments in 20th-century paleontological research. Prior to the 1970s, archaeologists interpreted the fossils they excavated simply and straightforwardly as evidence of hominin diets. Breaking with this "menu paleontology," taphonomists developed criteria for recognizing hominin involvement with bone modification and insights into how human activities and natural forces cause variation in the kinds of bones archaeologists recover from excavations. For example, skulls, jaws, and lower parts of limbs predominate among older sites. While this "heads and feet" pattern could reflect hominins scavenging bone left behind after a carnivore had left a carcass (Binford 1981), it could also reflect that fact that dense crania, mandibles, and lower limb bones resist erosion and decomposition better than other bones (Marean 1991).

---

[4] Recall how often people shopping in supermarkets lost their composure when their favorite food became unavailable during the Covid-19 pandemic!

Taphonomic research suggests important variables affecting vertebrate fossil preservation and the fossil record, including the following.

Differences in preservation due to bone density: Cranial/mandibular (skull/jaw) and distal (lower) limb bones are denser than most other bones. They resist mechanical weathering better than other parts of vertebrate skeletons.

Differences in identifiability: Skulls, teeth, and the ends of limbs are among the most diagnostic parts of animal skeletons. They are intrinsically likely to be identified during zooarchaeological analysis.

Differences in bone destruction due to human activity: Recent humans often pulverize limb bone shafts, ribs, vertebrae, and pelvises in order to extract marrow and fat from them by boiling them ("bone degreasing"). Domestic dogs and pigs also ravage vertebrate ribs, vertebrae, and fragments of pelvises left lying about on the surface at human habitation sites.

Differences in archaeological conservation practices: Many early archaeological excavations deemed anything other than cranial/mandibular and distal limb bones "unidentifiable" and discarded them. Today, sophisticated image analysis and computer-assisted methods help archaeologists to identify such bone fragments.

Actual scavenging: Recent hunter-gatherers sometimes drive carnivores off their kills, taking what they can. Large carnivores consume meat- and fat-poor cranial/mandibular and distal limb bones later rather than earlier, and for this reason "heads and feet" figure prominently among remains available to human scavengers with late access to large animal carcasses.

Exposure to heat and/or fire: When humans reside in one place, they nearly always keep one or more fire going. Centers of social activity, humans provision hearths with fuel constantly. One safely assumes that the ease or difficulty of gathering firewood and other fuel materials (e.g., large mammal dung) influenced prehistoric human settlement patterns, much as they do in many rural areas of the world today. Exposure to fire adversely influences fossil preservation, too. That is, if prehistoric humans were using fire and bones were present, some bones were lost to fire, either accidentally, for sanitary reasons, or as fuel when wood was scarce. Conclusive tests determining whether or not bones were exposed to lower heat levels more typical of cooking require geophysical testing.

Tool Marks versus Tooth Marks on Bone

When carnivores consume their prey, they use their teeth to separate muscle and fat from bones. The scratches they leave on bone ("tooth marks") have indistinctly defined margins and the same rounded profile as the tips of carnivore teeth. Lacking large and self-sharpening canines, humans use stone tools to separate meat from bone and to split open long bones to get at the fat-rich marrow those bones enclose. Sharp and jagged stone tool edges leave scratches on bones that have sharply defined edges and internal striations (scratches). Percussion-damaged bones also feature sharply defined compression fractures. By feeding bones to carnivores and by experimenting with stone tools, taphonomists have learned how to recognize differences between tooth marks and tool marks on fossils. This in turn allows them to identify those bones with which hominins demonstrably interacted and bones damaged by other causes.

The locations of tooth and tool marks on a bone can also show whether hominins or carnivores had early versus late access to a bone. Most of the meat and fat on limb bone are attached to a bone's proximal end (the part closest to the spinal column). Cut marks on proximal ends of limb bones indicate hominins had earlier access to those bones than carnivores.

Coprolites

Coprolites (fossilized feces) comprise remains of former meals. On those rare occasions when they are preserved, they offer indisputable evidence about human presence and dietary variability. Because coprolites contain human DNA and proteins, researchers can establish their anthropogenic origin beyond reasonable doubt. Far from being trivial evidence for human population movements, human coprolites from the Paisley Caves in Oregon (14.3 Ka) comprise some of the oldest indisputable evidence for human presence in the Americas.

ARTIFACTS: ARCHAEOLOGY

Archaeologists develop hypotheses about prehistoric human population movements and other behavior by studying artifacts and other residues they recover from excavations at archaeological sites. An archaeological site is any place at which archaeologists have observed occurrences of artifacts and other traces of past human and hominin activity. Archaeologists call artifacts, fossils, and other things found in the same level of an archaeological site an "assemblage." The principal artifacts prehistoric archaeologists study include stone tools ("lithics" or "lithic artifacts"), pottery ("ceramics") and artifacts made of organic materials, such as wood, bone, and shell.

Stone Tools

Stone tools consume a disproportionate amount of space in the archaeological literature because, being essentially indestructible, they occur pretty much everyplace humans do and thus offer a common point of comparison across time and space.

In stoneworking, or making and using stone tools, humans and earlier hominins sought percussors, abrasive surfaces, and sharp cutting edges. Prehistoric humans shaped stone tools using abrasion and retouch (small-scale fractures, or < 5 millimeters long), but they made the overwhelming majority of stone tools using larger-scale fractures. In fracture-based stoneworking, one forcefully strikes one rock (a core) with another rock (a percussor) or some other hard object (e.g., throwing it against another rock) until a fracture (cleavage plane) forms in the core, detaching one or more pieces of stone. Archaeologists call these detached pieces "flakes." If one wants to modify the flakes' shape, or to make small-scale modifications to a core edge, then one "retouches" these artifacts by lightly tapping or pressing their edges with a stone or some other percussor until fracture removals accomplish one's goals. Fracture-based stoneworking works best on brittle rocks with predictable fracture properties, the same sorts of conchoidal ("shell-shaped") fracture properties as those in glass. Common conchoidally fracturing rocks include quartz, obsidian (volcanic glass), basalt, rhyolite, flint or chert, slate, and quartzite. Conchoidal fractures leave scars whose distinctive features allow archaeologists to reconstruct where the fracture began, how it spread, and where it ended. Archaeologists who study stone tools distinguish stoneworking strategies for modifying stone, such as hard- versus soft-hammer percussion, abrasion, or pressure-flaking.[5]

Most Pleistocene-age stone tool assemblages include four kinds of stone artifacts (see Figure 2.2). Percussors (aka hammerstones) are rocks preserving crushing damage from repeated percussion against other rocks. Cores are rocks featuring one or more fracture scars longer than 10 millimeters. Most cores have a "worked edge" from which fracture scars spread out across their surface. Flakes are pieces of stone that fractures have detached from another rock. Most flakes feature a relatively flat "ventral" surface that formed during detachment and a convex "dorsal" surface, formerly the exterior surface of the core from which stoneworkers detached the flake. The core surface on which the fracture started and its remnant on a flake is the "striking platform." Retouched pieces are flake fragments featuring retouch, that is, one or a series of relatively small (< 20 millimeters long) fracture scars along their edge. Many Later Pleistocene and Holocene assemblages include preserved groundstone tools, artifacts humans modified and/or shaped using abrasion.

Archaeologists subdivide major stone tool categories into many specific artifact-types. Lists of formally recognized lithic artifact-types run into the hundreds and vary among different research traditions. Figures 2.3 and 2.4 show the considerably smaller number of major lithic artifact-types mentioned in this text.

---

[5] For jargon-free introductions to archaeological lithic analysis, see Andrefsky (2005), Odell (2004), Shea (2013b, 2017b, 2020a), and Whittaker (1994).

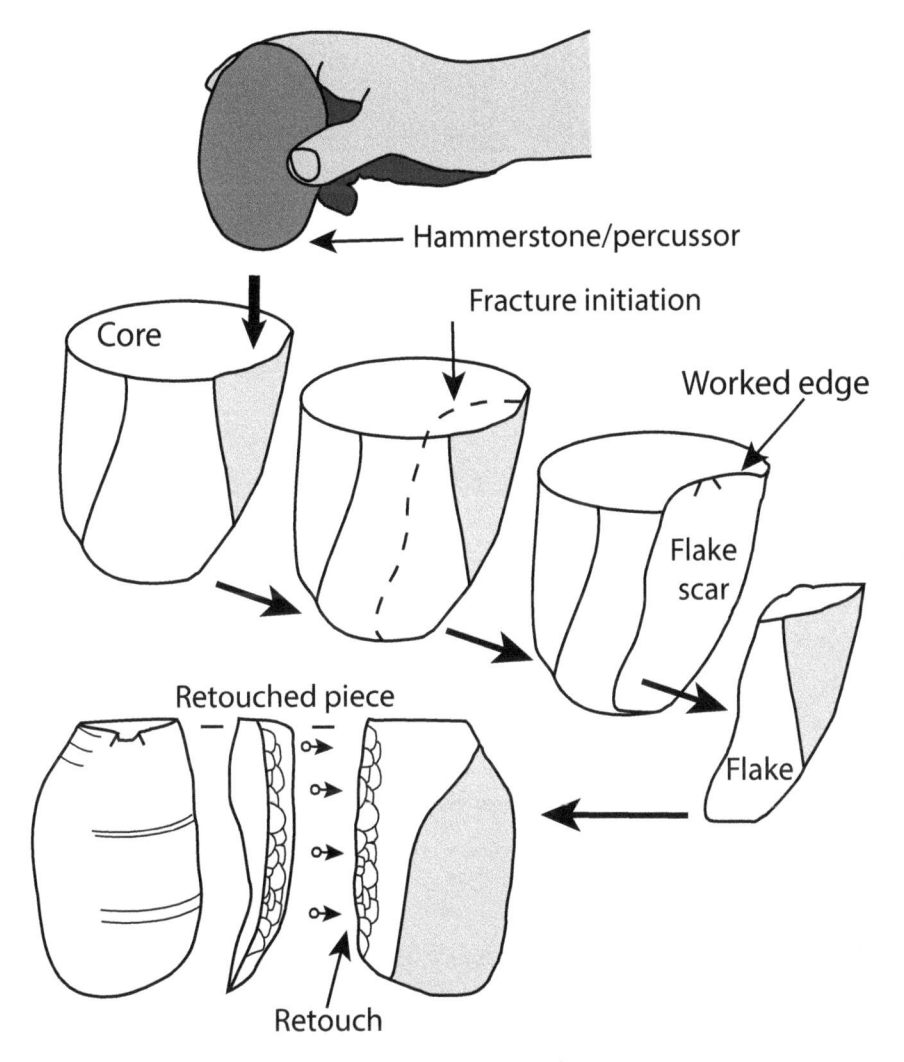

Figure 2.2 Basic stone tool categories. © John J. Shea.

Percussors, also known as pounded pieces or hammerstones, bear damage from repeated percussion against hard objects.

Bipolar cores are cores (and cores-on-flakes, see below) from which stoneworkers detached flakes by setting them on a hard surface and then striking them from above with a percussor. Though often derided as an inefficient way of obtaining cutting edge, experiments show that bipolar core reduction is actually a very efficient way of extracting cutting edge from stone (Pargeter and Eren 2017). It is also the oldest-dated method of hominin stoneworking.[6]

Short nonhierarchical cores (SNHCs) have roughly equal length, width, and thickness. Stoneworkers detached flakes to roughly the same extent on both

---

[6] That early hominins figured this out naturally begs the question of why they bothered developing so many other less-efficient stoneworking strategies.

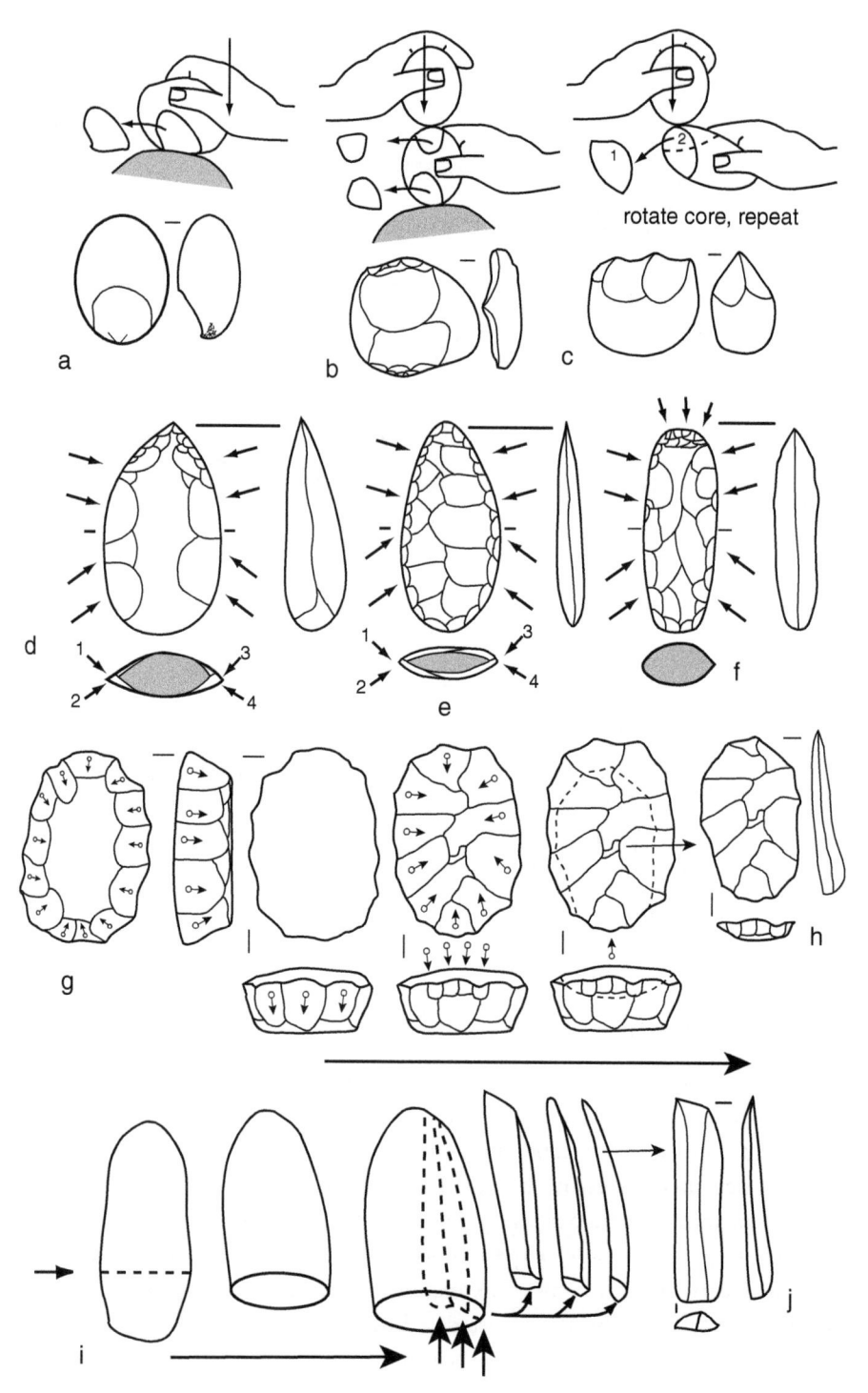

Figure 2.3 Major stone artifact-types discussed in the text, showing how they are made. (a) Percussor, (b) bipolar core, (c) short nonhierarchical core, (d)–(f) elongated nonhierarchical cores (d, long core tool; e, foliate point; f, celt), (g) bifacial hierarchical core (BHC) reduction, (h) "preferential" BHC flake, (i) unifacial hierarchical core (UHC) reduction, and (j) UHC flake, aka "prismatic blade." © John J. Shea.

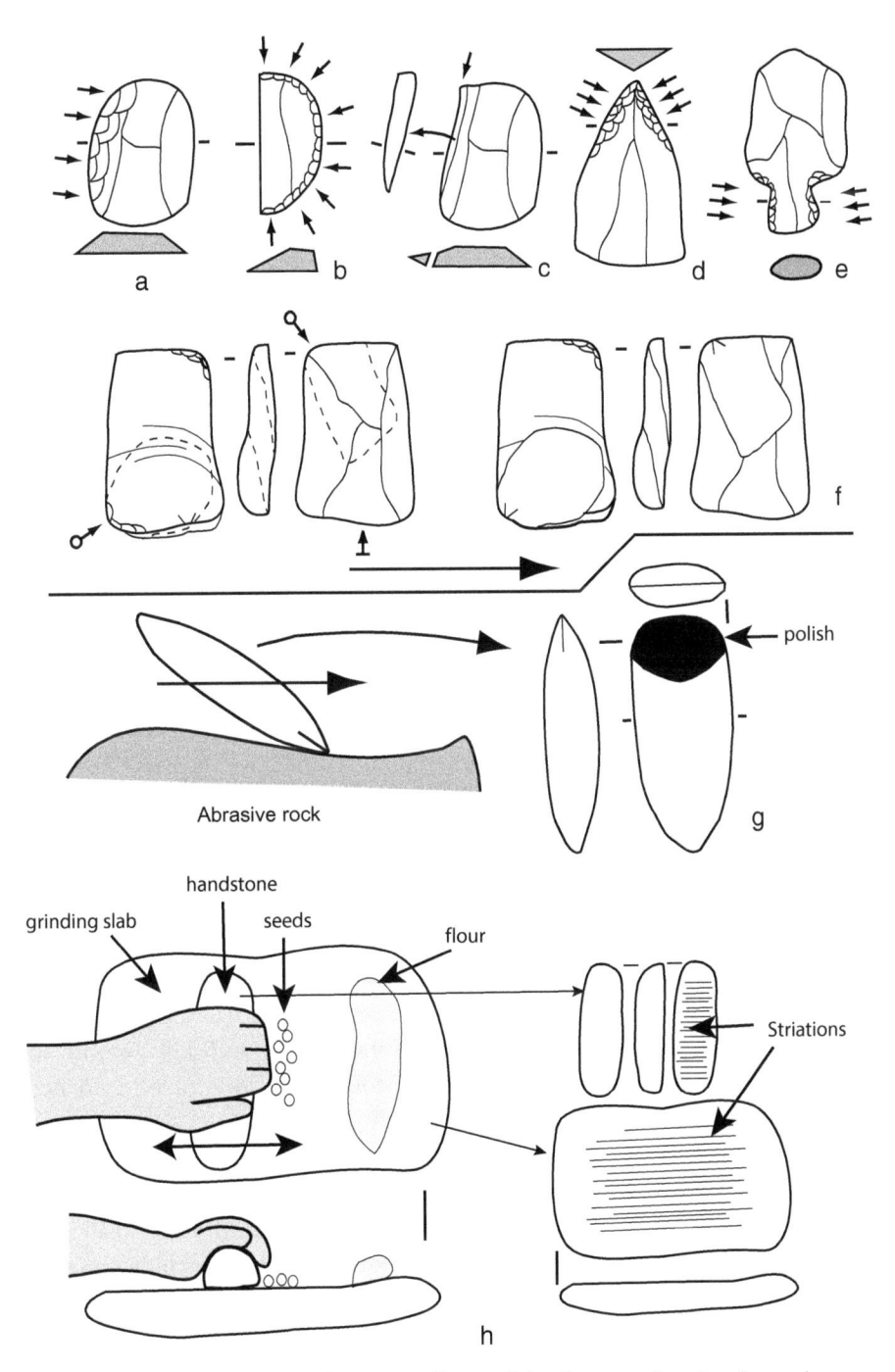

Figure 2.4 Major stone artifact-types discussed in the text showing how they are made (continued). (a)–(f) Retouched pieces (a, scraper; b, backed/truncated piece; c, burin; d, flake point; e, tanged piece; f, core-on-flake), (g) abraded-edge celt, (h) grinding slab/quern and handstone. © John J. Shea.

sides of their worked edges. SNHCs occur in nearly every archaeological stone tool assemblage from all time periods. Many archaeologists call SNHCs "pebble cores," even though they are made on larger and different rocks than those fitting geologists' definition of pebbles (rounded rocks between 4 and 64 millimeters long in any dimension).

Elongated nonhierarchical cores have unequal length, width, and thickness dimensions as well as flakes detached to roughly the same extent on both sides of their worked edges. The most important of these artifacts are long core tools (LCTs),[7] foliate points, and celts. LCTs are elongated nonhierarchical cores with acute ($< 90°$) retouched edges. LCTs have relatively thick cross-sections. They vary tremendously in size and shape, but on average and among large samples they are about the size of an adult human hand. Foliate points have relatively thin cross-sections and a convergently retouched edge at one or both ends of their long axis. Celts feature a convex, straight (but nonconvergent) retouched edge at one or both ends of their long axis. Some foliate points and celts were used while attached to a handle, or were "hafted."

Bifacial hierarchical cores (BHCs) have worked edges from which stoneworkers created systematically detached flakes of unequal length. "Preferential" BHCs have a relatively large and symmetrical flake scar on the more invasively flaked side of a worked edge, while "recurrent" BHCs have many large scars of roughly equal size.[8]

Unifacial hierarchical cores (UHCs) have worked edges from one side of which flakes roughly equal to the core's longest axis were detached. Short and/or small UHCs are often grouped together with "pebble cores." Archaeologists distinguish elongated UHCs and the long, thin, and narrow flakes detached from them as "prismatic blade cores" and the long, narrow flakes detached from them as "prismatic blades." Many archaeologists think prismatic blades were more difficult to make than shorter flakes and therefore especially informative about earlier hominin intelligence and skill. As with so much of what archaeologists believe about stone tools, little or no evidence supports this hypothesis.

Retouched pieces include flake fragments that feature groups of small ($<$ 30 millimeters long) fracture scars spreading either orthogonally (perpendicularly) to an edge or parallel to their edge. "Retouch" describes both these small scars and the act of creating them. The most important of these include scrapers,

---

[7] Many archaeologists use the acronym LCT to mean "large cutting tool." However, "large cutting tool" is inaccurate. Most LCTs are not particularly large, though archaeological illustrations tend to select larger specimens. Only a tiny number have preserved wear traces or other residues indicating they were used to cut things. Archaeologists also call LCTs "handaxes."

[8] Eurasian and some African archaeologists call BHCs and some of the flakes detached from them "Levallois" cores/flakes after the name of the Parisian suburb where 19th-century archaeologists first noticed them.

notches, and denticulates (SNDs); backed/truncated pieces; flake points; burins; and tanged pieces. SNDs have at least one relatively sharp retouched edge that is either straight, concave, or convex in plan view (i.e., set on a level surface looking at it from above). Backed/truncated pieces feature at least one steeply retouched edge (around 90° in cross-section). Archaeologists often distinguish large and elongated backed/truncated pieces as "backed knives" and those less than 20–30 millimeters long as "microliths" or "geometric microliths." Flake points feature at least one convergently retouched tip. Burins feature at least one large flake scar that spreads parallel to an edge. Tanged pieces feature one area (or more) of invasive and concave retouching at one end of their long axis that creates a rectangular or tapering projection. Archaeologists think this "tang" an aid to hafting (attaching a tool to a handle). Cores-on-flakes are flake fragments featuring relatively large flake detachment scars (i.e., ones more than half their maximum length).

Historically, archaeologists view some retouch patterns on artifact-types as signifying cultural differences; others see in retouch variation clues about stone tool function. Retouch imposed on artifacts during reuse and recycling can also affect artifact variation (Dibble 1995).

Groundstone tools have flat, concave, or convex surfaces shaped by repeated and prolonged abrasion (Adams 2014a). Abraded-edge tools feature an edge formed by the intersection of two surfaces, at least one of which has been shaped by abrasion. The most common such artifacts are abraded-edge "celts." Pulverizing tools feature extensive flat, concave, or convex abraded surfaces. Common examples of pulverizing tools include mortars and pestles and handstones and grinding slabs (aka querns). Perforated stone tools, such "digging stick weights," "maces," and stone beads, have a hole carved or drilled through them.

Percussors, bipolar cores, short nonhierarchical cores, and short/small UHCs occur in almost every archaeological lithic assemblage from all time periods. Most of the other lithic artifacts discussed above appeared in the African archaeological record long before *Homo sapiens* fossils first appear, ca. 200–300 Ka (Table 2.4). The principal exceptions to this are foliate points, tanged pieces, and abraded-edge and pulverizing tools.

Archaeologists' Names for Stone Tools What's in a name? Many stone tool names reflect 19th- and early 20th-century archaeologists' speculations about their functions based on comparisons with Industrial Age metal tools. *Burin*, for example, is French for an engraving tool. Scraper implies a tool used for "orthogonal" (edge-transverse) cutting. Analyses of wear patterns and residues on prehistoric stone tools show that many retouched pieces were essentially like pocketknives, or multipurpose tools carried during daily foraging expeditions and in movements between residential sites. Because stoneworking is reductive (the more one uses stone tools, the smaller they become), many of the forms in which lithic artifacts enter the archaeological record have more to

TABLE 2.4 *First appearance dates for important lithic artifact-types*

Artifact-type	First appearance dates (Ma)	Reference[a]
Percussors	3.4	1
Short nonhierarchical cores	3.4	1
Bipolar cores	3.4	1
Elongated nonhierarchical cores	1.7–1.8	2
Long core tools	1.7–1.8	2
Foliate points	0.1–0.2	3
Celts	0.3	4
Bifacial hierarchical cores	0.3–0.5	5
Unifacial hierarchical cores	3.4	1
Prismatic blade cores	0.3–0.5	5
Retouched pieces	1.6–1.8	6
Scrapers, notches, denticulates	1.6–1.8	6
Backed/truncated pieces	1.6–1.8	6
Microliths	0.2–0.3	7
Flake points	1.6–1.8	6
Burins	1.6–1.8	6
Cores-on-flakes	1.6–1.8	6
Groundstone tools	< 20 Ka	8
Abraded-edge pieces	< 20 Ka	8
Pulverizing tools	< 20 Ka	8
Perforated pieces	< 40 Ka	8

[a] References: 1, Harmand et al. (2015); 2, Lepre et al. (2011); 3, Shea (2008a) and Yellen et al. (2005); 4, Clark (2001); 5, Johnson and McBrearty (2010) and Wilkins and Chazan (2012); 6, M. Leakey (1971); 7, Barham (2000); 8, numerous sources, see Shea (2017b, 2020a).

do with their having reached the limits of being able to be grasped or attached to handles, to cut things, or (for cores) to provide flakes large enough to be held and/or used. Unretouched flake edges dull swiftly (Key et al. 2018), and many of them may have enjoyed brief use for single purposes.

Many archaeologists assume that the various sorts of named stone artifact-types they have identified were as functionally specialized, similar to the various sorts of metal and other implements we use today. This is almost certainly a mistake. Subject to some constraints of mass and size, with enough ingenuity, one can make pretty much any stone tool do any cutting task.

These same cautionary notes apply to archaeologists' names for ceramic vessels and for artifacts made of other materials.

Stone Tools, "Modes," and Prehistoric Dispersals Some archaeologists have proposed meaningful correlations between changes in stone tool technology and prehistoric hominin dispersals. The most commonly cited such efforts (Lahr and Foley 1994; Foley and Lahr 1997; Gamble 2013) have done so by seeking correlations between first appearance dates of particular hominin species and first appearance dates for various ways of making stone tools. The stone tool framework they use, Grahame Clark's Modes 1–6 (Clark 1970), is little more than traditional cultural periods of European Stone Age prehistory expressed with numbers (e.g., "Mode 4" versus Upper Paleolithic) (Shea 2017a, 2020a). Others have used a different and recently developed framework, Stoneworking Modes A–I for similar purposes (Shea 2013a, 2017b). Which of these competing "modes" frameworks offers up superior insights into the processes driving prehistoric population movements remains to be seen.

Ceramics

Ceramics are artifacts made out of fired clay. When heated, silica particles in these sediments fuse together, forming a hard material, essentially an artificial igneous rock. When pure, such fused silica can be brittle, like glass. To counteract brittleness and to toughen ceramics for daily use, "temper" is added, such as sand, crushed shell, or fibers, whose presence in the ceramics prevents fractures from spreading. Most prehistoric ceramic artifacts are either vessels ("pottery") or figurines (small, three-dimensional images). The earliest ceramics currently known are figurines made around 25 Ka in Central Europe; however, recent discoveries of ceramic vessels in China dating to around the same time (20 Ka) suggests ceramic vessel production is equally ancient. Archaeologists often equate ceramic vessel production with food production (agriculture and pastoralism). This assumption is, if not demonstrably false, then at least not simple. Numerous prehistoric, ethnographic, and historic food-producing societies did not make or use ceramics, and yet some prehistoric hunter-gatherers did.

In describing ceramic vessels, archaeologists use commonplace terms for major functional categories (Figure 2.5). A "plate" or "platter" is a broad and shallow vessel used for serving solid food. A "bowl" is hemispherical vessel used for cooking and for serving liquids. A "jar" is a cylindrical cooking/storage vessel, usually accompanied by a lid that covers its wide opening. A jug is a storage vessel with a relatively large enclosed space and a narrow opening.

Apart from handles, decorations on ceramics, such as slips (colored sediments applied to vessel surfaces), incised patterns, applications, and paints/pigments add little or nothing to vessel function. Archaeologists think choices among such decoration can reflect prehistoric people's cultural choices. Ceramic variation can be a valuable source of hypotheses about "who questions," but one has to consider its limitations. Large and conspicuously decorated ceramic vessels broadcast symbolic messages about their owners' identities. In circumstances where such messages have important social consequences, near borders between different ethnic groups, for example, inappropriate choices among ceramic decorations can have serious social consequences.

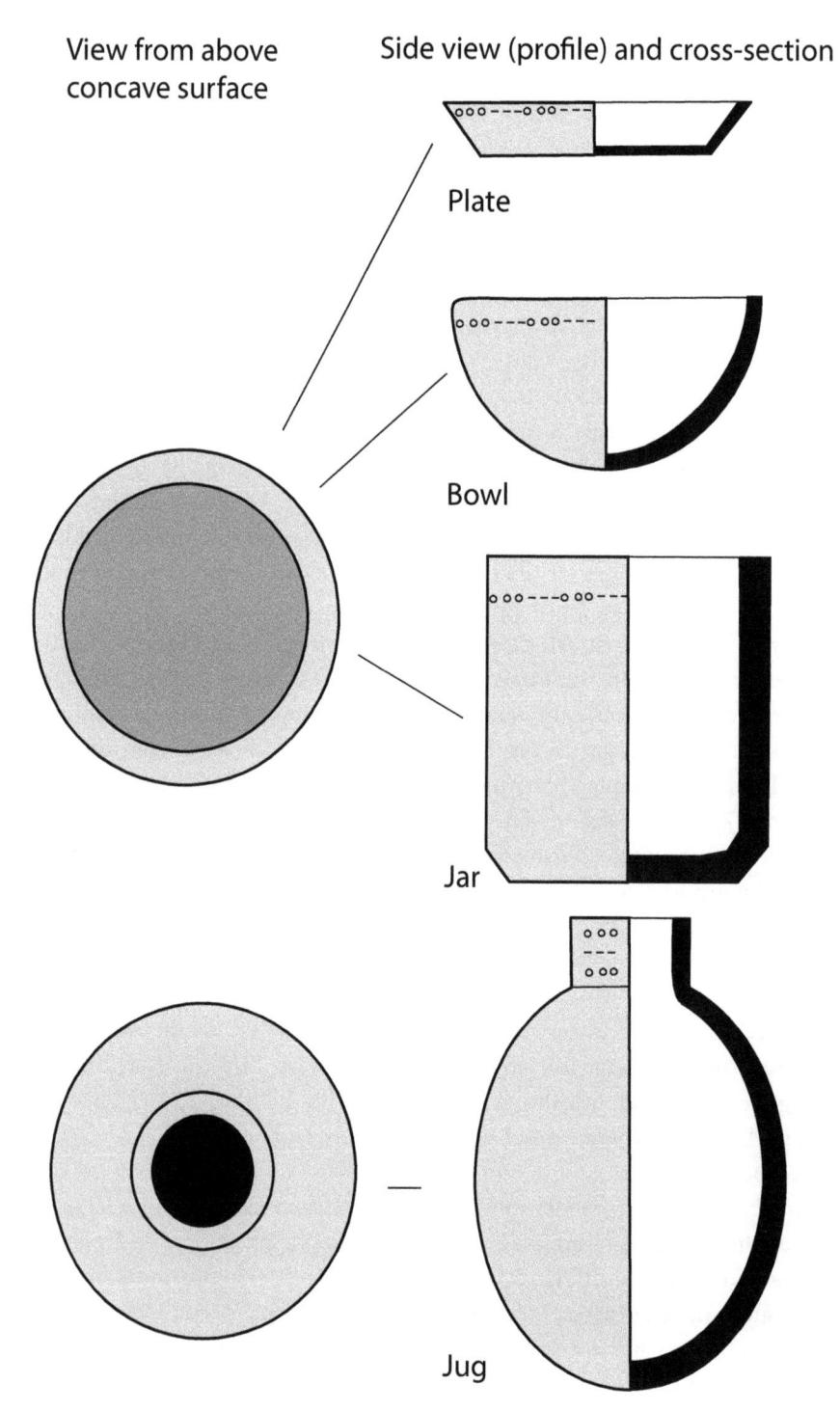

Figure 2.5 Ceramic plates, bowls, jars, and jugs. © John J. Shea.

For example, using ceramics decorated in the tradition of former allies who are now enemies might arouse suspicion about one's loyalties. In other situations, away from borders and possible encounters with strangers, choices of ceramic decoration may have few or no consequences, and as a result, choices may vary more widely (Hodder 1982). Though some ceramic designs may be uniquely associated with some smaller social groups, archaeologists express skepticism about hypotheses equating specific ceramic wares with social groups. Pots are not people.

Stone tools and ceramics covary with one another in complex ways. Sometimes their patterns correlate; other times, they do not. Much depends on how broadly or narrowly archaeologists have divided the lithic and ceramic evidence. In general, stone tool variation crosscuts variation in ceramic wares. That is, stone tools vary much less between assemblages of the same age and from the same region than ceramic wares do.

Artifacts Made of Wood, Cordage, Bone, and Shell

Carved wood, bone, antler, and ivory artifacts offer up a mixed bag of familiar and unfamiliar artifacts. Wooden artifacts are rarely preserved other than in waterlogged or extremely dry sediments. These artifacts range from weapons, such as javelins, to vessels and watercraft. Pleistocene-age cordage and basketry made from plant fibers are rarely preserved, but archaeologists can often infer their use from evidence associated with stone tools or from impressions on ceramics or other surfaces.

"Osseous" tools are artifacts made from ivory, antler, bone, horn, and shell. Early hominins appear to have recognized bone fragments as potential tool materials more than 2 Ma. More recent hominins of the genus *Homo* occasionally made fractured bone LCTs out of large mammal bones and elephant ivory in more or less similar ways to how they made stone tools at the same time. Carved osseous tools become considerably more common after 40 Ka, especially in Europe, Northern Asia, and the northernmost part of the New World, where cold conditions favor their preservation.

Interpreting organic artifacts can be tricky. First, preservation biases thrust nearly every inference about them into the "absence of evidence does not mean evidence of absence" debate. If one finds evidence for wooden javelin use in Germany 300 Ka, can one infer that hominins living earlier or at the same time and/or elsewhere used similar tools? Does such use vary geographically and chronologically, and can we estimate that variation with any confidence? Archaeologists assume specific kinds of artifacts were in widespread use after their first appearance dates in the archaeological record, but there is no consensus, and the risks of making that assumption are obvious.

Second, many of the organic artifacts recent humans use are fragments of multipart artifacts, such as traps, projectile weapons, or transport aids (boats, sleds). It can be difficult to deduce their role in such contraptions from their appearances alone. A preserved bit of cordage, for example, could be part of a net, a string used to lash a stone tool to a handle, part of a carrying bag, or part of a tourniquet. All too often archaeologists accept one particular hypothesis about organic artifacts' function without giving due consideration to alternatives, even though many ethnographic organic artifacts enjoy multiple functionally distinct uses. A series of carved bone points, for example, might be awls used for sewing or making baskets, barbs or tips attached wooden projectiles, parts of traps, pins for securing hair or garments, or several such uses in combination. Wooden bows are widely viewed as specialized hunting aids, but ethnographic studies document their use as digging sticks or for other purposes (Greaves 1997).

GENES: MOLECULAR ANTHROPOLOGY

Genes are segments of DNA molecules. They comprise sets of amino acids (base pairs) whose sequences cause cells to synthesize proteins in different ways, creating the various organs and tissues that comprise our bodies. These proteins influence our appearance, health, and behavior. During sexual reproduction, DNA in cell nuclei recombine. However, DNA in cell mitochondria (mtDNA), an individual cell's energy-producing organelles, do not. One inherits one's mitochondrial DNA intact from one's mother. Males inherit their nuclear Y-chromosomes intact from their fathers. Mutations, or copying errors that occur during cell division, create genetic differences among individuals. Some mutations can cause death anytime between early embryonic development and old age. Some parts of our DNA, so-called junk DNA, do not appear to code for anything in particular. Other than identical siblings and clones, all organisms have individually unique sequences of genes in their DNA.

Molecular anthropologists reconstruct historic and geographic patterns of human population movements by comparing DNA from living humans with DNA recovered from fossils (ancient DNA) and from sub-fossil (incompletely fossilized) human remains.[9] If the DNA collected from living Native Americans more closely resembles Asian DNA than European DNA, then that suggests Pleistocene Americans came to the Americas from Asia. Molecular anthropologists can then test that hypothesis by extracting DNA from Pleistocene American fossils and comparing it with the DNA of living Europeans and Native Americans.

---

[9] Molecular anthropologists study other things than genes, such as hormones, endocrines, blood, and proteins, but the overwhelming bulk of molecular anthropological research on issues in human evolution focuses on DNA.

Haplogroups

When molecular anthropologists write about human evolution, they discuss prehistoric humans in terms of haplogroups (from the Greek *haploûs*, "simple"), or groups of DNA samples that share the same specific combinations of alleles at specific places in their genome. Molecular anthropologists name haplogroups using hierarchical combinations of letters and numbers (e.g., L1, L2, L3, M). By working with geochronometric dates for when major mammal lineages diverged and deriving from those dates a general rate at which mutations accumulate among mammalian DNA, molecular anthropologists estimate branching points or divergences among human haplogroups.

The most important divergences among mitochondrial DNA haplogroups are those between haplogroup L (the most ancient and represented today mostly among Africans) and haplogroups N, M, R, and U, which are also found among Eurasians. These divergences are thought to date to between 35 and 70 Ka. The most ancient of the Y-chromosome haplogroups is haplogroup A00, whose appearance around 250 Ka in Africa correlates closely with first appearance dates for *Homo sapiens* fossils. A second cluster of Y-chromosome divergences occurs between 40 and 80 Ka and another between 13 and 30 Ka. The former aligns well with fossil evidence for human expansion northward and eastward from Africa and southern Asia. The second group of divergences bracket MIS 2 (the Last Glacial Maximum), and that group may have arisen from population fragmentation during this exceptionally cold period. That is, formerly widespread and interconnected regional populations became concentrated into smaller and temporarily-isolated groups.

Molecular anthropology is a relatively young, specialized, and fast-developing science. Higham (2021) provides an excellent and accessible overview of paleogenetics research challenges. Molecular anthropologists have thoroughly refuted the long-standing myth of "pure" races in prehistory (Reich 2018) (for which generations of anthropologists salute them!). And yet several common mistakes occur when scientists try to correlate the molecular evidence with other sources of evidence about human evolution, that is, linking genes to fossils and/or archaeological assemblages. First, scientists often mistake "gene histories" for population histories. British and German people, for example, enjoy very similar genes (Leslie et al. 2015), even though the two nations have fought two world wars against one another whose combined casualties almost certainly dwarf the population of their last common Anglo-Saxon ancestors.

Second, divergences among haplogroups were not necessarily evolutionarily important milestones. Humanity's last common female ancestor, "Mitochondrial Eve," lived in Africa around 200 Ka. We know she had at least one daughter, but that is all we know about her. After all, historically important people do not necessarily leave a correspondingly significant genetic legacy. A "genetic history" of the English people, for example, would miss both Elizabeth I (the "Virgin Queen" of England) and William Shakespeare. Neither has descendants among living humans, and so, from a "genetic history" standpoint, both are invisible.

"For" Genes

Finally, we come to a discussion of "for" genes, or specific genes purportedly for specific behaviors. Such genes are a myth. Geneticists have not found one-to-one demonstrably casual correlations between any specific gene and any important human behavior defined *prior to genetic research*. Any differences found by geneticists are usually noticed *after* obtaining samples and then "fishing for correlation." Press-release claims that someone has discovered a gene for musical talent, homosexuality, intelligence, risk-taking, or some similar characteristic receive much attention in popular media, but they rarely withstand skeptical experts' scrutiny. Why? Those touting them rarely specify just how the "for" gene actually causes the behavioral differences in question. Such negative findings are entirely predictable, of course, for an evolutionarily important behavior that depended on a single gene would be deeply vulnerable to loss to mutation.

SUMMARY

This chapter reviewed the "hard evidence," the principal sources of information out of which archaeologists and other paleoanthropologists construct hypotheses about human evolution. Because paleoanthropologists use every scrap of information from any scientific field to do this, this chapter has necessarily focused on the "centers of gravity" among these sources, namely geochronology, paleontology, archaeology, and molecular anthropology. The next chapter considers who we, *Homo sapiens*, are, our evolutionary origins, the differences between ourselves and other animals, and the differences among living humans.

Box 2.1: *Teleoliths, or Child's Play*

Dispersing people change their culture and social relations rapidly when they reach their destination, and children's activities may be the most important bellwethers of this process. In a migrating group, on the other hand, adults work to maintain their cultural and social identity. They take active measures to ensure their children keep established traditions, such as language, dress, cuisine, and other things that distinguish the migrating group from others. Such measures emphasize "negative feedback," efforts

Box 2.1: *(cont.)*

to reduce deviation from social norms. In a dispersal, in contrast, parents have incentives to encourage their children to imitate and adopt elements of their new cultural and novel social circumstances.

Why is this important and what are its implications for archaeology? Stoneworking appears to have been among earlier humans' survival skills. Human fossils appear nowhere after 300 Ka unaccompanied by stone artifacts of the same age. Stoneworking is a learned activity with virtually indestructible products and byproducts. If archaeologists can detect "teleoliths," or stone artifacts children made while learning how to make stone tools, then they may also be able to detect patterned variation in learning, including differences between how children among migrants and dispersers learn.

How should such teleoliths appear? First, one should expect to find teleoliths anywhere humans (and other hominins) resided for any length of time. If children were around stoneworking materials, they almost certainly interacted with them. Otherwise, stone tools would be unique among all human material culture.

Second, most children under the age of twelve lack the hand-eye coordination, strength, and impulse control to make flaked stone tools using controlled conchoidal fracture. They can imitate adult stoneworking gestures, but they often misjudge how a fracture will spread. Consequently, the objects on which they practice feature numerous incompletely propagated fractures (comminution), including edges too obtuse for such fractures to propagate.

Third, small hands make small tools. Much as a responsible parent would not allow a child to operate heavy machinery, one expects that children would use tools scaled to their size.

Finally, children are destructive little creatures. One ought not expect adults to have supplied small children with the best stone materials available. Teleoliths will probably be concentrated among rocks available nearby and on artifacts adults have discarded.

Historically, archaeologists have devoted surprisingly little attention to detecting teleoliths and/or other ways in which children influence the archaeological record. This issue remains an important frontier for research into prehistoric human population movements. A prehistory without children in it is no prehistory at all (Nowell 2021).

CHAPTER 3

WHO ARE THESE PEOPLE?

This chapter puts humans in our evolutionary context, answering such "who questions" as we need to before investigating "how questions." First, it explains where we fit in terms of broader patterns of primate evolution. Next, it shows how human behavior differs from that of other animals. Finally, it considers how we humans differ from one another. The most important differences among humans are cultural differences. Culture has several distinct properties for which we should expect to find evidence in the prehistoric record. Failing to find such evidence can suggest problems in our methods for investigating human evolution and prehistory.

HUMANS AS PRIMATES

Humans are primates, quadrupedal mammals with grasping hands. Living primates include lemurs, tarsiers, monkeys, apes, and humans. Among primates, we are catarrhines, or Old World monkeys. Catarrhines' distinctive features include closely positioned and downward facing nostrils, 32 teeth, and nongrasping tails (if any). Catarrhine fossils first appear around 23–34 Ma, during the Oligocene Epoch.

Among catarrhines, apes and humans are Hominidae. Hominidae include the African apes (gorillas, bonobos, chimpanzees), Asian orangutans, gibbons, and humans, as well as extinct hominins (bipedal primates). Hominidae differ from Old World monkeys in their larger body size, short trunk, more mobile shoulder joint, and lack of an external tail. Early Hominidae diverged from Old World monkeys around 20 Ma, during the Miocene Epoch.

Hominins

Ancestral hominins and apes shared a last common ancestor around 5–6 Ma, during the Pliocene Epoch. Hominins differ from apes in having reduced prognathism (a less-projecting lower face), shorter arms, longer legs, a more bowl-shaped pelvis, and other structural adaptations to habitual bipedal locomotion. Early hominins (those dating to 3.5 Ma or older) include *Sahelanthropus tchadensis*, *Ardipithecus kaddaba*, *Ardipithecus ramidus*, *Orrorin tugenensis*, and *Kenyanthropus platyops*. As their having both unique genus and species names suggests, these fossils differ markedly from one another. Most are also singular finds. That is, they come from one or a few localities close to one another in time and space. Understandably, paleoanthropologists maintain many competing hypotheses about these early hominins' evolutionary relationships to one another and to living humans.

This situation changes among fossils dating to the late Pliocene and Early Pleistocene epochs (1.5–3.5 Ma). These Plio-Pleistocene hominins include at least three hominin genera, *Australopithecus*, *Paranthropus*, and early *Homo*, each of which groups together more than one recognized species. Unlike early hominin fossils, those of these three Plio-Pleistocene genera appear at multiple sites scattered widely over Eastern and Southern Africa. Plio-Pleistocene hominins differ from earlier hominins in having smaller canine teeth, larger molars, and larger brains. *Australopithecus* has smaller molars than *Paranthropus*, but smaller brains than early *Homo*. These features suggest early *Homo* had a generalized diet. *Paranthropus* has very large molars, bony crests running front to back over the top of their skulls, and other features indicating powerful chewing. These features suggest a diet rich in foods requiring considerable chewing to extract nutrients, such as from fiber and other roughage. Early *Homo* has relatively smaller molars and somewhat larger brains. Brains are energetically expensive tissues. These features suggest early *Homo*'s diet included densely concentrated and high-quality nutrients, a signal feature of all living human diets. Paleoanthropologists infer early *Homo* engaged in considerable pre-oral food processing, such as pulverizing, cutting, and perhaps even cooking food before eating it.

Genus Homo

Fossils of early *Homo* dating to more than 1.6–2.3 Ma (e.g., *Homo habilis*) differ from those dating to younger periods. Earlier fossils had shorter legs, and longer arms, and other features thought to reflect retentions of earlier hominin adaptations to climbing around in trees (arboreal locomotion). Though height varies widely among fossils assigned to the genus *Homo* dating to less than 2.0 Ma, some are taller than earlier hominins. These younger hominins have an external nose, long legs, short arms, a true waist (a gap between their lowermost rib and the uppermost part of their pelvis), and a long and narrow foot with parallel toes and an elongated hallux (big toe). Paleontologists think these features reflect responses to selective pressures for more dedicated terrestrial locomotion, including prolonged walking and running on the ground. Tellingly, perhaps, these features occur among *Homo ergaster* and

Homo erectus, hominins whose remains occur in both Africa and Eurasia. They are less pronounced among fossils found only in Southern Africa (*Homo naledi*) or on islands in Asia (*Homo floresiensis*). The more widespread *Homo ergaster/erectus* younger than 1.6 Ma had larger brains than Plio-Pleistocene hominins, and brain volume seems to have enlarged over time. This evidence suggests these hominins maintained increasingly secure access to the dense concentrations of high-quality nutrients that larger brains require (Aiello and Wheeler 1995).

*Humans (*Homo sapiens*)*

Humans (*Homo sapiens*) differ from other species of the genus *Homo* in having a tall, globular skull with an orthognathic face (a face tucked under the front part of our brain), reduced brow ridges, and a projecting chin. These features reflect our flexed basicranium (bottom of the skull). Below the neck, we differ from earlier hominins mainly by having a more rounded, "basket-shaped" ribcage than earlier *Homo*. First appearance dates for *Homo sapiens* vary depending on criteria paleontologists use to diagnose the fossils as such, but the most widely accepted such fossils date to between 0.1 and 0.3 Ma and come from sites in Africa.

Living humans differ from Pleistocene *Homo sapiens* in having relatively less robust skeletal remains (thinner bones, smaller muscle attachments) and more dental pathologies. These features arise from many factors, mostly variation in activity levels and diets (D. Lieberman 2011, 2013), but they appear more or less worldwide after the end of the Pleistocene Epoch (since 12 Ka) and especially among remains from agricultural and urban-industrial societies. Though striking differences exist between recent (i.e., sub-fossil Holocene-age) human skeletons and Pleistocene human skeletons (Lieberman 2011), the current paleoanthropological consensus holds these differences insufficient to justify assigning them different scientific names.[1]

HOW DO HUMANS DIFFER FROM OTHER ANIMALS?

To truly appreciate how humans differ from other animals, we would need a nonhuman perspective. What would extraterrestrial biologists visiting and surveying Earth make of us? Laland (2018) proposes seven ways in which extraterrestrial biologists might find *Homo sapiens* remarkably different from other species.

---

[1] If one were to give them different names, then *Homo primigenius* for Pleistocene humans and *Homo familiaris* for Holocene ones would do the trick. *Homo sapiens* ("wise man") refutes itself daily.

Population Size

As of late 2022, about 8 billion humans inhabit the Earth. This is far more than for any mammal of our size and is multiple orders of magnitude larger than any of our nearest living primate relatives, chimpanzees (< 300,000), bonobos (50,000?), and gorillas (< 250,000). Africa's human population (1.2 billion) numbers around 1,200 times more than its ape population. Admittedly, insects, and ants in particular, outnumber us and exhibit signs and scales of social organization to rival our own (Moffett 2019), but our extraterrestrial observer would quickly discover that ants and other eusocial insects (bees, wasps) live within a narrow range of ecosystems and that their numbers ebb and flow with minor changes in climate. Humanity's numbers continue to increase independently of climate change.

Ecological Range

Humans live in a global diaspora, thriving everywhere from barren Arctic tundra to tropical forests teeming with life. To switch from living in one such extreme habitat to another, we merely change our clothing and modify our traditional architecture and diet. Our extraterrestrial visitors would doubtless note that other species, such as dogs, cats, rodents, cockroaches, and even some plants, have as wide geographic ranges as humans do, or very nearly so. Closer study would reveal some of these as "commensal" species, such as rats, mice, and sparrows, that subsist on our trash and in habitats humans have created. Others are plants and animals we domesticated as food sources. Still others are species we keep as pets, transport aids, or for other purposes. Exploring our nearest other planetary bodies, our visitors would undoubtedly notice that we have already begun littering the Moon and Mars with our artifacts, and they would surely note us as a species to watch.

Environmental Regulation

Humans control vast and diverse flows of energy and matter. As other primates do, they wrest such energy from their environment physiologically, by digestion. Preindustrial humans and earlier hominins used fire and other processes to liberate the energy available in wood and other plant matter, a renewable resource available nearly globally. Recent humans have expanded our energy sources to include fossil fuels and nuclear energy. Assuming our visitors could see both visible and infrared light spectra, they would certainly note correlations between light and heat emissions and human population distributions. They would also note that of the high carbon emissions pouring into our atmosphere and heating the planet, most result from human activity.

Global Impact

All organisms affect others. Ecologists call that network of relationships among any given organism and other organisms a "niche." The human niche is both uniquely broad and dynamically variable. Our activities affect other organisms for both better and worse. Domesticated plant and animals enjoy the same "extinction immunity" we do. On the other hand, human activities have also driven mass extinctions and biodiversity losses. Digging around a bit, our visiting alien surveyors would find correlations between first appearances of *Homo sapiens* in any given region and last appearances of countless animal species both large and small. They would also find correlations between high human population densities and occurrences of a very small range of domesticated plants and animals that comprise our principal food sources. If they were concerned about us, for good or ill, our visitors would note our small number of food sources as a potential vulnerability.

Cognition, Communication, and Intelligence

Cognition varies. A dolphin perceives its world differently from a bat, and both dolphin and bat perceive the world differently from a human being. Nevertheless, countless studies comparing human perception, learning, and problem-solving with those of our nearest living primate relatives confirm our distinctiveness. Some juvenile chimpanzees excel over human children of the same age in certain problem-solving tasks, but as humans mature, our children outperform the apes. Our spoken language and symbolic artifacts allow us to create infinite combinations of meanings in ways other species' vocalizations and gestural signals cannot. If our extraterrestrial biologists decide to make "first contact" with intelligent terrestrial species, one thinks they would find such contacts with humans vastly more informative than first contacts with apes.

Knowledge Acquisition and Sharing

Other animals move around searching for food, shelter, and mates. Eusocial insects (ants, bees) even systematically store food (Holldobler and Wilson 1990). Humans also move in search of information (e.g., attending college) and store it in artifacts (books, electronic media) that allow us to share that information broadly. Because our complex cognition allows us to treat artifacts as symbols, we accumulate knowledge and share it across large populations and over many generations. Most of what other primates need to learn they learn by observation and imitation. Instances of learning with "joint attention" – two or more pairs of eyes and hands applied on the same thing simultaneously – are uncommon among apes. Among humans, joint-attention-based learning is universal. Much human teaching/learning involves children observing adults, but adult-adult teaching is commonplace, too. Humans alone have formal institutions specifically intended to transmit learning (schools, libraries) and to generate new information (universities, research institutes).

Complex and Variable Technology

Humans invent, manufacture, and use more tools and more complex technology than other species. Many other animals use tools, but such tool use rarely involves more than bringing two or more objects into contact with one another, such as chimpanzees splitting stones with nuts and birds building nests. Human tools routinely involve the patterned imposition of nonintrinsic shapes – shapes that are not intrinsic to the raw material of which they are comprised – as well as objects of different and artificial materials (ceramics, metals, plastics) conjoined to one another, such as an axe, a house, or a piano. Our alien visitors might note the vegetation and feces our near primate relatives throw at them, but they would be on guard against our considerably more lethal weapons.

HOW DO HUMANS DIFFER FROM ONE ANOTHER?

Zoologists divide many widely dispersed species into subspecies, or genetically and morphologically distinct regional populations of a more widely distributed species. Subspecies differ, but not so greatly as to prevent interbreeding if and when opportunity arises. Domesticated animals are subspecies of their ancestors' wild-living descendants. Dogs (*Canis lupus familiaris*) belong to a subspecies of wolf (*Canis lupus*). Both dogs and wolves interbreed routinely wherever the two occur at the same time and in the same places.

Are human "races" subspecies? No, they are not. Human races are the opposite of subspecies. Morphological and genetic differences among living humans result from complex combinations of natural and sexual selection. Natural selection influences an organism's individual survival, while sexual selection influences its opportunities to mate (Mayr 2001). Some "racial" features, such as darker or lighter pigmented skin, confer survival advantages in environments with greater or lesser amount of sunlight. Others, such as blue eyes or blonde hair, possibly reflect shifts among what people considered attractive or unattractive at any given point in time. Among small early human populations, preferred physical characteristics could swiftly have become "fixed" (ubiquitous) without comprising barriers to interbreeding with individuals among other human groups who had different physical characteristics.

The most commonly recognized races are social constructs, "folk biology," categorical distinctions we make up for immediate purposes that, for one reason or another, persist onto historical timescales. They combine biologically based differences in appearance (skin pigment, hair color and texture) together with mutable behavioral characteristics, such as language and cultural differences (Saini 2019). Humans belonging to the major geographically defined human races (European, Asian, African, Australasian, Native American) have as much or more genetic and morphological variation within said groups as exist between them (Templeton 1999).

Races, Humor, Color, and Other Characteristics

Early scientific writing about human variation identified "white," "yellow," "black," and "red" races. One no longer hears the terms "yellow" or "red" races in polite society, but "white" and "black" persist in wide usage. Ostensibly referencing skin color, the modern use of color terms for race likely arose when Renaissance Era scholars tried to explain geographic variation in human groups' appearance and behavior in terms of the four "bodily humors" (white/yellow phlegm, black bile, blood) by which the ancient physician Hippocrates and his followers explained variation in individual temperaments. Prior to the 15th century AD, most scholars of human variation used alternative terms based on combinations of linguistic, cultural, and geographic variables – Greeks, Jews, Germans, Slavs, and so on. Renaissance and later scholars ascribed temperamental differences formerly applied to individuals based on imbalances in humors to entire peoples based on their skin color. Most of the pernicious myths about different modern-day races arose from this practice. Nineteenth-century pre-evolutionary theories about racial variation envisioned these "pure" races originating separately and remaining separate and distinct from one another until recent cross-racial intermarriage (aka "miscegenation").[2]

Measurable differences between DNA from fossils and DNA of living humans supports the hypothesis that modern "races," however defined, are but transient things (Reich 2018). Such fossil DNA may be more similar to DNA samples from one living group of humans than to others, but it is never identical. Geneticists always find differences. Pure races with ancient pedigrees are a myth. They bring nothing to scientific explanations of either differences among living humans or patterns in past human population movements. This is important because past efforts to reconstruct human population movements have often cast those movements in terms of migrating races, "peoples,"

---

[2] Nineteenth-century theories about race origins varied, but most incorporated the assumption that races were "pure," that such homogeneity was a good thing, and that racial mixing, much less intermarriage, was bad. "Pure race" theories enjoyed much support among slave-owners and slavery apologists, and later among segregationists, but World War II and the Holocaust removed most of the last vestiges of scientific support for these theories. There are no such things as pure races, and there never have been, either.

"folk," named haplogroups, or archaeological "cultures" of whose existence as self-conscious social entities enjoy not a trace of scientific support. These things are both figments and failures of the anthropological imagination.

It may seem difficult to imagine discussions about human variation that do not mention race, but it is important to remember how recently the human race concept developed. Typological thinking about human variation is, of course, very ancient. Egyptian artists, for example, painted their men and women with different skin colors and showed Libyans, Nubians, and Asians with different and distinctive skin colors, too. Classical and Medieval travelers rarely remarked on geographic variation in human appearance. Before the 16th to 18th centuries, short ocean voyages and caravan travel probably made differences among the people encountered by voyagers seem gradual, slight differences in peoples' looks and customs from one coastal town or desert caravanserai to another. Longer ocean voyages with fewer ports of call may have made variation in human appearance and behavior appear categorical, differences of kind rather that points on a continuum of variation. Scholarly misadventures with "race" begin shortly afterward.

"Definite-Article" Cultures

The most important differences among living humans are cultural differences, patterned choices among learned strategies for accomplishing one or another objective. Historically, anthropologists have sought patterns in human cultural variation and organized their observations in terms of specific named cultures (Harris 2013). One thinks of these cultures as "definite-article" cultures, for early anthropologists often identified the subjects of their studies as *the* Maasai, *the* !Kung San, or *the* Navajo. Ethnologists and, later, anthropologists did not mean any harm in using "the," but in doing so, they implied much less variability among the groups thus named than among those (typically Europeans) to whom they did not attach such names. That human cultural variation is simple, stable, and amenable to categorical classification came to cultural anthropology from its precursor, ethnology, and more specifically from the German *kulturkreislehre* (culture circle/culture area) school of early 20th-century ethnology. Exponents of this *kulturkreislehre* approach grouped together living human cultures based on patterns of similarities and differences in order to trace their origins back to hypothetical centers of innovation in human evolution. This approach to studying human cultural differences relied heavily on accounts of different cultures that missionaries, colonial officers, tourists, and other travelers recorded. Understandably, given these sources, ethnologists' accounts of other people living in distant lands emphasized modalities (norms and central tendencies) rather than variation and variability. When "cultural anthropologists" began conducting fieldwork and making their own observations during the early 20th century, they discovered human cultures were vastly more complex, dynamic, and variable than "culture circle" stereotypes (King 2019). The only places actual human cultures remained unchanging were in the books ethnologists and early cultural anthropologists wrote about them. This would all be an amusing anecdote in the history of cultural anthropology, except that archaeologists adopted the "definite-article" model of human culture at the very moment actual cultural anthropologists realized how wrong it was (Trigger 2006).

Archaeological Stone Tool Industries and Ceramic Wares

Archaeologists began grouping stone tools and ceramic wares together into named industries and cultures during the later 19th century and ever more extensively during 20th century. Early archaeologists envisioned these groupings as stages in a "stadial" (ladder-like) progression from primitive to advanced cultures, much as 19th-century ethnologists had done. As the archaeological record grew, however, archaeologists began viewing and naming prehistoric cultures nonhierarchically, treating groups of archaeological assemblages as the equivalents of different contemporary groups of living humans, specifically "definite-article" cultures. Much as *kulturkreislehre* scholars before them, 20th-century archaeologists tried to trace evolutionary relationships among prehistoric cultures offset from one another in time and space. Mid-20th-century syntheses of prehistory routinely summarized their findings using maps showing different sequences of named prehistoric cultures in different regions, sometimes connecting them to one another with arrows indicating hypothetical ancestor-descendant relationships. Archaeologists still do this, but our collective understanding of culture has improved. Most anthropologically trained archaeologists recognize culture as far more complex than early 20th-century archaeologists realized. Nevertheless, the idea that prehistoric cultural differences were categorical differences persists. It is "baked in" to the language we use to describe patterned variation in the prehistoric record (Clark and Riel-Salvatore 2006). One sees its expression in "Freudian slips," when archaeologists reference groups of prehistoric people with the "definite-article" names they gave to their industries and cultures, such as *the* Solutreans or *the* Clovis people.[3]

Some of the prehistoric people archaeologists explicitly or implicitly group together into named industries and cultures might have been part of the same hypothetically self-conscious human groups, that is, groups that would recognize their shared cultural identity. Then again, they might not. Unfortunately, we lack any way to test these hypothetical equivalences independently of the

---

[3] Doing so is, admittedly, less linguistically cumbersome than calling them "the people who made what we call Solutrean/Clovis artifacts," but it is still the academic equivalent of lazy screenwriting.

evidence that inspired them. To do so, one would need to interview and observe extinct humans. Answers that invoke the names archaeologists have dreamed up for prehistoric people are simply not scientific responses to "who questions."

Actual Cultural Differences among Living Humans

Culture is a biological phenomenon and an evolved human capacity. Other animals have approximations of culture, such as "chimpanzee cultures" (Whiten et al. 1999), but no other living animal has quite the same thing we do, culture supported by spoken language and other forms of symbolic communication.[4] A creature that cannot explain culture's complex emergent properties (the ways in which it is more than the sum of its parts) does not have culture as the anthropologists who coined the term understood it and as anthropologists understand it today.

One understands why primatologists might seek to describe nonhuman primate (or other animal) activities as "culture." It elevates the importance of those species and research on them into larger anthropological debates. It could also potentially aid efforts to conserve those animals and their habitats. Still, the fact of the matter remains that in the two decades since primatologists began writing about "chimpanzee cultures," noncaptive chimpanzee populations have plummeted. "Culture" does not seem to confer on apes the same extinction immunity it does on humans.

Human culture has five key properties with deeply important consequences for reconstructing our species' evolution, namely, variability, mutability, accumulation, virality, and complexity.

Variability: Culture varies. People in the same society make different choices. Students in my large morning lecture classes rarely dress identically. They present a mosaic of sartorial individuality and stereotypes: art student, business major, engineer, future professor, a few still in their pajamas. As my Stony Brook University students' choices demonstrate, culture encourages variation. For noncollegiate corroboration, one need merely survey differences in clothing among people in the same restaurant.

Mutability: Culture mutates and changes. That is, there exist historic patterns in cultural variability. When I began teaching in the 1990s, Stony Brook University had as its mascot "the Patriot," a thuggish-looking male figure dressed in the uniform of an American Revolutionary soldier. (Stony Brook and nearby Setauket were hotbeds of pro-independence activity during the Revolutionary War.) At some point, the university decided it needed a new mascot, and so it commissioned and trademarked "Wolfie the Seawolf," a

---

[4] An old "Indian" proverb holds, "It's never a good idea to have the same name for different things."

half-fish half-wolf chimera.[5] Gradually, over the course of 3–4 years, one saw fewer and fewer signs, shirts, and other Patriot logos and more and more Wolfies. Noncollegiate examples of cultural mutability abound. For corroboration, one need only visit an antiques store. Disconcertingly, your author all too often finds on display and for sale artifacts familiar from his childhood.

Accumulation: Culture accumulates. When people adopt new choices among ways of doing things, they often retain previous ones. During lectures, my students often take notes on laptops and tablet computers (as well as shop, email, and watch sporting events), but most of them also have a pen or pencil and notepaper handy. Culture can be cumulative (Tennie et al. 2009), but cultures do not always retain all previous ways of doing things. A few of my students know ancestral techniques for starting fire by wood-on-wood friction, because I have taught them how do so. But, mindful of how difficult making fire this way is, far more of my students carry butane lighters or matches in their "everyday-carry kits."[6]

Virality: Virus-like, culture spreads.[7] Each Wednesday afternoon, Stony Brook University has a class-free 90-minute "Prime Time" during which student activity groups meet. When the weather is favorable, these groups set up tables at the edge of the campus' academic mall that they staff with group members and promotional materials. These tables advertise fraternities and sororities, political groups, athletic clubs, ethnic-interest groups, academic majors, and pre-professional societies. These groups' organizational "cultures" differ, but all seek new members among the student population. Political parties host similar events on a regular basis, aiming to spread their messages among a new audience and to reinforce those messages' hold on those who are already members.

Complexity: Human cultural identities vary in complex ways. One can profess membership in "cultures" arranged hierarchically, in nested sets of ever-smaller categories, such as American, New Englander, college professor, archaeologist. My Stony Brook University students may self-identify as Chinese, nonbinary, art major, or varsity fencing team member. Or one can identify transcendently, as professing memberships in "cultures" that cross-cut other social divisions, such as memberships in fraternities, sororities, and various professional organizations. Humans can belong to or shift allegiances

---

[5] In paleontology, a chimera references a fossil made up of parts of different animals. The name refers to a Greek mythological creature that sported a goat's body, a lion's head, and a serpent's tail. Why a major research university with world-renowned programs in evolutionary biology and marine sciences has as its mascot a half-fish half-wolf chimera remains an enigma.

[6] A small packet of emergency essentials I urge my commuter students to carry with them to and from campus. These include an LED flashlight, whistle, penknife, matches/lighter, button compass, bandages, safety pin, aspirin, cell phone charging cord, pencil, and notepaper.

[7] Evolutionary biologist Richard Dawkins (1976) argued that "memes," bits of information that comprise culture, compete more or less like genes do, but for places in our minds and culture rather than positions in our genome.

among more than one cultural group simultaneously in ways that other primates cannot.[8]

Lessons for Prehistoric Research

Why are these qualities of culture important for research on prehistoric human dispersals? Uniformitarian principles require that we explain the past using processes we can observe in the world around us today. All recent human cultures have an evolved capacity for rapid change and wide behavioral variability. All of even the most self-professedly "conservative" living human cultures differ profoundly from humans who lived a mere 500 years ago and among themselves. Your culture may have only one approved way of cracking open eggs, or rules about what one can eat and what one cannot, but somewhere, someone among your group does these things differently.

Knowing these qualities of culture guides us in terms of what we should expect to find in an archaeological record prehistoric humans created. Among living animals, only humans have culture with all of these properties. No human culture lacks any one of them. Therefore, we should expect early *Homo sapiens'* culture had these properties, too (Shea 2011a, 2011b). If we find mismatches between our expectations and our observations about prehistoric human cultures, then we have to consider alternative hypotheses, namely, the following:

> *Hypothesis #1:* Preservation biases. Preservation bias and inadequate sampling create the illusion of absence, and thus, of differences.
> *Hypothesis #2:* Analytical errors. Flawed analytical methods create the illusion of differences between samples.
> *Hypothesis #3:* Actual differences. Early human cultures were genuinely and significantly different from recent human cultures. (One struggles to imagine what could have constrained early *Homo sapiens* from exploiting the full range of advantages culture affords, but failure of imagination is not a valid reason to accept or reject a hypothesis.)

Time and again the history of paleoanthropological research shows that preservation bias and analytical error (Hypotheses #1 and #2) more than adequately explain differences between archaeological cultures and recent human cultures. Hypothesis #3 remains a possibility, for evolution never stops, but as of this writing, no evidence whatsoever supports the existence of profound evolutionary differences in earlier versus current humans' capacity for culture.

---

[8] This remark may elicit arguments that apes, monkeys, lemurs, or whatnot shift among social alliance networks. The important difference is that, unlike these creatures, humans can explain why they do so, even when that explanation appears counterfactual.

SUMMARY

This chapter reviewed how our species differs from other hominins and now-extinct primates and how we differ from other forms of life on earth. It examined historical approaches to describing human variation, concluding that categorical distinctions among humans, such as "races," offer little to paleoanthropological research. Most of the important differences among humans are cultural differences, not genetic nor morphological ones. These observations suggest that important differences among prehistoric humans were cultural differences, too. That is, they reflect conscious choices among known and imaginable options rather than some sort of "innate cultural conservatism," or tradition's cold, dead hand. The next chapter considers how to go about answering "how questions" about prehistoric human population movements.

Box 3.1: *What's in a name? (Hominin alpha taxonomy)*

Historically, the formal naming ("alpha taxonomy") of fossils in the genus *Homo* veers between periods of "splitting" (many species recognized) and "lumping" (few species recognized). Late 19th- to early 20th-century paleontologists had few fossils, and so, differences among them appeared to warrant making major species- or even genus-level distinctions. As fossil evidence accumulated, paleontologists gained a greater appreciation of patterned variability in that evidence. During the middle part of the 20th century, paleontologists grouped together many formerly distinct species of fossil *Homo* into a smaller number of more inclusive species, such as *H. erectus* and *H. heidelbergensis*. Lately, this trend has reversed itself, with increasing claims identifying "new" species.

Several factors appear to be driving a return to "splitting." First, some newly discovered fossils, such as the so-called "hobbits" of Flores, Indonesia (*H. floresiensis*) and *H. naledi* from South Africa' Rising Star Cave Complex, are truly something new and very different from previously known hominin fossils. Second, paleontologists now have a dizzying array of multivariate statistical tools and other technological aids for discovering and quantifying differences among fossils. Finally, naming a new hominin fossil species attracts considerable attention in popular media. Scientists and research institutions value this attention, and in seeking it sometimes alter traditional criteria and procedures for identifying new hominin species.

Ordinarily, one identifies a new species of extinct hominin using a "type-specimen" (holotype) such as a fossil skull and/or jaw with well-documented geological provenience, solid geochronology, and using morphological criteria including measurements. And yet in 2010 scientists excavating at Denisova Cave in Russia identified "Denisovans" as a new

Box 3.1: *(cont.)*

hominin species based on DNA extracted from a fingerbone. More than ten years later these "Denisovan" fossils still lack a formal scientific name. In 2021, scientists announced a new species, *Homo longi* ("Dragon Man") based on their analysis of a Late Pleistocene fossil skull that had been hidden in Chinese well for the last 80 years.[9] Rather than announcing a new hominin species in prominent journals such as *Science* or *Nature,* as is customary, "Dragon Man" debuted in a new and obscure journal that, perhaps unsurprisingly, remains obscure.

---

[9] Only time will tell whether the larger field of paleoanthropology accepts *Homo longi*. Several experts have noted that it looks not much different from a fossil found in Dali, China, that is itself the subject of a controversial "new species" claim. To make matters even more amusingly complicated, some commentators have proposed the *H. longi* skull is that of a Denisovan. The fun never stops.

CHAPTER 4

HOW DID THEY GET HERE?

This chapter introduces a new approach to investigating "how questions" about prehistoric human population movements. Rather than speculating about specific population movement routes, "survival archaeology" asks how prehistoric humans solved essential survival problems as they moved to and settled in new habitats. Ethnographic studies of preindustrial humans as well as the modern-day wilderness survival and "bushcraft" literature shed light on what these "ancestral survival skills" were. The chapter argues that humans overcame prehistoric survival challenges by using complex combinations of ancestral survival skills. It closes by proposing some reasonable assumptions about how earlier humans used those skills.

ARROWS ON MAPS

The ease with which we can travel the world today influences our view of prehistoric human population movements. Prehistoric archaeology developed during the 19th to 20th centuries, an era of increasingly cheap, easy, and safe global movement. Today, one can journey from New York to Sydney, Australia, using either boat or aircraft, and upon arriving wear the same clothes, eat similar foods, and speak more or less the same language in both places. One does not need to learn radically different modern-day survival skills, such as how to drive a car, how to order lunch in a restaurant, or how to make a phone call. Unsurprisingly, archaeologists' answers to "how did they get here?" usually focus on routes connecting origins and destinations, hypotheses they express graphically as "arrows on maps" (Nicholson et al. 2021). For expressing hypotheses about population movements, arrows on maps offer several advantages. They are a clear way to depict a hypothesis and thus easy for one's audience to understand. They are also familiar. Historians, journalists, and others depict recent human population movements as arrows on maps, too.

Problems with Arrows on Maps

And yet arrows-on-maps hypotheses have several problems. First, they oversimplify. That most such arrows in paleoanthropological literature have points at only one end implies one-way population movements. This fits well with how migrations play out, but not so well with dispersals. Migrating populations cannot return from their new homelands for the simple reason that farmers, herders, and others who remained behind in the "old country" almost certainly took over any farms and pastures emigrants abandoned. Individual humans who fail at dispersing *can* go home again. Indeed, being able to return home if all else fails *encourages* dispersals.

Second, arrows on maps imply an unrealistic degree of precision. A narrow arrow implies movement along a very specific path. Some historic migrations play out this way. For example, many Euro-American pioneers moving across the North American plains and deserts followed advance-scouted, mapped, and well-marked trails. But this is not how other animals disperse. They move in many directions simultaneously and along multiple routes. For example, when coyotes dispersed into the Eastern United States during the 20th century, they did not form a "mega-pack" and follow one single interstate highway (Flores 2016). When they appeared in my hometown in Massachusetts, they did so one animal at time, and only after years did the "coyote chorus" announce that individuals had found one another and bred. When it comes to answers about by what routes animals disperse, the answer is: by any and all routes possible. The more specific the arrows-on-maps hypotheses about such dispersals are, the more likely they are wrong.

Finally, arrows on maps sometimes appear utterly divorced from geographic reality. Some of those published in textbooks and popular-science works show prehistoric humans and earlier hominins crossing oceans, fording rivers, blazing through jungles, and traversing mountain ranges, as if they were flying over them in aircraft. They offer no hint of either the difficulties in actually crossing through or around these obstacles or how dispersing hominins overcame those difficulties. Arrows on maps strip prehistory of much, indeed all, that would be interesting to learn about our ancestors.

From "Who Questions" to "How Questions"

Archaeologists' long-standing emphasis about "who questions" colors their efforts to answer "how questions." When archaeologists recognize prehistoric industries and cultures, they usually assign them to one and only one hominin. Archaeologists then use these hominin-industry linkages to construct hypotheses about population movement routes. Two problems afflict this strategy of using answers to "who questions" to answer "how questions."

First, archaeologists link industries and/or stoneworking strategies to specific hominins based on occurrences of hominin fossils in the same sediments as the artifacts. And yet such co-occurrences ("stratigraphic associations") merely indicate burial during the same time interval, an interval that could have spanned centuries or millennia. They do not prove that the specific hominins whose fossils occur in those deposits made all or any of the stone tools enclosed in the same sediments with them. Furthermore, vastly more sites contain stone tools unassociated with any hominin fossils. Who made and discarded stone tools at these sites is anybody's guess. If there is no way to prove such guesses wrong, then should one really bother guessing?

Second, conventions for naming stone tool industries and to whom to attribute them vary among different archaeological research traditions. Use of the term "Levallois" for bifacial hierarchical cores, for example (see Chapter 2), strongly tracks Francophone research activity. The term commonly appears in archaeological literature for Europe, the Near East, and former French colonial possessions in Africa, but it is virtually unknown in South Africa, Australia, and the Americas. Nor do any set of rules govern the naming of new stone tool industries.

In Africa and in much of Eurasia, the prior presence of hominins other than *Homo sapiens* often sparks debate over who made which sets of stone artifacts. Unsurprisingly, since no rules govern this process, debates about hominin-industry equations swiftly descend into appeals to authority and to past research practices – essentially an adult version of Pin the Tail on the Donkey, the children's game in which a blindfolded contestant tries to pin a paper tail on a poster of a donkey guided by other children yelling directions to them.[1]

Any one of these problems would be sufficient to cast doubt on hypotheses tracing prehistoric human population movements using such a "who-to-how" approach. Taken together, they show that hypotheses about population movements incorporating hominin-industry equations are almost certainly wrong.[2]

SURVIVAL ARCHAEOLOGY

Archaeologists devote surprisingly little attention to how earlier humans overcame challenges to their survival. All too often they do not mention them, or they assume ancestral humans somehow managed to survive. Such "silence and somehow" non-answers are not good enough. Would archaeologists accept such non-answers to questions about how earlier hominins made stone tools and hunted? Would they entertain theories about the origins of agriculture that failed to discuss how humans domesticated the plants and animals

---

[1] Watching children play this game can be near-deafening fun. Sitting through the archaeological version can be coma-inducingly tedious.
[2] Arguably worse, for one cannot prove them wrong.

involved? Would they consider adequate a theory about the rise of cities that did not consider how early cities became linked to other settlements on the landscape? They would not, and neither should anybody else.

A new approach to prehistory, "survival archaeology," seeks to fill this gap in our knowledge about ancestral human behavior (Shea 2020b). Survival archaeology asks the most important "how question" of all: How did early humans survive long enough to become ancestral humans? What, specifically, were the survival challenges early humans faced as they dispersed and migrated? At the very least, they had to solve the following "big six" survival challenges (listed below in order of priority):

1. First aid and medication: treating injury and illness
2. Thermoregulation: making fire and finding shelter
3. Hydration: obtaining potable water
4. Nutrition: procuring food
5. Transportation: moving across the landscape
6. Communication: signaling for and getting help.

All living human societies have solutions to these challenges, usually more than one, and in all cases those solutions differ from those used by other living primates.

To answer questions about early human survival strategies, survival archaeology uses insights from both familiar and somewhat more exotic sources. Familiar sources include the archaeological record itself, experimental archaeology, ethnography, and ethnoarchaeology. More exotic sources (or at least ones less often cited in the professional archeological literature) include works on bushcraft, wilderness survival, and nonhuman primate ethology. Each of these sources of hypotheses has strengths and weaknesses (Table 4.1).

Archaeological Evidence

The archaeological record offers up clues about human survival strategies, such as traces of fire, stone-cutting tools, ceramic containers, and animal bones. But it has some known limitations, first, "sample error." That is, archaeologists dig where they think artifacts and other remains are likely preserved, and modern-day terrain features such as vegetation and ease or difficulty of access influence those choices of excavation sites. Archaeologists excavate caves, for example, not because of some prior theory suggesting important things happened in caves. They do so because cave sediments preserve fossils and artifacts better than open-air sites.

Second, associations among excavated finds can invite multiple hypotheses. Finding stone tools together with zebra bones, for example, could suggests humans ate zebra. On the other hand, the zebra bones and stone tools could have been deposited separately, months, weeks, even years apart.

TABLE 4.1 *Strengths and weaknesses among sources of hypotheses for survival archaeology*

Source	Strengths	Weaknesses
Archaeological record	Clear evidence of particular solutions to problems	Preservation biases, sample error
Experimental archaeology	Can demonstrate possible activities, explicitly seeks criteria for recognizing them	Possible is not the same as actual; experimenter competency issues
Ethnography or ethnoarchaeology	Activity directly observable and verifiable	Risk of fabrications, memory culture
Bushcraft	Can demonstrate possible activities	Non-peer-reviewed literature, appeals to authority, rarely measurement-based
Wilderness survival	Identifies specific problems, ranks them in priority, shows what *not* to do	Short-term versus long-term solutions, reliance on modern technology
Nonhuman primate ethology	Allows one to scale comparisons of variation among human and other hominin survival strategies	Limited numbers of studies on noncaptive animals, especially African apes

Archaeologists need to be on guard against "time averaging," or assuming things enclosed in the same sediments were exactly contemporary with one another.

Preservation biases can also be a problem. Living humans use wood, cordage, and leather for countless tasks, but these materials decompose rapidly on the surface and rarely are preserved in ancient archaeological sediments. Human behavior can also affect preservation. Prehistoric humans might have regularly enjoyed elephant steaks but balked at hauling heavy elephant bones from distant butchery sites back to caves and other habitation sites whose accumulations of stone tools and smaller animal fossils confer high archaeological "visibility."

Experimental Archaeology

Experimental archaeology involves archaeologists simulating conjectural past human activities in order to verify whether or not a hypothetical activity is possible (butchering a zebra with one or another sort of stone tool, for example) and, if so, how to recognize evidence for it in the archaeological record (such as stone tool cut marks on zebra bones) (Schick and Toth 1993). Experimental archaeology demonstrates the possible rather than what prehistoric humans actually did. For example, showing that one can cross the shark-infested lower Red Sea between Africa and Arabia using simple watercraft suggests such voyages were possible. It does not show that prehistoric humans made those voyages.

A second risk involves experimenter competency. Put simply, many of those performing the experiments lack expertise in the activities being undertaken. Rather than having practiced these skills for years, as prehistoric humans almost certainly did, many archaeologists and their students make and use stone tools or other implements in experiments after only brief exposure to "the basics." Studies of even relatively simple stoneworking, for example, reveal significant differences between novices and experts (Duke and Pargeter 2015; Pargeter and Faith 2020). Even greater differences seem intuitively likely in activities more complex than stoneworking.[3]

Ethnography and Ethnoarchaeology

Ethnography refers to cultural anthropologists' studies of living preindustrial humans (e.g., Lee 1979; Marlowe 2010). When archaeologists conduct such studies in the service of specifically archaeological research goals, one calls the activity "ethnoarchaeology" (e.g., Yellen 1977; Hayden 1979; Gould 1980). Ethnography and ethnoarchaeology offer up documented examples of strategies for solving problems whose effectiveness one can observe directly. One can also ask one's research subjects why they chose one solution to a problem rather than a different one. Ethnographic studies seem to lack the "competency issues" that afflict experimental archaeology, but still, one has to be careful. Older such studies often fail to distinguish between what an anthropologist has actually seen and what ethnographic "informants" told them. Some such accounts can report "memory culture," or potentially flawed recollections of how things were done in the former times. Others can be outright fabrications. As my late colleague, cultural anthropologist William Arens (1940–2019), often warned his students, "Ethnographic informants are human, and humans lie." Needless to say, as more and more formerly nonindustrialized peoples come into contact with globalized economies, opportunities to study preindustrial activities dwindle. Such limited numbers of accounts create a risk of overgeneralizing from very small samples of high-quality ethnographic information.

Bushcraft

Bushcraft references ways of sustaining oneself in wilderness conditions (Kochanski 1987; Mears 2003). Some aspects of bushcraft involve modern techniques, such as navigating with a map and compass. Other others involve traditional skills, such as reading animal tracks and signs or making tools out of stone or other materials. Much like experimental archaeology, bushcraft can demonstrate the possible, but key differences exist. The bushcraft literature

---

[3] Archaeologists have taught a bonobo to make stone tools, but they have not taught these or any other animals to make fire or cordage.

serves mainly outdoor recreation enthusiasts. It is not peer-reviewed scientific research. Arguments among practitioners all too often devolve into appeals to authority. That authority is all too often established by citing factors such as past military service or appearances on television programs or in other popular entertainment media.[4] Good bushcraft sources can tell one what works and why, but they rarely do so in ways that can be documented and objectively evaluated. Because bushcraft works' authors and publishers market their books to outdoor recreation enthusiasts, many focus on strategies applicable to the sorts of habitats to which people travel for outdoor recreation. These destinations more often include temperate-zone forests and deserts, rather than Arctic tundra, steppe, tropical rainforests, or subtropical deserts. Because they also market their works to "armchair adventurers" (people interested in outdoor recreation but who may not have the opportunity or ability to do it), some bushcraft works offer up eclectic mixes of survival "hacks" from around the world, rather than the most common and simple solutions to specific problems in a given culture's repertoire of survival strategies. Raw materials or resources for solutions we see today among humans living in different habitats might not have occurred together in the same place and at the same time in the past. (They might have, but we have no basis from which to estimate such co-occurrences' likelihood.)

Wilderness Survival

Wilderness survival describes strategies for saving lives using any means necessary, emphasizing effective and immediate solutions to short-term problems (e.g., Lundin 2003; Towell 2020). Because much of the wilderness survival literature focuses on helping people avoid making life-threating mistakes, it can help archaeologists identify things ancestral humans did *not* do because doing so could have got them killed. For example, the wilderness survival literature focuses mainly on helping people who are lost and/or stranded in the wilderness survive long enough to be rescued.[5] Most successful wilderness

---

[4] In no way, shape, or form should these remarks be read as disparaging military service. However, there is a big difference between having taken the US military's Survival, Evasion, Resistance, and Escape (SERE) course or its equivalent in other countries as a matter of basic training and having designed and taught such courses to elite service members (e.g., McPherson and McPherson 1993, 1996). Students in SERE classes learn a few basic, time-tested skills designed for very specific situations, such as being temporarily stranded behind enemy lines or otherwise separated from one's comrades in battle. Those who design SERE classes and other survival classes have to make a choice from an almost unimaginably wide range of solutions to any specific problem based on years or even decades of learning and practicing those skills.

[5] Wilderness survival literature differs from the "prepper" literature. Prepper works offer advice on how to survive longer-term disasters, mostly political unrest, social collapse, or natural disasters that afflict urban societies (e.g., Lundin 2007; Begley 2021; Pogue 2021). The survival and prepper literature overlap in complex ways. In general, if a book spends an inordinate amount of time discussing firearms, home defense, and in-bulk food purchases, it is a work in the prepper genre.

search-and-rescue operations last 72 hours or less, after which the chances of success plummet. These works' audience, the "typical" civilian search-and-rescue victim, is usually a single person who is underequipped and has moved quickly into unfamiliar terrain and become lost (Koester 2008). Thousands of people become lost in remote areas every year. To judge from the geological sources of the rocks Pleistocene hominins used as tools (usually from less than 10 kilometers away), they spent most of their lives in familiar terrain. They might not even have had a word for "lost." The wilderness survival literature can suggest the specific nature of the survival challenges our ancestors faced as well as things they avoided doing.

Nonhuman Primate Ethology

Nonhuman primate ethology documents the behavior of living nonhuman primates. Most of this literature focuses on the behavior of the primate species rather than on comparisons between that species and humans (e.g., Goodall 1986). Nevertheless, observations of differences in how humans and other primates solved the same survival challenges can help "scale" variation among human survival strategies. Similarities between human and nonhuman survival strategies can also hint at possible ancestral behaviors, that is, things humans' and other primates' last common ancestors did, but one also has to keep in mind the possibility of evolutionary "convergence," of different evolutionary actors coming up with similar solutions independently of one another (Muller et al. 2017). For example, the observation that both humans and chimpanzees use rocks to split open nuts could suggest our last common ancestor (that lived around 5–6 Ma) did so, too (McGrew 1992). Conversely, chimpanzees might have only recently begun up splitting nuts with stones for any number of reasons. The oldest-known presumed chimpanzee nut-splitting site dates to only about 4,300 years ago (Mercader et al. 2007).

THE BIG SIX SURVIVAL CHALLENGES

What do these sources tell us about the "big six" survival challenges?

First Aid and Medication

In a survival emergency first aid is one's first priority. Blocked airways and arterial bleeding can kill in minutes. Most wilderness survival works cover basic first aid, including cuts, bruises, sprains, and broken limbs. Few discuss dealing with major broken bones, childbirth, and chronic illnesses (for such, see Werner et al. 2010). Many bushcraft works discuss plants with medicinal properties, but one has to be aware that these plants' presence and availability vary among different geographic regions. Bushcraft and related works that deal with first aid, medicine, and caregiving (e.g., Alton and Alton 2013) understandably emphasize modern techniques rather than conjecturally ancestral ones.

Thermoregulation

Recommendations about shelter vary with the geographic region, weather conditions, group size, and the anticipated duration of the emergency. A good general guideline holds that one needs shelter immediately if ambient temperatures drop below or above one's normal resting body temperature (98.6°F/37°C). Most people who perish from "exposure" actually succumb to either extreme cooling (hypothermia) or overheating (hyperthermia). Either one can kill in minutes or over a longer period, depending on circumstances. All wilderness survival works discuss how to make fire using both modern and "primitive" techniques. Those requiring no use of industrial technology involve wood-on-wood friction fire and collision products ("flint and steel," or more precisely silica and iron). Detailed instructions about how to construct lasting shelters appear in bushcraft works more so than wilderness survival works. The latter focus on short-term emergency shelters.

Hydration

Deprived of water, people in survival emergencies begin to suffer serious dehydration after three days or less. Agricultural and industrial pollution and human waste have contaminated so many waterways worldwide that nowadays one must assume any standing water unsafe to drink without prior treatment to make it potable. Wilderness survival works recommend a wide range of chemical-based strategies for doing this, but the two most common and relevant for prehistoric times include filtering (passing the water through fabric) and boiling. (At elevations below 6,500 meters above sea level, boiling for one minute will do the trick; for higher elevations, three minutes.) Most wilderness survival works' advice about transporting water focus on containers made of metal or plastic, rather than out of other organic materials. Bushcraft works sometimes cover how to make preindustrial water containers, but the ethnographic literature offers up a wider range of options.

Nutrition

Humans require between 2,000 and 2,500 calories daily. Healthy adults can survive up to three weeks without food. Securing food in a survival emergency is generally less urgent than obtaining water, though most wilderness survival works discuss the subject, possibly in order to give people a way to remain proactively "doing something" in an emergency to maintain morale. Wilderness survival references' recommendations for finding food contrast starkly with the archaeological literature's emphasis on big-game hunting. Instead, these works focus on potential plant foods, insects, and other small animals. Collecting such foods involves less risk of injury or failure than hunting larger animals. Plants and small animals vary widely with geography. Subtle differences distinguish edible plants from poisonous ones. Failure to recognize such differences can have fatal consequences.[6]

Transportation

Some wilderness survival works discuss making improvised transport aids for moving injured persons, but unless staying put endangers one's near-term survival prospects, survival guides advise against individuals without medical training moving an injured person in an emergency. Doing so increases the area over which rescuers must search, dramatically reducing their chance of finding lost people (Koester 2008). Bushcraft works offer up an impressive array of suggestions about transportation and carrying aids (e.g., rafts, boats, snowshoes, backpacks, stretchers), but many of these devices call for specialized knowledge, tools, and abundant time to make them. Almost without exception, improvised transport aids recommended by the bushcraft and survival literature are unlikely to leave a durable archaeological trace because humans made them using minimally modified wood and cordage made from plant fibers and/or animal tissues (leather, sinew, hair, etc.).

Communication

Wilderness survival books and other works generally recommend marking one's path through unfamiliar terrain and carrying devices that allow one to signal rescuers with both visual cues (mirrors, electric lights) and sounds (whistles and other noisemaking devices). Nearly all wilderness survival works recommend carrying maps, a compass, and electronic signaling and navigational aids (personal locator beacons, global positioning systems, cell phones, and the like). If prehistoric humans knew their habitats at least as well as recent human hunter-gatherers do, they would have rarely needed either to mark their trails or to signal to rescuers. Recent humans, such as hunters and others pursuing recreational activities in the wilderness, signal to others and to potential rescuers by wearing eye-catching colored garments (e.g., "hunters' orange"). Prehistoric humans might have done something similar, signaling

---

[6] As documented in Jon Krakauer's book *Into the Wild* (1997), adventurer Chris McCandless (1968–1992) managed to kill a moose with a low-caliber rifle, an impressive feat that should have sustained him for months during his self-imposed isolation in Alaska, but he probably perished shortly thereafter from consuming a plant, *Hedysarum alpinum*, whose seeds contain a toxic amino acid called L-canavanine (www.newyorker.com/books/page-turner/chris-mccandless-died-update).

their identity and intentions to strangers at a distance by varying clothing and other personal adornments, such as jewelry and/or pigments applied to their skin, hair, or other surfaces.

If prehistoric humans failed to solve all of these challenges swiftly and effectively, then they would not have lived long enough to become our ancestors. To answer questions about how they did these things, we need to consider which ancestral survival skills early humans possessed.

ANCESTRAL SURVIVAL SKILLS

What were early humans' survival skills? Five stand out above others, namely, powerful precision grasping, endurance bipedalism, predictive hallucination, language with quantal speech, and hyperprosociality. One calls these things "skills" because one can become better at them with practice, and "ancestral" because evidence suggests they were in place among the earliest *Homo sapiens* who lived 200–300 Ka (Table 4.2).

Powerful Precision Grasping

Humans' long thumb "opposes" (articulates with) all four fingertips (Christel 1994). This versatile arrangement provides us with powerful precision grasping, especially the "three-jawed chuck" grip (tips of thumb and first two fingers) (Marzke and Wullstein 1996; Marzke 2013). Powerful precision grasping allows us to do survival-related tasks that apes cannot do, such as using stone tools to carve artifacts of other materials; making cordage, baskets, and textiles (clothing); devising tension-based spring traps; butchering animal

TABLE 4.2 *First appearance dates for ancestral survival skills*

Ancestral survival skill	First appearance dates and durable evidence	Reference
Powerful precision grasping	3.5 Ma: Enlarged thumbs, stone tool cut marks on bone, small-scale stoneworking and tool use after 2.5 Ma	1
Predictive hallucination	2.5–3.3 Ma: Fracture-based stoneworking, pigments and symbolic artifact use	2
Endurance bipedalism	1.6–1.8 Ma: Lower limb elongation in *H. ergaster/erectus*, increased artifact transport distances	3
Language with quantal speech	0.2–0.3 Ma: Facial orthognathism, "quasi-linguistic" variation in stoneworking methods	4
Hyperprosociality	<0.5 Ma: Large neocortex (upper brain), larger-scale collaborative foraging, durable and labor-intensive symbolic artifacts (beads, carvings)	5

References: 1, McPherron et al. (2010), papers in Hovers and Braun (2007) and Pargeter and Faith (2020); 2, Harmand et al. (2015), Brooks et. al. (2018); 3, Bramble and Lieberman (2004) and Feblot-Augustins (1997); 4, Lieberman (2011) and Shea (2017b); 5, Gamble et. al. (2014) and Marean (2015).

carcasses; and hunting with projectile weapons. Evidence for powerful precision grasping becomes increasingly clear after 2.5–3.5 Ma. Such evidence includes enlarged thumbs, stone tool cut marks on bone, and (after 2.5 Ma) small flaked stone artifacts bearing use-related wear traces.

How would powerful precision grasping aid dispersing/migrating humans? Clothing allowed early humans to conserve heat in cold habitats and to shelter from the sun while on the move in warm habitats. Gaiters and leather footwear reduced their risk of easily infected foot and lower leg injuries. Cordage helped them carry things as they moved. Humans moving into new habitats encountered prey and other food sources different from those they were accustomed to exploiting. Nets, baskets, traps, projectile weapons, and other products of powerful precision grasping allowed human ancestors to sample a wide range of prey and to harvest food sources in bulk.

Predictive Hallucination

Compared with other primates, humans have an advanced capacity for "predictive hallucination," for accepting facts not in evidence in order to make predictions about future events. Not only do we restlessly experiment with alternative solutions to problems; we also include superfluous actions, such as wishing one another "good luck" on a skill-based examination. Humans excel at predictive hallucination due to our large and complexly structured brains. Our brains are much larger than apes' brains (1,400 vs. 400 cubic centimeters), and our larger cerebral cortex has more neurons (nerve cells) per unit volume than theirs. We also possess an enlarged prefrontal cortex, the part of the brain controlling "executive functions." Executive functions include judgment, impulse control, aggression management, emotional regulation, planning, reasoning, and social skills (P. Lieberman 2013). These qualities help us envision alternative interpretations of facts and to speculate about different consequences for our actions. For humans, indeed for any mobile vertebrates, feeding, reproducing, interacting with others of one's species, and avoiding predation all require some capacity to creatively envision future actions and to predict and evaluate the consequences for one's actions. It follows that predictive hallucination's antiquity extends deeply in hominin, primate, mammalian, and vertebrate evolution.

Stoneworking using controlled fracture requires one to weigh different combinations of strategies and tactics to obtain sharp cutting edges. The oldest-known purposefully fractured stone tools date to between 2.5 and 3.3 Ma, millions of years before the oldest *Homo sapiens* fossils. This observation suggests early humans possessed a capacity for predictive hallucination different from other nonhominin primates. One very distinctively human expression of predictive hallucination involves using symbolic artifacts, such as mineral pigments, as symbols. The oldest evidence for pigment use currently dates to around 500 Ka at Olorgesailie, Kenya, and becomes increasingly common thereafter (Brooks et al. 2018). Another such expression is reading animal tracks and signs, an activity so widespread among recent humans that it is almost certainly ancestral in at least *Homo sapiens* populations (Liebenberg 1990).

How does predictive hallucination aid prehistoric humans on the move? Nearly everything about dispersal requires those attempting it to envision different consequences for their actions. Should one remain in place and work harder, or "light out for the territories"? Does this river valley look like a better prospect than that other one? Do those clouds on the horizon indicate an island or a coming storm? Are those people going to be friendly or hostile? Symbolic artifacts can be especially useful in making predictions about social interactions. Recent humans who share similar ideas about the right way to dress, make tools, build houses and other things share other cultural values as well. Being able to accurately predict strangers' behavior from visual clues at a distance can be a valuable aid to predicting the course of future interactions.

Predictive hallucination is the beating heart of the scientific method. Science begins with imagining unobserved causes and circumstances different from those in which one finds oneself and then developing hypotheses that allow one to test, by careful observation, whether one is right or wrong. But predictive hallucination comes with some strings attached. As the term "hallucination" implies, we often get things wrong. Thinking takes a lot of energy, and in energetic matters, evolution looks for shortcuts. "Confirmation bias," accepting false hypotheses as true because they agree with our preëxisting biases, figures prominently among these, but those who study such issues have assembled impressive lists of other such biases and shortcuts (Adams 2014b).

Endurance Bipedalism

Humans excel at endurance bipedalism. We can walk, run, and swim impressively long distances without interruption (D. Lieberman 2013). The several features that help us do these things include our upright posture and a spinal column with a lumbar curve that positions our center of gravity close to our spine while walking and running. Our wide shoulders and narrow waist (the separation between lowermost ribs and uppermost part of our pelvis) allow us to store energy in our abdominal muscles between steps as we stride. A nuchal ligament connects the back of our skull to our shoulders, enabling us to stabilize our heads while walking or running. Large gluteal muscles and hamstrings, long legs, short arms, and a long, narrow foot with enlarged big toe aligned parallel to the other toes allow us to propel ourselves further forward with each step than apes can when they walk bipedally. Our abundant sweat glands further help us thermoregulate (e.g., cool down) between bouts of high-energy locomotion. The increased lower limb length and more robust hip joints that appear on *Homo ergaster* and *Homo erectus* fossils suggest that some form of endurance bipedalism had evolved by 1.6–2.0 Ma (Bramble and Lieberman 2004). A shift toward greater stone artifact transport distances (from less than 5 kilometers to more than 10 kilometers) begins around the same time as well. Early *Homo sapiens* fossils display essentially the same hallmarks of endurance bipedalism that living humans do. We are a species born to run.

Endurance bipedalism helped dispersing/migrating humans in numerous ways. First, it enabled them to survey vast areas for potential new habitats, food sources, and potential mates and social allies. Second, it allowed humans to track and chase fleeing prey animals.[7] Finally, we can swim. Immersed in water, apes "dog paddle" or drown. We do not swim particularly fast, but relatively few people out of the millions or even billions who immerse themselves in deep water actually drown. Rivers that have divided African ape populations for thousands of years teem with swimming African children and throng with watercraft. Being able to swim may have encouraged watercraft use in a similar way to how parachutes encouraged aviation.

Language and Quantal Speech

Other animals live in an eternal present tense. Their gestures and vocalizations express their immediate emotional states. They can communicate that they are happy or angry now, but they cannot tell one another whether they were happy yesterday or if they will be unhappy if something happens next week. Human spoken language involves "quantal speech," sounds broken up into short, distinct bits whose brevity ensures fewer copying errors in repetition. Humans excel at quantal speech because we have oddly shaped heads (Lieberman 2011). Other mammals are prognathic. Their large faces project out in front of their brains and their upper respiratory tracts are either unflexed or minimally flexed. This minimal flexion allows dogs, deer, mice, apes, and other animals to breathe while drinking, to ingest food quickly, and to avoid choking to death. But having an unflexed basicranium and relatively long oral cavity with a long tongue limits animal vocalizations' variability. Most such vocalizations are continuous and modulated mainly by repetition and increased or decreased volume (e.g., dogs barking.). They lack either syntax (rules about word order) or grammar (rules about word choices).

Humans are orthognathic. Our small face is tucked beneath the front of our brain. Human orthognathism sharply flexes our basicranium (the bottom of our skull) and our upper respiratory tract. Having a flexed basicranium, flexed

---

[7] Unlike quadrupedal runners, whose viscera lurch forward with each step, driving air from their lungs, humans' guts pull downward when we land between strides, pulling air into our lungs (Carrier 1984).

upper respiratory tract, and a short oral cavity and tongue allow us to break up sound into the short bits quantal speech requires (P. Lieberman 1973). Syntax and grammar are universal features of human language, spoken or otherwise, and so one assumes the two are equally evolutionarily primitive (Chomsky 2012). How primitive? Orthognathism varies among all fossil species of the genus *Homo*, but it becomes more pronounced and more common among fossils of *H. heidelbergensis* and *H. sapiens* than among earlier hominins. This suggests strong selective pressure for spoken language arose *before* our species appeared.

Spoken language undoubtedly played several important roles in prehistoric human population movements. First and foremost, spoken language allowed speculations about future events (predictive hallucination) to change from individual reflections to matters of discussion and debate among a larger number of minds. Time and again in the annals of wilderness survival, having "more minds on a problem" results in better outcomes than individuals working alone does.[8]

One might imagine immigrants' having to learn new languages could have made spoken language a barrier to dispersal, but instead, spoken language likely aided dispersal. Syntax and grammar allow any human to learn any language. For a variety of reasons, some physiological (delayed myelination of neurons in certain parts of the brain[9]) and others social (adults using "baby talk" with simple syntax and grammar), children and adolescents learn languages better than adults do (Ipek 2009), and so, bringing children along in dispersals and/or having them soon after arriving in new habitats provides all concerned with a supply of "universal translators."[10] One could even make the case that aiding theirs and their parents' dispersal was a source of selective pressure for children evolving the neurological basis for skill at learning new languages! After all, doing so successfully and retaining that capacity into adolescence would, through sexual selection, increase the copies of those children's genes in future generations.

---

[8] Druet's book *Island of the Lost* (2007) documents an almost unimaginable test case of this axiom. In 1864 two different ships wrecked on different parts of the same island in the South Pacific near New Zealand. One group worked together collaboratively; the other disintegrated into "every man for himself." The former group thrived, the latter did not.

[9] Myelin is a fatty sheath that encloses neurons. It stabilizes signal transmission between neurons and reduces the brain's ability to reroute new neural pathways. In a classic evolutionary trade-off, myelinization improves signal fidelity, but it reduces cognitive and behavioral flexibility. Myelination occurs earlier among neural pathways used often and early in life than those less often used. Neural myelination is, in a nutshell, the reason why it is so difficult for "old dogs to learn new tricks."

[10] Stony Brook University has a large proportion of first-to-college students from families who recently immigrated to the United States. Many among such students report having served as the "family translator," especially for their grandparents whose advanced age makes them struggle to learn English.

Finally, by using artifacts to convey symbolically encoded linguistic messages, in artworks, writing, or other notational systems, humans overcome proximity, truth, and indeed reality in impressively complex ways. Other animals can deceive, but only humans negotiate contracts and pass laws.

Hyperprosociality

Hominins, apes, and monkeys are "prosocial" creatures. Individuals seek out members of their own species not just for reproduction and child care but also for companionship and grooming (or the human equivalent, gossip). Humans are "hyperprosocial": we even seek out members of other species as "companion animals" (Marean 2015). Humans incur and tolerate relatively high costs[11] to seek out interactions with strangers and potential social allies. We do this so much better than other primates because of two diverging strategies for aggression management (Wrangham 2018, 2019). We have a high tolerance for "reactive" aggression. We put up with minor insults and other slights arising from members of our own social groups.[12] We also eagerly engage in "proactive aggression." We respond rapidly to threats from outside our social group. (Thanks to predictive hallucination, these can even include imaginary threats.) As a result, we can form large alliance networks that encompass individuals who may not be physically present in the same place at the same time. Estimating when hyperprosociality appears and how it varied among hominins is tricky. The most convincing such evidence includes the increase brain neocortex sizes after 0.5 Ma, signaling larger social groups, but evidence for collaborative foraging (hunting large game, gathering shellfish) dating to less than 0.2 Ma could signal changes in underlying capacities for hyperprosociality over the course of recent hominin evolution (Marean 2015, 2016). Carving durable personal adornments, artworks, and other symbolic artifacts seems fairly straightforward evidence for hyperprosociality, but such durable symbolic artifacts' occurrences may lag behind hyperprosociality's evolutionary emergence for, well, nobody knows how much time.

If we accept – and it seems reasonable – that distinctively human hyperprosociality evolved, then we must maintain multiple working hypotheses about its expression among early *Homo sapiens*:

1. That all early humans inherited a capacity for it from *H. heidelbergensis* ancestors
2. That it was expressed variably among early *H. sapiens*
3. That it evolved sometime after first appearance dates for *H. sapiens*.

---

[11] College tuition, for example.
[12] Sincerely spoken, the words, "just kidding" and "I apologize" may have saved more lives than penicillin.

How did hyperprosociality aid prehistoric human population movements? For dispersing individuals to become ancestral humans, they needed to form a stable society, one large enough to ensure everyone had a reasonable chance of finding a mate and social allies. To paraphrase anthropologist Irven DeVore (1934–2004), "a lone hominin is a dead hominin." Demographers estimate minimum viable human populations at around 400–500 reproductively active adults (Wobst 1974). By encouraging dispersing humans to form larger and internally tolerant groups that can work together against common threats (human or otherwise), and by rewarding people for maintaining themselves in such groups, hyperprosociality helped human populations form stable societies as they moved and in their destinations.

AN INTEGRATIVE ANCESTRAL SURVIVAL SKILLS HYPOTHESIS

How did early human use these ancestral skills? Though we have discussed them separately above, we have no reason to assume they actually worked in isolation, for they demonstrably do not do so among recent humans. What value does spoken language have without hyperprosociality? Why evolve endurance bipedalism if one cannot envision what to do at a fork in the road? Virtually all the components in modern-day wilderness "survival kits" require one to coordinate multiple ancestral survival skills with one another simultaneously.[13] Bandages, for example, require powerful precision grasping and predictive hallucination. To show how ancestral survival skills work together in combination to create solutions to survival challenges that are more than the sum of their parts, here we consider fire and cordage, universal components of all recent humans' survival strategies that also seem likely to have been aids to early humans' and other hominins' survival strategies.

Firemaking (as an Integrative Ancestral Survival Skill)

Of all the things humans do differently from our nearest primate relatives, making and using fire is the most consequential (Wrangham 2009). Fire is a human cultural universal. All humans make and use it; other primates avoid it. Fire allowed humans to extend our species' geographic range into cold habitats no other primates inhabited, such as Northern Eurasia during glacial periods.

Kindling fire using either friction or collision products requires powerful precision grasping in assembling a "tinder bundle," in manipulating the ember into the bundle, and in building up the fire from an ember to a flame. Endurance bipedalism allows one to transport fuel to hearths and, with a little

---

[13] In my classes, I bring to lecture the small "survival kit" that I carry on day hikes and camping. As I extract each of the kit's components, my students and I identify the ancestral survival skills involved in making and using that component.

ingenuity, to transport fire from one residential site to another. That humans maintain so many different ways to start fire is an impressive demonstration of our capacity for predictive hallucination (Hume 2018). Different sorts of fuels have widely variable combustion properties. Spoken language enables children and others to learn these properties rapidly, accurately, and far more efficiently than by individual trial-and-error. Hyperprosociality encourages the use of hearths as social hubs. One can converse in the dark, of course, but radiant flame lengthens the day, allowing us to supplement our words with facial expressions and gestures.

Fire is so useful in survival emergencies that all bushcraft and wilderness survival guidebooks recommend having the knowledge and means to make fire in several different ways. One can use fire to sterilize metal implements used in first aid. Fire can provide heat and can dry clothing, staving off hypothermia. Boiling water for a minute or so purifies it, killing the bacteria and other microorganisms that cause gastroenteritis and diarrhea. Cooking makes edible many foods that would otherwise be difficult or dangerous to eat, such as raw meat or tough roots and tubers. Charring and scraping wood allows one to make wooden vessels in which to boil and transport water, food, or other things. Last, of course, one can use fire and smoke to signal others from a distance.

Were early *Homo sapiens* the first hominins to make and use fire? Multiple lines of archaeological and biological evidence suggest that Lower Pleistocene hominins controlled fire, and evidence for fire usage grows steadily more common in more recent time periods (Wrangham 2009). This cumulative pattern for fire use is what one would expect to see if early *Homo* used fire widely and if fire use increased over time. It contradicts the hypothesis that hominins began making and using only fire recently. On the other hand, clear and convincing evidence for pyrotechnology, for mechanical production of fire and for the use of fire to transform other nonedible materials (ceramics, metallurgy), occurs almost exclusively in contexts associated with *Homo sapiens*. Recently discovered evidence suggests some of the most recent among European Neanderthals may have used collision-product (flint and iron) fire-making techniques (Sorensen et al. 2018).

Cordage (as an Integrative Ancestral Survival Skill)

Cordage refers to fibers from plant or animal tissues fashioned to form string or rope. To make cordage, one needs powerful precision grasping to separate plant fibers or animal sinews, to twist them against one another, or to cut leather into rawhide strips. Endurance bipedalism creates incentives for carrying things, which ropes, strings, bags, and textiles wrapped around the body make far more efficient than hand-carrying. Other than weaver-bird nests, few examples of cordage-based containers occur in nature. It follows that in order to make baskets, bags, textiles, and other cordage-based containers, humans had to "predictively hallucinate" them. Making cordage out of plant or animal tissues is neither easy nor intuitively obvious. It requires careful selection among possible materials and choices among alternative preparation recipes. It might be possible for humans or earlier hominins to have learned cordage production by careful imitation, but verbal instruction (spoken language) accelerates and refines the process. Among ethnographic humans, cordage production and allied crafts, such as basket and textile manufacturing, are hyperprosocial activities. Not only does artifact production usually occur among groups in public settings; those making the cordage, baskets, and textiles vary those artifacts' designs in order to transmit symbolically encoded messages. No one ancestral skill accounts for cordage, but together, they all do.

Were early *Homo sapiens* the first hominins to make and use cordage? Probably not. Evidence suggesting African *Homo heidelbergensis* attached stone tools to handles more than 500 Ka (at Kathu Pan 1, South Africa) (Wilkins et al. 2012) and evidence of cordage attached to Neanderthal stone tools (Hardy et al. 2020) suggests hominin cordage production is evolutionarily primitive among at least the larger-brained and geographically widespread hominins who lived from Middle Pleistocene times onward.

The "Integrative Ancestral Survival Skills Hypothesis" this work proposes asserts that as they moved, early humans overcame survival challenges using complex combinations of survival skills already in place among the hominins out of which *Homo sapiens* evolved. It further argues that the mere possession of those skills did not make us unstoppable, for other hominins with whom early humans overlapped geographically and chronologically possessed them, too. Rather, it was how our ancestors used those skills that mattered, and unless they were utterly different from their descendants, they used them integratively, turning them from stand-alone skills into "force multipliers" vastly more than the sum of their parts. In its concluding chapter (Chapter 14), this work will speculate about why *Homo sapiens* used their ancestral survival skills better than other hominins. For now, and in each of the "geography" chapters that follow (Chapters 5–10 and 12), this work will develop the Integrative Ancestral Survival Skills Hypothesis so that future researchers can test it using different evidence from that which inspired it in the first place. Before discussing this evidence, and to avoid repetition in later chapters, the next section considers some of what we can reasonably assume about early humans' particular solutions to survival challenges.

REASONABLE ASSUMPTIONS?

Knowing about *Homo sapiens*' ancestral survival skills allows us to propose some minimal reasonable assumptions about their solutions to survival problems.

First Aid and Medication

Injuries, infections, and other illnesses occur commonly among all human societies. All human societies maintain both emergency and nonemergency treatments for illnesses and wounds. Most of these treatments involve perishable media unlikely to be preserved in geological deposits. One thinks it reasonable to assume that earlier humans had first aid, long-term care strategies, and medicines. From the standpoint of hyperprosociality, it seems vanishingly unlikely that earlier humans simply disregarded their injured or abandoned their sick companions. Doing so systematically not only would create strong disincentives to collaborate in risky ventures but also sacrifices all the information injured and ill individuals carried about in their minds as well as such other practical skills they possessed.

Thermoregulation

Unclothed and unsheltered, humans can survive only within a narrow range of humid, low-altitude, tropical habitats. Clothing, artificial shelters, and fire use are human cultural universals; but particular ways of making clothing, shelter, and fire vary widely, sometimes in concert with variation in temperature and humidity, other times less clearly so. We can assume earlier humans made clothing (Gilligan 2010), artificial shelters, and fire, but we should also expect variation in prehistoric clothing, shelter, and fire use.

Hydration

Without water, human bodily functions begin to degrade in a matter of days. Chimpanzees, among other animals, will dig shallow pits ("wells") to reach water, and it seems reasonable to assume hominins did so, too, from a very early point in their evolution.[14] All recent human societies either live near potable water, treat water to make it potable (chiefly by boiling and/or filtering it), or devise means to transport water (e.g., containers, irrigation) to where it is not readily available. We should assume early humans did such things, too.

Nutrition

Humans fuel their large and energetically costly brains by focusing subsistence strategies on resources offering dense concentrations of high-quality nutrients

---

[14] A study published while this book was in production (Péter et al. 2022) documented forest-dwelling chimpanzees digging such "wells" near standing surface water presumably to take advantage of sediments' filtering properties. We do not know whether such sediment-filter wells are ancient practices now only recently discovered or recent innovations in chimpanzee behavior.

(Marean 2016). Hunter-gatherers, our best models for prehistoric pre-agricultural humans, do this using a division of labor (Kelly 2013). Some individuals pursue high-risk, high-return food sources such as large game, while others collect large quantities of lower-quality foods (e.g., insects, shellfish, plant foods). We can assume that earlier humans did these things, too, although we should reserve skepticism about whether divisions of labor differed between humans and other hominins (Kuhn and Stiner 2006).

Watercraft

Waterways crosscut our species' geographic range, but humans swim neither particularly fast nor particularly well and certainly neither faster or farther than sharks or crocodiles can. Nearly all humans who live near coastlines, rivers, lakes, and marshes design and use watercraft to traverse water barriers to movements. Their scarceness in the archaeological record may reflect humans' abandoning watercraft along riverbanks, lake edges, and ocean beaches where high erosion rates swiftly disintegrate them. We can assume that early humans devised and used watercraft as transport aids (Bednarik 2003), but we should keep an open mind about the particular sorts of watercraft they used. Much archaeological speculation about prehistoric watercraft assumes an "evolutionary" or "developmental" sequence from rafts to canoes to sailing vessels. These sequences derive from 19th-century ethnological theories about "progressive" evolution in technology, and they exist mainly in anthropologists' imaginations. No prior anthropological theory predicts them.

Communications

Symbolic artifacts allow those who use them to overcome obstacles to communication and cooperation and to make social interactions predictable. All humans use such symbolic artifacts as "social media" for these purposes. More often than not, these symbolic artifacts – textiles, for example – are made of organic materials unlikely to survive long-term burial. We can assume that if prehistoric humans used clothing, then they used clothing as social media, too. Ethnographic studies of symbolic artifact use show wide variation in the choices of media and motifs among contemporary societies (Hodder 1982). We should expect similar variation within and between prehistoric archaeological data sets from any given region or time period.

Are these assumptions reasonable? That they appear universally among recent humans in such a wide range of circumstances suggests so, but we have to be on guard against accepting such universality as evidence for practices in antiquity. In many circumstances we have to maintain "multiple working hypotheses" about such issues (Shea 2011c). After all, evolution never stops.

SUMMARY

This chapter examined how archaeologists try to answer "how questions," contrasting their "arrows-on-maps" approach to a new "survival archaeology" approach. It explained the questions survival archaeology considers important and reviewed the sources of hypotheses about those matters. It also discussed the suite of ancestral survival skills on which we think early *Homo sapiens* relied and what our knowledge about those skills suggests for our expectations of the archaeological record. Chapter 5 begins this work's "deep dive" into deep-time prehistory, starting with evidence for Ancient Africans and their evolutionary precursors.

Box 4.1: *Prehistory's "Atlantis Problem"*

Research investigating prehistoric human population movements suffers an "Atlantis problem." Put simply, we have no clear method for evaluating competing arguments/hypotheses about what happened on coastlines and islands before postglacial sea-level rise flooded them. Prehistoric human coastal adaptations are one of archaeology's "known unknowns."

The most fabled "lost continent," Atlantis, appears in two works by the Greek philosopher Plato (ca. 420–350 BC). "Dialogs" purportedly recording discussions among philosophers, or symposia, *Timaeus* and *Critias* described a powerful rival to ancient Athens located on a now-drowned continent in the Atlantic Ocean. *Timaeus*' and *Critias*' Atlantis was not a historical entity, but rather a fictional stand-in for the ideal society in much the same way Thomas Moore's 1516 work, *Utopia*, treated its "utopian" society. (In Latin, *utopia* means "nowhere.")

Prehistory's Atlantis problem arises from the fact that over the last 12,000 years, postglacial sea-level rise drowned most Pleistocene-age coastlines and lower river valleys that drain into them. Today they lie as much as 150 meters below modern sea level, depths inaccessible to scuba divers and thus also inaccessible to underwater archaeology.

These circumstances pose a dilemma. On the one hand, some former coastlines were attractive places for preagricultural human settlement, possibly harboring much larger and different human and hominin populations than those whose remains occur above sea level today and near modern-day coastlines. On the other hand, nothing constrains speculation about these matters, and so, archaeological speculation varies widely. Were the now-drowned bottom of the Persian/Arabian Gulf or Libya's Gulf of Sidra centers of high human population density during Pleistocene times, which might have been places from which populations dispersed? Or were they as

Box 4.1: *(cont.)*

sparsely populated as archaeological research suggests the contiguous and unflooded portions of nearby Africa and Asia were at the same time?

Few ethnographic hunter-gatherers living near cold ocean waters fail to use coastal and near-shore food sources (Kelly 2013), and yet archeological evidence for systematic marine resource use becomes commonplace worldwide only after 5–6 Ka, after sea levels reached their modern stands. Are sporadic occurrences of Pleistocene evidence for intensive shellfish collection in Southern Africa and Atlantic/Mediterranean Europe isolated occurrences with no lasting consequences ("flashes in the pan," as it were) or are they evidence of systematic and widespread aquatic resource use?

Speculations about such issues occupy a middle ground between currently unfalsifiable arguments and hypotheses that could be falsified using as-yet-unavailable remote sensing and robotic survey and excavation strategies. For the present, the best way for paleoanthropologists to cope with such uncertainties is by maintaining "multiple working hypotheses" (Isaac 1981; Shea 2011c). Having more than one such hypothesis in play complicates efforts to write prehistory using neat and tidy narrative explanations and "arrows on maps" scenarios. For the comparative approach to prehistory this work advocates, multiple working hypotheses pose no obstacles whatsoever. If one does not need to select one and only one hypothesis to explain a given set of observations, then why choose? Law requires one to do so, but science does not.

For thought and discussion: If the future sea level rose 100, 300, or even 500 meters above its current stand, nearly all of the world's major port cities would vanish beneath the waves. Other than by written records (haphazardly preserved from even recent past periods), how might far-future archaeologists reconstruct our current world's economy and political landscape without archaeological evidence from modern-day coastlines?

CHAPTER 5

ANCIENT AFRICANS

This chapter examines African evidence for human origins, behavior, and population movements between 50 and 600 Ka. It compares evidence associated with *Homo sapiens* and *H. heidelbergensis*. Both hominins solved survival challenges in broadly similar ways, with humans occasionally devoting more time and energy to technology ("technological intensification"). The African evidence is entirely consistent with dispersal, showing not even a hint of migration. This and other evidence suggest humans replaced earlier *H. heidelbergensis* not by an abrupt evolutionary event originating in one place and radiating outward, but instead by a gradual, continent-wide process, "infiltration," whose mode and tempo varied widely.

GEOGRAPHY: THE "FOUR AFRICAS"

This chapter considers African evidence dating to between 50 and 600 Ka. The 600-Ka benchmark reflects a generally accepted first appearance date for *Homo heidelbergensis*, the species out of which *Homo sapiens* evolved. By 50 Ka humans had established themselves across much of Africa and dispersed into at least southern Eurasia.

The commonly used Mercator projection map of the world makes Africa look small, smaller than Greenland (about 2,166,086 square kilometers, or 836,300 million square miles). In actuality, Africa is enormously larger (> 30 million square kilometers, or > 12 million square miles). It comprises at least four ecological "subcontinents," four Africas, with differing topography, hydrology, flora, and fauna (Figure 5.1).[1] Differences and similarities among these regions have important implications for human population movements.

---

[1] Though Madagascar is politically part of Africa, the island's indigenous population descends from Oceanian voyagers from Southeast Asia (see Chapter 12).

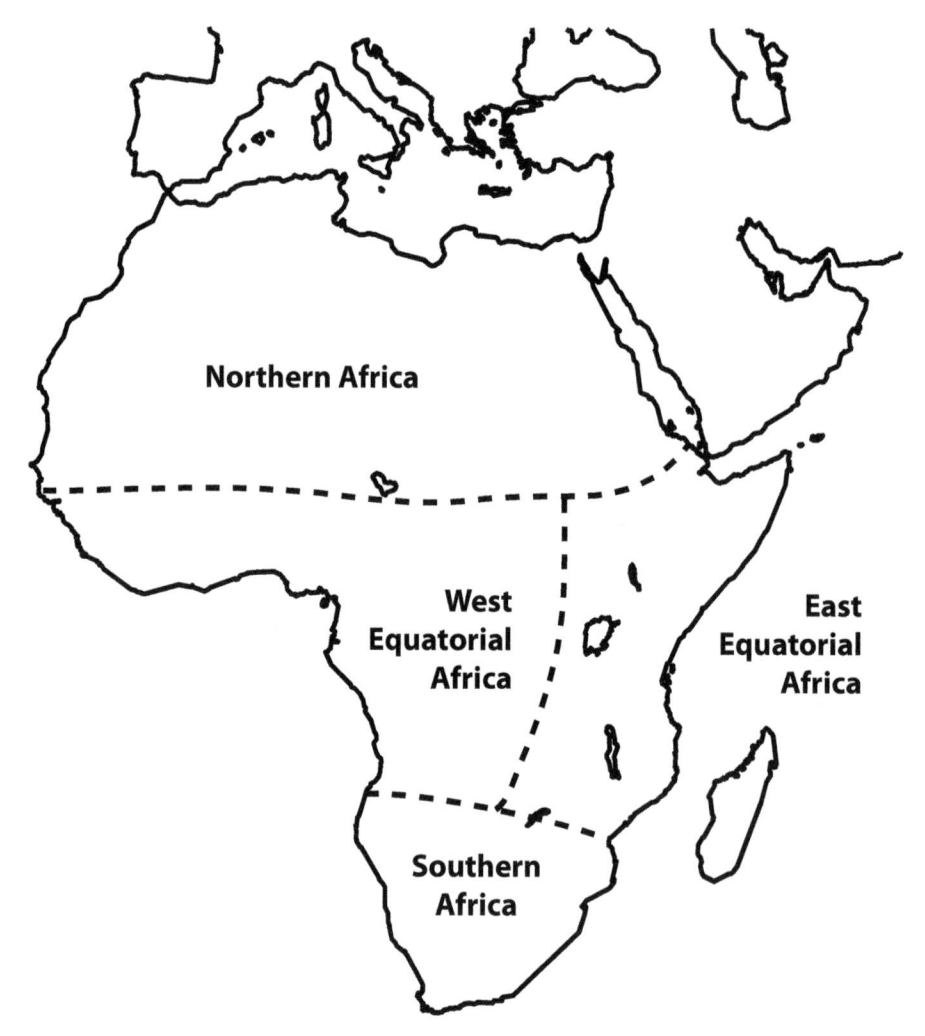

Figure 5.1 The "four Africas." © John J. Shea.

"Four Africas"

Northern Africa encompasses the Mediterranean Sea's southern coast, the Sahara Desert, and the lower Nile Valley, or essentially that part of the continent above 13° north latitude.[2] A region of deserts and mountains, Northern Africa was alternatingly more humid and more arid during Pleistocene times. During humid periods, savanna and open woodlands dominated the landscape, while numerous rivers crisscrossed the region. Extensive lakes formed in what are now Chad and Sudan. The modern-day Sahel Belt running along the Sahara's

---

[2] Modern geopolitical maps treat the East Mediterranean "Levant" and the Arabian Peninsula as parts of Southwest Asia. During prehistoric times, these regions had as much if not more in common ecologically with Northern Africa (temperatures, humidity, flora, and fauna) than they did with montane Western Asia.

southern margin is a remnant of these formerly more extensive savanna-woodlands. This region's main obstacles to human settlement and survival were its periods of hyperaridity and the drying-up of life-sustaining rivers and lakes.

West Equatorial Africa includes West African bight (the Mid-Atlantic Coast) and the greater Congo River basin. This region features relatively low topographic relief and numerous navigable rivers. Persistently humid and covered with dense woodland, forest, and jungle, West Equatorial Africa was the continent's stable core area of woodland, forest, and jungle for much of the Pleistocene. During arid periods, the Kalahari Desert expanded northward into West Equatorial Africa's southern margins leaving sands that deep excavations in this region routinely expose. This region's main challenges for human settlement and survival include (1) that so much of the equatorial forests' potential food sources comprise either plants whose edible parts occur in the forest canopy and (2) that many of the ground-dwelling animals are small, solitary, and mainly active at night. The Sahara Desert's periodic expansions southward posed further challenges along Western Africa's northern latitudes.

East Equatorial Africa groups together the Horn of Africa, the Ethiopian highlands, the East African Rift Valley, and the Indian Ocean Coast. This region features high topographic relief (including the continent's the highest and lowest places) and habitats ranging from deserts to montane forests. The filling and draining of Rift Valley lakes (Turkana, Victoria, Tanganyika, etc.) and the higher elevations surrounding them created complex mosaics of habitats. For animals that could not swim, or hominins that could not make boats, expanding Rift Valley lakes created barriers to movements within species' geographic ranges (Trauth et al. 2010; Kaboth-Bahr et al. 2021). Draining lakes reunited descendants of these populations, some of which may have evolved into different species. One obstacle to human settlement and survival in East Equatorial Africa was that the larger mammals, or "megafauna," that would have attracted hunters due to their large body size (elephants, rhinos, hippos, and Cape buffalo) were also long accustomed to dealing with hominin predators. Calling them "killer herbivores" is not entirely wrong.

Southern Africa encompasses the western and of interior parts of continent below about 17° south latitude. Its western end is hot and dry, its eastern end cooler and wetter. Its southern Cape features high topographic relief. Today's southern Cape has a "Mediterranean" habitat, one featuring cool, wet winters and warm, dry summers. Due to its nearness to Antarctica, however, Southern Africa was very cold during Pleistocene glacial periods. Compared with other parts of Africa, Southern Africa has very resource-rich coastal habitats. The main obstacles to human settlement and survival in this region were cold temperatures at higher elevations and aridity in inland and upland areas to the northwest, such as the Skeleton Coast and Kalahari Desert

Conditions Affecting Population Movements

These "four Africas" differ, but they share two important geographic characteristics relevant for prehistoric human population movements. First, navigable rivers crisscross each of them and connect all of them to one another. This means that hominins capable of making and using watercraft faced few major barriers to moving around the continent. Second, there exist within each region possible humid "refugia" during the hyper-arid episodes that occurred repeatedly during Middle and Later Pleistocene times. The most plausible of these hypothetical refugia lie in lower elevations and along rivers, but humans living in more humid uplands, such as the Ethiopian Plateau, could have coped with climate change simply by moving their settlements upslope or downslope in tune with shifts in vegetation belts and animal habitats. These geographic characteristics suggest that while such refugia may have existed, one should be skeptical about popular "regional refugium" hypotheses that envision continental-scale mass extinctions of humans, a population "bottleneck" (reduction of genetic diversity) among survivors in one region only, followed by a repeopling of the continent by migrations out of one and only one refugium (Ambrose 1998; Marean 2010; Brandt et al. 2012).[3] It is vastly more likely that multiple such refugia formed in multiple locations at the same or different times (Blinkhorn et al. 2022), each acting less as a castle refuge or "keep" than as a station on a metropolitan subway line – as a place to which people travel and from which they depart following complex individual and collective schedules.

IMPORTANT ANCIENT AFRICAN PALEOANTHROPOLOGICAL SITES

Table 5.1 lists important African paleoanthropological sites (see also Figure 5.2).[4] That evidence from Eastern Africa and Southern Africa dominate the list largely reflects differences in regional research histories and the ease versus difficulty of conducting research in different regions. Of these, the sites most notable for preserving long and well-documented sequences of archaeological deposits include the following:

- Haua Fteah Cave (Libya) offers a long Later Pleistocene sequence for Northern Africa from 150 Ka onward.
- The Middle Awash Valley's localities of Bodo, Herto, and Aduma (Ethiopia) preserve a series of deposits spanning the transition between *Homo heidelbergensis* and *H. sapiens*.

---

[3] One suspects some measure of paleoanthropologists' (and especially archaeologists') enthusiasm for "regional refugia" hypotheses springs from the conviction that they are conducting research in such a former refugium.

[4] Out of a vastly larger number of sites. Those sites plotted on Figure 5.2 are mainly those preserving important fossils and deep sequences of archaeological remains.

TABLE 5.1 *Important African paleoanthropological sites*

Site	Dates (Ka)	Comment
Abdur Reef (Eritrea)	125	Stone tools in coral and coastal deposits = coastal adaptation
Blombos Cave (South Africa)	70–100	Red ochre, perforated shell beads, carved bone tools, possible evidence for early use of poison arrows
Bodo (Middle Awash Valley, Ethiopia)	600	*H. heidelbergensis* fossil found together with stone artifacts.
Border Cave (South Africa)	50–170	Early *H. sapiens* fossil
Diepkloof Rockshelter (South Africa)	45–130	Ostrich eggshell water canteens
East Turkana FxJj 20 (Kenya)	1500	Pre-*H. heidelbergensis* fire use
El Mnasra Cave (Morocco)	62–124	Perforated shell beads
Elandsfontein (South Africa)	500	*H. heidelbergensis* fossil
Eliyeh Springs (Kenya)	200–300?	*H. heidelbergensis* fossil
Florisbad (South Africa)	260	Early *H. sapiens* fossil
Gademotta-Kulkuletti (Ethiopia)		Deep sequence of Middle to Late Pleistocene occupations
Grotte des Contrabandiers (Morocco)	90–120	Perforated shell beads
Grotte des Pigeons (Morocco)	82	Perforated shell beads
Haua Fteah Cave (Libya)	> 50 130	Long sequence of Later Pleistocene occupations near Mediterranean Coast
Herto and Aduma (Middle Awash Valley, Ethiopia)	165	Early *H. sapiens* fossils found together with stone artifacts
Hofmeyr (South Africa)	36	Later *H. sapiens* fossil
Iwo Eleru (Nigeria)	12–16	Later "archaic" human skull?
Jebel Irhoud (Morocco)	300	Early *H. sapiens* fossil
Kabwe (Zambia)	274–324	*H. heidelbergensis* (aka Broken Hill Man)
Kalambo Falls (Zambia)	> 50–500	Deep sequence of Middle and Later Pleistocene occupations, waterlogging-preserved wooden artifacts
Katanda (Democratic Republic of Congo)	90	Carved barbed bone point, possible evidence for fishing
Kathu Pan 1 (South Africa)	500	Early evidence for stone tools attached to handles (hafting)
Klasies River Mouth Cave Site Complex (South Africa)	60–115	Early *H. sapiens* fossils, evidence of hearths, systematic production of small backed/truncated pieces
Lake Ndutu (Tanzania)	400–600	*H. heidelbergensis* fossil
Melka Kunturé (Ethiopia)	< 300 Ka	Deep sequence of Middle to Late Pleistocene occupations
Mochena Borago Cave (Ethiopia)	36–59	Evidence of highland occupations
Mumba and Nasera caves (Tanzania)	> 50–100	Long sequence of Later Pleistocene occupations in East African Rift Valley

(continued)

TABLE 5.1 *(continued)*

Site	Dates (Ka)	Comment
Olorgesailie (Kenya)	320	Early use of red ochre pigment, long-distance stone transport
Omo Kibish (Ethiopia)	195–223	Fossils and archaeological sites associated with early *H. sapiens* fossils
Oued Djebana (Algeria)	100	Perforated shell beads at an inland site
Panga Ya Saïdi (Kenya)	< 78 Ka	Long sequence of Later Pleistocene occupations near Eastern Africa's Indian Ocean Coast, juvenile human burial
Pinnacle Point Cave 13B (South Africa)	40–165	Long sequence of Middle and Later Pleistocene occupations along South Africa's Indian Ocean Coast
Rising Star Site Complex (South Africa)	236–335	*H. naledi* fossils
Sibudu Cave (South Africa)	38–77	Long sequence of Later Pleistocene occupations in South African interior
Singa (Sudan)	120–150	Early *H. sapiens* fossil
Swartkrans (South Africa)	1500	Pre-*H. heidelbergensis* fire use
Twin Rivers Kopje (Zambia)	140–300	Early use of red ochre, small backed-truncated piece production, stone tools attached to handles (hafting)
Wonderwerk Cave (South Africa)	1700	Pre-*H. heidelbergensis* fire use

- Mumba and Nasera caves (Tanzania) and Panga Ya Saïdi (Kenya) preserve deep sequences of human occupation from less than 100 Ka.
- Kalambo Falls, an open-air site in Zambia, contains a long sequence of deposits spanning at least the last 500,000 years.
- In South Africa, the Klasies River Mouth Cave Site Complex, Pinnacle Point Cave 13B, and Sibudu Cave together comprise a long sequence of Later Pleistocene occupations running from 55 to 165 Ka.

ANCIENT AFRICAN HOMININ FOSSILS

Between 50 and 600 Ka, at least three morphologically distinct hominin species inhabited Africa: *Homo heidelbergensis*, *H. sapiens*, and *H. naledi*.

Homo heidelbergensis

Most *Homo heidelbergensis* fossils date to > 300–600 Ka and from sites in Europe and Africa. Much of what we think we know about *H. heidelbergensis* comes from European evidence. More than 70 percent of all *H. heidelbergensis* fossils known come from just one Spanish site, Atapuerca Sima de los Huesos. Dating to around 300–400 Ka, these fossils appear in the throes of evolving into

Ancient African Hominin Fossils 93

Figure 5.2 Map of Africa showing sites discussed in the text. © John J. Shea.

European Neanderthals. Generalizing from them to all *H. heidelbergensis* populations risks projecting the characteristics of European hominin evolution globally. The oldest African *H. heidelbergensis* fossil currently known appears to be Bodo 1 (600 Ka, Ethiopia). Other important African specimens include skulls or cranial fragments from Kabwe (Zambia), Lake Ndutu (Tanzania), Elandsfontein (South Africa), and Eliyeh Springs (Kenya).

Homo heidelbergensis skulls differ from the skulls of *Homo erectus* (their likely ancestor) mainly in having reduced lower facial prognathism, a more prominent nose, a less receding forehead, and larger brain cases. Estimates of *H. heidelbergensis* brain volume range between 1,100 and 1,390 cubic centimeters, and on average 1,206 cubic centimeters, whereas *H. erectus* brain volumes are mostly less than 1,000 cubic centimeters. (Living human brains range widely in volume, too, from 950 to 1,800 cm^3, and average around

1300–1500 cm^3.) These hominins' height, estimated from limb bones, suggests males stood around 170 centimeters (5 ft 7 in) and females around 158 centimeters (5 ft 2 in). Paleontologists often describe *H. heidelbergensis*' postcranial (below the neck) remains as "near modern." That is, they have broad shoulders, a rounded ribcage, and a bowl-shaped pelvis with strongly buttressed hip sockets. Their limbs have about the same proportions as seen among living humans, though they are generally thicker and with more prominent muscle attachments. These differences likely reflect subsistence strategies and mobility patterns requiring higher levels of physical exertion than those of recent humans.

Ancient African Homo sapiens

This work uses the term "Ancient Africans" for *Homo sapiens* who lived on the continent before 30 Ka.[5] The oldest generally accepted Ancient African fossils are those from Jebel Irhoud (Morocco, 300 Ka), Florisbad (South Africa, 260 Ka), Omo Kibish (Ethiopia, 195–223 Ka), Herto (Middle Awash Valley, Ethiopia, 165 Ka), Singa (Sudan, 150–170 Ka), Klasies River Mouth (South Africa, 60–115 Ka), and Border Cave (South Africa, 50–170 Ka). All of these fossils differ noticeably from both living humans and from human fossils dating to less than 40–50 Ka. Ancient Africans also differ among themselves, exhibiting variable combinations of primitive and derived features. The oldest African fossil exhibiting the same full suite of derived features living humans have is the Hofmeyr cranium (South Africa, 36 Ka). The firmness of these fossils' datings varies considerably. Taken at face value, the fossil evidence suggests that Ancient Africans originated around 200–300 Ka and had established themselves across at least Northern, Eastern, and Southern Africa by 100–200 Ka.

Humans differ from *Homo heidelbergensis* most obviously in their skull shape (Figure 5.3) (Lieberman 2011). We have a more vertically oriented frontal bone, and thus higher forehead. Our cranium is shorter front-to-back and its widest point is above our ears at the parietal bone. The bottom of our skull (basicranium) is flexed, and as a result, our face is under the front of our brain. We have a relatively small face, and our jaw features a three-sided "mental eminence," or chin. Pleistocene-age *H. sapiens*' and *H. heidelbergensis*' postcranial bones differ little from one another other than in overall robusticity. Both hominins' bones have thicker cortical bone and larger articular surfaces than recent (Holocene-age) humans, features indicating higher activity levels and possibly hormonal differences.

---

[5] The terms this work uses for various groupings of early humans are merely literary conveniences. It would be an extraordinary coincidence if they corresponded to actual cultural or biological differences among *Homo sapiens* populations other than the geographic differences their names imply.

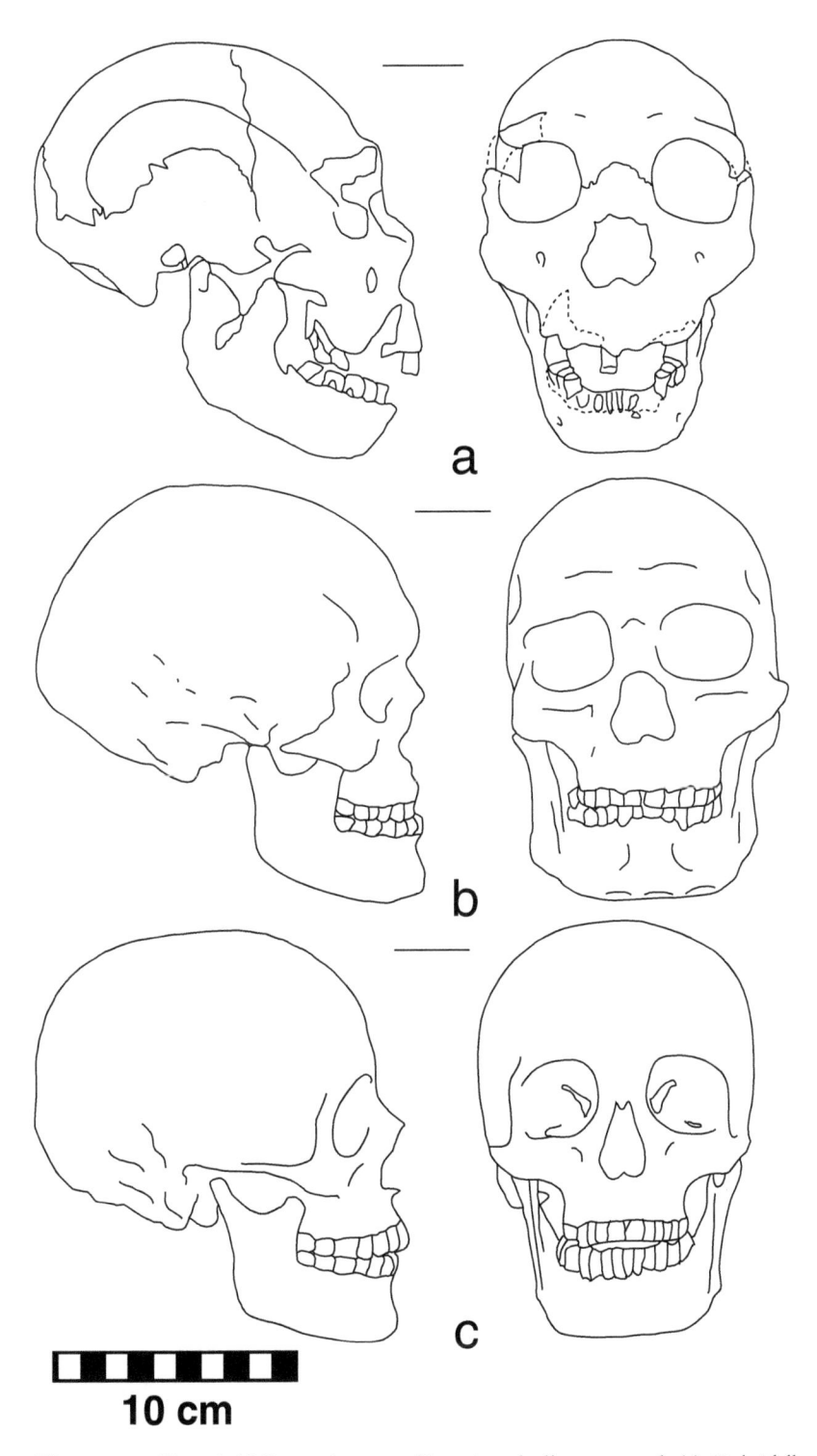

Figure 5.3 *Homo heidelbergensis* versus *H. sapiens* skulls compared. (a) *H. heidelbergensis*, Sima de los Huesos, SH-5; (b) Late Pleistocene *H. sapiens*, Zhoukoudian Upper Cave 1; (c) 20th-century *H. sapiens*. Redrawn after Lieberman (2011), © John J. Shea.

Paleontologists' views diverge over whether some specific fossils should be assigned to *H. heidelbergensis*, *H. sapiens*, or some other "transitional" species between them. Omo Kibish 2, Florisbad 1, Eliyeh Springs 1, and the Jebel Irhoud fossils could fit the bill for "transitional" specimens.

Other African Middle to Late Pleistocene Homo

Homo naledi is a relatively small-brained hominin known from skeletons tumbled together in an underground fissure at the Rising Star Site Complex (245 Ka, South Africa) (Dirks et al. 2015). Discovered only recently, we know too little about these creatures to speculate about their survival strategies. *Homo heidelbergensis* and *H. sapiens*, on the other hand, appear at multiple sites, including sites in Eurasia between 50 and 600 Ka. They are plainly germane to questions about prehistoric human diaspora in ways *H. naledi* does not appear to be.

The Ancient African human skull from Iwo Eleru (Nigeria) retains "archaic" features at a surprisingly young date, 12–16 Ka (Harvati et al. 2011), but this fossil does not necessarily indicate the late survival of *H. heidelbergensis* populations. It more likely reflects the fact that some late Pleistocene/early Holocene-age Africans retained "archaic" features, as do individuals in many other populations elsewhere.

ANCIENT AFRICAN ARCHAEOLOGY

Africanist archaeologists recognize the period 50–600 Ka as one in which the mode and tempo of hominin behavior changed significantly from the million-year-long period of apparent stability that preceded it.[6] Stone tool and bone artifacts and evidence of fire use, symbolic artifacts, and food remains all change and vary geographically, but neither synchronously nor in anything that could be remotely recognized as a single continent-wide sequence.

Stone Tools

A few changes in the archaeological record between 200 and 300 Ka hint at differences in how *H. heidelbergensis* and *H. sapiens* made and used stone tools and how they obtained food (Figures 5.4 and 5.5). Larger long core tools (LCTs) become less common and smaller. Smaller LCTs and thin foliate points become more common, as do flakes struck from bifacial and elongated unifacial hierarchical cores (prismatic blade cores). Archaeologists attribute these changes to increased use of hafting, of attaching stone tools to handles (Barham

---

[6] Archaeologists who work on African prehistory divide this period into the later part of an Earlier Stone Age and Middle Stone Age (ca. 50–250 Ka).

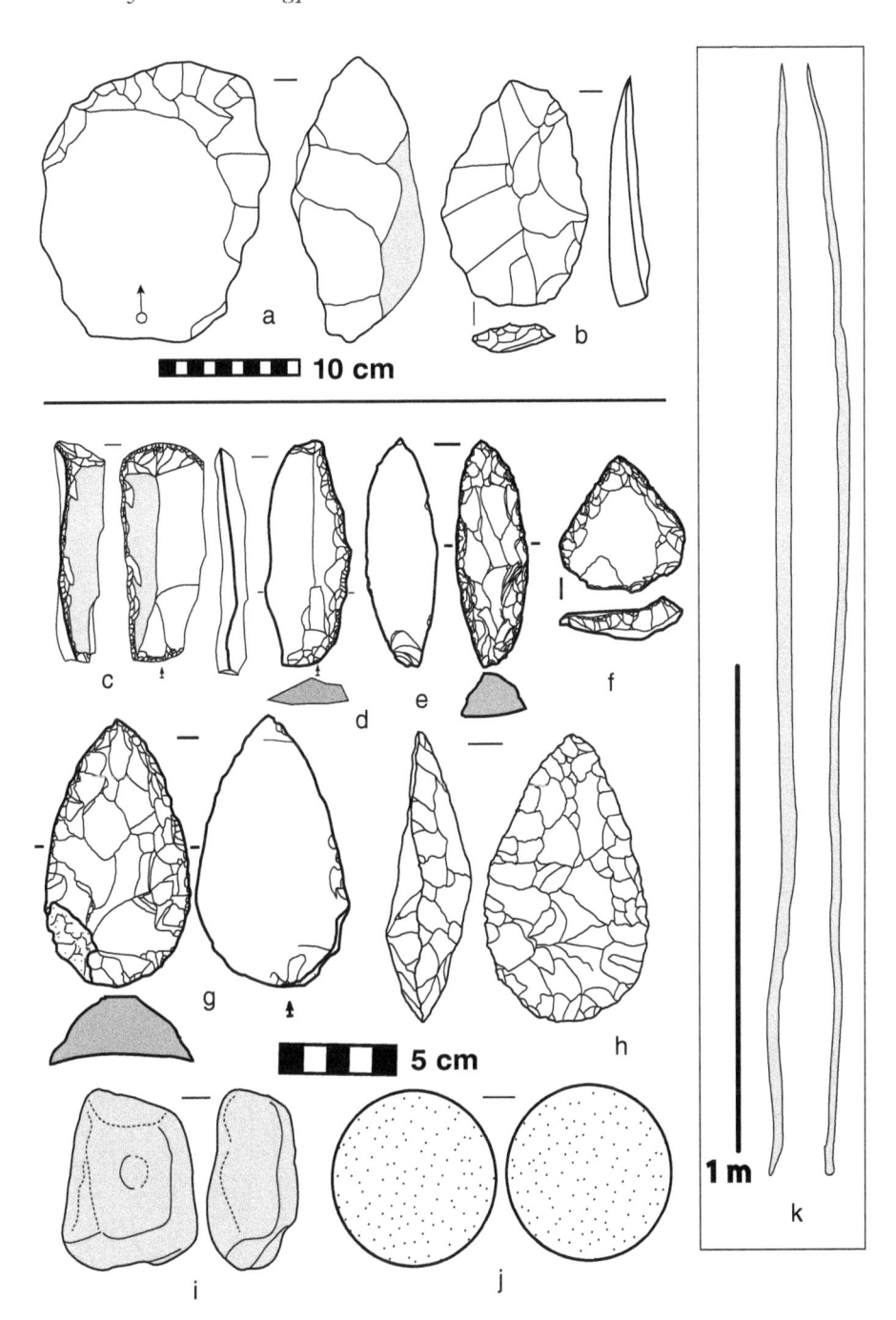

Figure 5.4 Artifacts associated with *Homo heidelbergensis*. (a) Bifacial hierarchical core with preferential removal scar, (b) large flake detached from bifacial hierarchical core, (c) end scraper on blade, (d) backed piece on blade, (e) and (f) convergently retouched pieces, (g) long core tool on flake, (h) long core tool, (i) pitted stone, (j) spheroid/pounded piece, and (k) wooden "javelin" from Schoeningen, Germany. Sources: Shea (2013b, 2017b, 2020a) and Theime (1997). © John J. Shea.

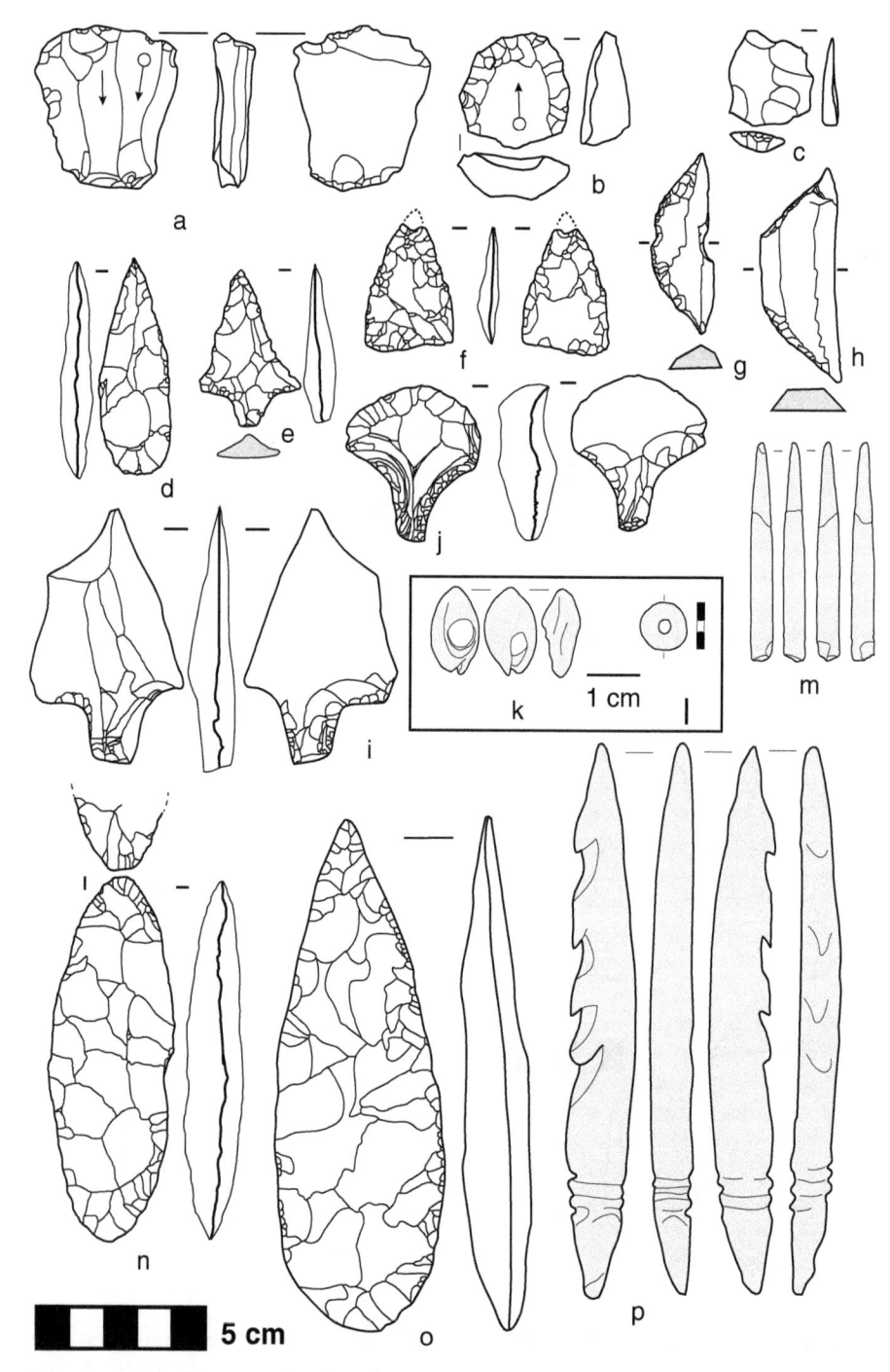

Figure 5.5 Artifacts associated with Ancient Africans. (a) Unifacial hierarchical core (blade core) on a truncated flake, (b) bifacial hierarchical core, (c) flake detached from bifacial hierarchical core, (d)–(f) foliate points, (g) and (h) backed/truncated pieces, (i) and (j) tanged pieces, (k) *Nassarius* shell bead, (l) ostrich eggshell bead, (m) bone arrow tips, (n) and (o) long core tools (n, core-axe; o, lanceolate), (p) barbed bone point ("harpoon"). Sources: Backwell et al. (2018), Henshilwood et al. (2004), Shea (2017b, 2020a), Tryon et al. (2018), and Yellen et al. (1995). © John J. Shea.

2013), but we should not reject the hypothesis that other selective pressures were involved. Making thinner foliate points and the sorts of thin flakes one can detach in bulk from hierarchical cores could also reflect efforts to reduce the amount of rock one had to carry while foraging or hauling back to residential sites.

Foliate points, tanged pieces, flake points, and small backed/truncated pieces become more common and widespread after 100 Ka. Some archaeologists link these developments to increased use of complex, stone-tipped projectile weapons. Much of what archaeologists think about these artifacts' actual uses remains speculation unmoored from actual evidence of their functions, such as wear traces or residues adhering to tool surfaces. Like many of the heavily modified stone tools recent hunter-gatherers carried around while on the move (Binford 1979), many such prehistoric artifacts were probably multipurpose tools.

After around 300 Ka, the African lithic (stone tool) record exhibits increasing regional variation. Suites of artifacts found together in one region do not appear together in others. This "quasi-linguistic" variation could indicate regional cultural differences developing among Ancient Africans (Clark 1988; Shea 2017b).

Bone Artifacts

Some Ancient Africans carved bone into points and other tools. Most of these points are bone splinters with one end carved or abraded into sharply tapering cone. A few have more extensive modifications (i.e., a cylinder pointed at both ends) or barbs carved into their sides. Carved bone points and other implements occur over such a wide range of Africa that one thinks it reasonable to assume they were in general use. A few bone points from Blombos Cave (South Africa, 70 Ka) bear striking similarities to poison-tipped arrows from ethnographic contexts (Lombard 2020).

Fire and Pyrotechnology

Evidence for pre-*H. heidelbergensis* fire use appears at multiple sites in Africa, such as Swartkrans (South Africa, 1.5 Ma), Wonderwerk Cave (South Africa, 1.7 Ma), and East Turkana FxJj 20 (Kenya, 1.5 Ma) as well as at Gesher Benot Yaacov (Israel, 0.7–0.8 Ma). One of the major innovations in fire use dating to 50–600 Ka involves pyrotechnology, using fire to alter materials' properties. Woodworking by "charring and scraping" is a type of pyrotechnology, and excavations have recovered carved wooden artifacts older than 200 Ka from Florisbad (South Africa) and Kalambo Falls (Zambia), but it remains unclear whether those who made them used the charring and scraping technique. The clearest such evidence for pyrotechnology comes from Pinnacle Point Cave 13B (South Africa) (Brown et al. 2009). Between 70 and 165 Ka, humans living at Pinnacle Point weakened tough silcrete rocks by exposing them to fire ("heat treatment" or "thermal alteration"), making them more amenable to precision stoneworking. Heat-treating rocks is a complex process, one that requires careful preselection of rocks, fuel, and other variables. Done wrong, the rocks can disintegrate or even explode. One thinks it unlikely Ancient African did such heat treatment repeatedly and successfully over thousands of years without teaching, learning, and experimentation. Considering the sheer number and complexity of variables involved, heat treatment almost certainly required spoken language.

Symbolic Artifacts

Rare traces of red ochre (iron oxide) dating to ca. 500–600 Ka at Olorgesailie (Kenya) (Brooks et al. 2018) suggest that *H. heidelbergensis* may have appreciated this mineral pigment's value for transmitting symbolically encoded social information, or conceivably for other purposes, such as preserving leather. Blombos Cave (South Africa, 70–100 Ka) preserves abundant early evidence for red ochre use, and similar such evidence grows considerably after 100 Ka.

Blombos Cave, together with Grotte des Contrabandiers ("Smugglers' Cave," Morocco, 90–120 Ka) and, further afield, Skhul Cave in Israel (80–120 Ka), preserves evidence for early humans using perforated gastropod shells as personal adornments. Remarkably, and in spite of the distances separating them, humans selected shells of the same genus, *Nassarius*, at all three sites.

Food Remains

Nonhuman animal fossils in African sites after 600 Ka feature a wide range of species, ranging from small bovids, such as duiker and hyrax, to megafauna (elephants, rhinos, hippos) and including both solitary and migratory species. Hominin hunters do not appear to have systematically hunted African apes or other large terrestrial primates, such as baboons. That tropical and equatorial environments receive so much solar radiation complicates interpreting this evidence. Such radiation exposure means that bones rarely preserve long, or well, especially in open-air sites. Prior to 200–300 Ka, such open-air sites dominate *H. heidelbergensis*' archaeological record. Ancient Africans seem to have used caves more often, and thus we have a richer zooarchaeological record for them (Smith et al. 2019).

ANCIENT AFRICANS' SURVIVAL STRATEGIES

This section compares what we think we know about Ancient Africans' and *Homo heidelbergensis*' solutions with the "basic six" survival strategies.

First Aid and Medication

No evidence shows that either *Homo heidelbergensis* or Ancient Africans provided medical assistance to one another or that they differed from one another in this respect. This does not mean *H. heidelbergensis* and *H. sapiens* enjoyed perfect health, or that they lacked strategies for treating the injured or ill among their numbers. After all, few traces of first aid or medicine survive in the archaeological record for ethnographic and historic populations with well-documented medical practices.

The Kabwe 1 fossil from Zambia has carious lesions all over its teeth and maxilla and must have suffered terribly before he died (Pycraft et al. 1928). What caused this unique injury and whether he received treatment for it remain unknown.

Thermoregulation

Homo heidelbergensis and Ancient Africans both sheltered in caves, but the archaeological record from less than 200–300 Ka shows somewhat more evidence for artificial thermoregulation. Evidence for fire use and for transporting fire into caves occurs at African and Eurasian sites much older than 500 Ka, but the evidence for fire use becomes more common after 200 Ka. Ashy deposits in Klasies River Mouth Cave feature the distinctive alternating pattern of black-and-white banding that results from prolonged combustion in the same hearth (Singer and Wymer 1982).

Genetic studies of human head and pubic lice suggest that the lineages of these insects diverged sometime between 83 and 170 Ka, a finding that suggests humans used clothing widely by at least that point in time, as clothing would isolate head and pubic lice from each other (Toups et al. 2011). One thinks it unlikely *H. heidelbergensis* lacked clothing entirely, for their fossil remains and archaeological traces occur north of the European Alps where winter nighttime temperatures, even in today's warm world, can cause lethal hypothermia (Gilligan 2010). The head/pubic lice divergence most likely marks changes in the kinds of clothing in use, perhaps garments secured with belts and drawstrings rather than loose cloaks.

Hydration

Stable sources of potable water at or near the surface seem to have "anchored" early hominin settlement patterns, much as they do those of other large primates. Most sites at which *H. heidelbergensis* and Ancient African fossils and archaeological remains occur are near springs, rivers, or lakes. Diepkloof Rockshelter (South Africa, 45–130 Ka) preserves numerous fragments of engraved ostrich eggs that are thought to have served as water canteens, a common practice among African hunter-gatherers (Texier et al. 2010), but the antiquity and extent of ostrich-egg canteen use remains unknown. Ostrich egg fragments found at archaeological sites younger than 600 Ka may have been canteens, food waste, or both. Other than the Diepkloof evidence, no other evidence suggests major differences between *H. heidelbergensis*' and early *H. sapiens*' strategies for finding and transporting water.

Nutrition

Both *H. heidelbergensis* and Ancient Africans procured meat and fat from large animal carcasses. Neither hominin seems to have systematically hunted Africa's "killer herbivore" megafauna, such as elephants, rhinoceros, and hippos, though they occasionally preyed on large bovids, such as Cape buffalo and *Pelorovis*, a large bovid (cattle-like creature), now extinct. The extent to which they killed the larger such animals or exploited other carnivores' kills themselves undoubtedly varied widely with habitat, season, and circumstance. Recent African hunter-gatherers do both things, and so it seems reasonable to assume their recent ancestors did them as well.

Sites dating to less than 200–300 Ka feature significantly greater quantities of bones from smaller animals and fewer remains of larger animals than older sites do (Smith et al. 2019). This could signal a change in human subsistence strategies, but it could also result from contrasting taphonomic differences in cave versus open-air sites. Many more of the younger sites are caves, and caves preserve smaller animal bones better than open-air sites do. When large mammals die they often do so near water sources, places where carnivores hunt and where water persists during droughts (Shipman 1981). Carcasses of large animals quickly develop into "carnivore magnets," and so one assumes hominins exploiting such large mammal death sites for food had few incentives for dragging these animals' heavy bones back to cave refuges and habitation sites. The scarcity of large animal bones at cave sites might reflect Ancient Africans having sensibly left the inedible parts of these carcasses at death sites.

Two other lines of evidence hint that *Homo sapiens* may have exploited aquatic resources in ways that *H. heidelbergensis* did not. Located along the Semliki River, Katanda (Democratic Republic of Congo, 90 Ka) preserves a series of barbed bone points thought to have been used to spear fish (Yellen et al. 1995). *H. heidelbergensis*' archaeological record preserves no similar such evidence.

Ancient Africans appear to have systematically gathered shellfish from coastal sources in South Africa, most clearly at Pinnacle Point Cave 13B (Marean 2014). That site preserves dense concentrations ("middens") of shellfish (mollusks and gastropods) like those that that appear in recent contexts around the habitation sites of shellfish-collecting hunter-gatherers and farmers. These shellfish middens contrast with occurrences of shellfish at sites older than 200–300 Ka. The global archaeological record preserves few Middle

Pleistocene-age archaeological sites. Located on the Mediterranean Coast, Terra Amata (France, 400 Ka) preserves some sparse shellfish remains but nothing anyone could credibly call a midden. Still, one has to be careful about overgeneralizing. Shellfish beds are "patchy" resources. Just because one fails to find middens on those parts of ancient landscapes that have fortuitously escaped the destructive forces at work on coastlines does not refute the hypothesis that hominins gorged themselves on shellfish elsewhere.

The archaeological record suggests *some* Ancient Africans used aquatic resources differently from *H. heidelbergensis*, but we do not yet know much detail about either species' behavioral variability in aquatic resource use.

Transportation

Hauling stone tools around the landscape appears evolutionarily primitive among hominins of the genus *Homo*. Rocks are heavy, and one expects that natural and sexual selection would favor survival strategies that minimized the energetic costs associated with transporting stone tools.[7] That is, carrying superfluous numbers of heavy rocks around, rather than, say, food or children, would earn one neither long life nor many marriage proposals.

The African evidence offers hints that humans' and *H. heidelbergensis*' strategies for transporting stone around the landscape differed, but the picture is complicated. The leverage a handle provides allows one to accomplish tasks with small tools that would otherwise be difficult or even impossible to do using tools held directly in the hand.[8] Beginning around 250 Ka, the Africa archaeological record features ever-decreasing numbers of larger long core tools whose size and thickness suggest they were used while held directly in the hand. At the same time, that record preserves increasing numbers of thin foliate points, tanged pieces, and small backed/truncated pieces, as well as thin flakes struck from hierarchical cores whose morphological consistency made them easier to attach to handles without much prior retouching and shaping.

Did a "hafting revolution" occur around 250 Ka (Barham 2013)? The main argument against this hypothesis involves various triangular and/or convergently retouched stone artifacts from Kathu Pan 1 in South Africa (Wilkins et al. 2012). Published dates for Kathu Pan 1 suggest these artifacts were made, used, and discarded around 500 Ka. If these dates are correct, then hafting stone tools long predates *Homo sapiens*' emergence.

---

[7] Natural selection describes forces affecting individual survival (e.g., avoiding a predator), while sexual selection references forces influencing individual reproductive success (e.g., having nutritious food and mating opportunities) (Darwin 1859). To help remember the difference, I tell my students to think of natural versus sexual selection as "life versus lunch." They, of course, prefer "life versus love" (or other terms).

[8] To demonstrate this, I sometimes invite skeptical students to try cutting a piece of wood with a metal axe head detached from its handle.

Attaching stone tools to handles appears something *Homo heidelbergensis* did occasionally but something Ancient Africans did more consistently over time. The mode and tempo of hafting's development remains a major research question in Pleistocene archaeology.

Communication

Early humans and *Homo heidelbergensis* almost certainly communicated verbally. Whether or not *H. heidelbergensis* had the sort of rapid-fire quantal speech we enjoy remains unclear.

Among humans generally, the color red catches attention and elicit emotional responses in ways that other colors do not (Maier et al. 2009). Both hominins appear to have used mineral pigments, such as red ochre, an observation suggesting red color–bias may be evolutionarily primitive. Most occurrences of symbolic artifacts, such as stones and bones with geometric patterns incised or painted on them and perforated shells used as personal adornments date to less than 200–300 Ka. All these things occur together in impressive combination at Blombos Cave (South Africa) between 70 and 100 Ka (d'Errico et al. 2005). Interpreting this evidence is fraught with problems. First, iron bonds with nearly everything, so the use of red ochre as a mineral pigment has high archaeological "visibility" in ways that other potential pigments (e.g., chalk or charcoal) do not.

The case for associating perforated personal adornments uniquely with *H. sapiens* seems stronger until one considers preservation biases. Many living and historic groups make and use beads out of wood, bone, seeds, and other materials that do not preserve long or well in sedimentary deposits. Increased evidence for personal adornments after 200–300 Ka might not reflect the inception of personal adornment use as much as a shift toward using more durable media, possibly the result of increasingly predictable contacts among strangers where such exosomatic symbolic artifacts can help overcome linguistic and cultural barriers to cooperation (Wobst 1977).

Does Ancient Africans' archaeological record preserve evidence for the sorts of extensive, symbolically reinforced alliance networks ethnographers observe among living Africans and other humans? Little or nothing in *H. heidelbergensis'* record does. Few of the artifacts associated with *H. heidelbergensis* pass the "archaeological where/when test," that is, can archaeologists correctly assign an artifact to a specific region and time period using visual clues only? Many, indeed most artifacts associated with Ancient Africans fail this test, too. Still, region-specific artifact designs and stoneworking strategies in the evidence dating from 30–300 Ka suggests something different afoot among these people. A few regional phenomena featuring distinctive artifacts such as the Southern African "Still Bay" foliate points and "Howiesons Port" small backed/truncated pieces, as well as the Northern African "Aterian" tanged pieces, might correspond to such extensive regional alliance networks along which ideas about artifact designs flowed, but these "complexes" extend far more widely and show fewer clear changes over time than artifacts linked to recent such alliance networks among ethnographic humans do. These observations do not refute the hypothesis that these archaeological phenomena correspond to such networks, for networks can change and vary. (That is kind of the whole point of having them.) Those patterns seen in some parts of Africa's Middle to Late Pleistocene archaeological record may be "lithic fallout" from networks spread out among human populations living at far lower population densities than recent African hunter-gatherers whose geographic ranges and population densities reflect circumscription by pastoralists and farmers.

INTERPRETIVE ISSUES ABOUT ANCIENT AFRICANS

Much remains unknown about what happened in Africa between 30 and 600 Ka. By the end of this period, and to judge from the paleontological record, more humans were inhabiting the continent than *H. heidelbergensis* populations, if indeed any of the latter persisted after 30 Ka. Below, we consider why this is.

Behavioral Differences between Ancient Africans and Homo heidelbergensis

Before we consider differences between *Homo heidelbergensis*' and early *H. sapiens*' survival strategies, we have to examine the quality of the evidence, specifically, how things other than prehistoric hominin behavior, such as "sample error," can create the appearance of differences.

Ordinarily, one tries to infer the qualities ("parameters") of unknown larger populations using only probabilistic samples, samples of evidence in which each observation has a knowable chance of being made. All archaeological and paleontological samples are judgmental samples. That is, some sites and fossils have a greater likelihood of discovery, investigation, and documentation. Proximity to major cities, ease of access, and other factors increase those odds. Distance, difficult terrain, and political unrest reduce them. These considerations do not make comparisons among archaeological data sets moot or meaningless. They just mean that one has to recognize one is comparing "filtered" samples and not the original hominin behavior. For example, that there are fewer artifacts indicating activity X in *Homo heidelbergensis*' archaeological record than in *H. sapiens*' archaeological record does not mean that *H. sapiens* performed activity X more often than *H. heidelbergensis* did. It may simply reflect the fact that more sites associated with *H. sapiens* survive geological attrition (deep burial and erosion) than those resulting from *H. heidelbergensis*' activities.

The archaeological evidence associated with both *H. heidelbergensis* and Ancient Africans is demonstrably both a historical and geographic chimera. The Chimera was a Greek mythological creature with a lion's head, a goat's body, and a serpent's tail. Paleontologists use the term "chimera" for reconstructed fossils made up of parts from different organisms. In this case, *H. heidelbergensis*' and Ancient Africans' archaeological records are made up from multiple sites across the continent dating tens of thousands of years or more apart from one another. It might be a mistake to interpret things some Ancient Africans did as things all or even many Ancient Africans did.

We have a far richer archaeological record for *H. sapiens* than for *H. heidelbergensis*. Well-documented African archaeological sites dating to 300–600 Ka number no more than a dozen or so, while sites dating less than 200 Ka number in the low hundreds. The larger numbers of sites in younger samples make it more likely that younger samples will preserve evidence for uncommon activities than older samples will.[9] We cannot write off evidence for *H. heidelbergensis*' versus *H. sapiens*' behavioral differences, but we need to be alert to the possibility and not overgeneralize from sparse evidence of unusual behaviors in the younger samples.

With these considerations in mind (which, incidentally, also apply to all of the comparisons among evidence in later chapters), we can now ask, do the differences between *H. heidelbergensis*' and early *H. sapiens*' survival strategies clearly and convincingly indicate additions to ancestral survival skills? No, they do not. Differences in the evidence associated with *H. heidelbergensis* and *H. sapiens* are largely matters of degree rather than of kind. Nothing humans did in Africa 50–300 Ka of these things required skills *H. heidelbergensis* did not also possess.

Technological Intensification

Most of the things Ancient Africans did differently from *Homo heidelbergensis* involved "technological intensification." That is, Ancient Africans expended more time and energy on technology than *H. heidelbergensis* did. Few of the stone tools *H. heidelbergensis* made require more than a few minutes' stone-working effort, and even novice "flintknappers" can reproduce them with ease (Shea 2015). Some Ancient Africans carefully selected high-quality rocks, such as obsidian and quartz, for tool materials. Those tools' shapes suggest they were attached to handles using cordage and glue, a process that can take hours. Carved bone tools, perforated shells and ostrich eggshell beads, and stone tools seemingly designed for hafting occasionally appear at African sites earlier than 200–300 Ka. These and other evidence for technological intensification grows

---

[9] When I teach about this subject, I bring a deck of playing cards to class, shuffle them, and then ask one group of students to select three cards and another twenty cards. I then ask them to tell us what they can infer about the deck of cards *solely from the cards they hold in their hands*. The students who have drawn twenty cards always have a more accurate picture of the full range of suits and denominations in the deck than those students who have three cards. This lesson teaches that comparing archaeological evidence for *Homo heidelbergensis* behavior with evidence for *Homo sapiens* behavior is like comparing three-card versus twenty-card draws.

ever more common after 200–300 Ka and in more recent time ranges (Barham and Mitchell 2008).

What created these differences? Differences in technological intensification between *H. heidelbergensis* and early *H. sapiens* may indicate contrasting dependence on tool use. Humans today are obligatory tool users, even in the African habitats in which we evolved, but *H. heidelbergensis* might have been less obligatory tool users than early *H. sapiens* were (Shea 2017a, 2017b). Long-term changes in the global stone tool evidence suggest a shift from occasional stone tool use before 1.8 Ma and more habitual stone tool use afterward – as reflected in increased evidence for the artifacts whose shapes are not intrinsic to the rocks of which they were made. After 200–300 Ka, the stone tool record shows increasing evidence for hafting, for more careful rock material selection (more use of uncommon, fine-grained quartz-rich rocks), and for carrying stone longer distances. These added efforts at artifact design (costs) suggest that, much like someone who has made a dugout canoe (or, nowadays, bought a boat), once humans became more dependent on tools, they earned greater returns on the time and energy they invested into making them (benefits), provided they continued investing.[10]

No evidence supports the argument that such intensification arises from a specific genetic cause.

Migration versus Dispersal

With hominin fossils being scarce and ceramics appearing widely only in Holocene times, archaeologists seeking evidence for Pleistocene-age human migrations have turned to the stone tool evidence. Is any of the stone tool evidence from Africa dating to 50–600 Ka more consistent with migration than with dispersals? Here, we consider both traditional archaeological perspectives as well as the integrated paleoanthropological perspective on this question. Neither perspective supports the hypothesis that Ancient Africans ever migrated anywhere.

Humans appear in Africa during a period of increasing "regionalization," a time when different parts of the "four Africas" increasingly preserve evidence for distinctive stoneworking traditions. If humans originated in one of these regions and migrated from there to other regions, one would expect to see one or another region's distinctive stone tool "signature" appear earlier in that region and at steadily younger ages further away from it. Archaeologists' speculations have focused on three artifact categories: foliate points, tanged pieces, and small backed/truncated pieces.

Foliate points occur all over sub-Saharan Africa, Northern Africa west of the Nile River Valley, and mostly in assemblages younger than 100 Ka. It is not

---

[10] A popular proverb defines a boat as "a hole in the water into which one pours money."

clear that they appear earlier in one part of Africa than in any other. Remarkable similarities appear among foliate points from widely distant parts of Africa, but remarkable differences occur among foliate points from the same sites, too. Further study may reveal geographic and chronological patterning among these artifacts consistent with migration, but as of this writing we cannot reject alternative hypotheses (1) that these points result from a convergent selective pressure for artifact designs that recruited ancestral stoneworking skills or (2) that ideas about foliate point production flowed along extensive social networks connecting Ancient Africans to one another.

Tanged pieces occur mainly in Northern Africa west of the lower Nile River Valley between 20 and 150 Ka. Some of these artifacts are foliate points that have had concavities removed from their base. Others are triangular flakes or convergently retouched pieces modified in this way. Still others are flakes, scrapers, burins, or other artifacts. Stone tool assemblages with tanged pieces differ little from those roughly contemporary with them that lack such tanged pieces (Dibble et al. 2013; Scerri 2013). Dates for sites preserving tanged pieces show no obvious point of origin from which they spread outward. That tanged pieces and foliate points occur only to the west of the lower Nile, but not to the east, is a unique case among African prehistoric stone tools. Most such artifacts appear on both sides of major sub-Saharan rivers (Clark 1967). It remains unclear why the lower Nile bounds their distribution.

Early (> 50 Ka) occurrences of small backed/truncated pieces ("microliths") occur mainly in Southern and Eastern Africa. After 30 Ka, they appear continent-wide. A few examples from Twin Rivers Kopje (Zambia) date to around 140–300 Ka (Barham 2002), but a long gap separates these from archaeological assemblages in which a large number of small backed/truncated pieces appear (Ambrose 2002). Most of those younger assemblages date to less than 80–100 Ka. Occurrences of small backed/truncated pieces appear to be marginally older in Southern Africa than in Eastern Africa, but the distinctive trapezoidal shapes one sees among the Southern African artifacts do not commonly appear among their Eastern African counterparts. There, crescentic, triangular, and other forms predominate. This last observation seems to tip the scales against migration, suggesting that much as with foliate points and tanged pieces, we are observing either toolmaking convergences or the diffusion of stoneworking habits along social networks.

Neither foliate points nor tanged pieces nor microliths match the predicted consequences of Ancient African migrations within Africa.[11]

---

[11] The single greatest obstacle to investigating Ancient African population movements (or indeed anything else) using the African lithic record is that archaeologists, especially those working in Eastern Africa, use many and variable ways of measuring and describing stone artifacts (Shea 2020a).

What are we to make of *Nassarius* shells having been selected for use as personal adornments at opposite ends of the continent in Southern Africa's Cape and along the Mediterranean Coast? Nothing in the stone tool evidence supports the hypothesis that people from Africa's Mediterranean Coast moved to Southern Africa or vice versa. Foliate points occur in both places, but the distinctive tanged pieces one finds among Northern African sites do not appear in Southern Africa. Nor do the distinctive trapezoidal small backed/truncated pieces one finds in Southern African sites appear at sites of the same age along the Mediterranean Coast.

To invoke convergence (similar choices made independently of one another) to explain these far-flung occurrences strains belief, but until we learn as much about the variation among these regional bead-making occurrences, we cannot take this hypothesis off the table. It is possible that ideas about *Nassarius* shell bead use spread over the Continent along exchange networks like the "chains of connection" that moved shells and other items across Australia (Mulvaney 1976). However, no such perforated *Nassarius* shells have turned up at any sites of the same or greater age in interior Africa or its coastlines. In the end, testing hypotheses about possible connections between Northern and Southern African shell bead use requires more evidence from Equatorial Africa, especially its Atlantic and Indian Ocean coastlines than archaeologists currently have at their disposal.

Allowing that there is much we do not know about what causes variation in the stone tool (and shell bead) evidence, does the hominin fossil evidence support migration hypotheses about Ancient Africans? Claims for older and oldest *Homo sapiens* fossils grow apace, but the same pattern in this evidence persists.

- The oldest such fossils retain a complex mosaic of derived and primitive features. None could by any stretch of the imagination be mistaken for a recent human fossil dating to less than 40–50 Ka, much less the skeletal remains of a living human.
- These early human fossils do not appear earlier in one region and in progressively younger ones with greater distance.
- These fossils' archaeological associations (stone tools and other artifacts) differ from one another and are, in most cases, more similar to the evidence that precedes them locally than to contemporary evidence from one of the other "three Africas".

These observations are entirely consistent with recent analyses of living human DNA variation that suggest human ancestry extends continent-wide rather than to one or another region within Africa (Scerri 2018; Bergström et al. 2021). Paleontological and molecular evidence largely agree in answering, "Did Ancient Africans migrate from one part of the continent to the rest of it?" with a resounding, "No." No evidence supports the hypothesis that there once existed an African "Garden of Eden" from which humans spread outward in all directions conquering the world, driving all other hominins before them. Such "migrate and conquer" scenarios have deep roots in 19th-century ethnology and prehistory (Kossina 1911; Robinson 2016), but they do not align well with the evidence available to 21st-century paleoanthropology.

The Infiltration Hypothesis

If Ancient African *Homo sapiens* did not migrate, then how did they become so widely distributed? Several telling, if inconvenient facts suggest an alternative to migration.

First, early *H. sapiens* did not really expand *H. heidelbergensis'* geographic range all that much. Second, few major changes in the archaeological record occur between last appearance dates for *H. heidelbergensis* fossils and first appearance dates for *H. sapiens* fossils other than changes in stoneworking strategies, whose causes remain unclear, and variation in zooarchaeological remains arising from changes in climate or in the sources of the evidence (i.e., caves vs. open-air sites). These observations suggest Ancient Africans replaced *H. heidelbergensis* by dispersing, by infiltrating local *H. heidelbergensis* populations, and then out-reproducing them (sexual selection). For brevity, we shall call this the "Infiltration Hypothesis." In naming it "infiltration," one does not assert that such infiltration was a centrally directed initiative, planned process, or conspiracy. Nor does one think it something they did out of altruism, "for the good of the species." Rather, individuals adopted this social and reproductive strategy in response to costs and benefits and to serve their own individual evolutionary goal, getting more copies of their genes into the next generation ("inclusive fitness").

What short-term advantages might individual *H. sapiens* have enjoyed over *H. heidelbergensis* populations among whom they lived? Possibly none. But rather like football, soccer and lacrosse, dispersal is not a game one plays alone. Small groups of humans cohabiting with *H. heidelbergensis* and who possessed some capacities for behavior those other hominins lacked could have leveraged those capacities to their own reproductive advantages. What were such advantageous capacities?

Early Ancient Africans might have been more intelligent that *H. heidelbergensis*, but intelligence is such a difficult quality to measure even among living humans that one struggles to imagine how one would test this hypothesis using paleoanthropological evidence.

Spoken language? Our oddly shaped heads or, more specifically, our flexed basicranium confer a capacity for quantal speech – rapid speech with distinct elements and few copying errors (Lieberman and McCarthy 2014). Modest basicranial flexion on many *H. heidelbergensis* fossils suggests some sort of speech, but perhaps not quantal speech. If this were the case, quantal speech could have been among early humans' advantages. Being able to warn someone, "Look out for that lion" in 2 seconds rather than 10 seconds could comprise an advantage in sexual selection (opportunities to mate) and inclusive fitness. Some of the newly emergent behaviors we see in evidence among Ancient Africans, such as heat-treating rocks, assembling multicomponent tools, and astronomical timing of shellfish gathering (collecting shellfish exposed by extremely low tides) suggest activities that would be difficult to teach and learn without spoken language of the sort our species possesses uniquely among primates. How quantal speech arose remains a mystery, but because the basicranial flexion that allows it also makes it easy to choke on food, one suspects it arose in concert with some change in foodways among early *H. sapiens'* immediate *H. heidelbergensis* precursors.

A second thing *H. sapiens* does universally and in contrast with other primates is collaborative child-rearing (Kramer 2019), an offshoot of our hyperprosociality. Other primates may look after one another's young for brief periods or correct their misbehavior, but only humans willingly, indeed enthusiastically, entrust their children's daily care and education to strangers (teachers, college professors) who could, in principle, be the parents' reproductive rivals. In singling out spoken language and collaborative child-rearing for discussion here, one does not assert that they alone were the behaviors that enabled *H. sapiens* to out-reproduce *H. heidelbergensis*. Still, they are ones whose effects this author observes daily in college classrooms. The better-prepared students study together and reject overtures from would-be "free-riders" among their less-studious classmates.

The evolutionary transition between *H. heidelbergensis* and *H. sapiens* in Africa may have involved a move away from individual self-sufficiency to more dependence on extensive social networks (Gamble et al. 2014), a shift from living as the protagonist in Gary Paulsen's inspiring novel of individual wilderness survival, *The Hatchet* (1986) to the setting of William Golding's (1954) much darker work, *The Lord of the Flies*. Collaborative child-rearing's origins remain unclear, too, but that other primates practice something like it suggests deep evolutionary roots. Considering the African evidence, one thinks it possible that *Homo ergaster/erectus'* and *H. heidelbergensis'* activities around large mammal death sites, at which the children on hand would have been exposed to rival carnivores, provided selective pressure for collaborative child-rearing either on-site or elsewhere in return for a transported share of the haul from the "meat jackpot."

One principled objection one could raise about the Infiltration Hypothesis asks why Ancient Africans sharing the capacities for spoken language and collaborative child-rearing of the sort humans practice today would have anything to do with *H. heidelbergensis* in the first place. Wouldn't they have been better off as a people apart, living among their own kind, or at least among others with similar abilities? To answer this question, we consider a thought experiment. Imagine there appeared among us a heritable mutation that made humans immune to other humans' counterfactual claims. Let us call it the "Skeptic Gene." Advertising would mean nothing to those who had this capacity. Politicians' appeals to their passions would fall on deaf ears. Supernatural claims would evoke laughter rather than reverence, much less martyrdom.[12] In today's interconnected world, individuals inheriting such a mutation might group together to form a community on some island or remote mountain, but such a community would face several problems. First, it would pit those who had the Skeptic Gene in direct reproductive competition with one another. Second, the entire population would be vulnerable to environmental "insult," such as a drought, meteor impact, large-scale volcanism, epidemic, or targeted coalitionary violence from those who lacked this capacity. Third, from a "gene's-eye" standpoint (Dawkins 1976), these "*Homo skepticus*" would be better off (i.e., create more copies of their genes) by infiltrating populations lacking the Skeptic Gene and seeking out such reproductive advantages as that gene afforded them in those populations. Their optimal reproductive survival strategy would be to live among populations with sufficient numbers of more credulous people whom they could "outwit, outplay, and outlast."[13]

Did "dispersal and infiltration" require different skills than those *H. heidelbergensis* already possessed? One thinks not. *H. heidelbergensis*' and other Lower and Middle Pleistocene species of the genus *Homo* have similarly murky evolutionary origins. That is, one cannot peg them to a specific time or place, but rather to two or more competing "hot spots" that reflect fossil discoveries rather than probable zones of origination identified from prior evolutionary theory. (That is, just because the oldest fossil of *Homo erectus* occurs in, say, South Africa does not mean *Homo erectus* originated in South Africa.) Dispersal and infiltration may be deeply ancestral in at least the genus *Homo*. How much older it may be in hominin and other primate evolution remains to be discovered.

SUMMARY

This chapter argued that Ancient Africans established themselves throughout Africa by a continent-wide process of dispersing and infiltrating. Ancient Africans' most distinct archaeological difference from *Homo heidelbergensis* involved "technological intensification," or devoting more time and energy using tools to solve basic survival challenges. The evidence hints at increased hyperprosociality in some parts of Ancient Africans' geographic range, but Ancient Africans do not appear to have added to the suite of ancestral survival

---

[12] For other advantages such a hypothetical "skeptic gene" might confer, see Novella (2018).
[13] The motto for CBS Television's long-running *Survivor* show.

skills. They simply did the same things *H. heidelbergensis* did, only differently, and in the long run, better than them. Chapter 6 reviews the evidence for early human population movements in Southwestern and South Asia (the Levant, Arabia, and India).

> **Box 5.1:** *Boats, bows, and beads*
>
> If one is looking for activities in evidence among Ancient Africans that might predict their success in wider dispersal, combined evidence for "boats, bows, and beads" certainly fits the bill.
>
> Navigable rivers teeming with fish so crisscrossed Africa during the Pleistocene Epoch's wetter phases that it is unimaginable Ancient Africans lacked watercraft. Proof of Pleistocene watercraft remains elusive, but it does not escape notice that few African rivers mark any major change in the stone tool evidence on either side of them. Some of these same rivers have apparently divided chimpanzee, bonobo, and gorilla populations for hundreds of thousands of years.
>
> Before firearms became widely available, the bow and arrow were humanity's most versatile and widespread hunting aids (and domesticated dogs, of course). African apes routinely use the sudden release of energy stored in bent wood to move through trees, but they do not use this understanding to make subsistence aids utilizing stored tension. One reasonably assumes at least Middle Pleistocene humans understood this energetic principle, too. Wherever ethnographic humans use the bow and arrow and spring traps, they serve as a "niche-broadeners." They allow hunters to prey on both large and small game at the same time, opportunistically. Though archaeologists' speculations about the origin of the bow and arrow tend to focus on their use against terrestrial game, many ethnographic Africans fish using bows and arrows (Maclaren 1958; Inskeep 2001). No evidence suggests we should view bow fishing as a recently developed activity. It might even predate bow-and-arrow use against terrestrial prey. Singly or together, bow and spring trap use would have helped dispersing humans tailor their food-getting strategies to novel habitats. Evidence for the antiquity of bow use in Africa currently hovers around 75 Ka (Lombard 2021), but one suspects future research will reveal its use in considerably more ancient contexts.[14]
>
> Beads might seem an unlikely aid to dispersal, but dispersals involve individuals and small groups moving into new habitats, assimilating, and

---

[14] This author is confident that the oldest dates for the bow and arrow will eventually converge with first appearance dates for *Homo sapiens* in Africa, but (as with much else in this book) his is a minority position in prehistoric archaeology.

Box 5.1: *(cont.)*

reorganizing their social networks in those habitats. Local linguistic and cultural differences can pose obstacles to such assimilation and reorganization. By transmitting visual messages about individuals' status and social identity, beads and other symbolic artifacts could have helped dispersing humans overcome these linguistic and cultural differences. Being modular, one can arrange beads quasi-grammatically, recombining and reordering them to convey different messages (Kuhn and Stiner 2007). Beads, moreover, are durable. Some of the beads that Ancient Africans made and used persisted for nearly 100,000 years. We do not currently know how much further back in time hominins' use of beads and other symbolic artifacts extends, but inasmuch as making and using beads requires evolutionarily ancestral skills, such as powerful precision grasping and predictive hallucination, one thinks their use at least as old as our species, and probably much, much older.

Ancient Africans' archaeological record offers up sparse evidence for boats, bows, and beads being in use at the same place at the same time, but recent history provides some measure of their power in combination. Nearly all of the major historical population movements between the Old and New Worlds were accomplished using watercraft – initially, ocean-going vessels and later riverboats – to reach continental interiors. By the late 1500s, European armies had largely replaced the bow and arrow with firearms and cannons, but many colonists' success hinged largely on advances in light firearms and horsemanship. Industrially mass-produced glass and metal beads figure prominently among the trade goods European and Asian merchants brought to the Americas and to Africa from the 1500s onward. So common are glass beads that archaeologists use their occurrences as "horizon markers" for contacts with foreign trade networks across much of the Americas, sub-Saharan Africa, and Australasia. How important were beads? In many parts of the world to which Europeans migrated and dispersed from the 17th century onward, handmade beads already served as "social media" as well as currency in exchange networks. A possibly apocryphal 17th-century account holds that Dutch explorer Peter Minuit purchased Manhattan from the Native American Lenape tribe for "beads and other trinkets" worth about $24 today.[15]

These observations suggest that we should expect to find that as Ancient Africans extended their geographic range, evidence for their using boats, bows, and beads should appear in their archaeological record. Such

---

[15] Historians speculate that in "selling" Manahatta (Manhattan Island) the Lenape were granting permission for the Dutch to hunt, fish, farm, and live there, but not to do so to the exclusion of others who had used the land previously or who might ask to do so in the future.

Box 5.1: *(cont.)*

evidence should neither surprise us nor constitute "big news," for in using these things, early humans would simply be relying on ancestral skills long in use previously. Rather, finding evidence for human population movements unaccompanied by such evidence should attract close archaeological scrutiny, for such a finding would suggest either that some novel suite of innovations aided human population movements or that selective pressure worked against using boats, bows, and beads.

For thought and discussion: That early humans made and used boats should surprise no one. Humans make and use boats pretty much everywhere they live near coastlines and navigable waterways. But what can we assume about earlier hominin watercraft usage? Watercraft are rarely preserved, even in recent contexts where historical accounts attest to their use. The African and Eurasian rivers that both challenged and aided human dispersal flowed long before *Homo sapiens*' first appearance dates in the fossil record. How did Neanderthals and other hominins deal with crossing rivers? One cannot rule out that they swam or paddled/poled across smaller rivers using rafts assembled expediently using local vegetation. Swimming or rafting across larger rivers, on the other hand, might have posed more problems. Making a dugout canoe or a substantial raft using stone tools is the work not of hours but of days, even weeks. Learning how to assemble and navigate such watercraft is not intuitively obvious. Crocodiles infested many African and Asian rivers and sharks patrolled near coastlines. Fed by glacial meltwater, Eurasia's rivers almost certainly posed risks of near-instantaneous hypothermia. The paleoanthropological record offers up contradictory evidence about Pleistocene watercraft. Hominin fossils and archaeological remains such as those found at Mata Menge (Flores, Indonesia, 730 Ka) suggest *Homo erectus* possessed the capacity to cross tens of kilometers of open ocean one way or another. On the other hand, the virtual absence of similar such evidence of Pleistocene hominin activity on the larger and more remote Mediterranean islands suggests limited use of ocean-faring watercraft, even during times when humans living in Europe would have had to have used boats to move around the continent.

CHAPTER 6

GOING EAST

First Asians

This chapter surveys the evidence for *Homo sapiens* behavior between 30 and 600 Ka in Southwest and Southern Asia (the East Mediterranean Levant, the Arabian Peninsula, and the Indian Subcontinent). These regions have much in common with those parts of Africa on roughly the same latitude, and their paleoanthropological record differs little from one another. Moving into these regions seems to have required few major changes to Ancient Africans' survival strategies. Alternatively, Southern and Southwest Asia could have been part of a larger Afro-Asiatic region in which *H. sapiens* evolved out of *H. heidelbergensis*.

GEOGRAPHY: THE LEVANT, ARABIA, AND INDIA

Southwest and Southern Asia together comprise a land bridge (the East Mediterranean Levant) and two peninsulas (Arabia and India), all stretching southward from a west-east mountain range, the Taurus-Zagros-Himalayas (Figure 6.1). This work draws the line between Southern Asia and Southeast Asia at 90° east longitude, in the Bay of Bengal.

The East Mediterranean Levant

During Pleistocene times, the East Mediterranean Levant (Lebanon, Syria, Israel, Jordan, and parts of adjacent countries, hereafter "the Levant") offered the only permanent "feet dry" land route out of Africa. The Levant's Middle to Late Pleistocene climate alternated between colder and drier conditions during Northern Hemisphere glaciations, but throughout it maintained a core area of resource-rich Mediterranean oak-terebinth (*Quercus-Pistacia*) woodlands along the coast. Steppes dominated by scrub wormwood (*Artemisia*) and grasses flanked these woodlands to the south and east. During cooler

Geography: The Levant, Arabia, and India 117

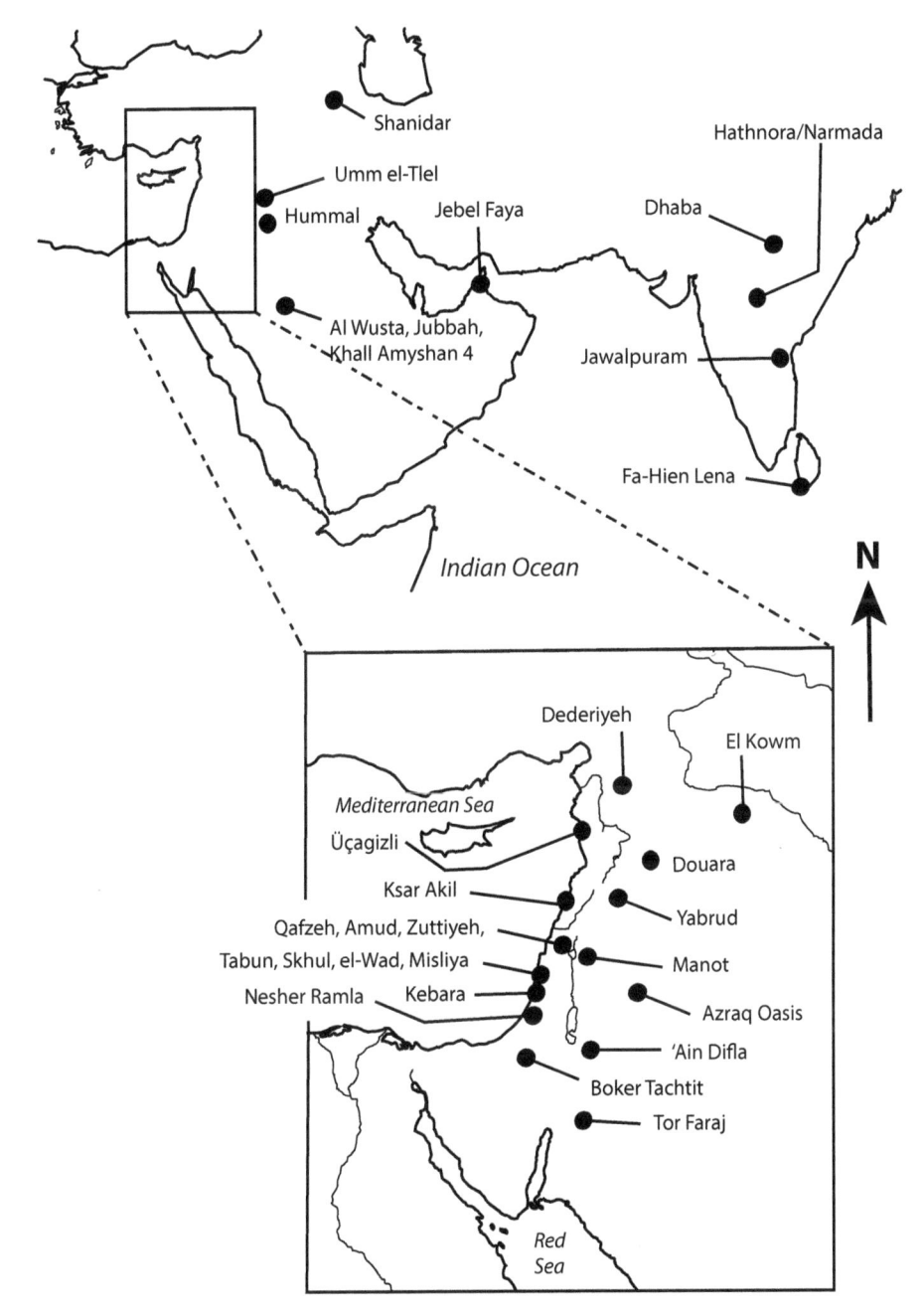

Figure 6.1 Map of Southern Asia showing sites discussed in the text. © John J. Shea.

phases, a large lake (Lake Lisan) covered much of the central and lower Jordan Rift Valley. The Levant posed few if any major obstacles to human population movements from Africa, except during extreme dry periods when the Saharan and Arabian deserts "joined hands" to its south.

The Arabian Peninsula

The Arabian Peninsula is a northward-tilted basin with mountain ranges on its western and eastern margins. Like the Levant, the Arabian Peninsula periodically went through wetter and drier phases. During wetter phases rivers flowed northward across what is now desert. Lowered sea levels exposed much of the Arabian/Persian Gulf. There, lower river valleys and swamplands rich in plant and animal life undoubtedly attracted human settlement. Hyperaridity posed the main obstacle to human population movements into and through Arabia. Because the bulk of the peninsula lies so far from the Mediterranean's moisture-rich seasonal cyclones and the Indian Ocean monsoons, during dry phases, large swaths of the Arabian interior could have been too arid to support human life.

The Indian Subcontinent

The Indian Subcontinent stretches south from the Himalayan Plateau into the Indian Ocean. The Indus River drains its northwest, and the Ganges River drains its northeast. In its southernmost regions, the line of hills running north-south along its western coastline capture some of the monsoon rains, but most of the rainfall tracks across Sri Lanka northward up India's eastern coast into the Ganges Basin. This well-watered eastern region (Sri Lanka, eastern India, and Bangladesh) would have attracted Pleistocene humans.

Conditions Affecting Population Movements

In moving from Africa to Southern Asia the most likely routes by which hominins reached and transited these regions would have been by traversing the Lower Nile River Valley and the Mediterranean Coast northward, or eastward around the northern end of the Red Sea – or by watercraft, across the southern end of the Red Sea.

Lowered Pleistocene sea levels exposed the Nile Delta much further north of its present position, sometimes bringing it north to the same latitude as modern-day Tel Aviv, Israel. Hominins living in the Nile Delta during such times could have simply walked northward and eastward into the region as many terrestrial mammals both large and small did repeatedly over the last 3 million years (Tchernov 1988).

Scarce water sources make the northern end of the Red Sea a path of greater resistance. However, hydrostatic springs (springs that flow during lowered sea levels) dot the coastline, and these prehistoric "rest stops" could have aided humans moving from Africa to Asia along this route (Faure et al. 2002).

At the southern end of the Red Sea, Arabia and Africa lie so close to one another that one can see across the Bab al-Mandeb ("Gate of Tears"). Further north, along the Eritrean Coast, clouds boiling up over Arabia disclose the presence of land over the horizon. If humans had ocean-capable watercraft, this could have been a third route by which Ancient Africans moved into Eurasia (Beyin 2006). Landings on the islands in Eritrea's Dahlak Archipelago and Arabia's Farsan Islands could have shortened voyages across the widest parts of the Red Sea. Archaeologists sometimes treat these routes as alternatives, but hominins could have used all of them at the same or different times.

By arriving in colder and drier Eurasian habitats, early humans would have left behind the lethal scourge of malaria (*Plasmodium*) (Bar-Yosef and Belfer-Cohen 2001). Freed from malaria and other zoonotic diseases with which Ancient Africans coevolved likely caused rapid population increases among early First Asians. These, in turn, may have conferred reproductive advantages over later local *H. heidelbergensis* populations.

IMPORTANT FIRST ASIAN PALEOANTHROPOLOGICAL SITES

Table 6.1 lists important Southern Asian paleoanthropological sites (see also Figure 6.1).

FIRST ASIAN HOMININ FOSSILS

This work uses the term "First Asians" for early humans who lived in Asia south of the Taurus-Zagros-Himalaya mountain ranges. Southern Asia's hominin fossil record for the period 30–600 Ka is unevenly distributed in time and space. Most of the evidence and the most complete fossils date to less than 130 Ka and come from the Levant. The sparseness of Arabia's and India's Middle Pleistocene fossil record could reflect these regions' periodic reversion to desert and correspondingly small hominin populations. Political obstacles to field research may have prevented further evidence being found as well.[1]

One can group hominin fossils from Southern Asia into *Homo sapiens*, Neanderthals (*H. neanderthalensis*), and older later Middle Pleistocene fossils with less clear affinities. Specifically, fragmentary human cranial remains from Zuttiyeh, Tabun (C2), Neser Ramla, and Misliya defy efforts to pigeonhole them as being *H. heidelbergensis*, *H. neanderthalensis*, or *H. sapiens*. Dating as they do to the period when Neanderthals and humans were diverging from *H. heidelbergensis*, paleontologists' difficulties assigning them to one species may simply reflect nearness to their last common ancestor.

---

[1] Saudi Arabia's 1990s opening to foreign paleoanthropological field research has resulted in a dramatic increase in information about the Peninsula's prehistory. Iranian prehistoric archaeology also seems to be undergoing a renaissance.

TABLE 6.1 *Important Southern Asian paleoanthropological sites*

Site	Date (Ka)	Comment
'Ain Difla Rockshelter (Jordan)		Well-documented sequence of Late Pleistocene archaeological remains
Al Wusta (Saudi Arabia)	85	*H. sapiens* finger bone
Amud Cave (Israel)	50–75	Neanderthal adult and child burials
Azraq Oasis (Jordan)	30–300	Well-documented Middle Pleistocene archaeological deposits
Biqat Quneitra (Israel)	65	Lake-margin activity area
Boker Tachtit (Israel)	47–46	Well-documented open-air site, evidence for changes in stoneworking
Dederiyeh Cave (Syria)	50–70	Neanderthal child burial
Doura Cave (Syria)	> 30	Well-documented sequence of archaeological remains
El Kowm Oasis (Syria)	> 30	Well-documented sequence of archaeological remains
Fa-Hien Lena (Sri Lanka)	38–43	Cave preserving early occurrence of carved bone arrow points, together with microlithic stone tools, human fossils ca. 30 Ka
Hathnora/Narmada (India)	300	*H. erectus/heidelbergensis* fossil
Hummal (Syria)	> 30–700	Deep sequence of Middle and Later Pleistocene archaeological deposits
Kebara Cave (Israel)	< 45–65	Deep sequence of Neanderthal and post-Neanderthal archaeological remains, fossils; levels younger than 45 Ka document changes in preagricultural adaptations across the Pleistocene/Holocene transition.
Ksar Akil Rockshelter (Lebanon)	20 > 50	Deep sequence of archaeological deposits, human fossils from ca. 42–43 Ka
Manot Cave (Israel)	55	*H. sapiens* skull
Misliya Cave (Israel)	250	Early *H. sapiens* fossil?
Mughr El Hamamah (Jordan)	39–45	Early prismatic blades, ochre use
Nesher Ramla (Israel))		Early human or late *H. heidelbergensis* fossil
Qafzeh Cave (Israel)	93	Numerous *H. sapiens* fossils and burials in terrace deposits, shells collected and used for personal adornments. Younger deposits ca. 30 Ka preserve *H. sapiens* fossils, too.
Qesem Cave (Israel)	350–450	Exceptionally well-documented Middle Pleistocene site
Shanidar Cave (Iraq)		Montane Neanderthal habitation, many fossils
Skhul Cave (Israel)	80–120	Numerous *H. sapiens* fossils and burials, shells collected and used for personal adornment

(continued)

TABLE 6.1 *(continued)*

Site	Date (Ka)	Comment
Tabun Cave (Israel)	45–500	Long sequence of archaeological remains Tabun C1 Neanderthal burial, Tabun C2, a *H. heidelbergensis*/early *H. sapiens* fossil
Tor Faraj Rockshelter (Jordan)	55–65	Well-documented later Pleistocene human and/or Neanderthal habitation site
Üçagizli Cave (Turkey)	39–44	Archaeological deposits, human teeth, perforated shell beads
Umm el-Tlel (Syria)	> 30–70	Deep sequence of Later Pleistocene archaeological deposits
Yabrud Cave (Syria)	> 45–> 500?	Deep sequence of Middle and Later Pleistocene archaeological deposits
Zuttiyeh Cave (Israel)	> 250	*H. heidelbergensis* or early *H. sapiens* fossil.

Later Middle Pleistocene Fossils

Hominin fossils dating from 130–600 Ka are isolated teeth and cranial fragments whose affinities remain unclear. The most complete of these, found at Zuttiyeh Cave 1, a frontal bone and upper face recovered during the 1920s, appears "intermediate" between *H. heidelbergensis* and *H. sapiens*. The Tabun C2 jaw fragments enjoy a similar diagnosis. Paleontologists view the cranial fragment from Narmada/Hathnora (India, 300 Ka?) as either *H. erectus* or as some variant of *H. heidelbergensis*.

Homo sapiens

The earliest generally accepted Southwest Asian *Homo sapiens* fossils come from Skhul Cave (Israel, 80–120 Ka) and Qafzeh Cave Terrace (Israel, 93 Ka). Both sites feature multiple burials (skeletons in anatomical articulation) with grave goods as well as more numerous fragmentary remains. The interior of Qafzeh Cave also features a set of younger human fossils dating to around 30 Ka. The calvarium (braincase) from Manot Cave (Israel, 55 Ka) and two juvenile burials from Ksar Akil (Lebanon, 45 Ka) round out this Levantine First Asians fossil sample. Arabia's sole human fossil (as of 2022) is a finger bone from Al Wusta (Saudi Arabia, 83 Ka). Fossils from Fa Hien Cave (Sri Lanka, 28–30 Ka) preserve evidence of human occupations further east.

Southwest Asian Neanderthals

Relatively complete Neanderthal fossils appear at Tabun, Kebara, and Amud caves in Israel, Dederiyeh Cave in Syria, and Shanidar Cave in Iraq. Most of these "Levantine Neanderthal" fossils date to 45–75 Ka. Several appear to

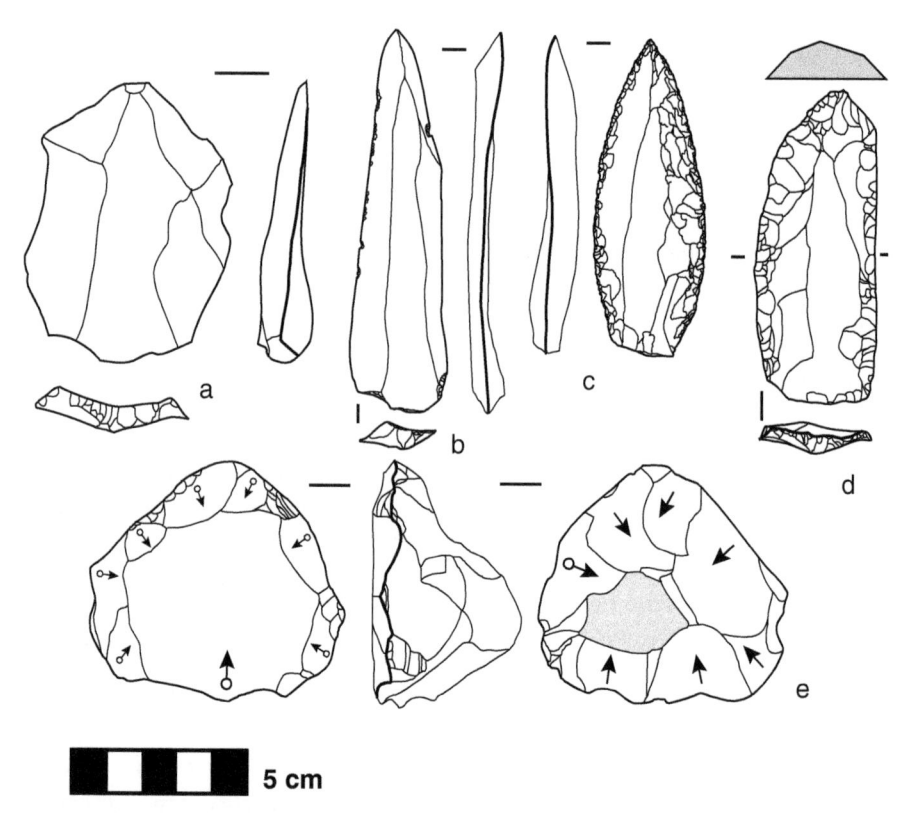

Figure 6.2 Artifacts associated with First Asians. (a) and (b) bifacial hierarchical core flakes, (c) convergently retouched piece, aka "Abu Sif knife," (d), convergently retouched scraper, (e) bifacial hierarchical core with preferential flake removal scar. Sources: Shea (2013b, 2017b). © John J. Shea.

be deliberate burials. The age of the Neanderthal fossil from Tabun Cave (Tabun C1) remains unclear due to uncertainties about its place in the cave stratigraphy. An older age (122 Ka) based on ESR dates could hint at an earlier Neanderthal presence in the Levant. Isolated Neanderthal teeth, cranial fragments and other bones occur at other sites in the region. (Chapter 8 discusses Neanderthals and other extinct Eurasian hominins.)

FIRST ASIAN ARCHAEOLOGY

Southern Asia's archaeological record for around 600 Ka is more or less the same as Africa's. Hominins made stone tools using a variety of strategies. The most distinctive artifacts they discarded included long core tools (LCTs), which range from objects not much larger than one's thumb to pieces 20–30 centimeters long or longer. Between 30 and 600 Ka, there occur two major inflection points in the archaeological record, one around 250 Ka, the other around 50 Ka (Figure 6.2).

Changes around 250 Ka

Much as in Africa, the period around 250 Ka sees hominins abandoning large LCT production and making greater use of flakes detached from bifacial hierarchical cores (BHCs). The particular methods of BHC flake production and their products vary widely, with two or more such methods usually in evidence in the same assemblage. In the Levant, older stone tool assemblages feature many elongated pointed pieces (aka "Abu Sif knives"), while younger assemblages do not, or at least less so. The archaeological sites at Douara and Zuttiyeh caves, 'Ain Difla and Yabrud rock shelters, and open-air sites at Hummal, El Kowm, and Azraq oases provide evidence of these stoneworking practices.

Unlike in Africa, foliate point production does not follow dwindling LCT production and discard. A few such points appear in Arabia and India, but they are uncommon there and in the Levant. Many appear little more than short and narrow LCTs or "elongated discoidal cores" of the sort that also continue to appear in Africa after 250 Ka. The retouched pieces hominins made included many varieties of scrapers and convergently retouched pieces ("flake points"). Tanged pieces of the same sort found in North Africa around the same time are either unknown (in the Levant) or uncommon (elsewhere).

This period also sees a shift in the zooarchaeological record paralleling events in Africa, namely, fewer remains of very large animals, more remains of smaller ones. As in Africa, this may reflect the greater number of cave or rock shelter sites in younger samples. The onset of cooler conditions after 130 Ka and colder ones after 75 Ka seems to have led to more persistent and recurring use of caves as habitation sites. Younger cave sites feature greater quantities of stone tools and animal remains, burials, and clearer evidence of hearths and other fire use than older cave occupations do (Kuhn and Clark 2015).

At Qafzeh Cave (Israel, 93 Ka), early humans exposed different sorts of red ochre to fire in order to change those pigments' color (Hovers et al. 2003).

Changes around 50 Ka

After around 40–50 Ka, First Asians largely stopped using the "preferential" form of BHC reduction (one that detached a single large flake from a core surface). In place of preferential BHC reduction, they adopted elongated unifacial hierarchical core (UHC) reduction. First Asians shaped "prismatic blades" that they struck from these UHCs into a various kinds of retouched points, backed/truncated pieces, burins, and other tools. Many more of these retouched pieces are relatively small, narrow (< 30–50 mm long) backed/truncated pieces and flake points than the stone tools found among artifacts dating to more than 50 Ka. After around 20–30 Ka, small backed/truncated pieces ("geometric microliths") become increasingly common (Shea 2013b).

The date of 40–50 Ka does not mark a major change in the kinds of large animal prey represented at cave or rock shelter sites. Remains of small game, such as tortoises, rabbits, and hares, presumably collected locally, grow increasingly common. Stiner and colleagues (1999) interpret this change as evidence for human population increase. The period after 50 Ka also sees an increase in the occurrences of carved bone tools and of perforated shells and teeth used as personal adornments (Bar-Yosef Mayer 2005).

It is crucially important to remember that much of what is written above is based on evidence from the Levant (Shea 2013b; Enzel and Bar-Yosef 2017). Future research will determine the extent to which similar changes occurred in Arabia and India, too.

FIRST ASIANS' SURVIVAL STRATEGIES

In comparing Southern Asian and African evidence for survival strategies, one has to deal with the fact that between 45 and 130 Ka, Neanderthals and early humans were present in the Levant (see Box 6.1 below, "The Rise and Fall of Mount Carmel Man"). They might not have resided in the same place at the same time for very long, but they created remarkably similar, if not entirely identical, archaeological records. Here we assume any evidence not associated *solely* with Neanderthals reflects shared ancestral survival strategies.

First Aid and Medication

Ancient African and First Asian evidence for first aid and caregiving do not differ significantly, but any such evidence for such caregiving is sparse for all Pleistocene hominins. Two of the fossils from Qafzeh preserve such evidence (Tillier 2002). Qafzeh 12, a 2- or 3-year-old, suffered from hydrocephaly (excessive fluid buildup inside their braincase). The child was profoundly mentally incapacitated before they died. Qafzeh 11, a teenager, sports a partly healed puncture wound to their frontal bone. Whether or not this wound became infected (very likely), the resulting behavioral anomalies could have contributed to their death (Coqueugniot et al. 2014). Ancient African fossils preserve no such incapacitated juveniles, but this may reflect the relative scarcity of juvenile Ancient African fossils.

Thermoregulation

The First Asian evidence for shelter and thermoregulation is essentially the same as for Ancient Africans. Both sheltered and resided in caves and rock shelters. Both used fire for light and heat. We have neither stronger nor weaker evidence for First Asian's use of clothing or for such artificial structures that they created.

Hydration

Much like their African counterparts, Southwest Asian archaeological sites dating between 30 and 600 Ka are usually located near stable sources of potable water, such as springs, rivers, or lakes. "Pulses" of chronologically offset human occupations around desert oases suggest First Asians lacked the means by which to move long distances over deserts and to sustain themselves in hyperarid environments (Groucutt et al. 2021).

Excavations of First Asian sites have not thus far turned up evidence for ostrich eggshell canteens like those from Africa, but it seems reasonable to assume they availed themselves of these useful storage devices. First Asians may have used pine pitch, acacia gum, or even bitumen upwelling from natural sources to make watertight baskets, but traces of such artifacts have thus far not come to light. Southwest Asians used bitumen to attach stone tools to handles (Boëda et al. 1996), but not, apparently, to make watertight containers.

Nutrition

Southern Asia preserves trends in faunal records similar to evidence from Africa. Older sites in both regions conspicuously preserve remains of larger mammals and megafauna (elephants, rhino). Archaeological remains at some of these "large mammal death sites" sites suggest hominins "camped on" such death sites and fended off carnivores much as *Homo ergaster/erectus* and *H. heidelbergensis* seem to have done now and again (Howell et al. 1995; Pitts and Roberts 1997). After 200 Ka, more faunal assemblages come from cave sites. These assemblages feature partial remains of many different kinds of animals (though less and less often megafauna) and greater quantities of smaller animals (Ben-Dor and Barkai 2020). Shellfish present at coastal sites in Africa and Southern Asia show humans on both continents utilized coastal resources, though nothing in Southern Asia quite approaches shell middens dating to Holocene times.

We do not know much about how Ancient Africans dealt with dense forest and jungle, but First Asians seem to have done so by using versatile complex projectile weapons like the bow and arrow to hunt birds, arboreal animals, and ground-dwelling species. The Sri Lankan site of Fa-Hien Lena (38–43 Ka) preserves carved bone arrow points, together with microlithic stone tools likely used for a similar purpose (Langley et al. 2020). Stone and bone artifacts from Levantine sites dating to less than 40 Ka exhibit damage similar to experimental arrowheads (Bergman and Newcomer 1983; Newcomer 1987; Yaroshevich et al. 2021).

Transportation

We have little direct evidence for Early Eurasians' transportation aids, but observations suggesting increased systematic collection of tortoises and other small animals after 40–50 Ka suggest some forms of cordage, basketry, or other carrying aides were in use by that point, if not (as seems likely) considerably earlier.

Communication

The practice of transmitting messages using symbolic "social media" was widespread among humans from at least 100 Ka onward. Qafzeh Cave (Israel, 93 Ka) preserves shells from the Mediterranean Sea (then some 30 Ka distant, due to lower sea levels) including shells that have had red ochre pigments applied to them (Taborin 2003; Bar-Yosef Mayer et al. 2020). Qafzeh also features evidence for the use of red ochre, presumably to decorate artifacts, for personal adornment (beads), or to color skin, hair, and clothing. Skhul Cave (Israel, 80–120 Ka) and Üçagizli Cave (Turkey, 39–44 Ka) also preserve remains of marine shells with no nutritional value, including perforated *Nassarius* shell beads like those found in Africa at Grotte des Contrabandiers, Grotte des Pigeons, and El Mnasra Cave (all in Morocco); Oued Djebana (an inland open-air site in Algeria); and Blombos Cave (South Africa)(Vanhaeren et al. 2006; Ben Arous et al. 2022). In this, Skhul appears preserve not just evidence for *similar* strategies for using symbolic artifacts as Ancient Africans did, but evidence for *exactly the same strategies* in use at about the same time at opposite ends of the African continent.

As among Ancient Africans, First Asians' early archaeological record shows few traces of short-term, regional-scale social networks reinforced using symbolic artifacts that grace more recent (< 30 Ka) phases of Southern and Southwest Asian prehistory. One thinks the most likely explanation for this lack of patterning in the evidence is more or less the same as among Ancient Africans. Humans may have been so few in number and so widely dispersed that their networks and the symbolic artifacts used to reinforce them had properties different from those in use among later, more populous human societies. The shell beads found at Levantine sites clearly attest to such networks' existence, indeed hint at networks extending to the other end of the Mediterranean Basin, but their stone tool evidence offers up nothing similar.

Sea-level rise complicates this assessment of First Asians' social networks. Many of the most attractive places for early humans to have lived between 30 and 300 Ka were estuaries and lower river valleys along the Mediterranean coastline, in the Arabian/Persian Gulf, and along the Indian Ocean coastline that postglacial sea-level rise has now flooded to depths beyond archaeologists' reach. Archaeologists are, in effect, looking at First Asian's inland adaptations, which may have involved smaller and more dispersed populations whose social networks had different, perhaps less clearly identifiable expressions than those in place among more densely populated coastal regions.[2] Testing this hypothesis requires further research, but it is an hypothesis more congruent with the facts than alternative hypotheses, such as ones equating the scarcity of symbolic artifacts with the absence of social networks among First Asians.

INTERPRETIVE ISSUES ABOUT FIRST ASIANS

Behavioral Differences between First Asians and Ancient Africans

The Southern Asian archaeological record offers up little evidence for important behavioral differences between Ancient Africans' and First Asians' solutions to survival challenges, certainly nothing that requires additions to our list of ancestral survival skills. First Asians living in the Levant and Arabia adopted geometric microlith production and/or complex projectile technology later than their African and Asian counterparts, but this might reflect contrasts in how different archaeological research traditions define microliths (Pargeter and Shea 2019) and how they recognize complex weapon armatures (Rots and Plisson 2014; Lombard 2021). In terms of the larger shift from relatively large bifacial hierarchical cores to elongated unifacial hierarchical cores, First Asians were "in sync" with their Ancient African relatives.

Should we be surprised to find so few differences between Ancient Africans' survival strategies and those that First Asians employed in Southern Asia? One thinks not. Ancient Africans had to cope with woodlands, steppe/savanna grasslands, and deserts much like those inhabited by First Asians. Both regions have similar carnivore and herbivore communities. Lions, leopards, baboons, ostriches, pigs, equids (horses, donkeys), hippos, elephants, and rhinos ranged across both regions in prehistory. Deer would have been a novelty for humans moving into Southern Asia from Africa, as would have been bears and wolves. That Asia harbored tigers, large predatory cats that can swim and indeed enjoy doing so, might have been an exciting revelation!

To keep this finding of "no significant differences" in perspective, one needs to remember that the geopolitical rationale for distinguishing Africa from Asia is utterly irrelevant to human evolution. Taken at face value, the archaeological record suggests that our modern-day geopolitical distinction between

---

[2] Consider, for example, such clear expressions of exclusive social networks as "no trespassing" signs. Such signs appear everywhere in the United States. But while one might drive for miles across sparsely populated inland parts of the United States without seeing more than a few such signs (usually clustered around lakes and rivers), once sees them on virtually every parcel of private property along the country's densely populated coastlines. As the perceived need for such symbols varies geographically today, one thinks it both reasonable and in keeping with uniformitarian principles to expect them to have varied in similar ways among earlier humans.

Africa and Asia does not meaningfully divide either prehistoric humans or variation in their activities.

Much like Ancient Africans, First Asians were tough and resilient. At Jawalpuram Locality 3 (India, 74–76 Ka) and at Dhaba (India, 74–76 Ka), stone tools from levels immediately above ash deposits from the Mount Toba supervolcano differ little from those below it (Petraglia et al. 2007; Clarkson et al. 2020). Petraglia and colleagues interpret this as evidence that, rather than abandoning the ash-blanketed landscape, First Asians remained in place and adapted. First Asians appear to have done so, too, in the Levant during the Heinrich H5 Event, an abrupt shift to cold conditions around 45 Ka, one that either killed off the Levantine Neanderthals or caused them to abandon the region (Shea 2008b).

Migration versus Dispersal

Does anything in the First Asian or Southern Asian evidence support the hypothesis that early *H. sapiens* migrated into or through this region? Surprisingly, considering the reputation that Southwest Asia, and the Levant in particular, enjoys as the "crossroad of the continents" and historical records of migrations stretching back thousands of years, little or no actual evidence supports hypothetical Pleistocene-age migrations either from Africa or within Southern Asia. First, there is no evidence for the necessary preconditions for migration. Archaeological excavations have revealed no evidence for food production or for in-bulk storage of transportable foodstuffs in the Levant, Arabia, or India prior to 10 Ka. Nor has research in any of these regions revealed evidence of watercraft capable of carrying large numbers of people on far oceanic voyages before 10 Ka. Second, even though the Levant boasts several deep sequences of hominin occupations (Tabun and Yabrud caves, Azraq Oasis, Hummal), none of these sites provides clear evidence of a horizon in which artifacts previously known only from Africa suddenly appear, as one would expect if a migration had occurred, and as one actually does find in recent (<10 Ka) phases of Levantine prehistory (Levy 1995). Nevertheless, here we consider two recent hypotheses about population movements to Southern Asia based on the stone tool evidence sometimes characterized as "migrations."[3]

Nubian Cores as Evidence for Afro-Arabian Movements

Rose (2004) argues that occurrences of "Nubian cores" on either side of the Red Sea indicate a human population movement across the Red Sea from

---

[3] Not usually by those who proposed/identified the evidence, but more often in popular media coverage of their findings.

Africa to Arabia. Nubian cores are a distinctive form (usually triangular and four-sided) of bifacial hierarchical core on which a series of small flake-detachment scars at the core's narrow end causes a large triangular flake to detach when a stoneworker strikes the core's wider opposite end (Figure 6.3a, b). Some Nubian cores come from excavations, but many, indeed most, are undated surface finds. First identified in Sudan (ancient Nubia), it remains unclear whether they are more ancient in Africa or Asia. Some have identified Nubian cores at sites in the East Mediterranean Levant (Blinkhorn et al. 2021), but others dispute this claim (Hallinan et al. 2022). Such occurrences could result from either diffusion of an idea or dispersing humans bringing their stoneworking strategies with them (Rose and Marks 2014); thus, one does not need to invoke a migration to explain these occurrences so near to one another. That archaeologists have also identified Nubian cores among stone tools from South Africa (Will et al. 2015) suggests our notions about Nubian cores' geographic distribution may owe much to how archaeologists describe stone tools. That is, archaeologists formally recognize Nubian cores in some parts of the world (Northeastern Africa, Southwest Asia), but not in others (sub-Saharan Africa, Europe, and East Asia).

Microliths as Evidence for Afro-Asiatic Movements

The late Sir Paul Mellars (2006) contended that occurrences of small backed/truncated pieces ("microliths") in Africa and Southern Asia (India and Sri Lanka) indicate a population movement between these regions around 65 Ka (see Figure 6.3c–k). Such a "microlith-assisted dispersal" is not impossible, but one also has to keep alternative hypotheses, such as convergence, in play – especially, as in this case, if the only things connecting source and destination are stone tools. Small backed/truncated pieces are lightweight, versatile, and easy to make. One can (and prehistoric people did) use them to cut and pierce things while held in the hand, embedded in mastic (glue), or attached to handles in any number of configurations. That they occur episodically in Africa and Asia could reflect stoneworkers independently arriving at similar solutions to the problem of provisioning themselves with lightweight, versatile, and easy to make cutting tools.

What about dispersals? In sediments around water sources in the Hall Amayshan 4 and Jubbah Basins in northwestern Saudi Arabia, Groucutt and colleagues (2021) have identified deep and complex sequences of sedimentary deposits that seem to chronicle "pulses" of Middle to Late Pleistocene hominin population movements out of the Levant and possibly parts of Northeastern Africa into "Green Arabia." Though one should not necessarily accept the hypothesis that chronologically sequential differences in the stone tool evidence necessarily indicate differences in the stoneworkers, this reconstruction

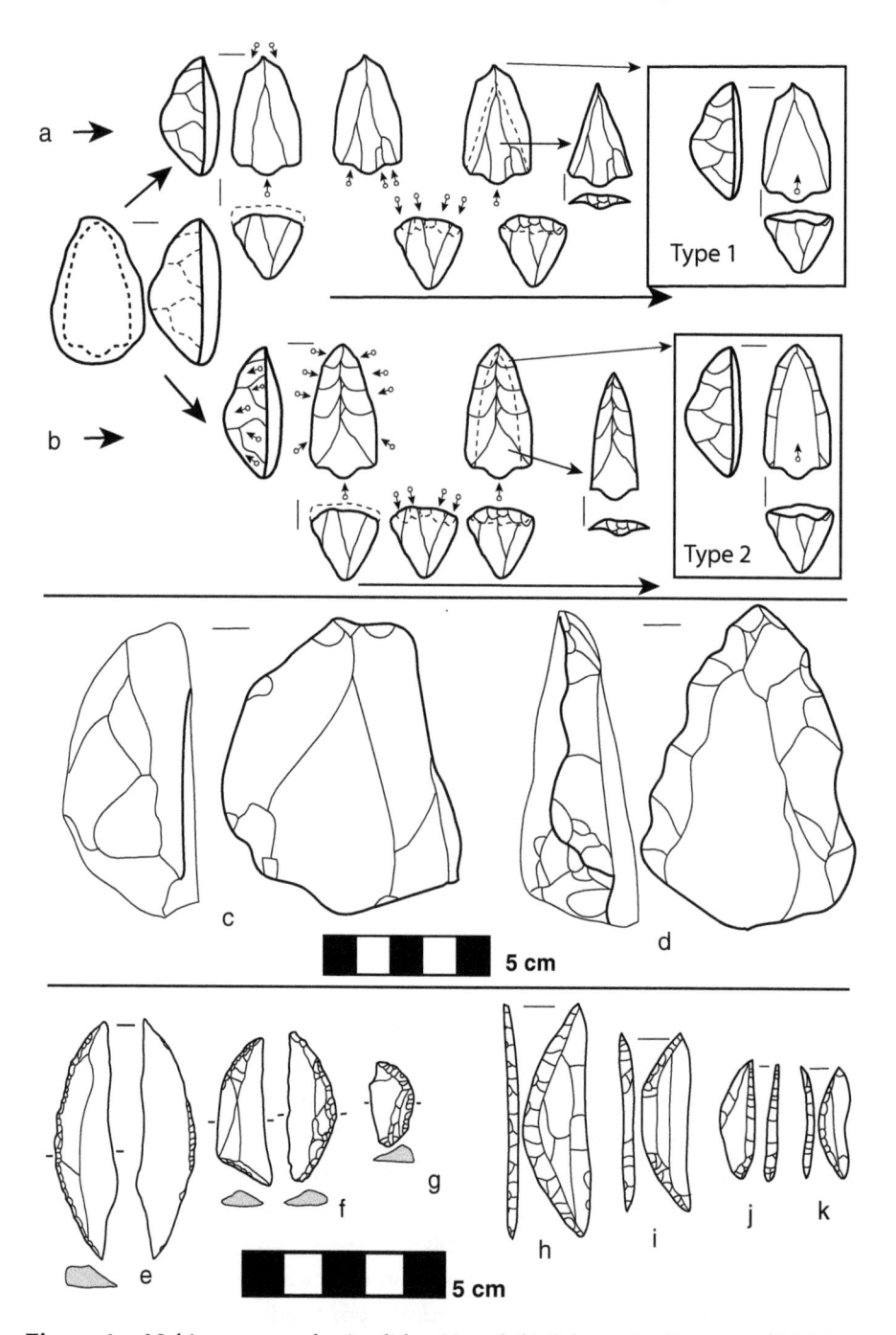

Figure 6.3 Nubian cores and microliths. (a) and (b) Schematic diagrams of Nubian core reduction, (c) and (d) Nubian cores from Arabia, (e)–(h) small backed/truncated pieces (microliths) from Eastern Africa and (i)–(k) from Sri Lanka. Sources: Groucutt et al. (2015), Rose et al. (2011), Shea (2020a).

Interpretive Issues about First Asians

agrees well with climatic reconstructions for the Arabian Peninsula. If, as the evidence from the Levant suggests, humans and other hominins were well entrenched along the Eastern Mediterranean Coast, then one reasonably expects that the greening of Arabian deserts, such as the Nefud, would attract dispersing humans.

An Afro-Asiatic Human Origination Zone?

If humans did not migrate from Africa to Southern Asia, then how did they get there? There could have been multiple and distinct climate-driven waves of dispersals from Africa into and across Southwest Asia during Middle to Later Pleistocene times. Groucutt and colleagues (2021) report occurrences of distinct "pulses" of human occupation around Nefud Desert paleolakes dating to around 400, 300, 200, 130–75, and 55 Ka. Each of these dates corresponds with "Green Arabia" conditions, that is, increased humidity. That the artifacts associated with these pulses differ from one another suggests there may be discontinuities between them. Like waves on a beach during a rising tide, these dispersals might have involved short-lived movements that either extinctions or retreats interrupted when arid conditions reasserted themselves. This hypothesis's weak point, however, lies in its extrapolating a plausible scenario for sparsely populated inland steppe-desert habitats to a much larger and ecologically diverse region. No evidence supports the hypothesis that hominins long abandoned the food-rich woodlands hugging the Eastern Mediterranean coastline. They might have, but one does not see the sort of long, deep sequences of artifact-sterile cave deposits one would expect to find if hominins had quit the region for prolonged periods.

Alternatively, Southern Asia or at least the Levant could have been part of a larger "Afro-Asiatic human origination zone." Humans might have dispersed from Africa to Southern Asia in more or less the same way Chapter 5 proposed for Ancient Africans, by infiltrating regional *Homo heidelbergensis* populations already established and by remaining "networked" to one another while advantages in sexual selection ran their course. The marine shell ornaments at Skhul and Qafzeh caves in Israel, Üçagizli cave in Turkey, and other sites in Algeria and Morocco may be traces of those far-flung networks.

Future Research Directions

Clearly, paleoanthropologists need more evidence about Southern Asia's Middle Pleistocene hominin populations. The region's Middle Pleistocene hominin fossil record remains sparse. This chapter has assumed the Levant's, Arabia's, and India's pre-*Homo sapiens* populations were either *H. heidelbergensis* or something very much like them. This is an assumption that needs to be tested with evidence. We also need to learn more about the Skhul and Qafzeh people. As things stand today, any number of hypotheses remain in play concerning their origins, fate, and relationships with other hominins (Shea and Bar-Yosef 2005). For example, can we reject the hypothesis they were Denisovans?

In addition to more evidence, we need better evidence, especially better stone tool evidence. Lithic artifacts are often the only common point of comparison among Southwest Asian, Southern Asian, and African archaeological assemblages, and yet archaeologists working in these regions use classifications and measurement conventions (systematics) utterly different from one another. Those in use in Southwest Asia vary between time periods, and to an extent between Francophone and Anglophone research traditions (Shea 2013b). Those in use among Africanists archaeologists exist in a state of "lithics systematics anarchy" (Shea 2020a). Terms and measurements vary within and between time periods, countries, and research traditions.

SUMMARY

This chapter has argued that the relatively minimal evidence for differences between Ancient African survival strategies and those First Asians employed suggests that dispersing to Southern Asia required few major changes to preexisting human behavior. Alternatively, it could well be that humans did not so much move into Southern Asia as evolve locally out of local populations connected to social networks linked to Ancient Africans. Chapter 7 considers the evidence for the peopling of Southeast Asia and Australasia, regions in which humans faced different challenges and in which they left a different archaeological record than they did in either Africa or Southern Asia.

Box 6.1: *The Rise and Fall of Mount Carmel Man*

Medieval geographers placed Jerusalem and the East Mediterranean Levant at the center of the world as they knew it. They did this for religious reasons, but probably also recognized that the East Mediterranean coastline and Jordan Rift Valley were important for secular reasons, too. The Levant is a crossroads of the continents conjoining the Mediterranean Basin, Indian Ocean, and Nile River watersheds. No major development in human evolution or culture history has passed from one of these regions to another without leaving a trace in the Levant. Indeed, early 20th-century discoveries of human fossils at sites in the Valley of the Caves (now in Israel)[4]

---

[4] Like many landmarks in Israel, the Valley of the Caves is known by different names: Wadi el-Mughara (Arabic) and Nahal HaMearot (Hebrew).

Box 6.1: *(cont.)*

furnished the first clues of more complex patterns in recent human evolution than preserved in the European evidence.

Mount Carmel towers 524 meters over the Israeli port city of Haifa. This "mountain" (actually more of an escarpment) then trails off southeastward to lower elevations. Wadis (Arabic for valleys cut by seasonal streams) crosscut Mount Carmel's western escarpment. In the late 1920s, Palestinian workmen quarrying limestone in the Wadi el-Mughara (Valley of the Caves) for the nearby town of Atlit discovered stone tools and vertebrate fossils. Following some trial excavations, the British School of Archaeology in Jerusalem dispatched a young archaeology professor, Dorothy Garrod, to investigate and to oversee excavations. She and her team did so, tackling the most easily reached cave, El Wad ("the Gate") first, and the less accessible Tabun ("the Oven") later. At some point, a young Theodore McCown, then a graduate student and later an important physical anthropologist, joined Garrod's expedition. Garrod set McCown to digging a small collapsed rock shelter, Skhul ("Cave of the Kids," or young goats). Garrod worked patiently in the Valley of the Caves, assembling evidence to document the full sweep of "Paleolithic" (Pleistocene) prehistory (Table 6.2) (Garrod and Bate 1937). For definitions of age-stages, see Appendix A.

At El Wad in Level B and on the terrace in front of the cave Garrod's team found remains of a sedentary hunter-gatherer culture now known

TABLE 6.2 *Cultural stratigraphy of the Valley of the Caves*

El Wad level	Tabun level	Skhul level	Age-stage	Culture/industry
A	A		Historic: Bronze Age	
B			Epipaleolithic	Natufian
C			Upper Paleolithic	Atlitian
D–E		A	Upper Paleolithic	Middle Aurignacian
F			Upper Paleolithic	Middle and Lower Aurignacian
G	B		Middle Paleolithic	Upper Levalloiso-Mousterian
	C–D	B–C	Middle Paleolithic	Lower Levalloiso-Mousterian
	E		Lower Paleolithic	Upper Acheulian (Micoquian)
	F		Lower Paleolithic	Upper Acheulian
	G		Lower Paleolithic	Tayacian

Box 6.1: *(cont.)*

as the Natufian. Below these, in Levels C–F, they found unifacial hierarchical cores (UHCs), prismatic blades struck from them, and other characteristically Upper Paleolithic retouched pieces. The lowest level (Level G) preserved Middle Paleolithic stone artifacts similar to those found in the uppermost levels of Tabun Cave.

Tabun Cave is fully 60 meters or more deep. Its uppermost layers (Levels B–D) featured Middle Paleolithic artifacts, such as bifacial hierarchical cores (BHCs) and various scrapers and short retouched flake points. Level C also contained a female Neanderthal fossil buried with a neonate (young baby) whose remains were not recovered and a fragmentary jaw. Level D contained somewhat different Middle Paleolithic artifacts with elongated BHCs and long, convergently retouched points. Long core tools (LCTs) first appear in Levels E and F, but disappear in lowermost Level G. Following the practice at the time, Garrod identified the stone tool industries in Tabun Levels B and C–D to Upper and Lower phases of the Levalloiso-Mousterian industry, Level E–F to a Micoquian variant of the Lower Paleolithic Upper Acheulian Industry, Level F to the Upper Acheulian, and Level G to a Tayacian industry.

Skhul had three levels. The uppermost, a thin Level A, contained a mixture of Upper and Middle Paleolithic tools. Resting on bedrock and also thin, the lowermost Level C contained abraded Middle Paleolithic tools. In between Levels A and C, Level B preserved a much thicker layer (about 2 meters) of Middle Paleolithic remains that McCown arbitrarily divided into upper B1 and lower B2. Numerous hominin fossils appeared in Level B, several of whose bones lay in anatomical articulation. McCown and Garrod interpreted these as deliberate burials. The stone tools accompanying the Skhul fossils were similar to those in Tabun Level C.

The big surprise in all of this was not really the archaeology. Segments of the Valley of the Caves' archaeological industry/culture sequence came to light during excavations at other Levantine sites during the 1930s-1940s (e.g., at Yabrud Cave in Syria and at Ksar Akil Rockshelter in Lebanon). Rather, the surprise involved the hominin fossils. Skhul Level B and Tabun Levels B–C featured very similar suites of stone artifacts, but they preserved rather different-looking hominin remains. During the 1930s, McCown worked with eminent British anatomist Sir Arthur Keith to describe the Valley of the Caves fossils (McCown and Keith 1939). Initially, they treated them as separate Neanderthal (Tabun) and early human (Skhul) fossils, but later revised their interpretation, uniting them into a single fossil sample, one colloquially known as "Mount Carmel Man."

Box 6.1: *(cont.)*

Over the course of the 1930s–1960s, additional discoveries of early human fossils at Qafzeh Cave near Nazareth[5] and Neanderthal fossils in Amud Cave in the Galilee and Kebara Cave on Mount Carmel established that the Levant's "Middle Paleolithic" hominin population varied in ways distinct from either Europe or Africa. By the 1960s, paleoanthropologists had largely stopped viewing Mount Carmel Man as a single undifferentiated population and started viewing them more or less along the lines McCown and Keith had originally envisioned, as distinct sets of Neanderthals and early humans (Howell 1959). The latter were (and are) sometimes called the "Skhul-Qafzeh people," even though there are marked differences among them (Shea and Bar-Yosef 2005). At the time, Neanderthals were widely thought to be human ancestors, and so, paleontologists assumed the Levantine Neanderthals were older that the Skhul-Qafzeh fossils (Trinkaus 1984). All this changed dramatically during the 1980s–1990s, as geophysicists applied the newly developed dating methods of thermoluminescence and electron spin resonance to these fossils and the stone tools found with them (Shea 2003). The Skhul-Qafzeh fossils turned out to be tens of thousands of years older than at least some of their putative Neanderthal ancestors (i.e., Amud and Kebara). The Tabun C1 Neanderthal's age remains somewhat unclear due to uncertainty about her place in the cave stratigraphy (Bar-Yosef and Callander 1999). These findings, and other recent fossil discoveries at Manot and Misliya caves suggest the hominin fossil sequence in the Levant was, like much else about that region, complicated. As of 2022, the paleoanthropological consensus holds that humans and Neanderthals both lived in the Levant between 45 and 130 Ka, but other hominins could have lived in the region, too. No evidence shows humans and Neanderthals lived in the same place at the same time, at least not to the exclusion of the hypothesis that they did not do so.

Levantine Neanderthals and the Skhul-Qafzeh people differ so morphologically from other Eurasian Neanderthals and from Ancient African fossils that we must be careful about assuming they migrated/dispersed from either region, as opposed to having evolved in place from local ancestors and from hominins that dispersed into the Levant from adjacent regions.

---

[5] Located on a steep escarpment overlooking the central Galilee, Qafzeh ("the precipice") has an interesting backstory. Local folklore has it that at this place during the first decade of the Common Era, some Nazarenes, had had just about enough of young Jesus' antics. (A teenager who can outargue the rabbis and turn water into wine ... what could possibly go wrong?) Irate villagers carried young Jesus to the cliff above the cave and tossed him over it, after which he miraculously floated to the ground unscathed.

Box 6.1: *(cont.)*

Stone artifacts found with these hominins differ from those found with Neanderthals in Europe and Western Asia and from artifacts found with Ancient Africans. These artifacts differ from those preceding Neanderthal and early human fossils in the Levant > 130 Ka and from those following on after Neanderthals' last appearance dates around 45 Ka.

Stone tools and animal remains found with Levantine Neanderthals and the Skhul-Qafzeh people differ from one another, but they do so in subtle ways that likely reflect variation in mobility patterns and subsistence strategies on scales comparable to variation among recent human hunter-gatherers.

Evidence for symbolic artifact use is more strongly associated with the Skhul-Qafzeh people, but this could be an artifact of method. That is, archaeologists routinely assign "authorship" of the entire contents of a stratigraphic level, or even all levels of entire sites, to one hominin versus others based on fossil discoveries. Far more sites/levels lack fossils than preserve them, and in any case these fossils' occurrences merely establish the hominins' presence, not their authorship of the stone tools and other remains.

For thought and discussion: Paleoanthropologists do not reject the hypothesis that Levantine Neanderthals and the Skhul-Qafzeh people were part of a single morphologically variable population, as McCown and Keith put it, in the "throes of an evolutionary transition." On the other hand, it does not escape notice that Neanderthal and human fossils do not occur together in the same stratigraphic level of any of the many sites that preserve such fossils. In fact, neither fossil nor archaeological evidence supports the hypothesis that Neanderthals and First Asians ever set eyes on one another in or around the Mount Carmel caves. The stone tools that occur together with them differ in subtle ways, but the same sorts of artifacts occur across much of Western Eurasia and Northern Africa at the same time. This suggests their occurrence in the Levant reflects evolutionarily ancestral stoneworking strategies rather than a shared culture expressed in stone artifact design variation. The Levantine evidence poses an interesting question, namely, what evidence would prove that Neanderthals and First Asians lived in the same place at the same time?

CHAPTER 7

DOWN UNDER

Early Southeast Asians and Sahulians

This chapter reviews the evidence for the peopling of Southeast Asia and Australasia before 30 Ka. These regions' sparse fossil record lacks firm geochronology, but it appears humans established themselves in Southeast Asia sometime between 45 and 75 Ka. Archaeological evidence from these regions contrasts with that from Southern and Southwest Asia. Nevertheless, Southeast Asian and Australasian sites preserve some of the world's oldest-dated representative artworks and the oldest evidence for oceangoing watercraft. Humans' arrival in Southeast Asia coincides with last appearances of several other hominin species. Their arrival in Australia precedes mass extinctions of that continent's marsupial megafauna (large animals).

GEOGRAPHY: SUNDA, SAHUL, AND WALLACEA

Paleoanthropologists and others who study prehistoric Southeast Asia and Australasia divide the region into three major subregions: Sunda, Wallacea, and Sahul (see Figure 7.1).[1] "Sunda" describes the peninsula that formed when lowered sea levels conjoined mainland Southeast Asia to islands in the Indo-Malaysian archipelago. "Sahul" references the continent that formed when lower sea levels conjoined New Guinea, Australia, and Tasmania. Wallacea encompasses the islands in between Sunda and Sahul.

Tropical jungle covers much of former Sunda, or at least those parts as yet unaffected by industrial-scale logging. During glacial periods when cooler temperatures prevailed, lowered sea levels exposed the Sunda Shelf, which

---

[1] Sunda takes its name from the Sunda Strait between western Java and eastern Sumatra. Wallacea is named for Alfred Russell Wallace (1823–1913), the naturalist who identified the major biogeographic frontier ("Wallace's Line") running through this region that separates Eurasian and Sahulian plants and animals. (Wallace was also, with Charles Darwin, codiscoverer of the principle of evolution by natural selection.) Sahul refers to a submerged sandbank between East Timor and Australia. As with the "Levant" (Chapter 6) archaeologists use these names for their brevity and lack of overt political implications.

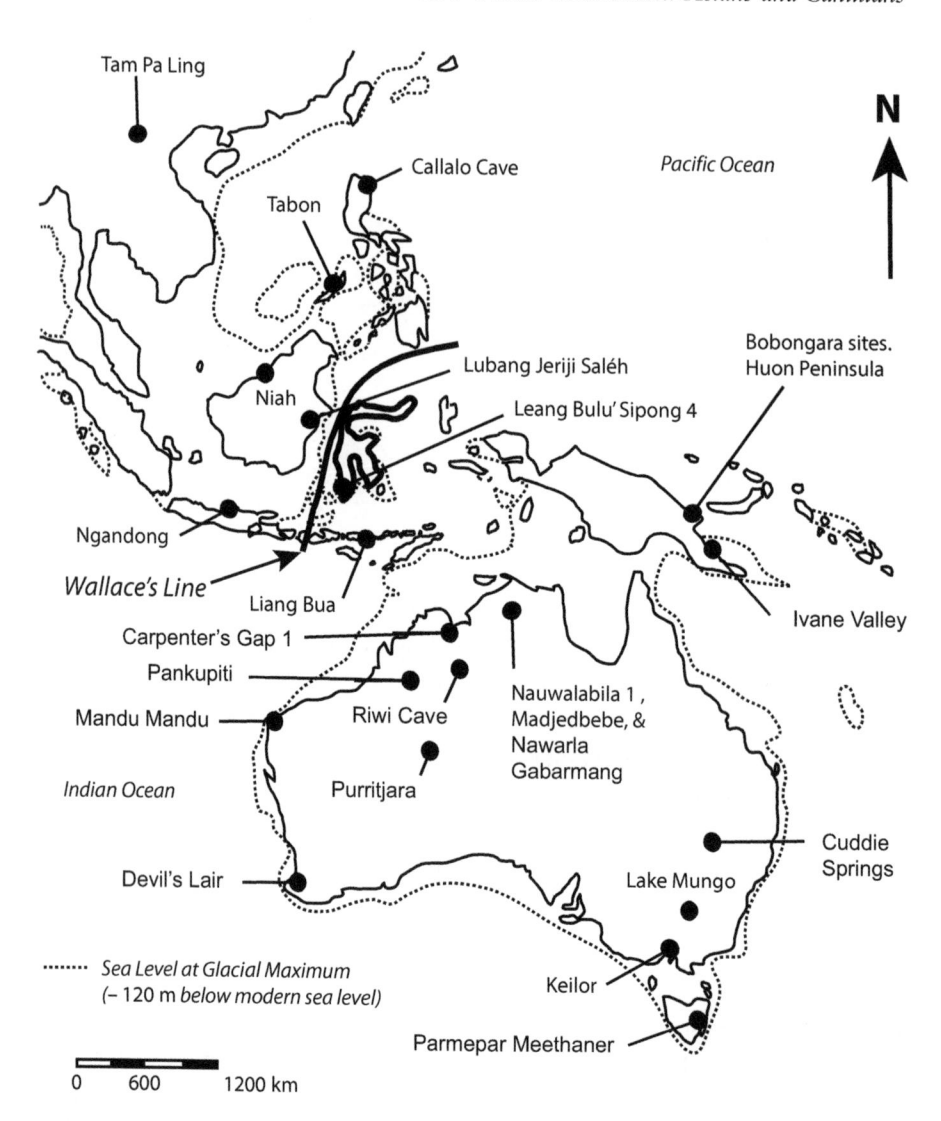

Figure 7.1 Map of Sunda, Wallacea, and Sahul showing locations of important sites. © John J. Shea.

supported mosaics of more open woodlands and grasslands. An eastward-draining basin in between what is now Vietnam, Borneo, and Malaysia connected to the Philippines and the Pacific Ocean beyond. Volcanism posed the principal obstacle to human settlement in this region. In fact, the Mount Toba (Indonesia) supervolcano eruption around 75 Ka was one of the largest such eruptions in recent Earth history. Ash from Toba occurs in geological deposits and archaeological sites as far away as Eastern Africa.

Like Sunda, jungles dominated Wallacea's islands, much as they do today, though cooler conditions may have made them more open than today's closed-canopy jungles. Lower sea levels connected some of Wallacea's islands to one another, but throughout the Pleistocene there remained tens of kilometers of open ocean separating Wallacea's islands from Sahul. The principal obstacles to human settlement in Wallacea were the need for watercraft capable of open-ocean voyaging and the difficulty of finding adequate food in subtropical jungles located on oceanic islands (Emory 1943).

Sahul was a continental basin bounded to the north by New Guinea's east-west running mountains, to the east by Australia's Great Dividing Range, and by several smaller ranges and plateaus to the west. Desert and grasslands dominate the interior of Australia today, but during cooler periods wetter conditions, including navigable rivers, prevailed. Some of Tasmania's higher elevations supported glaciers during these colder periods. The principal obstacles to settling Australia included coping with desertification and adapting to a very different suite of plant and animal resources than those in Sunda and elsewhere in mainland Eurasia. During the 50 million years that Wallace's Line separated Eurasia from Sahul, Sahul's marsupial-dominated fauna evolved distinct species, including rhinoceros-sized wombats and giant kangaroos with no counterparts in either Wallacea or Sunda.

Conditions Affecting Population Movements

In terms of their overall prospects for human settlement, Sunda, Wallacea, and Sahul were attractive destinations. The temperatures and humidity variation humans encountered there were similar to those in which Ancient Africans evolved and those into which First Asians moved as they dispersed eastward into Asia. Indeed, Sunda, Wallacea, and Sahul probably required even fewer adjustments to Ancient African survival strategies that South Asia did. Pleistocene Southeast Asians and Sahulians did not have to deal with the prolonged hyperaridity and extreme cold temperatures that afflicted First Asians. (Much of interior Australia's desertification is a recent phenomenon.) On the other hand, movement in and around these regions required watercraft, not just dugout canoes or rafts of the sort than can ply small rivers and lakes but rather the sort of sail-assisted and outrigger-stabilized vessels that transition easily from rivers to oceans. Making and maintaining such watercraft require fixed bases of operation at long-term residential sites. Such sites have thus far eluded archaeological detection, but one predicts archaeologists will find them, perhaps in sediments on now-drowned Pleistocene coastal landscapes.

IMPORTANT SOUTHEAST ASIAN AND SAHULIAN PALEOANTHROPOLOGICAL SITES

Table 7.1 lists important Southeast Asian and Australasian paleoanthropological sites.

TABLE 7.1 *Important Southeast Asian and Australasian paleoanthropological sites*

Site	Date (Ka)	Comment
Bobongara (Huon Peninsula, New Guinea)	38–60	Grooved stone celts
Callao Cave (Luzon Island, Philippines)	67	Fossil of *Homo luzonensis*
Carpenter's Gap 1 (Australia)	44	Stone tools, abraded-edge celts
Cuddie Springs (Australia)	40	Stone tools associated with extinct marsupial megafauna
Devil's Lair (Australia)	> 48	Stone artifacts
Ivane Valley (New Guinea)	43–49	Grooved stone celts
Keilor (Australia)	31	*H. sapiens* fossil skull
Lake Mungo (Australia)	40	*H. sapiens* fossil skull, burial, archaeological remains
Leang Bulu' Sipong 4 (Indonesia)	44	Early cave art
Liang Bua (Flores, Indonesia)	60–100	*H. floresiensis* fossils and archaeological remains
Lubang Jeriji Saléh (East Kalimantan [Borneo])	45	Early cave art
Madjedbebe Rockshelter (Australia)	53–65?	Early Sahulian archaeological site; evidence for abraded-edge tools, pulverizing roots, nuts using stone tools
Mandu Mandu Creek Rockshelter (Australia)	37	Red ochre, shell beads
Nauwalabila 1 (Australia)	53	Early Sahulian site
Nawarla Gabarmang (Australia)	47	Rock paintings, abraded-edge celts
Ngandong (Java, Indonesia)	108–117	Late-dating *H. erectus* fossil
Niah Cave (Sarawak, Borneo, Malaysia)	43–45	*H. sapiens* fossil skull
Pankupiti (Australia)	45–50	Stone artifacts
Parmepar Meethaner (Tasmania)	40	Stone tools, charred bone
Purritjara (Australia)	40–45	Stone artifacts, ephemeral rock shelter habitation
Riwi Cave (Australia)	41	Hearth, *Dentalium* shell beads
Tabon Cave (Palawan Island, Philippines)	37–58	*H. sapiens* fossil tibia
Tam Pa Ling (Laos)	46–51	*H. sapiens* fossil skull

SOUTHEAST ASIAN AND SAHULIAN HOMININ FOSSILS

This chapter retains the term "First Asians" for Sunda and Wallacea's earliest human inhabitants, but it uses the term "Sahulians" for Pleistocene residents of what is now New Guinea, Australia, and Tasmania.

Homo sapiens

Eastern Asia and Australasia appear to lie outside the hypothetical Afro-Asiatic human origination zone (see Chapter 6). Unlike Africa or South Asia, these regions lack human fossils dating to later Middle Pleistocene times (ca.130–330 Ka).[2] The oldest human fossils come from Tam Pa Ling (Laos, 46–51 Ka), with Niah Cave's "Deep Skull" (Sarawak, Malaysia, 43–44 Ka) a close second. A tibia from Tabon Cave (Palawan Island, Philippines) may be a bit older, at 37–58 Ka.

The oldest Sahulian fossils come from Lake Mungo (Australia), a dried Pleistocene lake bed in Southeastern Australia (New South Wales). They currently date to around 40 Ka.[3] Interestingly, the Lake Mungo fossils preserved evidence for both burials with grave goods (ochre powder) and for cremation. Like most Pleistocene humans, the Mungo people had relatively thick skulls and large faces. The Keilor fossil skull (Victoria, Australia, 31 Ka,) preserves these features as well.

Compared with the evidence from Western Eurasia during the same period, Southeast Asian and Australasian fossils are relatively sparse. Nevertheless, this evidence suggests humans established themselves throughout Sunda, Wallacea, and Sahul by at least 30 Ka (O'Connor and Hiscock 2014; Kirch 2018). The start date for human population movements into Sunda and Wallacea remains unclear (Bae et al. 2017) and the subject of persistent controversy. If the claimed date of 65 Ka for the Madjedbebe Rockshelter archaeological site in Arnhem Land, Australia, is correct (Clarkson et al. 2017), then human population movements into Southeast Asian and Australasia could either have begun considerably earlier (i.e., > 70 Ka) or unfolded considerably faster than generally supposed. On the other hand, if the date is wrong and younger (O'Connell et al. 2018), then human dispersals into Southeast Asian and Australasia would align chronologically with the timing of human population movements into Northern Eurasia around 45 Ka (see Chapter 9). By 40 Ka, humans had reached some of the nearer Pacific Islands off the Sahul's northeastern coast, including Manus Island in the Admiralty Islands and New Britain and New Ireland in the Bismarck Archipelago (see Chapter 12).

Other Southeast Asian Hominins

Homo erectus appears to have been the first hominin to settle Southeast Asia, after around 1.8 Ma Fossils of *H. erectus* from Ngandong (Java, Indonesia)

---

[2] Early fossils from China along with other Northern Eurasians are discussed in Chapter 9.
[3] The dates for the Lake Mungo fossils have undergone several revisions, from 30 Ka to 60 Ka, but 40 Ka appears to be the current consensus.

suggest these hominins may have survived in Sunda as recently as 108–117 Ka (Rizal et al. 2020), but it remains unclear if they overlapped with early humans' settlement of Sunda. *Homo erectus* does not appear to have reached Sahul.

Humans were the first hominins to settle Sahul, but it appears that descendants of earlier hominin dispersals survived on Wallacean islands, including Flores (Indonesia) and Luzon (Philippines). *Homo floresiensis* and *H. luzonensis* were diminutive creatures (a little over a meter tall) with relatively small brains. Little is known about *H. luzonensis* (mainly because paleontologists discovered it so recently), but the archaeological remains associated with *H. floresiensis* at Liang Bua (a cave) suggest they made stone tools. Both are thought descendants of earlier hominin populations that became isolated on islands and who underwent "island dwarfing." Island dwarfing is when limited food supplies on islands create selective pressures for smaller body sizes among larger animals.[4] Though initial studies suggest *H. floresiensis* might have overlapped with early humans on Flores, it now appears they became extinct at or around the time humans first appeared in the region.

PLEISTOCENE ARCHAEOLOGY OF SOUTHEAST ASIA AND SAHUL

Southeast Asia's and Australasia's archaeology is unevenly documented (White and O'Connell 1982; Bellwood 1987; Higham 2014). Other than in a few parts of Australia, those areas do not feature "hot spots" of long-term and sustained paleoanthropological research comparable to those in Western Europe or the Levant. Rather, the region has many "spotlight" sites, one or a few well-documented sites surrounded by vast "blank spaces on the map."

Stone Tools

Due to poor preservation of organic remains, stone tools dominate Southeast Asia's and Australasia's archaeological records (Figure 7.2). Short nonhierarchical cores, bipolar cores, short unifacial hierarchical cores, and flakes detached from the latter dominate Southeast Asian and Australasian stone tool assemblages older than 30 Ka. Retouched pieces are mostly scrapers/notches/denticulates. Burins and backed/truncated pieces are uncommon. On the whole, and except for a few artifacts discussed below, Southeast Asian and

---

[4] A similar process affected the elephants on Flores Island, too. Several Mediterranean islands also preserve evidence of island dwarfing among their elephants and hippos. Interestingly, birds, reptiles, and rodents vulnerable to predation by raptor birds sometime experience a reverse process, island gigantism, that makes them less attractive prospects to avian predators. Komodo dragons, the large monitor lizards that coinhabited Flores with *H. floresiensis*, may have grown so large for this reason. Large flightless birds, also presumably results of island gigantism, flourished on Madagascar and New Zealand before human settlement.

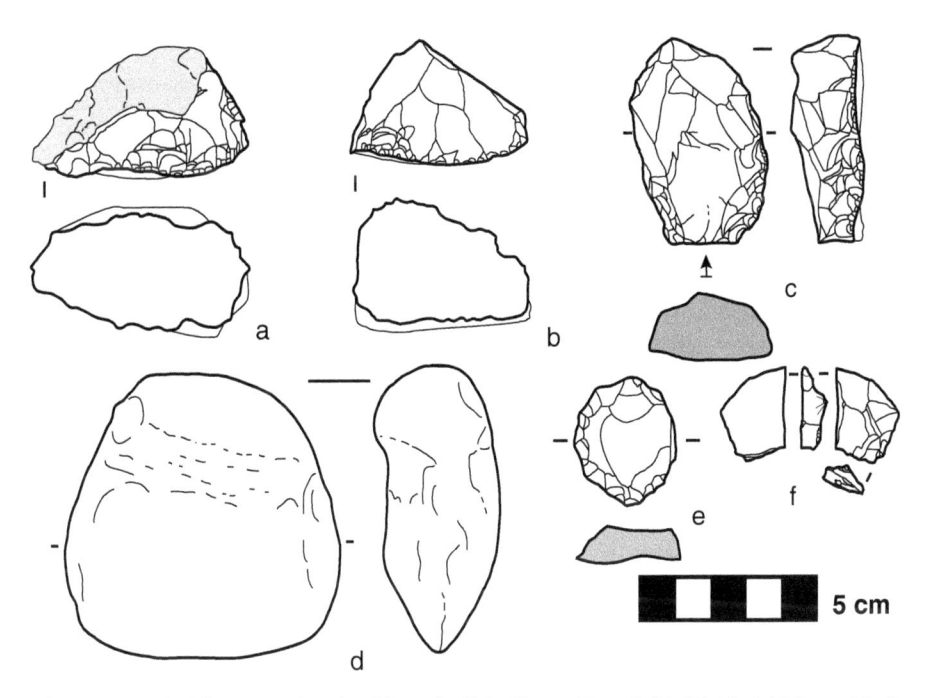

Figure 7.2 Artifacts associated with early Sahulians. (a) and (b) Unifacial hierarchical cores, (c) scraper, (d) "waisted" axe or celt, (e) scraper, (f) backed/truncated piece. Sources: Shea (2013b, 2017b). © John J. Shea.

Australasian stone tools appear "expedient." That is, they were made quickly, used briefly nearby, and then discarded. But this is not at all remarkable. Similar such expedient-looking tools dominate stone artifact assemblages from the earliest times to the ethnographic present. Expedient stoneworking minimizes time spent making tools, freeing up time for more evolutionarily consequential subsistence, social, and reproductive activities. (Smart people do not necessarily need complex tools to solve essential survival challenges.) Southeast Asian and Australasian stone tool assemblages are not distinctly simple or primitive; they merely lack the elongated bifacial core tools and hierarchical cores that occur in stone tool assemblages of the same age elsewhere. When one gets right to it, the expedient/primitive nature of Southeast Asian and Australasian stoneworking is not that remarkable. Much as in a survival emergency, spending as little time as possible smashing razor-sharp rocks against one another is simply common sense. Rather, the widespread occurrence of more time- and energy-costly "curated" stoneworking one sees elsewhere in Africa and Eurasia requires explanation (Shea 2017a). Had these people nothing better to do with their time than chip away at stone tools longer than minimally necessary?

In other respects, Sahulian stoneworking actually appears ahead of the Afro-Asiatic curve. Some Sahulian sites located in interior Australia (e.g., Madjedbebe Rockshelter) preserve evidence for the abraded-edge tools (presumably celts) like those that occur in many more sites after 30 Ka. Similar artifacts do not turn up in African, European, or Western Eurasian sites until early Holocene times and among agricultural societies.

Food Remains

What First Asians and Sahulians ate remains little known and dominated by evidence from a few sites. The regions abound with rivers and coastlines that could have provided fish, shellfish, and other aquatic prey. Wild pigs roamed throughout much of the Sunda and Wallacea, and their bones appear in archaeological sites. Animal remains from Niah Cave suggest First Asians hunted or otherwise captured a wide range of smaller mammals, birds, and reptiles (Barker 2014). Many sites preserve remains of fish, shellfish, and other aquatic prey, though mostly species found near coastlines rather than "pelagic" fish from deeper offshore waters, though recent discoveries of pelagic fish remains on Wallacean islands and islands off the coast of Sahul suggest suggests they may have done more such fishing than generally supposed (O'Connor et al. 2011).

Though Sahul supported many large terrestrial marsupial mammals, surprisingly little evidence shows Sahulians systematically preying on these creatures. It seems unlikely that humans ignored larger mammal food sources, for humans and other hominins preyed on them consistently from at least Middle Pleistocene times onward. Instead, they may have left these creatures' heavy and inedible bones at open-air kill/butchery sites where intense solar radiation and widely variable temperatures and humidity caused them to swiftly decompose and disintegrate. (Africa, too, suffers a similar sort of equatorial zone of poor faunal preservation.)

Many edible fruits, nuts, roots, and tubers occur throughout Southeast Asia. It seems reasonable to assume Pleistocene humans used them, as they and their descendants continue to do, but there is little direct evidence for their having done so. Madjedbebe Rockshelter in Australia preserves starch residue and charcoal evidence for the use of *Pandanus* nuts as well as grinding slabs presumably used to pulverize seeds, nuts, roots, and tubers (Florin et al. 2020).

SOUTHEAST ASIANS' AND SAHULIANS' SURVIVAL STRATEGIES

First Aid and Medication

We do not see evidence for major differences between first aid and medicinal practices in Southeast Asia and Australasia before 30 Ka and those used in Africa or South Asia at the same time, but we are almost certainly missing much. Hot and humid conditions like those that prevail over much of

Southeast Asia and points eastward encourage rapid bacterial growth. Superficial cuts and other wounds that would be inconsequential in colder, drier habitats can turn septic and become life-threatening in very short order (Werner et al. 2010; Schimelpfenig 2016). That humans moving into these regions encountered such bacteria and other pathogens for the first time undoubtedly created strong incentives to explore medicinal plants. These regions' recent human inhabitants use an impressive array of such plants, but archaeological sites thus far preserve no direct evidence for which, if any, medicinal plants First Asians and Sahulians used.

Thermoregulation

Sunda's, Wallacea's, and Sahul's archaeological records preserve evidence for the use of caves and rock shelters as habitation sites but no evidence for freestanding artificial shelters. In both respects, these regions' archaeological records do not differ from their counterparts in Africa and South Asia. Recent African, Asian, and Australasian hunter-gatherers' traditional architecture consists of lightweight structures unlikely to survive long in tropical habitats (Oliver 1987). Traces of fire at many sites affirm, unsurprisingly, that humans used fire to thermoregulate, to cook food, and for other purposes as well, such as cremation at Lake Mungo (Australia).

Hydration

The archaeological record preserves no evidence for how humans in Southeast Asia, Sunda, or Sahul found, treated, or transported water. As in much of the world, these regions' Pleistocene humans could have drunk surface water safely, or, if animals contaminated such sources, they could have obtained potable water by excavating shallow "wells" a short distance away. Another strategy could have involved boiling contaminated water in vessels made from the hollow sections of large bamboo stalks. Clearly, however, we are missing much. If First Asians in this part of the world undertook ocean voyages tens of kilometers or more, then they would have had to store supplies of water on their vessels to drink on route and as a hedge against making landfalls in places with scarce drinking water or none at all. Voyages of more than 100 kilometers such as those made to the Bismarck Archipelago and the Solomon Islands must have included impressively large water storage vessels, such as watertight baskets or wooden barrels.

Nutrition

Like humans to their west, First Asians in Sunda hunted terrestrial game, gathered diverse plant foods, and exploited coastal resources, including shellfish. Tropical Afro-Asiatic habitats offer a wide range of plants with starch-rich roots and tubers that can be gathered and replanted near habitation sites. This sort of "proto-horticulture" does not alter those wild plants' reproductive strategies, and so does not technically result in domestication. Ethnographic Africans do this (Fuller and Hildebrand 2013), as do living people in Sunda and Wallacea. One reasonably assumes that First Asians and Sahulians did so, too.

First Asians living in Sunda and Wallacea may have used the bow and arrow, for evidence for bow and arrow use now stretches back to 71 Ka in Africa (Lombard 2021) and to at least 48 Ka in South Asia (Langley et al. 2020). New Guineans adopted the bow and arrow during Holocene times, but no evidence shows Aboriginal Australians ever used them. Instead, Sahulians used the spear-thrower and dart (Churchill 1993) along with boomerangs and other simple (hand-cast) projectile weapons. Also known as atlatls in the Americas, spear-throwers are wood or bone/antler pieces usually less than a meter long. A hook, often made of bone, at one end of the spear-thrower fits into a concavity at the base of a spear or "dart." The opposite "handle" end of the spear-thrower often features a crossbar or cordage straps on which one hooks one's fingers while throwing the dart. A spear-thrower lengthens one's arm (much as a lacrosse stick does), increasing the velocity at which one can project a missile. Throwing a spear-thrower dart is not exactly a "stealthy" activity. Nearly every joint in one's body moves when one throws a spear-thrower dart. Just why the bow and arrow failed to find an eager reception in Australia remains unclear. Many historic and ethnographic cultures used both bow and arrow and spear-thrower and dart at the same time (Oswalt 1973).

Transportation

Evidence for watercraft use in Pleistocene Southeast Asia and Australasia differs from Africa and elsewhere in Eurasia by preserving incontestable proof of voyaging to and settlement of islands more than 10 kilometers offshore. Voyages to the islands in the Bismarck Archipelago and the Solomon Islands involved distances of more than 100 kilometers. Pleistocene humans could not have survived such voyages without using sail-assisted watercraft.

All early humans living in Africa and Eurasia probably used dugout canoes with or without outriggers to navigate rivers and ocean coastlines, but the sorts of oceanic voyages that took place between Sunda, Sahul, and Western Pacific islands almost certainly required more substantial watercraft. We do not know when people first developed such watercraft, but among the plants humans were processing for food at Madjedbebe Rockshelter 53–65 Ka there occur traces of *Pandanus* (Florin et al. 2020), a plant out of whose fibers ethnographic Polynesians made sails (Thomas 2021).

Communication

First Asians' and Sahulians' archaeological records preserve evidence of personal adornments (red ochre, shell beads), mural artworks (painting and hand-markings on cave walls), burials with grave goods, and what appears to be the world's oldest-known cremation (Langley et al. 2019). Much of this evidence appears after 30 Ka, and thus after the period with which this chapter concerns itself, but there are enough early occurrences of all these symbolic artifacts to assure us that earliest humans in Sunda, Wallacea, and Sahul possessed the full range of capacities for symbolic artifact use as Ancient Africans and First Asians did, and as those reading these words do.

Though some of the motifs in the Indonesian cave art, such as monochrome figures and human-animal ("therianthrope") images, repeat themselves in cave art found at later dates in Europe and Africa (as well as at Holocene-age sites in the Americas), the archaeological consensus sees these artistic traditions as having developed independently of one another (Bahn 2016). That children from many of the world's cultures also use such motifs could suggest that such similarities arise from ancestral and possibly biologically-based ways of graphically representing three-dimensional views of animals and other humans with two-dimensional media (Guthrie 2005, Nowell 2015).

As with First Asians (Chapter 6) sea-level rise complicates efforts to assess early Southeast Asian' and Sahulians' use of symbolic artifacts in forming and reinforcing social alliance networks. Many of the coastlines and lower river valleys that were likely destinations for humans moving into these regions are now underwater. Southeast Asians' artworks demonstrate symbolic capacities no less complex than those seen among earlier humans in Africa or elsewhere in Eurasia, but their stoneworking remains relatively simple.

Sahul's early prehistory offers up few hints of regionally patterned stone tool industries or stoneworking traditions like those archaeologists identify in Africa or Western Eurasia at the same time (Holdaway and Stern 2004). Tellingly, when sea levels reached their near-modern stand around 5–6 Ka, Sahul's archaeological record begins to show precisely the same sorts of patterned regional and chronological variation in artifact design that archaeologists interpret as evidence for symbolically reinforced social networks elsewhere. One thinks it less likely that Sahulians suddenly discovered the merits of such networks 5–6 Ka and more likely that 5–6 Ka marks the earliest point at which the "lithic fallout" of their social networks, which could have been more complex along densely settled coastlines, began falling on those parts of Australia, New Guinea, and Tasmania that remain above sea level today.[5]

---

[5] It might also be that archaeologists working in Southeast Asia and Sahul have not organized these regions' lithic archaeological record into named stone tool industries as their colleagues in Africa and Western Eurasia have done.

INTERPRETIVE ISSUES ABOUT SOUTHEAST ASIANS AND SAHULIANS

Behavioral Differences among Southeast Asians, Sahulians, and First Asians

None of the derived (newly appearing) features of Southeast Asia's or Australasia's archaeological records requires additions to our species' six ancestral survival skills. Rather, it appears that they tailored those skills to new habitats and novel circumstances.

The most obvious differences between First Asians' and early Sahulians' archaeological records and earlier humans' archaeological records elsewhere at the same time involve stone tools. Bifacial hierarchical cores, prismatic blade cores, foliate points, and backed/truncated pieces occur throughout Africa and other parts of Eurasia between 30 and 75 Ka, but they rarely appear among Pleistocene Southeast Asian and Australasian stone tools. These differences in the stone tool evidence might not mean all that much. They could result from differences in the uses of nonlithic tool materials as cutting tools. That Pleistocene humans living in Sunda and Wallacea made fractured-shell tools out of marine mollusks suggests they were actively seeking lighter and, along coastlines, easier-to-procure alternatives to stone cutting tools.[6]

Southeast Asia supports forests of bamboo that might have served as an alternative to some stone cutting tools, as they do among some indigenous and historic Southeast Asian peoples (Pope 1989). Bamboo's woody tissues contain dense concentrations of silica particles (opal phytoliths) that confer cutting abilities more or less equivalent or even superior to stone cutting tools (Bar-Yosef et al. 2012). One does not have to risk permanently blunting or fracturing the tool while retouching it. One can shape bamboo easily enough using simple cores and flakes, and bamboo cutting edges can be "resharpened" by peeling away a strip of use-abraded wood. Bamboo cutting tools have the further advantage of buoyancy. Dropped in water, they float – a not inconsiderable advantage in a region so cross-cut with rivers and oceanic waterways. This "bamboo cutting tool" hypothesis remains controversial, for archeologists have not yet discovered actual evidence humans used bamboo in this way. Brumm (2010) provides a summary of arguments against this hypothesis.

The one explanation we can dismiss about the reason for differences between Southeast Asian stoneworking elsewhere in Eurasia and Africa is the "cultural retardation" argument (Movius 1944).[7] Long ago, Hallam L. Movius, Jr., an influential archaeologist, observed that the traditional benchmarks for major changes in stoneworking occurred later in South and East Asia than in

---

[6] Other hominins living elsewhere did this, too, but the practice is somewhat better-documented in Southeast Asia and Australasia.

[7] For a succinct review of this issue, see Lycett and Bae (2010).

Interpretive Issues about Southeast Asians and Sahulians

Europe or Africa. Movius' use of the term "retardation" jars modern ears, but during the 1940s, it expressed "slow" or "slower than expected" growth rather than pathological and immutable cognitive deficiency. In any case, the archaeological evidence no longer supports Movius' interpretation. Why prehistory textbooks continue to divide Pleistocene Eurasia into LCT-making Western Eurasia and non-LCT-making Southeastern Eurasia divided by a "Movius Line" remains an enigma.

If Pleistocene Southeast Asians were any less capable of changing their culture than other humans, then one would hardly expect to find carved and polished bone points, such as the one found at Niah Cave (Borneo, 45 Ka). That bone point is not older than its African counterparts, but it is older than any carved bone point found with humans in Europe.

One would not expect to find abraded-edge tools and grooved stone celts to appear as they do at Madjedbebe and at the Bobongara sites on New Guinea's Huon Peninsula dating to around 38–60 Ka (Groube et al. 1986; Hiscock et al. 2016). These artifacts date to tens of thousands of years earlier than the oldest such artifacts in Africa and Western Eurasia.

One would definitely not expect to find the world's oldest two-dimensional depictions of animals and human-animal figures, as one does on the walls of Lubang Jeriji Saléh Cave (Indonesia, 45 Ka) and Leang Bulu' Sipong 4 Cave (Sulawesi, Indonesia, 44 Ka) (Aubert et al. 2018; Aubert et al. 2019). Early Eurasians would not even begin painting animal figures and other images on European caves until the pigments on these Indonesian caves had set and dried for 10,000 years or more.

Migration versus Dispersal

Is the evidence for the early peopling of Southeast Asia and Sahul consistent with migration? The simple answer is "no," but the evidence is complicated and varies between Sunda, Wallacea, and Sahul. Though some have argued for continuities between *H. erectus* and *H. sapiens* in this region (Wolpoff and Thorne 2003), this remains a minority position among paleoanthropologists. Nothing in the archaeological record points unambiguously westward to India or north to East Asia as the source of Sunda's human populations.

There are persistent claims for finds of *Homo sapiens* fossils at cave sites dating to > 61–130 Ka in the People's Republic of China at Bailong, Luna, Fuyan, Zhiren, Laibin, and Liujang. These claims remain controversial for a variety of reasons, including unclear stratigraphy, geochronology, and morphological proof for species-level identifications (Hublin 2021). Many of the caves in South China formed around fissures in relatively soft limestone, and as a result, flowing water has often disturbed the deposits they contain. In several cases, flowstones dating to 100 Ka overlie deposits containing fossils radiocarbon dated to 30 Ka or even younger.

The peopling of Wallacea and Sahul involved something more complicated than dispersals but something less than migrations. For individuals or small families to have set forth in search of distant island homes would not lead to long-term success, due to risks of foraging failure and inadequate numbers of possible mates.[8] Communities that shipwreck survivors founded would likely fail for the same reasons. Among ethnographic peoples living in this part of the world, deep-water fishing is an almost exclusively male activity (Thomas 2021). Coordinated movements of dozens of individuals using rafts or other large watercraft seem more plausible, but we have little evidence for Pleistocene-age flotillas of the sorts Oceanian and Polynesian explorers used (Chapter 12).

The Wallacean and Sahulian evidence is not sufficient to reject the "no migrations before food production" hypothesis," but it is close. If one were looking to prove that hypothesis wrong (as readers should), then this is the part of the world most likely to offer convincing evidence to the contrary. On the other hand, early Southeast Asian and Australasian humans might have managed to combine wild plant and animal foods, root crops, and aquatic resources in ways that were the functional equivalents of food production. Testing this hypothesis requires further research focused on deposits containing well-preserved plant and animal fossils.

What did early humans have to do differently in order to settle Southeast Asia and Australasia? The simple answer is "not much" or "surprisingly little." First Asians' and early Sahulians' archaeological records preserve little or no support for the hypotheses that there were major differences between these people and either their First Asian or Ancient African precursors and contemporaries. Both used watercraft, foraged along coastlines and in near-shore waters, and hunted both large and small animal prey in jungles and woodlands. Watercraft, especially watercraft capable of making longer oceanic voyages, seems likely at as least as important here, or even more so, than in Africa or other parts of Eurasia, but poor preservation of coastal habitats and of wooden artifacts limits our ability to test this hypothesis.

Is this finding unexpected? Not really. The peopling of South Asia and Sunda were both latitudinal movements within the Old World tropics. People moved into similar sorts of tropical habitats in which their ancestors evolved. Sahul's uniquely evolved flora and fauna likely posed challenges, but the archaeological record suggests early Sahulians managed them with aplomb or, at the very least, without having to add much truly new to their suite of ancestral survival skills.

Why did humans disperse into Southeast Asian and Australasia? The least complex hypothesis for human dispersal into these regions invokes simple

---

[8] Johann David Wyss' 1812 novel, *The Swiss Family Robinson*, explores some of these difficulties.

population growth among those living along the Indian Ocean's northern coasts. Having arrived in these places and established themselves on coastlines, people seeking new homes for themselves could simply have moved eastward along the coast, a path of lesser resistance that would have brought them to Sunda and thence onward to Wallacea and Sahul. Movements inland, to upriver valleys and higher elevations and latitudes, would have brought them into colder, drier habitats that required more substantial changes to preexisting survival strategies developed for use in warm and humid tropical and coastal habitats. They did this eventually, of course (see Chapter 9), and at likely around the same time as others dispersed along the coast, but one suspects the coastal dispersals were the preferred option, for they required the fewest changes to preexisting survival strategies.

The Mount Toba Volcanic Eruption

We do not know whether humans were living in Sunda when the Mount Toba supervolcano erupted, ca. 75 Ka. If they were, then those people were in deep trouble. The eruption covered parts of Sunda in volcanic ash tens of meters thick. This ash buried plant food sources, killed terrestrial animal prey, and poisoned near-shore fisheries.[9] If humans lived in Sunda at this time, then the Toba eruption could have provided an incentive for rapid dispersals, or even migrations, eastward into Wallacea and beyond to Sahul.

We lack direct evidence that First Asian movements beyond Sunda were migrations, but it also seems unlikely that they would venture out to remote islands in ones and twos in small canoes rather than in larger groups on sail-powered rafts or on other large watercraft sailing against the wind on their way out and with it on return. The archaeological consensus currently holds that Pleistocene humans and earlier hominins did not have such sail-assisted watercraft, but if not, then one struggles to imagine circumstances that would more powerfully provide incentives to develop them than in the Mount Toba eruption's aftermath. In paleoanthropology, the swiftest way to be proven wrong is to underestimate one's ancestors' ingenuity.

Future Research Directions

What do we need in order to improve the archaeological record for human dispersals to Southeast Asian and Australasia? Simply put, we need more evidence, especially from former Sunda and Wallacea. War, political unrest,

---

[9] Breathing in sharp-edged particles of silica-rich volcanic ash can shred the alveoli in one's lungs, causing death from asphyxiation. Even if humans figured out that covering their mouths and noses with water-soaked cloth allowed them to breathe, none of the animals on which they subsisted would have survived.

and various circumstances conspired to slow the development of prehistoric research in these parts of the world at the very same time that archaeology and paleontology underwent rapid improvements and professionalization elsewhere. Aspiring young archaeologists who want to make a disproportionate contribution to prehistory should focus their research on these regions.

Last, far too much of Southeast Asian and Australasian prehistory remains "a story written in stone," that is, a lithics-centric view of prehistory. Paleoanthropology needs more information about how First Asians and Sahulians used plants and animal resources. The emerging field of proteomics (analyses of ancient proteins preserved on tools and in sediments) offers tremendous opportunities to shed light on these issues in regions where fossils remain scarce.

SUMMARY

This chapter reviewed the evidence for the Pleistocene peopling of Southeast Asia and Australasia (Sunda, Wallacea, and Sahul). When this process began remains unclear, but humans were living over much of these regions by at least 30 Ka. The most important change to Ancient African and First Asian survival strategies involved advances in watercraft and water storage/transport that allowed voyages to near oceanic islands. The next chapter, Chapter 8, takes a step backward in time, examining the archaeological record for the extinct indigenous Western Eurasians that we call "Neanderthals." It does this so that in Chapter 9 we can compare Neanderthals' survival strategies with those that humans employed in Western and Northern Eurasia after Neanderthals became extinct.

Box 7.1: *Ghost marriages: Fossils and stone tool industries*

Paleoanthropological "ghost marriages" needlessly complicate research into prehistoric human population movements. A phenomenon in many ethnographic cultures, actual "ghost marriages" unite unmarried deceased ancestors. Reasons for doing this vary within and between cultures, but ghost marriage connects unrelated individuals in larger families to one another using "fictive kinship," a uniquely human form of predictive hallucination in which we imagine and act toward unrelated persons as if they were close biological kin. Paleoanthropological ghost marriages link stone tools and other artifacts and ecofacts in a given level of an archaeological site to the (usually far less numerous) human and other hominin fossils found in that same level and/or elsewhere. Arguably the best-known such paleoanthropological ghost marriage links so-called Mousterian stone tools to

Summary 153

Box 7.1: *(cont.)*

Neanderthals (Shea 2014). Le Moustier Cave (France) did indeed preserve Neanderthal fossils, but so-called Mousterian artifacts also occur in direct stratigraphic association with *Homo sapiens* across much of Northern Africa and Southwest Asia as well as with Denisovans in Eastern Europe. Vastly more Mousterian stone tool occurrences lack any associated hominin fossils than preserve them.

The geological principle of association holds that objects enclosed in the same sedimentary deposit (e.g., one level of an archaeological site) were deposited "at the same time," but "at the same time" merely means between the oldest and youngest dates for that level. It does not mean at the same instant, by the same people, or for reasons related to one another. No less so than at open-air sites, levels of cave or rock shelter sites are soft and permeable when they are at or near the surface, less so after burial, compaction, and consolidation. Many such levels accumulate slowly, over the course of decades, centuries, even millennia, potentially combining archaeological and paleontological "inputs" the whole time. Upper levels of caves in many parts of the world demonstrably combine artifacts made millennia apart.

Is this the only problem paleoanthropological ghost marriages present? No, not even close. Further problems result from how archaeologists arrange these marriages. They commonly assign the entire contents of a given level to one or only one named stone tool industry. Further, they assign individual such stone tool industries to one and only one hominin.

Why is doing these things a problem? First, neither prior geological principles nor anthropological principles show that breaks in sediment deposition and changes in levels at an archaeological site coincide with changes in who was living at the site at the time. Second, no formal rules (systematics) govern the naming of stone tool industries. Third, archaeologists assign occurrences of stone tools to industries and, by implication, to particular hominins in spite of the fact that most such archaeological occurrences lack hominin fossils. Finally, assigning one or more artifact assemblages to a specific hominin accepts that paleontologists' categorical distinctions among hominins (e.g., Neanderthals vs. *H. sapiens*) correspond to actual social and biological divisions among hominins living at the time the sediments accumulated. They might, but this is an assumption.

If paleoanthropological ghost marriages' flaws are so head-slappingly obvious, why do paleoanthropologists continue creating and accepting them? At least two reasons suggest themselves. First, superficially, they convey the appearance of an "integrative" approach to the

Box 7.1: *(cont.)*

paleoanthropological evidence, that is, an approach integrating fossil, archaeological, and other (e.g., aDNA) evidence. In this case, paleoanthropologists err out of good intentions. Second, because stone tools are essentially indestructible and vastly more numerous than hominin fossils, stone tool industry-hominin fossil "ghost marriages" seem to offer a shortcut to identifying who made which sets of stone tools without fossil evidence. They allow paleontologists and archaeologists alike to use one another's evidence without doing the hard work of learning and understanding those different sources of observations' weaknesses.

CHAPTER 8

NEANDERTHAL COUNTRY

This chapter reviews evidence associated with the Neanderthals, extinct hominins who lived in Europe and Western Asia before humans settled these regions after 40–50 Ka. It compares evidence for Neanderthals' survival strategies with those Ancient Africans practiced. Many of the differences between Neanderthals and Ancient Africans seem to have arisen from Neanderthals' living in persistently small, highly mobile groups and from their investing less time and energy in technology.

GEOGRAPHY: NORTHWESTERN EURASIA BEFORE 45 KA

Neanderthals lived in Europe and Western Asia between 45 and 300 Ka (see Figure 8.1). The westernmost fossil sites appear in Spain, Portugal, and Gibraltar, the easternmost in Afghanistan. Their northernmost fossils occur in Britain, Belgium, and central Germany, but advancing glaciers during Marine Isotope Stages 2–3 may have obliterated sites located further north during warmer times. Their southernmost fossils appear at Shukbah Cave in the territory of the Palestinian National Authority and Kebara Cave in Israel. Even though abundant mammal fossil sites dating to 45–300 Ka occur in Africa, Eastern Asia, and the Americas, Neanderthal fossils have never been found at them.

Claims that Neanderthals lived outside Europe and Western Asia rest mainly on archaeologists and others equating Mousterian stone tools with Neanderthals. Such tools indeed occur with Neanderthals in Europe and Western Asia, but Mousterian tools also co-occur with *Homo sapiens* fossils in Southwest Asia and Northern Africa and with Denisovan fossils in Western-Central Asia. Further complicating matters, archaeologists' criteria for identifying stone tools as Mousterian vary among individuals and between research traditions.

"Neanderthal Country," such as it was, centered around the Alps-Himalayas and the mountain ranges and plateaus connected to them: the Pyrenees,

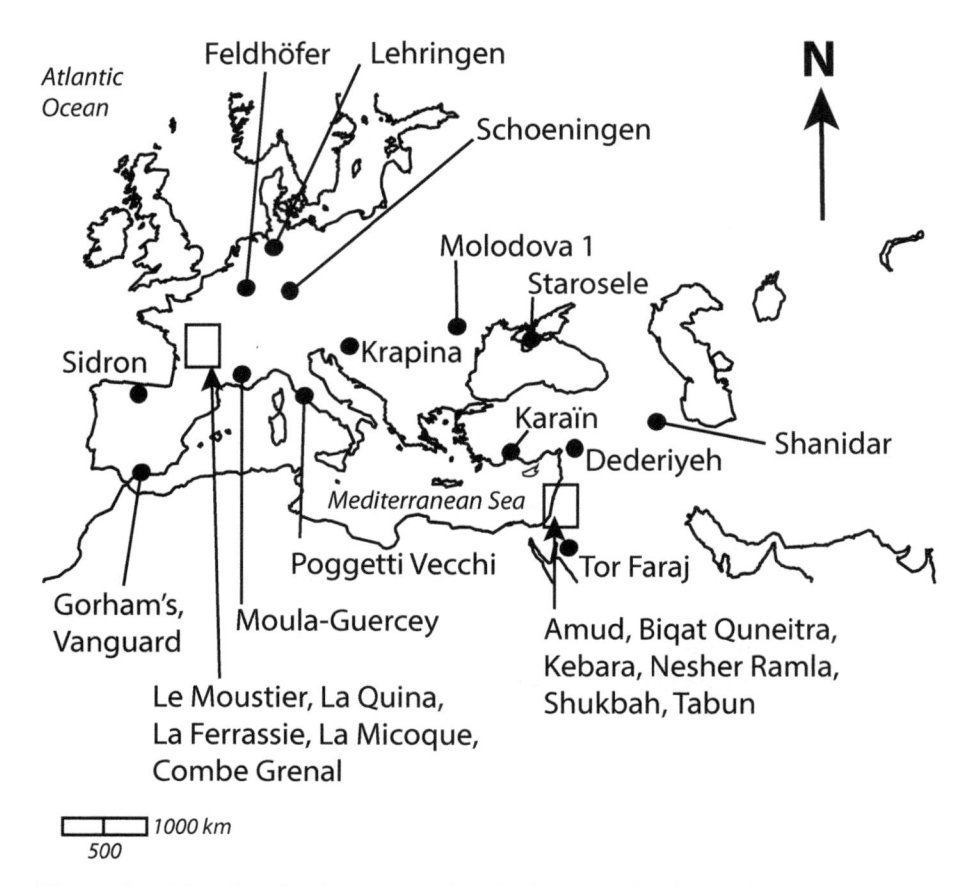

Figure 8.1 Map showing important Neanderthal sites. © John J. Shea.

Balkans, Taurus, and Zagros. Neanderthal fossils appear to the north and south of these mountains, as well as within them at sites on the Anatolian and Iranian plateaus. Neanderthals were not specifically "adapted" to montane habitats. Rather, the changes in vegetation and animal communities along these mountains' topographically complex foothills allowed Neanderthals to exploit diverse resources while making relatively few and short-distance changes in residential sites. Neanderthal sites seem clustered around ecotones, regions in which several different ecological zones conjoin one another. No consensus exists over what characterizes a "typical" Neanderthal site, but most Neanderthal sites archaeologists have investigated are caves located in sheltered valleys located near springs, rivers, or other stable water sources and close to the sources of the rocks they made into tools.[1] Animal bones from these sites suggest that, unlike many recent human hunter-gatherers, Neanderthals were

---

[1] Caves and rock shelters dominate evidence for Neanderthal settlement patterns because archaeologists prefer to excavate such sites due to their superior fossil preservation, not necessarily because they think Neanderthals preferred to live in caves or rock shelters.

mainly "locavores"; that is, and though it varied, they appear to have eaten mainly locally sourced foods. Creatures that live on rocky "crag" terrain, such as ibex, and near water sources, such as deer, aurochs (wild cattle), and boar are especially common among fossils at these sites.

Artistic reconstructions often show Neanderthals living in arctic-looking landscapes. Some did indeed inhabit cold regions and higher elevations, but the locations of fossil and archaeological sites dating 45–300 Ka in Western Eurasia suggest most Neanderthals lived in temperate woodlands and steppe margins at lower elevations along montane foothills and along the coasts of the Atlantic Ocean and the Mediterranean Sea. These places are, after all, where most of the potential plant and animal food sources lived and grew during Pleistocene times.

Much archaeological speculation about Neanderthal behavior focuses on how they coped (or failed to cope) with cold glacial conditions. Actually, for most of their time on Earth, 45–300 Ka, Neanderthals lived during something other than peak glacial conditions (MIS 3, 5, and 7 = 211,000 years) rather than full glacial conditions (MIS 4 and 6 = 75,000 years). They likely spent more time stalking deer, aurochs, and wild boar in dense woodlands than chasing reindeer and musk ox across tundra.

The Mammoth Steppe

North of the Alps-Himalayas during colder periods lay the Mammoth Steppe (Guthrie 1990, 2001). The Mammoth Steppe has no exact counterpart among contemporary ecosystems. It combined plants and animals that we today find in tundra, taiga (conifer-dominated boreal forest), and steppe, but at lower latitudes than these habitats now occur. Located closer to the Equator, Mammoth Steppe plants received more sunlight, grew more abundantly, and supported larger and more diverse animal communities than modern-day steppe, taiga, and tundra. Much as in Northern Eurasia today, warm Atlantic Ocean currents made the western end of this region (Europe) more humid, and thus a more attractive place for hominin settlement than interior and eastern regions (Siberia).

Conditions Affecting Population Movements

The principal forces that caused Neanderthal population movements were those nudging them toward altitudinal shifts in habitation sites. That is, either annually (between summer and winter) or over longer periods (glacial vs. interglacial periods), Western Eurasian climates pushed Neanderthals into sheltered intermontane valleys during colder periods and out into adjacent steppes or woodlands during warmer periods. That glaciers extended down-slope from the major mountain chains in these region was one obstacle to

Neanderthal population movements during colder periods, but one struggles to imagine any obstacle that could have constrained their movements within or beyond Europe and Western Asia during warmer periods. Indeed, Neanderthal fossils appear in the Levant (see Chapter 6).

IMPORTANT NEANDERTHAL PALEOANTHROPOLOGICAL SITES

Table 8.1 lists important Neanderthal paleoanthropological sites discussed in this chapter.

NEANDERTHAL FOSSILS

The name "Neanderthal" comes from a German valley, at which the first fossils from the Feldhöfer site were excavated and recognized as extinct hominins in 1858.[2] The current paleoanthropological consensus holds that Neanderthals evolved in Europe after around 300 Ka. Several European Middle Pleistocene *Homo heidelbergensis* fossils, such as those from Petralona (Greece) and Atapuerca Sima de los Huesos (Spain), exhibit cranial features seen widely among Later Pleistocene Neanderthals. Still, one cannot reject the hypothesis that Neanderthals evolved over a wider area in Eurasia, much as humans appear to have done in Africa and in Southwest Asia.

Neanderthals stood around 1.5–1.6 meters tall (5.0–5.5 feet), on average, and weighed around 68–77 kilograms (150–170 lb) (Figure 8.2). They were stocky creatures with large, "barrel-shaped" chests, little or no waist, and wide hips. Fleshed out, they would have had large noses, a projecting middle face, thick and prominent double-arched brow ridges, and a receding chin and forehead.[3] Analyses of European Neanderthal aDNA shows some had red hair and pale skin.

Neanderthal skeletons differ from *Homo sapiens* in at least two major ways (Trinkaus 2006; Churchill 2014). First, their skulls retain some "archaic" human features (i.e., ones shared with *H. heidelbergensis*), such as prognathic faces, thick brow ridges, receding chin, a long low skull shape, and thick cranial vault bones. Second, Neanderthal skeletons exhibit features that appear to have evolved in response to living in cold and/or dry habitats, such as large noses and sinuses. These features warm and moisten air before one aspirates it. Neanderthals' short forearms and lower legs conserve body heat by reducing

---

[2] British soldiers excavating at Forbes' Quarry (Gibraltar) had found a Neanderthal fossil in 1848, but it was heavily covered with carbonate concretions and not recognized as a hominin until much later.

[3] The Hanna-Barbera cartoon *The Flintstones* characters of Fred Flintstone and Barney Rubble exhibit these stereotypical Neanderthal features. Their wives, Wilma and Betty, have more human body shapes (high foreheads, narrow waists, long limbs).

TABLE 8.1 *Important Neanderthal paleoanthropological sites*

Site	Date (Ka)	Comment
Amud Cave (Israel)	50–60	Levantine Neanderthal fossils (and burials), archaeological remains
Biqat Quneitra (Israel)	65	Neanderthal (?) lake-edge activity area
Dederiyeh Cave (Syria)	> 45	Neanderthal child burial
Feldhöfer (Germany)	> 45	Original Neanderthal (Neander Valley) fossil site
Gorham's and Vanguard caves (Gibraltar)	45–55	Well-documented Neanderthal habitation sites, evidence for use of coastal resources, bird feathers as symbolic artifacts
Karaïn Cave (Turkey)	150–200	Neanderthal (?) habitation site
Kebara Cave (Israel)	45–65	Well-documented Neanderthal habitation site, traces of fire use and burials
Krapina (Croatia)	130	Large sample of Neanderthal fossils, evidence of cannibalism, symbolic behavior
Lehringen (Germany)	125	Wooden spear found with elephant skeleton
Molodova Site 1 (Ukraine)	> 44	Level 5 preserves traces of freestanding architecture
Moula-Guercey (France)	100	Bone breakage suggests Neanderthal cannibalism
Le Moustier, La Quina, La Ferrassie, La Micoque, Combe Grenal (France)	> 45–130	A group of French rock shelters at which early investigations discovered Neanderthal fossils (including burials) and archaeological remains
Nesher Ramla (Israel)	120–140	Neanderthal (?) open-air habitation site, hominin fossil
Poggetti Vecchi (Italy)	171	Carved wooden artifacts (digging tools?)
Schoeningen (Germany)	337–300	Wooden javelins, horse remains
Shanidar Cave (Iraq)	45–65	Montane Western Asian Neanderthal site with burials
Shukbah Cave (Palestinian National Authority)		Southernmost known Neanderthal site
El Sidron (Spain))	49	Residues on Neanderthal teeth show plant food consumption
Starosele (Ukraine)	40–80	Long sequences of Neanderthal occupations
Tabun Cave (Israel)	110?	Levantine Neanderthal fossils (and burial), archaeological remains
Tor Faraj Rock Shelter (Jordan)	69	Well-documented Neanderthal habitation site, traces of fire use; separate activity areas suggest prolonged or repeated occupations.

their body surface area/volume ratio, but they also confer greater strength than longer limbs.[4] Neanderthal teeth have enlarged pulp cavities, undivided molar

---

[4] Neanderthals' limb proportions resemble those of the most successful athletes in sports that involve short bursts of speed and power, such as wrestlers, hockey players, and rugby and American football players. Ancient Africans and other early humans' limb proportions are more like those of successful runners, soccer players, and basketball players.

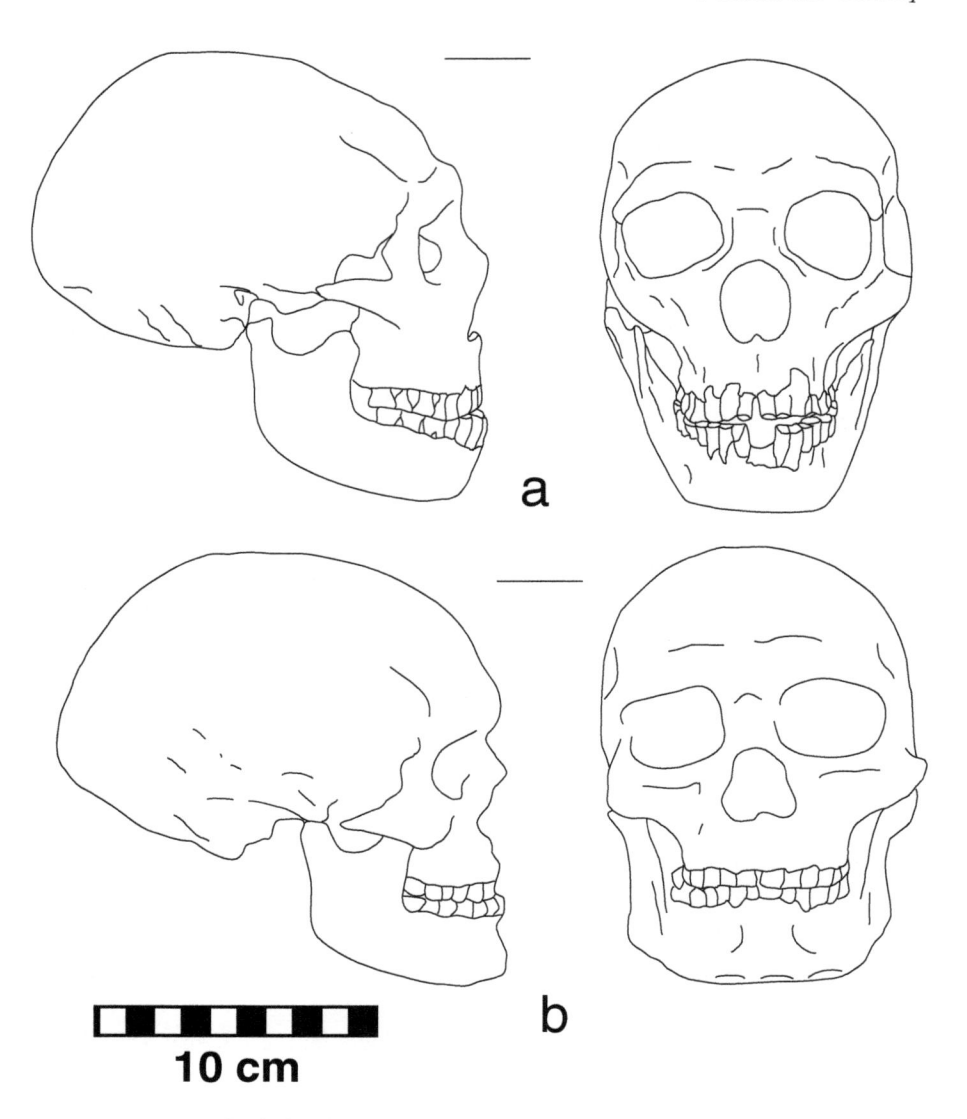

Figure 8.2 Neanderthal and Early Eurasian human skulls compared. (a) Neanderthal, Shanidar Cave 1, (b) Late Pleistocene *Homo sapiens*, Zhoukoudian Upper Cave 1. © John J. Shea.

tooth roots, and other features that can allow paleontologists to identify individual teeth as Neanderthal teeth or those of some other hominin. Neanderthal limb bones have thick cortical bones and enlarged joint articulation surfaces. These are both signs of extreme strength and higher activity levels than seen among living humans, but fossils of early humans with whom Neanderthals were contemporaries and some of their *H. heidelbergensis* ancestors exhibit similar levels of skeletal robustness. Still, a modern-day martial arts athlete would count themselves fortunate to survive a fight with a Neanderthal.

Neanderthals' brains were on average around 1,410 cubic centimeters in volume, a little less, on average, than Later Pleistocene humans (1,600 cm^3), but a little larger than many recent humans (1,350 cm^3). Their prefrontal lobe (the part of the hominin brain involved in planning, reasoning, and emotional regulation) is a bit smaller than ours, but their occipital lobe (the part of the brain that controls visual perception) is a bit larger. Historically, some anthropologists have interpreted these features as indicating inferior intelligence and superior visual perception, but this hypothesis enjoys little current support, or at least considerable skepticism among paleoneurologists (Wynn and Coolidge 2011). After all, it's not necessarily brain size or shape that affects behavior but rather the neural structure of the brain, something very difficult to infer from that organ's impressions on the inside of hominin skulls.

Variation: Progressive versus Classic Neanderthals

Neanderthal fossils vary. Since the 1950s, paleontologists have recognized that younger fossils from Europe (i.e., those dating to MIS 3–4) exhibit more divergent features from *H. sapiens* fossils than those from the East Mediterranean Levant. Some older works distinguish later European Neanderthals as "Classic" or "Würm" Neanderthals and their Southwest Asian counterparts as "Progressive" Neanderthals (Howell 1952).[5] This latter name notwithstanding, it remains unclear whether Southwest Asian Neanderthals enjoyed a closer evolutionary relationship to humans than Classic Neanderthals did.

Neanderthals' Relationships to Living Humans

That living non-Africans have 1–4 percent Neanderthal DNA shows some ancestral humans interbred with at least some Neanderthals (Green et al. 2010). Where, when, and how often this occurred remains unclear, for such variation does not exhibit strong geographic patterning. That is, Spaniards who live in the heart of former "Neanderthal country" are not more closely related to Neanderthals than Han Chinese who live outside it and at the opposite end of Eurasia. Greater or lesser amounts of Neanderthal DNA do not demonstrably correlate with major behavioral differences among living humans.

NEANDERTHAL ARCHAEOLOGY

The name archaeologists use for stone tool industries associated with Neanderthals, "Mousterian," comes from Le Moustier, a French rock shelter

---

[5] Würm, a river in Germany, is the name of the final Alpine Ice Age (here, Marine Isotope Stages 2–4).

first excavated in 1863. Early archaeological excavations in southern France, such as those at La Micoque, La Ferrassie, Combe Grenal, and La Quina, disproportionately influence archaeologists' notions about "typical" Neanderthal behavior. These French caves continue to attract international and interdisciplinary research projects (Jelinek 2013), but well-documented sites outside Western Europe, such as Starosele (Ukraine, 40–80 Ka), Dederiyeh Cave (Syria, > 45 Ka), Kebara and Amud caves (Israel 45–65 Ka), and Tor Faraj Rock Shelter (Jordan, 69 Ka), increasingly inform us about Neanderthal behavioral variability.

Stone Tools

Stone tools found with Neanderthal fossils show essentially the same range of stoneworking methods and techniques seen in Africa and Southern Asia at around the same time (Figure 8.3). Short nonhierarchical cores and flakes detached from them occur in all assemblages. Hierarchical cores and their products are somewhat less common at montane sites and in caves than at lower elevations and on the Northern European plain. When they occur, bifacial hierarchical cores and flakes detached from them are usually more common than elongated unifacial hierarchical (blade) cores and prismatic blades. Retouched pieces are mostly scrapers, notches, denticulates, larger backed-truncated pieces, and convergently retouched pieces ("flake points"). Burins and small backed/truncated pieces are uncommon.

Neanderthal stoneworking shows a strong degree of "environmental forcing." That is, the characteristics of the stone artifacts vary in ways one can predict from environmental variables, such as nearness to rock sources (fewer retouched pieces), more complex terrain (more retouched pieces), and colder conditions (more retouched pieces and more heavily retouched pieces) (Rolland and Dibble 1990; Jelinek 2013).[6]

Neanderthal stoneworkers varied their toolmaking strategies. The stone tools they left in Levantine caves differ from those Neanderthals left in cave sites to the north in the Taurus and Zagros Mountains and further away, in Europe. The stone tools found with Neanderthals in the East Mediterranean Levant are so similar to those First Asians left there that archaeologists refer both to the same "Later Levantine Mousterian" industry (Shea 2013b).

The main ways in which Neanderthal stoneworking differs from Ancient African and First Asian stoneworking include the following:

---

[6] Some Eastern African stone tool assemblages preserve similar covariation with geological variables (Tryon and Faith 2013), but it is not yet clear that other assemblages elsewhere on the continent do so.

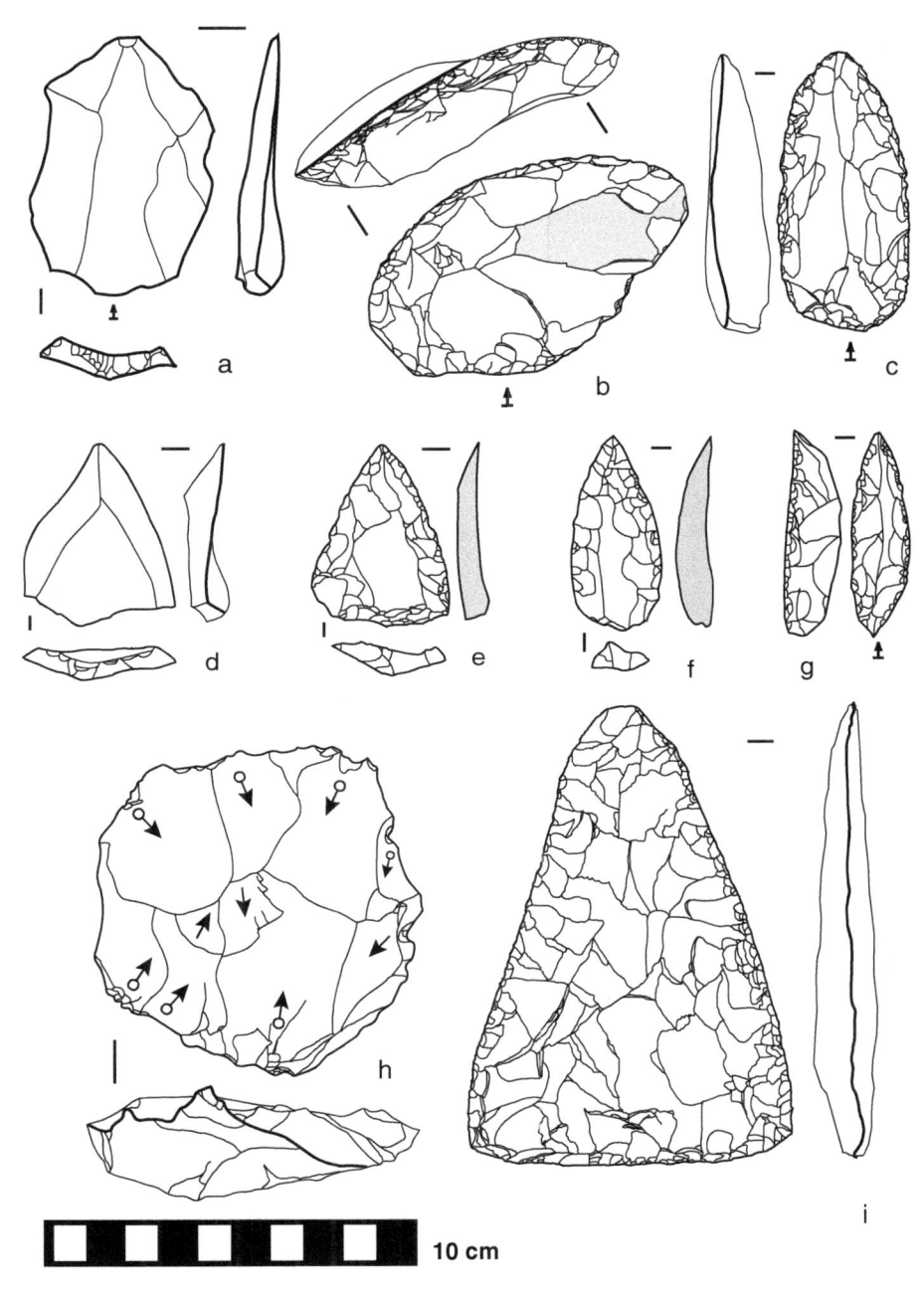

8.3 Neanderthal stone tools. (a) Bifacial hierarchical core ("Levallois") flake, (b) and (c) scrapers, (d) Levallois point, (e)–(g) convergent scrapers/retouched points, (h) bifacial hierarchical core, (i) long core tool. © John J. Shea.

- European Neanderthals continued making, using, and discarding large long core tools after 200 Ka, long after Ancient Africans and First Asians largely stopped doing so.

- They occasionally made foliate points and small backed/truncated pieces, but neither as often nor as widely throughout their geographic range as Ancient Africans did.
- Although some stone artifacts preserve wear traces and glue residues suggesting they were attached to handles, such evidence is uncommon. Few Neanderthal artifacts preserve tangs or other obvious modifications for hafting.
- Retouched pieces are common, and those from European and montane Western Asian sites preserve steep and deeply invasive retouching, indicating repeated use and resharpening. Retouched pieces are relatively uncommon in African stone tool assemblages, and such retouching as appears on their edges is usually shallow and not very invasive.
- Neanderthal stoneworking shows some chronologically patterned changes. These are most clear in places such as Western Europe, where archaeologists have sought such chronological patterns for more than a century (Mellars 1996a). Other than the differences between montane and lower elevations previously discussed, Eastern European and Western Asian Neanderthal stoneworking shows less clearly patterned geographic variation.[7]
- Whereas the period 30–50 Ka saw humans adopting similar methods for making stone tools across vast areas throughout their geographic range, the same period saw Neanderthal stoneworking fragment into local and regional stoneworking industries.

Neanderthals do not appear to have spent a lot of time making stone tools. Though vastly more of the stone tools found with their fossils are simple unretouched flakes, archaeologists tend to choose illustrations showing large, symmetrical, and retouched pieces.[8] When they did more than expedient stoneworking they made large, transportable stone tools (LCTs, foliate points, hierarchical core reduction flakes) whose edges they could resharpen repeatedly and from which they could detach smaller flakes as needed. Ancient Africans did much the same sort of thing, but they seem to have devoted more time and effort to making large numbers of small tools that either could have been or had to have been used while attached to handles. This difference may be real, or it may reflect differences in archaeological methods. Retouched pieces are rare among African stone tool assemblages dating 45–250 Ka.

---

[7] European archaeologists recognize many named regional varieties of "Mousterian" industries. Most of these regional Mousterian industries feature the same range of artifacts found continent-wide. They differ little from one another.
[8] Such "illustration bias" afflicts the stone tool evidence from nearly all regions and time periods. Essentially, the more unusual an artifact is with respect to others found with it, the more likely it is to appear in an archaeological illustration. Needless to say, this creates the impression that unusual artifact designs are, in fact, common (Shea 2011d).

Perceiving retouched pieces as more analytically important for answering "who questions" than unretouched flakes, Africanist archaeologists closely examine small (< 30–50-mm-long) unretouched pieces for evidence of use-related damage and/or small-scale retouch (Shea 2020a). Having long ago rejected the hypothesis that Neanderthals and earlier hominins used small stone tools without retouching them, some European archaeologists do not give such small artifacts much close scrutiny (Burdukiewicz and Ronen 2003).

Artifacts Made of Organic Materials

Neanderthals carved tools out of wood. Wooden artifacts ("digging sticks") recovered from waterlogged deposits at Poggetti Vecchi (Italy, 171 Ka) offer tangible proof of Neanderthal fire-assisted carpentry (i.e., carving wood by charring and then scraping it) (Aranguren et al. 2018). Most analyses of microwear traces on Neanderthal stone tools also identify damage from woodworking (Béyries 1987; Anderson-Gerfaud 1990). Residues of cordage and glue on stone tools show that Neanderthals were able to join together different kinds of materials (Niekus et al. 2019; Hardy et al. 2020).

Neanderthals used pieces of bone as percussors for stoneworking and for other piercing and scraping tasks, but they rarely carved bone extensively. A few teeth and bones from some possible Neanderthal sites dating to around 45–55 Ka have perforations and rings carved around their circumference to allow suspension from cordage, but such finds remain rare, as they do in Africa around the same time. Most of these Neanderthal artifacts are singular finds, either unique objects or artifacts found at one site only. Their attribution to Neanderthals rests mainly on their dating to a little more than 45 Ka, the widely accepted "date" of Neanderthal extinction and humans' arrival in Europe.[9] Many could be artifacts humans lost or discarded during those periods when their and Neanderthals' geographic ranges overlapped with one another. Other than these, little evidence supports the hypothesis that Neanderthals systematically carved tools out of bone or antler.

Wear traces on stone tools consistent with those tools having been hafted, and stone tools with thinning retouch or other accommodations for hafting, occur at many Neanderthal sites but with little clear patterning or trends in the evidence. Ancient Africans' artifact designs to accommodate hafting, in contrast, take similar forms and appear at multiple sites in the same region and at around the same time. Taking this evidence at face value suggests Neanderthals attached stone tools to handles occasionally, perhaps only in response to unusual circumstances, rather than doing so habitually or

---

[9] The latest dating evidence (Djacovik et al. 2022) shows that humans and Neanderthals overlapped with one another in Europe for thousands of years.

systematically. Attaching flake points to spears, for example, might be something they did only when hunting especially large and dangerous prey or when other circumstances, such as food shortages, forced Neanderthals to boost their "probability of kill" by putting more effort into weapon design (Geist 1981; Shea 1997).

NEANDERTHALS' SURVIVAL STRATEGIES

First Aid and Medication

Neanderthal bones preserve evidence for much mechanical damage (e.g., healed fractures, arthritis), though, as with early humans, they lack evidence for healed-over major lower limb fractures. One impressively innovative study (Berger and Trinkaus 1995) compiling evidence for injuries to Neanderthal bones found a near match among injuries to "rodeo clowns," athletes/entertainers who jump into the rodeo ring to distract a bull that has thrown its rider so that the rider can escape safely. This evidence suggests Neanderthals may have engaged in more close-quarters encounters with large animal prey than either earlier hominins or Ancient Africans.

Some Neanderthals survived an impressive array of injuries. Shanidar 1, an older male individual from Shanidar Cave (Iraq, 45–65 Ka), suffered a blinding injury to his eye and lost one arm below the elbow. Another adult male, Shanidar 3, survived a stab wound that left a healed-over scar on his ribs (Trinkaus 1983). While some paleontologists see Shanidar 1 and 3 as evidence for Neanderthal health care, their injuries are unique. They might simply have been extraordinarily tough and resilient individuals. Alternatively, someone other than their fellow Neanderthals may have cared for them. That Neanderthal fossils occur at Shanidar Cave does not mean only Neanderthals lived there. After all, how many of our parents lie buried next to their physicians?

Plant remains recovered from Neanderthal dental calculus (tartar) include traces of plants and herbs with palliative (pain-reducing) properties (Henry et al. 2014). Such plant remains might be evidence of first aid, but they could also be traces of plants that Neanderthals ate principally for nutritional reasons. For example, traces of poplar (*Salix*) in tartar from a Neanderthal from El Sidron (Spain, 49 Ka) could reflect self-medication (poplar bark contains salicylic acid, the active ingredient of aspirin) (Radini et al. 2016). Alternatively, the individual could have eaten poplar inner bark because it is a source of carbohydrates (Sandgathe and Hayden 2003).

Insufficient dental calculus evidence for early human fossils precludes comparison, but in general, neither Ancient African nor First Asian fossils preserve evidence for quite the same degree of wear and tear as Neanderthals do. The fossils from Qafzeh Cave in Israel preserve some evidence for caregiving to disabled infants and injured juveniles (see Chapter 6), but that's about it. Clearly, we are missing much.

Thermoregulation

Neanderthals sheltered in caves and rock shelters, much as other hominins have done since Middle Pleistocene times and earlier, but caves may have been more important sources of shelter for Neanderthals. Cold quickly saps one's energy, and hypothermia can kill in minutes. Even a relatively small fire, properly positioned, can warm a large cave. Some Neanderthal cave occupations were short-term "refuges" used by individuals or small groups. Others might have been used during seasonal or even multiseasonal encampments. Some European sites, such as Combe Grenal (France), preserve sequences of short-term Neanderthal occupations stretching out over tens of thousands of years. A few Levantine caves, such as Kebara and Tor Faraj, preserve evidence for different sorts of activities (hearths/cooking, tool making, waste disposal) taking place in correspondingly different areas of the cave. Archaeologists working in recent contexts customarily interpret such "intra-site spatial organization" as evidence for prolonged occupations of the same site by large groups of people (Kelly 1998).

Thus far, the only generally accepted evidence for Neanderthals' building freestanding architecture comes from Level 5 of Molodova Site 1 in (Ukraine, 44 Ka). Excavated in the 1930s, Molodova preserves a 5 × 8 meter roughly circular arrangement of mammoth tusks and other large animal bones within which occur several traces of hearths. A shallow pit excavated nearby contains many bones of other animals. Archaeologists initially reconstructed Molodova 1 as a domed hut with a framework of mammoth bones supporting a hide roof. More recent studies suggest it may instead have been either a windbreak or an open-roofed hut. As of this writing, Molodova remains a unique find. This does not mean Molodova 1 was genuinely unique. It does mean that we lack a firm basis for inferring how often Neanderthals made similar such structures, if indeed Neanderthals constructed it.

Unless Neanderthals had evolved physiological resistance to cold no other primates possess, they had some form of clothing (Gilligan 2010) and used fire. It is unlikely they had fur, for those tissues would reduce the skin surface area available for sweat glands, a necessary feature for large hominins with high activity levels. Wear traces similar to those on modern-day stone tools used to scrape animal hides (presumably to turn them into leather) appear on some tools from Neanderthal sites, but this is about all the direct evidence we have for Neanderthal clothing. Given the range of habitats in which Neanderthals lived between 45 and 300 Ka, the specific forms of their garments almost certainly varied widely. Neanderthal clothing must have covered those parts of the body through which humans in cold conditions lose most of their body heat to convection (contact with cold air), namely their head, neck, shoulders, forearms, hands, lower legs, and feet. They might also have carried about reed mats or larger animal skins upon which to sleep and thereby minimize heat loss to conduction (prolonged contact with cold surfaces).

Archaeologists have long debated whether or not Neanderthals made fire, as opposed to capturing, transporting, and using natural fires (Roebroeks and Villa 2011; Dibble et al. 2017). The current consensus holds that Neanderthals both made and used fire, though they may have made and used it differently from early humans.[10] Neanderthals' hearths may not have been as archaeologically conspicuous and enduring social hubs as some ethnographic human hearths. Rather, they might have been short-lived "survival fires," like the one in Jack London's 1908 short story "To Build a Fire." Neanderthals and older hominins might even have dispersed their hearth ashes to warm themselves by sleeping on them, deliberately minimizing their "fire footprint," to avoid attracting predators (including other hominins), and to prevent fire from spreading uncontrollably. That the better bushcraft/survival guides also recommend doing these things suggests they are all reasonable and intelligent things to do (Kochanski 1987: 47).

If one assumes the most widespread fire-making methods among living humans are the most evolutionarily ancient ones, then Neanderthals probably used some wood-on-wood friction-based techniques. However, the recent discovery of Neanderthal handaxes damaged from use as "strike-a-lights" (Sorensen et al. 2018) suggests Neanderthals also made fire using collision products (aka "flint and steel" or, in this case, flint and iron pyrite or marcasite).

The archaeological record points to few obvious differences between Neanderthal and Ancient Africans' and First Asians' strategies for thermoregulation, though Neanderthals probably endured more encounters with potentially lethal cold than Ancient Africans did.

Hydration

Unlike early humans who lived in habitats ranging from subtropical deserts to jungles, Neanderthals mostly lived in cold and dry habitats. Most of their fossil and archaeological sites are located near water sources of one kind or another. One assumes Neanderthals drank water from clean surface occurrences and that they excavated for water when necessary. Assuming they had fire at their disposal, they may also have obtained water by melting ice and snow.

---

[10] As University of Tübingen (Germany) Professor Nicholas Conard put it, "All those burnt bones from Neanderthal sites didn't result from spontaneous combustion" (personal communication, 2020).

The only difference in evidence for Neanderthal and early human strategies for hydration appears to be that some Ancient Africans used ostrich eggs as canteens to transport water.

Nutrition

Neanderthals had differing nutritional needs from recent humans. Living humans require about 2,000–2,500 calories per day, of which our large and energetically costly brains alone consume around 400–500 calories. Estimates of Neanderthal caloric requirements based on their body shapes and temperatures prevailing where they lived suggest they needed considerably more calories per day than humans do (Froehle and Churchill 2009; Sorensen 2009). Daily, Neanderthals needed 3,100–4,500 calories; pregnant or lactating females would have needed 5,500 calories daily, roughly the equivalent of ten McDonald's Big Mac sandwiches. Unsurprisingly, Neanderthal teeth often preserve "Harris lines," pathologies in enamel formation indicating severe nutritional stress during childhood (Molnar and Molnar 1985; Smith et al. 2018). We do not know much, if anything, about what Neanderthals thought, but we can be confident that they were often hungry and that they thought about food a lot.

What did Neanderthals eat? The larger animal bones at Neanderthal cave sites often seem a representative "grab bag" of whatever species were present in the area. That is, very large animals (mammoth, rhino) are uncommon, while smaller species (ibex, boar, and various sorts of deer) are more common. Larger animal remains often include aurochs (wild cattle), wisent (European bison), horses, and reindeer. Gazelle often appear at Southwest Asian sites. Carnivore remains are uncommon except in places where Neanderthals and carnivores used the same sites as shelters at different times. Such Neanderthal/carnivore "condominium time share" site use may explains finds of cave bear (*Ursus spelaeus*) remains at some sites, though a few Alpine sites preserve evidence suggesting Neanderthals attacked hibernating bears in their dens (Tillet 1996). Other than in the particular animals involved, which reflect geography rather than dietary choices, Neanderthals' zooarchaeological record for land mammal exploitation does not differ all that much from early humans' zooarchaeological record. Faunal remains are rarely preserved at Neanderthal open-air sites, but two sites in the Levant, Nesher Ramla and Biqat Quneitra, show contrasting patterns. At Nesher Ramla (Israel, 120–140 Ka) hominins brought animal bones back to a shallow depression they apparently used as a habitation site (Zaidner et al. 2021). At Biqat Quneitra (Israel, ca. 65 Ka) hominins hunted and scavenged along the shore of a large freshwater pond (Goren-Inbar 1990). Archaeologists assume the hominins associated with these sites were Neanderthals, but humans were also in the region at around the time.

Both Neanderthals and early humans consumed plant foods, including cooked starches (Fellows Yates et al. 2021), but plant foods were fewer and scarcer in Neanderthal country's colder and driers habitats than in the warmer and more humid tropical habitats in which early humans lived. Unsurprisingly, wear patterns on Neanderthal teeth show they depended more on animal food sources in their more northern habitats and more on plant foods in the southern parts of their range (El Zaatari et al. 2011).

Persistent hunger in cold habitats may explain occasional evidence of cannibalism among Neanderthals. Neanderthal fossils from Moula-Guercey (France, 100 Ka) show breakage and cut marks similar to those of nonhominin remains (Defleur et al. 1999). A few other sites preserve similar such evidence, which could suggest cannibalism was fairly common, much as it is in many species (Schutt 2017). The ethnographic record provides no evidence whatsoever of human societies practicing "culinary cannibalism" (treating other humans as food) (Arens 1979). Neanderthal cannibalism may have been "survival cannibalism" similar to what sometimes occurs among groups of humans stuck in survival emergencies, such as the 1846–1847 Donner Party in the Sierra Nevada, California (Brown 2015).

Neanderthals appear to have avoided food sources with high "handling costs," those requiring specialized procurement tools, such as spears, nets, traps, or carrying devices, and time-consuming pre-oral food processing, such as seed-grinding or cooking. Both Neanderthals and early humans resided along rivers and coastlines and used near-shore marine resources (Zilhão et al. 2020), but Neanderthals do not seem to have done so to quite the same extent as early humans did in Southern Africa, Sunda, and Wallacea (Marean 2014).

Oddly, considering the amount of nutrients Neanderthals seem to have gathered by preying on large, dangerous terrestrial mammals, little evidence supports the hypothesis that they made and used complex projectile weapons. Though at least some Ancient Africans and First Asians used the bow and arrow before 45 Ka, no evidence for this or other complex projectile weapons (spear-thrower and dart, blowgun, slingstone) appear in Eurasian contexts with Neanderthal remains (Shea and Sisk 2010). The closest things to projectile weapons found with Neanderthal remains or those of their *H. heidelbergensis* precursors are heavy wooden-tipped spears from the Schoeningen and Lehringen sites in Germany (300–337 and 125 Ka, respectively) (Movius 1950; Serangeli and Conard 2015). These long, heavy wooden weapons were either hand-cast spears or thrusting spears, weapons used at close quarters against animals already immobilized one way or another. Alternatively, some of these sticks might have been "snow probes" used to find large animal carcasses buried under snow (Gamble 1987).

Transportation

Whether Neanderthals had watercraft such as rafts or dugout canoes and whether they made and used carrying aids such as wooden bowls or baskets remains unknown, but neither more nor less so than among evidence associated with early humans. Some Neanderthals and some Ancient Africans occasionally gathered shellfish, a task in which recent humans near-universally employ baskets, bags, or some other carrying aids.

Communication

Neanderthals' archaeological record contrasts with Ancient Africans' and First Asians' records in featuring little or no evidence for their using durable artifacts as "social media." A few sites preserve mineral pigments, shell or bone beads, or decorated and/or perforated artifacts that could have been suspended on string, tied to their hair, or sewn onto clothing. Finds of such "candidate" symbolic artifacts exhibit little clear repetitive patterning. Rather, they are idiosyncratic. Most are unique artifacts and/or objects found at one or a few sites close to one another in time and space. Many if not most such finds occur so late in time (ca. 45 Ka) that they could be artifacts early European humans made that became commingled with Neanderthal artifacts in soft cave sediments.

When they used mineral pigments, early humans preferred red-colored minerals, such as red ochre (iron oxide). Red ochre can have a practical use in manufacturing glues (to prevent the glue from fracturing), but in this ochre is not unique; any oxide will work just as well (Wadley et al. 2004). Red ochre turns up from time to time in Neanderthal sites, but Neanderthals do not appear to have collected it systematically or to have used fire to alter its visual qualities as early humans did in South Africa and the Levant. The most plausible evidence for Neanderthal mineral pigment use appears to involve black-colored media, such as manganese oxide. And yet, unlike red ochre, manganese oxide can be used in collision product fire-starting using, and so we cannot rule out a nonsymbolic interpretation of this evidence (Heyes et al. 2016).

It seems vanishingly unlikely that Neanderthals abstained from using artifacts as social media. Indeed, there is evidence that they used perishable media for symbolic purposes. For example, Finlayson (2019) argues that Gibraltar Neanderthals systematically captured corvids (ravens, crows) and broke off their wings to use their black feathers for symbolic purposes. Whether early humans did this, too, remains unknown.

INTERPRETIVE ISSUES ABOUT NEANDERTHALS

Neanderthals' solutions to survival challenges differed from those early humans devised mainly in ways that reflect physiological adaptations to living in extremely cold habitats. Those solutions do not seem to have either added to or failed to use any of the six ancestral survival skills Neanderthals inherited from their *Homo heidelbergensis* ancestors.

Behavioral Differences between Neanderthals and Humans Who Lived before 45 Ka

Archaeological speculation about behavioral differences between Neanderthals and *Homo sapiens* usually focuses on Neanderthals and the humans who replaced them in Western Eurasia after 45 Ka. This work has taken a different approach, comparing evidence associated with Neanderthals and early humans who lived *at the same time as one another*. This comparison suggests we cannot explain Neanderthal versus early human differences in terms of some one specific quality that evolved uniquely among recent humans. Instead, it suggests Neanderthal versus human behavioral differences had more complex underpinnings (see Table 8.2).

Neanderthals had relatively high nutritional requirements (energy budgets) and lived in small groups in persistently cold, dry habitats (Sorenson and Leonard 2001; Churchill 2014). Few of their sites preserve evidence for prolonged habitation. Their default settlement and subsistence strategies appear, for want of a better expression, "dine and dash."

Cold, dry habitats create wide seasonal variation in plant foods, and thus wide seasonal variation in potential animal prey availability. Neanderthals coped with this seasonal resource fluctuation by living in persistently small

TABLE 8.2 *Behavioral differences between Neanderthals and early humans*

	Neanderthal	Humans
Nutritional requirements	Relatively high, because of cold habitats	Relatively low, because of warm habitats
Habitat characteristic	Persistently cold and dry	Wide variation in temperature and humidity
Group size variability	Persistently small	Variable, large or small
Settlement choices	Residential sites in and near ecotones supplied with food transported in bulk from sites dispersed over varying distances	Residential sites along coasts and rivers and other habitats with dense concentrations of renewable high-quality nutrients available nearby
Response to shortfalls of larger game	Residential movements ("dine and dash")	Switch to other small animal and plant food resources ("intensification")
Social media	Lived mostly among social intimates, little need for durable social media	Common encounters with strangers, greater need for durable social media
Reproductive consequence	Slow renewal rates	Rapid renewal rates

groups at residential sites near ecotones, the boundaries between different habitats. Living in ecotones allowed Neanderthals to switch between resources available in different ecozones, such as steppes and woodlands. To retain control and to defer the cost of moving away from these ecotonal sites, some Neanderthals provisioned their longer-term habitation sites with parts of large animals killed at sites dispersed over varying distances in and near the ecotone. Even though hauling pieces of large animals across the landscape incurs energetic costs, large animals yield higher "post-encounter" energetic returns than smaller animals. (Killing a bison yields thousands of times more calories than killing a hare.) Even though smaller animals may be more common locally, harvesting them efficiently and in bulk requires considerable time and energy in advance to prepare specialized tools for capturing and transporting them. Using small animal food sources might have allowed Neanderthals to occasionally aggregate in large numbers, perhaps seasonally, but if they were already living close to the edge of starvation on a regular basis, they simply may not have had the time to invest in technologies (bows, arrows, traps, nets, fishing gear) that allowed them to gather small prey in bulk. Their responses to shortfalls of large game likely involved abandoning residential sites and seeking their fortunes elsewhere. If these assumptions are correct, then Neanderthals lived much of their lives among social intimates. Living among social intimates does not preclude using symbolic artifacts to transmit social messages, but such messages can be redundant with lived experience. If Neanderthals rarely encountered strangers, then they would have had little incentive to divert precious time and energy away from subsistence and toward fabricating durable symbolic artifacts that they rarely needed. On those rare occasions where they needed such symbolic artifacts, they may have devised them on the spot or on an *ad hoc* basis. If so, and inasmuch as anything can be a symbol, then two or more Neanderthal groups living far away from one another would probably not devise identical symbolic artifacts. Indeed, putative Neanderthal symbolic artifacts exhibit precisely such idiosyncratic quality. No two identical such artifacts appear at different sites, much less at sites far apart from one another in time or space (as those such as the *Nassarius* shell beads found with Ancient Africans and First Asians do).

Ancient Africans and First Asians lived in a complex mosaic of habitats with widely variable temperatures and humidity. Many of these habitats were relatively warm and supported greater densities and diversity of plant and animal life. These circumstances may have allowed early humans to live in larger groups, especially near coastlines and rivers, places where there were persistent and renewable dense concentrations of high-quality food sources, such as spawning fish or shellfish beds. If they had relatively lower energetic requirements than Neanderthals, then early humans may have better met their nutritional needs by switching among different locally available plant and smaller animal food resources. The specific sorts of plants and small animals available varied from region to region, and so one thinks early humans had strong incentives to develop subsistence aids that allowed them to harvest a wide range of plant and animal prey, such as spring traps, nets, and the bow and arrow. (One also thinks large wooden bowls or buckets that could be heated to boiling by hot rock–immersion and thereby used to detoxify plant foods, shellfish, and other seafoods, would have been even more useful, but archaeologists have not yet discovered evidence of such devices' use.) Being able to "intensify" by switching from large animal prey to smaller animals and plants might have encouraged early humans to persist in larger numbers around the most favorable residential sites and to treat them as "territories," places to which access is restricted and actively defended. Movements into and out of such sites would have brought early humans into recurring contact with strangers, increasing energetic returns for devising durable symbolic artifacts with widely accepted meanings. Indeed, some of the shell beads Ancient Africans devised have remained intact for nearly 100,000 years.

Migration versus Dispersal

Neanderthals almost certainly engaged in seasonal transhumance, moving between higher and lower elevations or between coast and interior. In doing this, they followed their larger mammal prey, herbivores that moved between seasonally available plant foods. Many recent hunter-gatherers move seasonally, and it seems reasonable to suppose Neanderthals did something similar, although the scale of their seasonal transhumance movements may have differed. The lack of clear evidence for traps, projectile weapons, or storage of any kind (assuming it is real and not just an artifact of poor preservation) suggests Neanderthals required larger territories than recent human hunter-gatherers living under similar conditions.

Is there any evidence that Neanderthals migrated in the larger sense, moving as a large group from one region to another previously uninhabited one? The strongest possible case for such a migration comes from the East Mediterranean Levant, but it is not a very strong case. All but one Levantine Neanderthal fossil, Tabun C1, date to 45–75 Ka. Tabun C1, may date to around 110 Ka, but her position in the Tabun Cave stratigraphy remains unclear. If we allow that Tabun C1's age will never be resolved to everyone's satisfaction and set the fossil aside, then one can make a case for a Neanderthal migration into the Levant around 75 Ka.

The date of 75 Ka coincides closely with the Mount Toba supervolcano eruption (Chapter 7), and it also coincides with an abrupt global shift to colder temperatures during the onset of Marine Isotope Stage 4. Whether or not these two events are related to one another (Rampino and Self 1992), montane Southwest Asia got very cold, very fast. Neanderthals living in Taurus-Zagros mountain foothills might have abandoned the area, relocating south into somewhat warmer habitats in the Levant and the Arabian Peninsula. Is there any evidence for such movements, and if so, does that evidence suggest they were migrations? Put simply, the answer to both questions is no.

Hominins of some sort were living in Anatolia (Turkey and adjacent countries) and the Iranian Plateau before MIS 4, but little or no evidence indicates that they were only Neanderthals. When Neanderthal fossils show up in Levantine caves (Amud, Kebara, Shukbah, Tabun, and elsewhere) they do so along with stone tools virtually identical to those in use in the Levant before 75 Ka. Those stone tools contrast starkly with the lithic artifacts found in montane Western Asian cave sites, such as Karaïn Cave in Turkey before MIS 4 and at younger sites featuring Neanderthal fossils (Lindly 2005). Where did Levantine Neanderthals come from? Nobody knows. We should not reject the hypothesis that the Levant was part of a larger "Neanderthal origination zone" or one of the places our last common ancestor with Neanderthals lived (Hershkovitz et al. 2021).

Neanderthal Extinction

Why are Neanderthals extinct? Paleoanthropologists have an obsession with Neanderthals' demise far out of proportion to their interest in Neanderthal survival. And yet, we are here today, and Neanderthals are not. What explains our divergent evolutionary fates? Was it bad genes or bad luck? Paleoanthropologists have spent more than a century pursuing the "bad genes" argument, that Neanderthal extinction was predictable due to something wrong with them or that they lacked some single specific quality that *Homo sapiens* possessed. None of these "bad genes" arguments withstands either close scrutiny or an encounter with observations other than those that inspired the hypothesis in the first place. Up to 50 Ka, Neanderthals lived a hard-knock life, but they were doing fine. An extraterrestrial visitor would have no basis whatsoever for predicting their imminent extinction.

So, what of bad luck? Might Neanderthals have become extinct because they lived in the wrong place at the wrong time? To keep their extinction in perspective, one has to remember that hominins are tropical animals. Neanderthals lived in the coldest habitats any primate ever occupied during a time of unique and dynamic climate change (Finlayson 2003; Burroughs 2005). Moreover, they had very high nutritional requirements that they satisfied by hunting large prey animals. What they were doing plainly worked well for a very long time under a wide range of conditions. On the other hand, sudden and prolonged drops in temperature would have depressed plant productivity, which in turn reduced herbivore populations, and therefore populations of carnivore and omnivores, such as Neanderthals, who depended on larger animal prey.

The current consensus holds that Neanderthals became extinct throughout their geographic range around 45 Ka (Higham et al. 2014). This widespread and apparently synchronous extinction means that we can reject hypotheses invoking Neanderthals' slowly assimilating into human societies and hypotheses that roving bands of humans systematically exterminated them.[11] Whatever killed off the Neanderthals took place over a vast area simultaneously (on a geological timescale). The most likely such cause for Neanderthal extinction is rapid climate change (Shea 2008b).

The date of 45 Ka coincides with the Heinrich H5 event, an interruption in the North Atlantic thermohaline circulation, the northward flow of warm water from the tropics that keeps Europe warm and humid (Heinrich 1988). During a Heinrich event, icebergs and glacial meltwater flood the North Atlantic, causing the North Atlantic thermohaline circulation to slow. When this happens, Europe freezes.[12] The H5 event appears to have begun rapidly and been especially severe in its effects. When the H5 event occurred, it simply may no longer have been possible for Neanderthals to collect enough energy to reproduce themselves at replacement levels. They had been running as fast as they could for around 200,000 years, but as their habitat got swiftly colder and food suddenly scarcer, Neanderthals could no longer run fast enough. First appearance dates for human fossils in Europe and Asia north of the Levant date to after the H5 event. Neither bad genes nor bad luck did them in, nor was it bad neighbors, but in a nutshell, bad real estate choices: wrong place, wrong time.

SUMMARY

This chapter surveyed the evidence for Neanderthal behavior. It finds no evidence Neanderthals lacked any of the ancestral survival skills. Neanderthals used them differently, most likely as a result of living in small groups in cold habitats and with correspondingly higher individual energetic costs than early humans. Neanderthals dispersed, and they might have migrated seasonally within their habitats, but no evidence shows that they migrated in large groups from one region to another, at least not to the exclusion of competing hypotheses. The most likely cause for Neanderthal extinction was rapid climate change, specifically cooling – essentially the opposite of the climate change problems we now face. Chapter 9 reviews how differently early Northern Eurasian humans coped with the cold habitats of former Neanderthal Country.

---

[11] If modern-day industrial states intent on genocide routinely fail to completely exterminate their targets, then one can scarcely expect Stone Age hunter-gatherers to have done so.
[12] Were such an event to happen today, agriculture would probably be impossible north of the Alps and a dicey proposition in the Mediterranean Basin for centuries, if not millennia.

Box 8.1: *Imagining Neanderthals*

Humans and Neanderthals overlapped with one another in the East Mediterranean Levant for at least 65,000 years (45–110 Ka). Evidence for strict face-to-face contemporaneity between these hominins remains elusive and will probably always remain so. Still, molecular evidence shows that humans interbred with Neanderthals somewhere, and such interbreeding appears vastly more likely to have occurred in Southern Asia than in Europe, where Neanderthals and *Homo sapiens* overlapped more briefly with one another around 45 Ka.

So, how did Neanderthal-human encounters play out? Did they welcome one another as long lost brothers and sisters? Did they treat one another as "eternal enemies," as African lions and hyenas do in competing for the same food sources and territory? Did they more or less ignore one another as some African apes do members of other ape species? Did they even see one another as different, as our use of different names for them implies?

Paleoanthropologists have largely avoided expressing what they think actually happened when Neanderthals and humans met, leaving novelists to explore this issue.[13] Few fictional works envision Neanderthals' behavior as entirely identical to humans in all respects. Many imagine Neanderthals as like us, but missing some essential quality held universally among living humans.

- Neanderthals in William Golding's novel *The Inheritors* (1955) lack the ability to lie.
- Jean Auel's ur-feminist novel *The Clan of the Cave Bear* (1980) envisioned Neanderthals as physically violent, patriarchal, conservative, and tradition-bound.
- Björn Kurtén's *Dance of the Tiger* (1980) and its sequels imagined Neanderthals as "barefoot bush hippies," gentle beings closer to nature than humans, less social, and unlike their human contemporaries unable to lie.
- The female protagonist of Claire Cameron's *The Last Neanderthal* (2017) is tough, self-reliant, and yet humane enough to "adopt" an orphaned human child.

The idea that Neanderthals were in some way utterly different from the humans with whom they were contemporaries owes much to mythology. Early paleoanthropologists envisioned Neanderthals as physically strong but

---

[13] Off the record and after a few drinks at the bar of the hotel hosting their scientific meetings, many paleoanthropologists become far more forthcoming and colorfully expressive on the subject.

Box 8.1: *(cont.)*

unintelligent, living in small groups in the wilderness and who occasionally resorted to either cannibalism or to preying on humans (Trinkaus and Shipman 1993). As H. G. Wells put it in his 1921 short story "The Grisly Folk,":

> Many and obstinate were the duels and battles these two sorts of men fought for this world in that bleak age of the windy steppes, thirty or forty thousand years ago. The two races were intolerable to each other. They both wanted the caves and the banks by the rivers where the big flints were got. They fought over the dead mammoths that had been bogged in the marshes, and over the reindeer stags that had been killed in the rutting season. When a human tribe found signs of the grisly folk near their cave and squatting place, they had perforce to track them down and kill them; their own safety and the safety of their little ones was only to be secured by that killing. The Neandertalers thought the little children of men fair game and pleasant eating.

These visions of Neanderthal life align strikingly well with traditional European folkloric descriptions of trolls, ogres, satyrs, "wild men," and tales of humans' interactions with them. Indeed, Shackley (1986) proposed that such mythological figures are memories of encounters between humans and late-surviving Neanderthals. This is not impossible, but the tens of thousands of years separating Neanderthal fossils' last appearance dates in Europe from the oldest records of such folkloric creatures suggests this hypothesis is unlikely. One thinks it vastly more likely that early paleoanthropologists and others incorporated folkloric ideas about ogres, trolls, and the like into their reconstructions of Neanderthals.

Last, it bears remembering that calling all Neanderthals "Neanderthals" conceals important behavioral differences among them (Sykes 2020). European Neanderthals living in Northern Europe during MIS 3–5 were probably "thin on the ground" (Churchill 2014), but it is not necessarily true that Neanderthals living elsewhere were similarly sparsely distributed. Warmer Mediterranean coastlines might have supported larger and more densely aggregated Neanderthal populations. Archaeological remains found at Kebara Cave (Israel, 45–65 Ka), for example, preserve complex hearths and abundant remains of small animals consistent with prolonged occupation and a Neanderthal version of subsistence intensification (Lieberman and Shea 1994; Speth and Clark 2006). No similar such evidence has thus far come to light from Neanderthal sites north of the Alps. "One size fits all" might not be the best way to think about Neanderthals (or indeed any hominin).

Box 8.1: *(cont.)*

For thought and discussion: From the 1960s onward, paleoanthropologists began accepting Neanderthals as human ancestors (Trinkaus and Shipman 1993). During that period, reconstructions of Neanderthals portray them less and less along the lines that H. G. Wells imagined in *"the Grisly Folk"* and instead more like humans but lacking some essential quality that we possess, such as spoken language, complex thinking, or some other universal human behavior. If we accept that evolution never stops, it follows that Neanderthals did not simply stop evolving after our evolutionary lineages diverged around half a million years ago. Not all the differences they evolved were necessarily inferior to those evolved by early humans. Can we imagine ways in which Neanderthals' solutions to survival challenges could have been equal or superior to those Ancient Africans and First Asians practiced?

CHAPTER 9

GOING NORTH

Early Eurasians

This chapter reviews how humans settled Northern Eurasia between 12 and 45 Ka, comparing their survival strategies with those that Neanderthals deployed under similar circumstances. Both hominins shared the same suite of ancestral survival skills, but they used them differently and in distinctive ways. Humans devised calorie-conserving superior insulation from cold (clothing, artificial shelters) and innovative strategies for extracting calories from landscapes lacking sufficient plant foods. They used artifacts as "social media" to create and maintain extensive alliance networks, a strategy that resonates with contemporary audiences but also one with deep roots among ancestral survival skills.

GEOGRAPHY: NORTHERN EURASIA AFTER 45 KA

"Northern Eurasia" encompasses Europe and Asia north of the Alps-Himalayas as well as Europe's Mediterranean watershed. This vast region included most of former Neanderthal country (Chapter 8) as well as colder and drier parts of Siberia in which Neanderthals do not seem to have gained an enduring foothold. And yet Northern Eurasia is not really that big and those parts of it capable of supporting human life during Later Pleistocene times were even smaller.[1] Although some parts of eastern China were sometimes more like Sunda (Chapter 7), this work treats them together with Northern Eurasia (Figures 9.1 and 9.2). This chapter uses the term, Early Eurasians, for the humans who lived in this region ca. 12–45 Ka, rather than the older term, "Cro-Magnons."[2]

---

[1] The Mercator projection effect exaggerates Scandinavia's and Siberia's size.
[2] Nineteenth-century paleoanthropologists called early European humans "Cro-Magnons," after the French Cave at which their remains first came to light in 1868. One still sees that term, from time to time in popular media (Fagan 2011; Holliday 2023), but less often in the professional scientific literature.

Geography: Northern Eurasia after 45 Ka 181

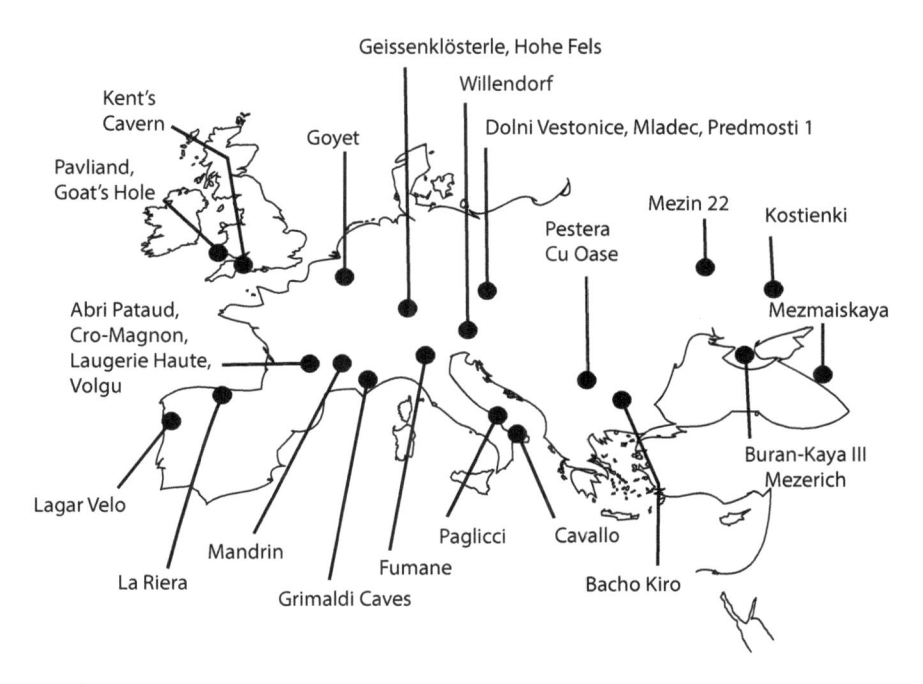

Figure 9.1 Map of Europe showing important Early Eurasian sites. © John J. Shea.

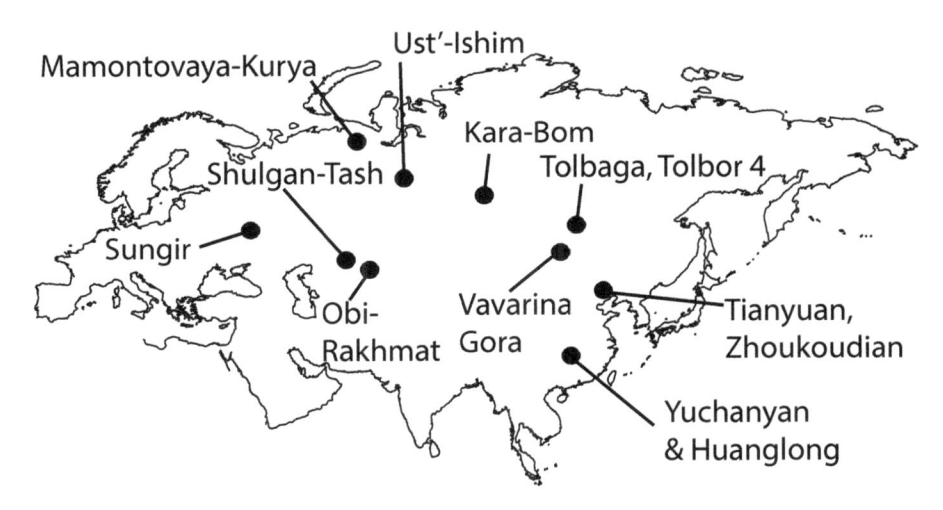

Figure 9.2 Map of Northern Eurasia showing important Early Eurasian sites. © John J. Shea.

Humans arrived in Northern Eurasia during Marine Isotope Stage 3 (29–57 Ka), also known as the "Interpleniglacial." MIS 3 was a cold period with wide and short-term climatic variability leading up to MIS 2 (12–29 Ka), the Last Glacial Maximum (LGM). During the LGM glaciers covered Scandinavia, northern Germany, Poland, the Baltic States, and much of Russia and

Siberia. Lowered sea levels conjoined Britain and Japan to mainland Eurasia. It was so cold that reindeer and musk oxen appeared at LGM sites in Britain and France, places formerly home to forest elephants and hippos.

Interpleniglacial Northern Eurasia was similar to that in which Neanderthals lived previously, but it was also becoming different, and in important ways. During most of the time Neanderthals spent in Northern Eurasia the region was cooling in fits and starts toward brief periods of peak glacial conditions and shorter, warm interglacial conditions. Humans arrived in a Northern Asia that already cooled and remained so for tens of thousands of years. Between 12 and 45 Ka much of Northern Eurasia was largely treeless other than in sheltered river valleys. Seasonal variation in snow cover and plant growth likely encouraged long-distance seasonal migrations among larger herbivores, such as reindeer, bison, horses, and mammoth.

Early Eurasians encountered many large mammals with which their First Asian ancestors had much previous experience. These included aurochs (wild cattle), ibex, equids (horses, wild asses), wild boar, and various cervids (red, fallow, and roe deer). Others, such as reindeer, musk ox, European bison, mammoth, steppe ("woolly") rhino, and cave bear, were novelties. The carnivores with whom Early Eurasians competed for these herbivores' carcasses included hyena, lion, leopard, brown bear, and *Homotherium*, a large (190 kg/ 420 lb) saber-toothed lion.

For all but the very coldest periods, Neanderthals enjoyed a landscape with considerable vegetation, woodland and grasslands arrayed in complex combinations. Early Eurasians, in contrast, inhabited a landscape in which wood was so scarce that in Eastern Europe, Early Eurasians burned bones for fuel and used mammoth bones in place of wood as architectural materials.

Extreme cold curtailed Early Eurasians' access to the many sorts of plant foods available in temperate woodlands and along rivers in boreal forests that sustained Neanderthals. Nudged in the direction of increased carnivory, Early Eurasian humans had to either move their short-term residential sites often or supply prolonged habitation sites with food gathered elsewhere and transported in bulk. (Most likely, their settlement patterns combined both strategies as circumstances allowed.)

Conditions Affecting Population Movements

In Northern Eurasia, Early Eurasians encountered a narrow (north-south) but wide (east-west) corridor wedged between ice sheets that extended south from the Arctic Ocean onto continental land mass and montane glaciers stretching northward from the Alps-Himalayas. Once humans figured out how to survive in such Mammoth Steppe habitats anywhere, they could have swiftly dispersed latitudinally from one of these corridors to the other. Radiocarbon and other

Early Eurasian Fossils 183

dates suggest they did just this. Consistent with such a rapid-dispersal hypothesis, dated archaeological first appearances of either Early Eurasian fossils and/or their associated archaeological remains show little or no clear north-south or east-west geographic trend.

During the LGM, humans seem to have largely abandoned much of the Northern European plain, Siberia, and higher elevations along the Alps-Himalayas. One has to hedge on this hypothesis a bit, because glacial meltwater scoured lower elevations along rivers, those very parts of the landscape that continued to offer food and fuel resources during colder periods.

Deglaciation began in earnest around 15 Ka, until the "brief" (on a geological timescale) return to colder conditions during the Younger Dryas Event, 11.7–12.5 Ka. After this point, Northern Eurasia warmed. Woodlands and forests expanded as the former Mammoth Steppe and its more cold-tolerant flora and fauna retreated northward. Some of Early Eurasians' descendants, no doubt, swiftly followed them into modern-day Scandinavia and Siberia, while others remained in place, adapting as forests and other life returned to a warming postglacial world.

IMPORTANT EARLY EURASIAN PALEOANTHROPOLOGICAL SITES

Table 9.1 lists important Early Eurasian paleoanthropological sites. More so than for earlier periods, archaeologists' attribution of particular sites to *Homo sapiens* often depends on assumptions about the authorship of certain named stone tool industries. Therefore, Table 9.1 also indicates whether or not human fossils appear at these sites.

EARLY EURASIAN FOSSILS

Western European evidence dominates our understanding of Early Eurasians and their behavior. This is not because we know this evidence is broadly representative of Early Eurasian adaptations. Mirroring the relationship between the Levant and Southern Asia (Chapter 6), it is because archaeologists have excavated more Early Eurasian sites in Western Europe for a longer time than anywhere else.

The easternmost Early Eurasian fossils come from the Upper Cave at Zhoukoudian (34–35 Ka) and Tianyuan Cave (39–42 Ka), both in China, near Beijing. The westernmost Early Eurasian fossils come from Lagar Velho (Portugal, 26 Ka). The northernmost fossils come from Paviland Cave (England, 33 Ka). Various sites in Spain, Italy, Bulgaria, and Iraq compete for the southernmost Early Eurasian fossils. The oldest European Early Eurasian fossils are those from Pestera Cu Oase (Romania, 37–42 Ka) and Bacho Kiro (Bulgaria, 44–47 Ka). Early Eurasian fossils older than 36 Ka mostly

TABLE 9.1 *Important Early Eurasian paleoanthropological sites*

Site	Date (Ka)	Human fossils?	Comment
Abri Pataud (France)	20–35	Yes	Rich and well-documented sequence of rock-shelter occupations
Bacho Kiro (Bulgaria)	44–47	Yes	Early Eurasian fossil site
Buran-Kaya III (Crimea, Ukraine)	36–39	Yes	Rich archaeological deposits
Cro-Magnon (France)	28	Yes	Site where the original "Cro-Magnon" fossils were excavated in 1868
Denisova Cave (Russia)	35–> 50	Yes	Denisovan fossils, archaeological remains
Dolni Vestonice (Czech Republic)	31	Yes	Burials, multiseasonal occupations, architecture, ceramic pyrotechnology, possible evidence for wolf domestication
Fumane Cave (Italy))	39–41	Yes	Mediterranean Early Eurasian site
Geissenklösterle (Germany)	42–44		Well-documented sequence of Early Eurasian cave occupations
Goat's Hole Cave (England)	33–34,	Yes	Burial with red ochre
Goyet Cave (Belgium)	35–37	Yes	Burials, possible remains of dog
Grimaldi Caves (Monaco)	> 30?	Yes	Includes Grotte dei Fanciulli, Barma Grande; burials with grave goods, including children, indicates ascribed status
Grotta de Cavallo (Italy)	44–45	Yes	Shell beads, isolated hominin teeth
Hohe Fels (Germany)	35–42		Well-documented sequence of Early Eurasian cave occupations, bone sculpture, ivory flutes
Huanglong Cave (China)	34–44	Yes	Isolated teeth
Kara-Bom (Russia)	30–50		Shows Early Eurasians in Northern Asia
Kent's Cavern (England)	41–45	Yes	Early Eurasian fossil site
Kostienki Site Complex (Russia)	> 26–44	Yes	Rich group of Early Eurasian open-air occupations (Sites 1, 12, 14, 15, and 17); possible dog remains
Lagar Velho (Portugal)	26	Yes	Early Eurasian fossil site
Laugerie Haute (France)			Well-documented sequence of Early Eurasian cave occupations
Mamontovaya-Kurya (Russia)	44		Site located in Arctic Circle shows Early Eurasian cold tolerance
Mandrin Cave (France)	52–57	Yes	Very early European site, human teeth fragments
Mezerich (Ukraine)	14–15		Mammoth bone used as architectural material
Mezin 22 (Ukraine)	24		Mammoth bone used as architectural material

(continued)

TABLE 9.1 (continued)

Site	Date (Ka)	Human fossils?	Comment
Mezmaiskaya Cave (Russia)	37–38		Early presumed Early Eurasian site in Caucasus
Mladec Cave (Czech Republic)	28–34	Yes	Early Eurasian fossils
Obi-Rakhmat (Uzbekistan)	36–49	Yes	Early Eurasian fossils
Paglicci Cave (Italy)	32–33	Yes	Early Eurasian fossils
Paviland Cave (England)	33	Yes	Northernmost Early Eurasian fossil site
Pestera Cu Oase (Romania)	37–42	Yes	Early Eurasian fossil site
Predmosti 1 (Czech Republic)	31	Yes	Early Eurasian fossils, burials, possible dog remains
La Riera Rockshelter (Spain)	13–20		Rich and well-documented sequence of rock-shelter occupations
Shulgan-Tash (Kapova) Cave (Russia)	15–36		Eastern example of cave art
Sungir (Russia)	34–35	Yes	Burials of children, adult with ochre, ivory beads, other grave goods
Tianyuan Cave (China)	39–42	Yes	Eastern Early Eurasian fossil site
Tolbaga (Siberia, Russia)	30–43		Shows Early Eurasians in Northern Asia, near Lake Baikal; artworks, storage pits, architecture
Tolbor 4 (Mongolia)	> 42		Shows Early Eurasians in Northern Asia
Ust'-Ishim (western Siberia, Russia)	43–47	Yes	Siberian site shows Early Eurasian cold adaptations
Vavarina Gora (Siberia, Russia)	31–42		Storage pits, remains of large architectural structure
Volgü (France)	18–22		Long, thin "Solutrean" points examples of "extreme flintknapping"
Willendorf (Austria)	44		Early Eurasian occupations, "Venus" figure
Yuchanyan Cave (China)	15–18		Ceramic vessels
Zhoukoudian Upper Cave (China)	34–35	Yes	Easternmost Early Eurasian fossil site

Note: Dates for these sites are in calibrated radiocarbon years, as given in Hoffecker (2017).

consist of isolated teeth or other fragmentary bones. After 36 Ka, *Homo sapiens* fossils appear more regularly and include burials (complete skeletons whose bones retain anatomical articulation). Dolni Vestonice (Czech Republic, 31 Ka) and the Balzi Rossi (aka Grimaldi) Caves in Monaco (Grotte dei Fanciulli, Barma Grande) preserve an especially rich sample of such burials dating to

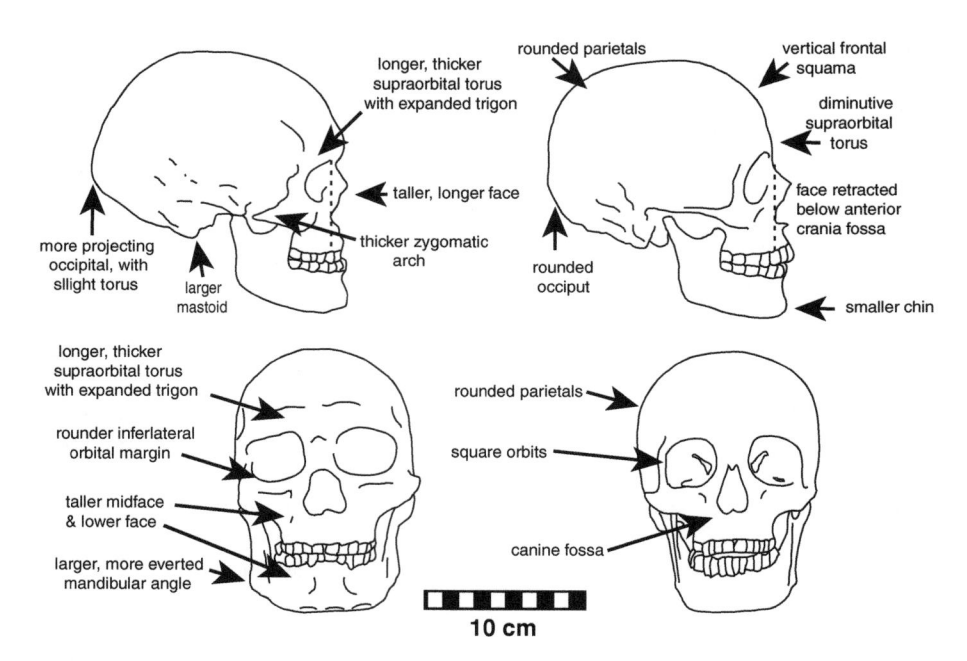

Figure 9.3 Comparison of Early Eurasian human skull (left, Zhoukoudian Upper Cave 101) with recent (Holocene-age) human skull (right). Adapted from D. Lieberman (2011: figure 13.7).

around 30 Ka. Grave goods ("mortuary furniture") accompany many of these fossils. One would naturally expect richer evidence from more recent contexts due simply to geological attrition, but it is also possible that formal mortuary practices became more common after 36 Ka. Alternatively, extreme cold conditions during MIS 2 and 3 may have led to more prolonged occupations that prevented carnivores from disturbing bodies buried in shallow pits.

Early Eurasian fossils feature our species' distinctive chin, high forehead, globular cranial vault, and orthognathic face (Figure 9.3). At 1,514 cubic centimeters on average, their brains were a bit larger than the living human average, 1,350 cubic centimeters. Early Eurasian limb bones differ from those of living industrial/agricultural humans mainly in greater robusticity (thicker cortical bone, larger joint articulation surfaces). Older (MIS 3) Early Eurasian fossils are relatively tall (men 1.8 m, women 1.6 m, on average, or 5 ft 9 in and 5 ft 2 in, respectively). Pre-LGM fossils retain Ancient Africans "heat-adapted" body shape of narrow hips and long limbs. Younger fossils are shorter and stockier, suggesting that extreme cold conditions during MIS 2 had begun overwhelming Early Eurasians' cultural defenses against cold. Artistic reconstructions of Early Eurasians often show people who look like living Northern or Central Europeans (pale skin, moderately curled hair, blue eyes). Studies of aDNA show they more closely resembled living Northern Africans and Asians in having darker skin and more variable eye color.

EARLY EURASIAN ARCHAEOLOGY

Though this work has tried to avoid invoking named stone tool industries, these terms are so deeply embedded in Early Eurasian paleoanthropology that one cannot avoid mentioning them. For evidence associated with Early Eurasians, archaeologists use the term "Aurignacian," a stone tool industry named after a French commune (village) in the Haute Garonne region where excavations during the 1860s uncovered evidence of Early Eurasians' activities. The term has since come to be applied more widely, to evidence from Central and Eastern Europe, the Levant, and Northern Asia. That archaeologists apply the term "Aurignacian" so widely may reflect the history of research and Western Europe's disproportionate influence on prehistoric archaeology in other regions. On the other hand, archaeological assemblages from these regions dating to between 30 and 45 Ka share some distinctive similarities in stoneworking and other artifact designs. We cannot reject the hypothesis than Early Eurasians maintained continent-spanning networks along which flowed specific ideas about artifact designs and other cultural practices in much the same way Ancient Africans and First Asians did (see also Chapter 10's discussion of the North American Clovis phenomenon).

Nineteenth- and early 20th-century investigations of Early Eurasian archaeology focused on caves, rock shelters, and a few open-air sites in southern France and northern Spain dating between 15 and 35 Ka (Laville et al. 1980). Unfortunately, 19th- and early 20th-century excavation methods missed much. Excavators routinely discarded unretouched stone tools and nonhuman fossils. More recently excavated sites that provide a more complete picture of Early Eurasian archaeology include Abri Pataud (France, 20–35 Ka), Dolni Vestonice (Czech Republic, 31 Ka), Hohe Fels (Germany, 35–42 Ka), La Riera Rockshelter (Spain, 13–20 Ka), the Kostienki Site Complex (Russia, > 26–44 Ka), and Yuchanyan Cave (China, 15–18 Ka).

Stone Tools

Many of the same sorts of stone tools and stoneworking strategies Neanderthals employed continue among Early Eurasians' archaeological record.[3] Figure 9.4 shows examples of Early Eurasians' stone tools and other artifacts that differ from those found with Neanderthals.

---

[3] Unhelpfully, archaeologists use different systematics (classifications and measurements) for early Eurasian and Neanderthal evidence (that from the Middle and Upper Paleolithic periods, respectively). This creates the appearance of a sharp break in the paleoanthropological record for Northern Eurasia and the Mediterranean Basin. There may well have been such a sharp break in human occupation, for after all, Neanderthals became extinct around this time; nevertheless, differences in archaeological systematics may make that break appear sharper and more all-encompassing than it actually was.

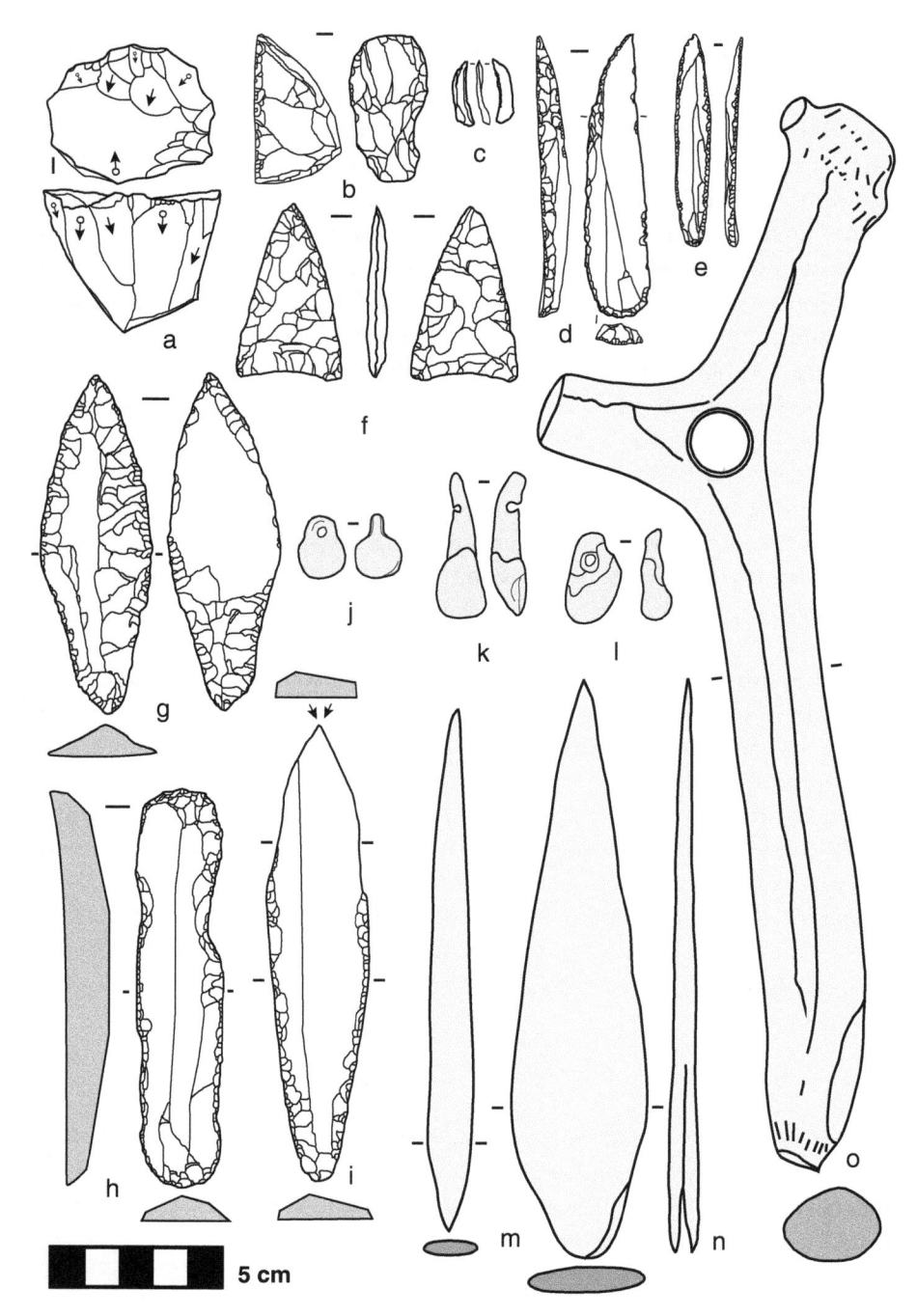

Figure 9.4 Early Eurasian stone tools and other artifacts. (a) Prismatic blade core, (b) carinated scraper/core, (c) bladelet (struck from carinated scraper/core, (d) blacked blade, (e) backed bladelet, (f) concave-based foliate point, (g) tanged piece, (h) endscraper, (i) burin (j) "basket" bead, (k) and (l) perforated teeth, (m) conical-based bone (antler) point, (n) split-based bone (antler) point, (o) perforated and carved antler *baton de commandment*. Sources: Shea (2017b), Conard (2006), Cheynier (1958) (m) and (n), Rigaud (2001) (o). © John J. Shea.

Some of the most obvious ways in which Early Eurasian stoneworking differed from Neanderthal stoneworking include the following:

- Early Eurasians rarely made large or heavy long core tools (LCTs).
- They brought stone to habitation sites from greater distances than Neanderthals did.
- Early Eurasians made more prismatic blade cores (elongated unifacial hierarchical cores [UHCs]) and fewer bifacial hierarchical cores (BHCs). Neanderthals' choices among core-reduction strategies show the opposite pattern (more BHCs, fewer UHCs).
- Many more artifacts feature retouch patterns and wear traces, showing they were attached to handles. Most notable among these are various kinds of "points," long, narrow pieces with convergent retouch at one or both ends and/or tangs. Many such points preserve damage, suggesting use as projectile weapon tips or barbs.
- The retouched pieces Early Eurasians made include elongated flakes (prismatic blades) retouched at their end ("endscrapers"). Some of these endscrapers are relatively small and may be cores from which stoneworkers detached small prismatic blades ("bladelets").
- Burins and backed/truncated pieces commonly appear, and these are smaller, thinner, lighter, and usually far more numerous than those Neanderthals made. Some such burins grade into UHCs and cores-on-flakes.

Early Eurasian stoneworking and other aspects of their material culture, such as carved bone tools and personal adornments, show complex regional and chronological patterning (Larsen-Peterkin 1993; Straus 1995; Vanhaeren and d'Errico 2006). That is, some artifacts occur in one region, but not in neighboring regions at the same time. For example, some older assemblages from Northern Central and Eastern Europe preserve relatively large foliate points, but otherwise these artifacts are uncommon until around the LGM (MIS 2). Then, between 17 and 22 Ka, "Solutrean" (a stone tool industry) assemblages from Western Europe feature many foliate points of widely variable sizes (Smith 1964). After the LGM, foliate points become uncommon again. Unlike groupings of Neanderthal artifact-types, which differ little from one another over tens of thousands of years or longer, specific combinations of Early Eurasian artifacts change and vary recognizably over a few thousand of years. Such variation more closely resembles variability among the stone tools and other artifacts that recent human hunter-gatherers used.

Bone Tools and Other Artifacts

Early Eurasians made extensive use of bone, antler, and ivory (hereafter "bone") as tool materials. In addition to shaping bone tools by fracture, as Neanderthals and earlier hominins did, Early Eurasians also carved, drilled, and abraded bone. Some individual northern Eurasian sites dating to 12–45 Ka preserve more carved bone, antler, and ivory tools than archaeologists have found at any African and Eurasian sites dating to more than 12 Ka. Early Eurasian bone artifacts include various kinds of carved points, barbed harpoons, perforators (including eyed needles), and flutes, as well as many other artifacts whose purposes remain unknown, though much speculated about.[4] Early Eurasians decorated many of these artifacts with abstract patterns and realistic engravings.

Early Eurasians' rich bone tool record is, in part, a result of geography. Bone, antler, and ivory preserve better and longer in cold, dry habitats than in hot, humid ones. Even today, Siberians routinely find Pleistocene mammoth ivory so well preserved that sculptors carve it into jewelry or other artifacts. Neither African nor Southern Asian Pleistocene-age ivory preserves so well.

Art and Personal Adornment

Early Eurasian archaeological sites preserve evidence for nearly every form of art and personal adornment that early Holocene-age sites do. Mural or wall art ("cave art") occurs as carvings, monochrome and polychrome paintings, and bas-relief sculptures. Motifs range from strikingly realistic depictions of animals to abstract images, such as groups of rectangles, lines and clusters of dots, crisscrossed lines, and hand-prints (both positive imprints and stenciled images). Sculptures that combine human and animal motifs, such as the "lion-man" at Höhenstadel (Germany, 31–45 Ka), the "bird-man" at Lascaux Cave (France, 16 Ka), and the "sorcerer" (a human figure with antlers) at Trois Frères Cave (France, 15 Ka), express visual metaphors whose meanings are lost to time.

Though since its earliest recognition as "the childhood of art, but not the art of children" (de Mortillet 1877) archaeologists have tried to arranged cave art into some form of developmental sequence (simple to complex or vice versa) (Bahn 2016). These "culture evolutionary" models find little support among contemporary scholars of the phenomenon. That cave art appears fully formed,

---

[4] For example, 20- to 30-mm-long pieces of antler with a 2-cm hole drilled in one end (see Figure 9.4). Early archaeologists called such artifacts *batons de commandment* (French, "stick of command"), implying they were like 19th-century royal scepters or military commanders' "swagger sticks." Why small groups of ostensibly egalitarian hunter-gatherers would need such durable symbols of authority remains something of a puzzle. Hypotheses concerning alternative mechanical functions include "shaft-straighteners" (levers for straightening projectile weapons' wooden shafts), spindles used to make cordage, and spear-throwers used with straps of leather wrapped around spear-thrower dart shafts that put a spin on the missiles (Rigaud 2001). A former Stony Brook student suggested (aloud in class, of course) that these artifacts might have been handles for leather-strap whips used in, as she put it, darkly, "ceremonies."

complex, in so many media over tens of thousands of years suggests both that it expresses cultural practices with deep evolutionary roots among Early Eurasians' ancestors and that it served many purposes over its > 30,000-year-long run. No evidence supports hypotheses tracing cave art's origins to Neanderthals. Those few occurrences putatively assigning Neanderthal authorship to one or another art site all cluster around first appearance dates for stone tool industries associated with human fossils. No significantly older such artworks appear in Neanderthals' impressively long archaeological record.

Evidence for the use of mineral pigments, especially red ochre/iron oxide, occurs all over northern Eurasia between 12 and 45 Ka. Such pigments are uncommon in Neanderthal sites.

Perforated animal teeth, bones, stones, and seashells occur at sites ranging from Lagar Velho (Portugal, 26 Ka) to Zhoukoudian Upper Cave (China, 34–35 Ka). Three burials at Sungir (Russia, 34–35 Ka) contain more than 10,000 ivory beads. Bead fragments occur at many Early Eurasian sites, suggesting these artifacts were not just worn as pendants but also sewn onto clothing or suspended from hair. A few perforated bones grace very late Neanderthal occurrences, but that's about it.

Early Eurasian cave art is concentrated mainly in Western Europe, where deep limestone caves favor its preservation, but enough examples occur in Eastern Europe, such as Shulgan-Tash (Kapova) Cave (Russia, 15–36 Ka), to show the practice extended eastward. That portable art, sculptures, decorated artifacts, and mineral pigments appear across Northern Eurasia suggests that gaps in evidence for cave art as likely reflect gaps in the occurrence of caves deep enough to preserve art on their walls rather than actual geographically patterned variation in Early Eurasian art production.

Pyrotechnology

Traces of fire are so common at Early Eurasian sites as to scarcely require comment. If, as Chapter 8 argued, Neanderthals took measures to conceal their "fire footprint" for one reason or another, Early Eurasians, in contrast, were indifferent about this. Several hypotheses about this include the following:

- Destructive wildfires might have been less likely to catch and spread across the largely treeless landscapes Early Eurasians inhabited.
- Equipped with projectile weapons (and possibly wolf-dogs) Early Eurasians could have been less concerned than Neanderthals were about attracting predators to their habitation sites.
- Some of the things humans did using fire, such as bone degreasing and heat-treating flints (discussed below), leave clearer and more distinctive evidence than the ashy sources of heat and light Neanderthals left behind.

- Last, Early Eurasians might have used conspicuous fires and smoke arising from them to signal their presence to other humans in the same area.

Some Early Eurasians seem to have heat-treated flints to improve their fracture qualities. This evidence is especially well documented in Western European contexts dating to the LGM (Schmidt and Morala 2018), but is almost certainly more widespread than this. Evidence from Dolni Vestonice (Czech Republic, 31 Ka) shows Early Eurasians used fire to transform clay into ceramic figurines (Vandiver et al. 1989). In southeastern China, the Yuchanyan Cave (15–18 Ka) preserves evidence that Early Eurasians made ceramic vessels (Boaretto et al. 2009), but pottery is not (yet) known from elsewhere in Northern Eurasia until postglacial times.

Biotechnology: Wolf-Dogs

Domesticated dogs are essentially biotechnology, living beings "intelligently designed" (bred) to help humans do things that would otherwise be difficult (hauling sleds across snow and ice) or impossible (hunting at night). A small but significant number of Early Eurasian sites, such as Goyet Cave (Belgium, 37 Ka), Predmosti 1 (Czech Republic, 31 Ka), and Kostienki Site Complex (Russia, 26–44 Ka), preserve evidence for possibly domesticated wolf-dogs (Shipman 2015). The oldest visibly domesticated dogs date to early Holocene times, but it is possible that like Australian dingoes, early wolf-dogs came and went into "quasi-domestication" again and again until human-dog mutual dependence "locked in" at some later point in time (Shipman 2021). Wild wolves probably avoided close contact with humans, but accumulations of nutrient-rich waste, including human feces, around winter habitation sites might have brought Early Eurasians and wolves into closer and more complex contact than in Southern Asia, where organic waste decomposes more rapidly. This all being said, few issues in Later Pleistocene paleontology are as controversy-wracked as those surrounding dogs versus wolf identifications. Given the tens of thousands of years that separate Later Pleistocene "dogs" and their clearly domesticated Holocene-age counterparts, one must reserve judgment about this issue.

EARLY EURASIANS' SURVIVAL STRATEGIES

First Aid and Medication

Many Early Eurasian fossils are burials. These burials may not be representative of their populations in general. Indeed, their most iconic fossil, Cro-Magnon 1 (France), exhibits a unique bone infection in his mid-facial region. In general, however, skeletal remains of Late Pleistocene Northern Eurasians paint a picture of individuals in good health who lived active lives and who occasionally suffered the kinds of injuries active people incur (Holt and Formicola 2008). A few individuals have healed-over fractures to their limbs. Many teeth preserve enamel hypoplasias that indicate acute food shortages at a young age, but otherwise dental pathologies mainly appear among older individuals with advanced tooth wear. Cranial fractures are distressingly common. In these respects, skeletal evidence for Early Eurasians' health does not differ all that much from skeletons of Ancient Africans and First Asians, or even Neanderthals. We have direct evidence for neither Early Eurasian first aid practices nor medical interventions. Nevertheless, some individuals suffered congenital deformities that required some forms of long-term care, including (for separate individuals) hydrocephaly, dwarfism, and an inherited form of rickets. European Early Eurasians dating to the LGM and afterward show somewhat more skeletal lesions and pathologies than their MIS 3 counterparts (Trinkaus and Svoboda 2005).

Thermoregulation

Early Eurasians developed effective strategies for insulating themselves from cold. Hearths and other evidence for controlled use of fire occurs commonly at Early Eurasian sites. This evidence includes hearths/combustion features, charcoal, burnt bones, and fire-cracked rock, as seen at Abri Pataud (France, 20–35 Ka). Early Eurasians may have used heated rocks for bone degreasing (see below), for roasting food, or to warm people sleeping on top of them. We do not know how Early Eurasians kindled or transported fire. A few perforated artifacts suggest they understood how rotary drilling worked, and rotary drilling is a simple, fast, and effective way of making friction fire today. It enjoys wide use among both ethnographic preindustrial humans and among primitive technology enthusiasts (Hume 2018). Flint and marcasite (iron oxide) artifacts preserving percussion damage show they understood collision-product firemaking, too (Sorensen et al. 2014).

Early Eurasians used caves and rock shelters as earlier humans did, but they also constructed freestanding structures at open-air sites. In Central and Eastern Europe they used mammoth bones as parts of these buildings' foundations, walls, and superstructure (Gladikh et al. 1984; Soffer 1985). The Mezin 22 (Ukraine, 24 Ka) and Mezerich (Ukraine, 14–15 Ka) sites preserve examples of these structures. Reconstructions of these buildings often show them as having been covered with the hides of mammoths or other large mammals. Considering that such hides would take months to make, weigh hundreds of kilograms, and need to be dragged from site to site, it seems at least as likely that Early Eurasians lined these buildings with brush and cut blocks of turf. Neither the African, Southern Eurasian, nor Neanderthal archaeological records preserve similar evidence for such durable and labor-intensive freestanding structures prior to 45 Ka.

Early Eurasians lived in habitats so cold that they could kill an unclothed human in minutes. Carved bone and ivory eyed needles show they made tailored leather garments that created a warm, humid air layer between one's skin and the clothes' inner surfaces. Tailored and waterproofed leather footwear and gloves prevented Early Eurasians from losing heat from their feet and hands, body parts with high ratios of surface to volume. (One suspects, but cannot prove, that they used bird feathers for insulating their clothing.) Stone scrapers worn from working hides appear at nearly every Early Eurasian site, as does red ochre and other minerals recent humans use to preserve leather. We do not know whether Early Eurasians also made clothing from textiles, but textile impressions in clay at Dolni Vestonice (Czech Republic, 31 Ka) suggest they did.

That pre-LGM Early Eurasians retain "tropical" limb proportions suggest they made and used tailored (sewn) clothing with drawstrings or other fasteners that minimized heat loss in the event of punctures or tears. Projecting ethnographic Arctic peoples' garments developed over millennia back into Pleistocene times is probably a mistake, but shared features among such garments (separate pants and shirts, hood with drawstrings, boots and mittens) can provide some notion of how Early Eurasian clothed themselves.

Improved heat retention has potentially huge evolutionary payoffs. Calories retained using more thermally efficient clothing can be redirected to reproduction. Early Eurasian parents could have been among the first Eurasian hominins to not have to worry about their unattended children dying from hypothermia.

Hydration

Like most known Neanderthal sites, Early Eurasians' habitation sites sit close to rivers, springs, and other sources of potable water. Their archaeological record for water use is, unfortunately, as mute as that for earlier periods elsewhere. Early Eurasians do not *appear* to have modified earlier African or Eurasian strategies for obtaining potable water in ways that leave detectable archaeological traces. Inasmuch as Early Eurasians were capable of making and sewing leather, it seems reasonable to envision them making and using lightweight water containers out of animal skins, as many ethnographic and historic groups do.

Nutrition

Popular artworks reconstructing Early Eurasians' life often depict them as specialized reindeer hunters, contrasting them with Neanderthals, who hunted more opportunistically. This is, of course, "archaeo-mythology" – a demonstrably false hypothesis retained due to its enduring presence in popular media. Early Eurasian and Neanderthal sites close to one another in age exhibit few major differences (Chase 1989). Most differences between animal remains at Neanderthal and Early Eurasian sites may reflect differences in the climate and the landscapes surrounding the sites at the times hominins occupied them. Both hominins hunted aurochs, wild boar, horses, and various sorts of deer. Reindeer remains become more common at Early Eurasian sites after MIS 3 and during MIS 2 for the simple reason that during MIS 2–3 Northern Eurasia became ever more like the tundra habitats in which reindeer outcompete other cervids.

One mystery about Early Eurasian foodways (of which there are many) concerns the use of coastal and marine resources. Cold habitats like Northern Eurasia offer rich sources of marine, riverine, and other aquatic foods. These include fish, shellfish, marine mammals, and birds. Often, and in cold seasons, there is more food in the water than on the land nearby. Early Eurasians' artworks depicting seals, salmon, and aquatic birds show they were aware of such potential prey, but their archaeological record preserves little evidence for aquatic food use. If Early Eurasians did not systematically use such aquatic resources, they were unique among hunter-gatherers who lived in cold habitats. This is possible, but one thinks it far more likely that preservation biases prevent us from detecting their subsistence strategies' aquatic components. Recent hunter-gatherers do not generally move the foods they procure along coastlines or in lower river valleys very far inland. (Such food spoils quickly.) The archaeological "fallout" of Early Eurasian aquatic resource use, therefore, may have been lost to postglacial sea-level rise or to glacial meltwater scouring river-edge settlements.

Another mystery about Early Eurasian subsistence concerns hunting weaponry. Throwing sticks, boomerangs, and hand-cast spears are so widespread among ethnographic hunter-gatherers that we assume they are evolutionarily ancient. Cordage would have allowed Early Eurasians to make and use nets, to set up spring traps, even to use fishing line, but we have little direct evidence for these practices.

All but very few recent hunter-gatherers[5] use complex projectile weapons, weapons systems with separate missile and launcher components, such as spear-throwers and darts or the bow and arrow. This suggests such complex

---

[5] Everyone except 19th-century Tasmanians, apparently. In this and many other ways, 19th-century Tasmanians appear anthropological outliers. Some have chalked up this divergence to their long isolation from mainland Australia following postglacial sea-level rise. It seems at least as likely that some of the odd things reported about them, such as their being unable to make fire (Gott 2002), result from ethnographic studies carried out among refugee populations during and after an attempted genocide and massive population losses to disease following contact with European colonists (Henrich 2004).

projectile weapon use is deeply primitive/ancestral, but it remains unclear how widely these weapons were in use among Early Eurasians.

Archaeologists know that some Early Eurasians used spear-throwers, for they have recovered examples of these artifacts carved out of antler. The antiquity of the bow and -arrow, and the question of its use among Early Eurasians, remains very much unsettled. Wear pattern studies and morphological comparisons between ethnographic stone arrow tips and barbs suggest Ancient Africans used bows and arrows more than 65 Ka (Lombard and Shea 2021), long before humans settled Northern Eurasia. On the other hand, bow use in Southern Africa > 65 Ka does not mean that all humans everywhere used the bow and arrow. Aboriginal Australians never adopted the bow and arrow (Chapter 7), and the archaeological consensus holds that bows and arrows appeared in the Americas only after 6 Ka (or less) (Bingham et al. 2013). The oldest-known preserved wooden bows hail from Holmegaard (Germany) and date to early Holocene times, but these are almost certainly not the first bows (Cattelain 1997). Unless Early Eurasians were unlike nearly all recent hunter-gatherers, their food-getting technology included complex combinations of projectile weaponry that varied over time and space.[6] First Asians' archaeological record suggests bows and arrows were in use by at least 40–50 Ka. It would be strange indeed if humans did not bring this versatile technology with them into Northern Eurasia, but on the other hand, Sahulians' ancestors do not appear to have done so.

Concentrations of fire-cracked rocks from Early Eurasian sites may be byproducts of "bone degreasing," extracting fat from animal bones by boiling them. To do this, one fragments the bones, immerses them in a water container, and then raises the water to a boil by adding heated rocks into the water one after another in relay. Fat "migrates" out of the bone, accumulating at the water's surface from which one can collect it after the water cools. Thermal shock from rapid heating and cooling leaves distinctive damage on the fire-cracked rocks thus used. Traces of this practice have not turned up at Neanderthal, First Asian, or Ancient African sites. Thus, it appears to be an Early Eurasian innovation.

Lastly, dogs. If Early Eurasians hunted with dogs or wolf-dogs, then they would have been able to easily capture smaller animal prey, to hunt at night, and to locate and pursue prey animals beyond visual range. They could have used dogs to bring a large animal at bay (immobilize it) and then kill it from a distance

---

[6] Among archaeologists there exists a widespread belief that projectile weapons systems followed a unilinear developmental trajectory, from javelins and other simple hand-launched missiles to spear-thrower and dart to bow and arrow. This assumption appears to have arisen in 19th-century ethnologists' efforts to chart quasi-evolutionary trajectories for changes in technology. The javelins-darts-arrows sequence appears in the order in which first evidence for these weapons appears in Europe (Cattelain 1997), but no anthropological theory justifies extrapolating it wider than this (or even justifies assuming that it is true in Europe).

Early Eurasians' Survival Strategies

by using projectile weapons. This is a big "if," of course, for as noted earlier, identifications of Pleistocene canine fossils as dogs rather than as wolves remain controversial, and framing the matter as dog versus wolf imposes a dichotomy on a complex continuum of morphological and behavioral variability.

Transportation

Ethnographic humans living in tundra, boreal forest, and similar northern habitats employ an impressive array of transport aids, including snowshoes, skates, skis, sleds, and boats. It does not take too much time trudging through even moderately deep snow to realize that increasing the surface area beneath one's feet reduces not only the energetic cost of moving but also the loss of body heat to contact with cold surfaces (conduction). One thinks it likely that both Neanderthals and Early Eurasians made something like snowshoes, perhaps improvised devices, but no physical evidence supports this hypothesis. No evidence supports the hypothesis that there were important differences between Neanderthals' and Early Eurasians' strategies for moving on foot across snow and ice.

Given that boats allow nearly friction-free transport, that wood was scarce on Northern Eurasian landscapes during MIS 2–3, and that Early Eurasians were demonstrably skilled at sewing leather, it seems reasonable to assume they made and used and wooden framed and hide-covered boats, perhaps vessels resembling traditional Inuit kayaks. If they supplied winter residential sites with food in bulk, Early Eurasians must have used sleds. Some archaeologists have proposed that Early Eurasians may have domesticated horses, dogs, or even reindeer to pull sleds, but such proposals remain controversial and a minority position among archaeologists.

Communication

A far stronger case for important and archaeologically detectable differences between Neanderthals and Early Eurasians concerns communications, specifically, Early Eurasians' use of artifacts as "social media." Put simply, the entire inventory of putatively symbolic artifacts associated with Neanderthals would scarcely cover a card table (1.3 × 1.3 m). Early Eurasian symbolic artifacts (mural art, personal adornments, decorated artifacts, etc.) would fill a museum gallery to bursting. Claimed Neanderthal and earlier hominin symbolic artifacts are almost all unique and idiosyncratic finds. Those associated with Early Eurasians include singular finds, too, but many more are artifact-types found at multiple sites across vast areas.

Consider "Venus" figurines. Definitions vary, but most of these artifacts are small (< 20 cm long) figurines or bas-relief carvings that appear represent women with exaggerated breasts and buttocks (Figure 9.5). Their vulva is often

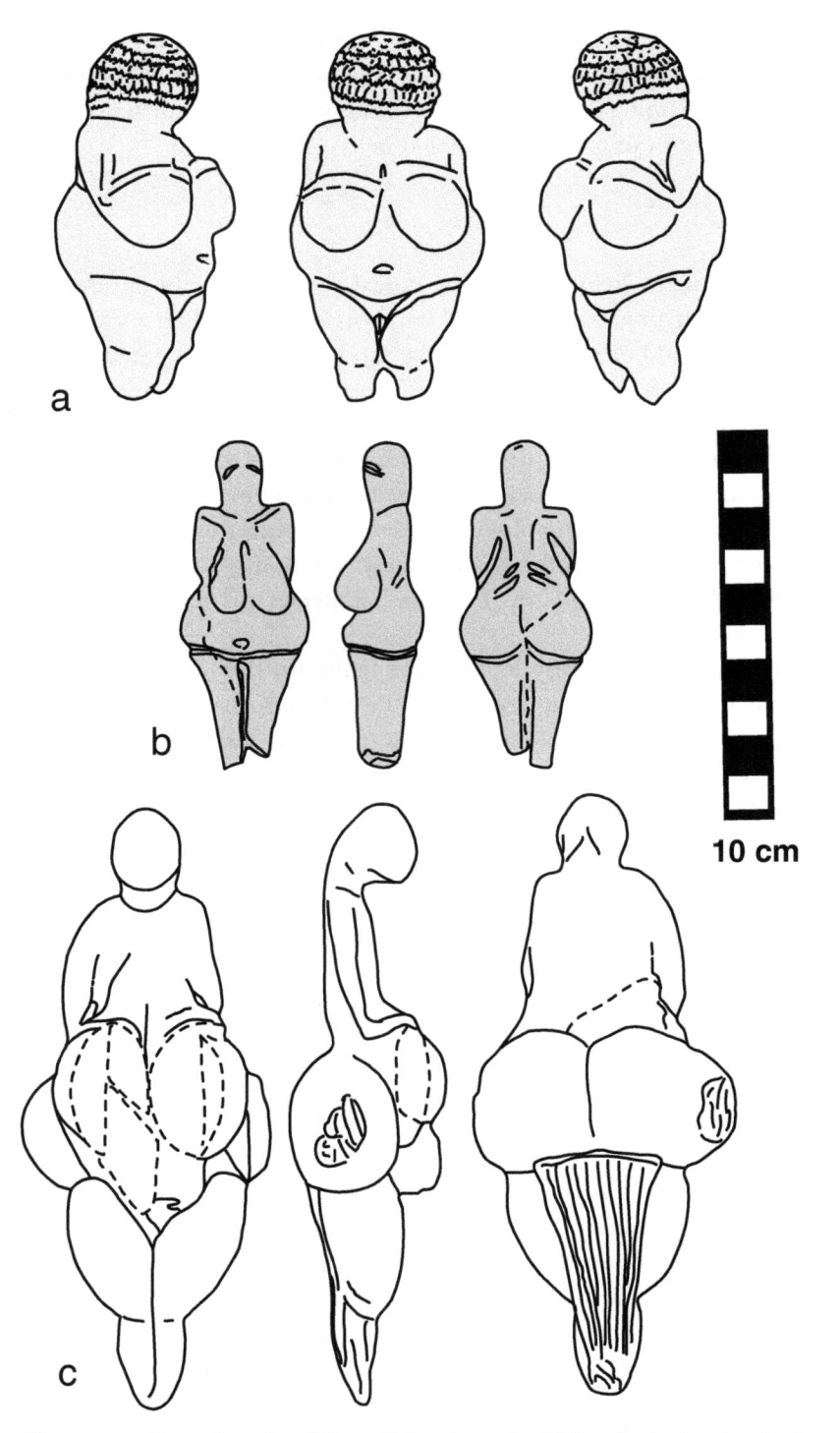

Figure 9.5 Early Eurasian "Venus" figurines. (a) Willendorf, Austria, (b) Lespugue, France, (c) Dolni Vestonice, Czech Republic. © John J. Shea.

show higher and more frontally than among actual women. Their faces and lower limbs (hands/feet) are either blank or lack detail. Most Venus figurines date to around 21–26 Ka and are spread out over the full breadth of Europe for more than 5,000 years. We will never know what these images meant to the people who made them, but their wide and enduring geographic distribution suggest that Early Eurasians maintained shared conventions for encoding their thoughts and beliefs over distances and time periods. (In comparison, not one word written more than a few thousand years ago remains intelligible to all but a miniscule number of archaeological specialists in ancient languages.) Abundant evidence exists for variation and variability among at least Early Eurasian symbolic artifact production and use (d'Errico et al. 2003). Such evidence contrasts starkly with the relatively scarce and idiosyncratic occurrences of claimed Neanderthal and earlier human symbolic artifacts.

All recent humans use clothing and personal adornments to transmit symbolic messages to "strangers," persons other than social intimates who share the same culture (or at least the same links between specific symbols and specific meanings). Artifact-assisted social media messages have less value among social intimates, for whom they are redundant with lived experience. That Early Eurasians made so many of these small and portable symbolic artifacts out of durable materials suggests they encountered strangers more often and that they planned accordingly.

The long-established psychological principle of "in-group favoritism" argues that people are more willing to help, or more generous with donations to, people who show evidence of similar cultural beliefs and practices (Taylor and Doria 1981; Efferson et al. 2008). Using symbolic artifacts to broadcast information (true or false) about one's social identity can ease tensions and encourage cooperation among strangers. Easing tensions and encouraging cooperation among strangers may have helped Early Eurasians build more extensive and more resilient social networks than earlier hominins could. More extensive and resilient social networks would have dispersed risks of subsistence failure broadly across a regional human population, not only ensuring demographic stability and growth, but also a providing greater range of potential social allies and mates. In short, Early Eurasians acted as members of fraternities, sororities, or labor unions, and Neanderthals and early humans as unaffiliated "independents."

INTERPRETIVE ISSUES ABOUT EARLY EURASIANS

Behavioral Differences between Early Eurasians and Neanderthals

Early Eurasians' archaeological record differs both from what Neanderthals left behind and from earlier and contemporary *Homo sapiens* archaeological records elsewhere. Many popular accounts of this evidence focus on Early Eurasians' artworks' undeniably impressive aesthetic qualities (White 1986; Guthrie 2005; Fagan 2011; Bahn 2016). From a "survival archaeology" standpoint, however, the following Early Eurasian innovations stand out:

- Thermoregulation: Superior insulation from cold by using clothing and artificial shelters
- Nutrition: Using complex projectile weapons (and probably traps, too) to extract calories from plant-food-impoverished landscapes
- Communication: Using symbolic artifacts and other "social media" to form extensive alliance networks among populations spread out over vast areas at low population densities.

Did these innovations require additions to ancestral survival skills? No, they did not. Evidence for clothing, artificial shelters, complex projectile weapons, and symbolic artifacts occurs in Africa, Southern Asia, and Sahul long before Early Eurasians moved into Europe and Northern Asia. Early Eurasians possessed the same survival skills as earlier humans living elsewhere. They simply used them differently in habitat-specific ways.

Why Is the Early Eurasians' Archaeological Record So Distinctive?

Historically, archaeologists have seen Early Eurasians' archaeological record as something special, not just a shift in *Homo sapiens*' geographic range but a "human revolution," something evolutionarily divergent from other Pleistocene hominins (Mellars and Stringer 1989; Mellars 1990). Also, and historically, speculation about Neanderthal versus Early Eurasian differences almost inevitably focuses not so much on *whether* Early Eurasians were superior to Neanderthals so much as *how* they were superior to Neanderthals. Much of this "they invented inventing" view of Early Eurasians arises because Early Eurasians left behind impressively elaborate stone and bone tools, personal adornments, and artwork. Why are Early Eurasians' artifacts so "over the top" compared with the artifacts other Pleistocene humans made elsewhere at the same time or earlier?

Superior preservation of organic artifacts in colder habitats certainly plays a role. The wooden artifacts, baskets, cave art, and other things ethnographic humans use worldwide do not appear in the Early Eurasian record, but they are missing (again due to preservation bias) from Ancient Africans' and First Asians' archaeological records. Bone artifacts are sparse in tropical archaeological deposits. These preservation issues create the illusion that Early Eurasian artworks sprung forth, fully formed like Athena from Zeus' forehead. It is vastly more likely they arise from a long-standing human social media strategy that for one reason or another encouraged Early Eurasians to use more durable media than Neanderthals did.

Early Eurasians lived in a colder and more risky Northern Eurasia than the one Neanderthals inhabited. Greater risks at our species' northernmost outposts during the peak of an Ice Age might have nudged them to adopt social strategies to minimize such risks. Any one of us would do the same. Few people pack professional-grade survival gear and tell others our itinerary for a short day hike. Professional explorers and field scientists do so in their work, for they have learned just how fast and unpredictably things can go seriously wrong.

One theme unifying much of Early Eurasians' archaeological record, and one that distinguishes that record from Neanderthal and earlier hominin adaptations, is what one might call greater "peak procedural complexity." A variant of costly signaling – doing things that broadcast one's value as a mate or social ally (Zahavi and Zahavi 1997) – peak procedural complexity refers to complex sets of actions that have to be performed in correct sequence and contingencies, or options to do things differently along the way. Because they are signals, these actions can include both mission-critical and superfluous actions. Not all Neanderthal stoneworking was "quick and dirty," but much of it involves little more than striking a one rock with another repeatedly until one obtains a sharp retouched edge or a small flake suitable for light cutting tasks. Making thin prismatic blades and foliate points, attaching artifacts to handles, carving decorations into bone tools, and drilling holes in ivory and stone beads offer up countless opportunities to do things wrong and wrong in ways that require one to start again from scratch. A few Neanderthal artifacts may exhibit these qualities, too, but examples of such artifacts of peak procedural complexity appear in nearly every Early Eurasian archaeological site. The open-air site of Volgü (France, 17–22 Ka) preserves what is arguably the acme of this "extreme stoneworking," a dozen or more thinned foliate points more than 20 centimeters long, less than a centimeter thick, and made out of heat-treated flint (Schmidt et al. 2018). Clearly, these visibly complex toolmaking strategies were under strong and "directional" selective pressure. That is, there accrued benefits for doing them well and costs for doing them poorly or not at all. Early Eurasian toolmaking seems to have had a more social and "performative" component than Neanderthal or earlier human technological strategies.

No one hypothesis currently "on the table" in prehistoric archaeology explains the totality of evidence for "peak procedural complexity" among Early Eurasian artifacts, but a survival archaeology perspective offers up insights. In learning bushcraft and survival skills, it is not enough to just read about them. To gain expertise, one has to practice. To gain authority, one has to demonstrate competence. Not one of the most successful "bushcraft/survival" school websites lacks video footage and/or photographs of their instructors and students performing the activities those schools teach. If, as their symbolic artifact record suggests, Early Eurasians frequently encountered strangers as they formed and reformed their communities, then requiring strangers, and especially juveniles, to demonstrate competence in stoneworking could have been a way for communities to ensure that those preparing to embark on a hunt or some other risky venture could understand and follow complex instructions.[7] It is not clear that we can test this hypothesis with currently available evidence, but thinking about it may inspire future researchers to seek such evidence. Making prismatic blades and shaping overly large foliate points and symmetrical long core tools might have functioned as "competency test" among earlier human societies in Africa and Asia.

If Early Eurasians did this, then why do archaeologists find so little similar such evidence elsewhere in prehistoric humans' geographic range? The evidence might be there, but archaeologists may not recognize it as such.

Migration versus Dispersal

Does the paleoanthropological evidence support the hypothesis that Early Eurasians migrated? It does not. In the balance, evidence associated with their population movements is consistent with dispersal.

Though colder temperatures' potential for natural refrigeration and the use of smoking to dry and preserve food might have allowed Early Eurasians to store sufficient food to undertake migrations, evidence for storage pits at Early Eurasian sites dates to long after initial human settlement in Northern Eurasia. Storage of smoked meat and dehydrated plants remains a theoretical possibility only. (It would be odd if Early Eurasians did not do these things, but we lack evidence that they did.) A few storage pits grace a few larger Early Eurasian sites, but neither these nor other sites dating 12–45 Ka offer up anything like the abundant evidence of storage pits and ceramic storage vessels found throughout Northern Eurasia since middle Holocene times (< 6 Ka). Lacking evidence for migrations' economic/energetic basis, one has to reserve skepticism about hypotheses invoking migration to explain Early Eurasians' initial settlement of Northern Eurasia.

So, how did they do it? How did Early Eurasians settle Northern Eurasia? They likely moved from Southern Eurasia to Northern Eurasia, by dispersing upriver and over mountain passes, and also by moving along Atlantic and Pacific coastlines. They almost certainly used watercraft to accomplish these things. Their dispersal unfolded swiftly after 45 Ka and in such ways that left no clear trail leading from one source to another destination (Higham et al. 2014). Sites in northern Spain date to roughly the same age as ones in northern China and in Russia. The Campanian Ignimbrite eruption (Italy, ca. 39 Ka) that

---

[7] The writer/director, Albert Hughes, proposed exactly this scenario in his 2018 film, *The Alpha* (Columbia Pictures).

blanketed much of Greece and the Balkans with volcanic ash (Fedele et al. 2004) does not seem to have slowed Early Eurasians down or to have interrupted their settlement of Europe, as one might expect it to have done to large groups of migrating humans depending on stored food supplies.

Individuals or small groups of humans probably moved into the margins of Neanderthal country, infiltrating and assimilating with the indigenous populations (Neanderthals, Denisovans, and anybody else running about) and outcompeting them in a "long game" of sexual selection. Alternatively, in circumstances where Neanderthals and others enjoyed "home court advantage," Early Eurasians could have avoided contact with them until gaining sufficient strength in numbers to overcome any resistance. Neanderthals' and Early Eurasians' archaeological records offer up contrasting pictures of these hominins' "connectedness." Neanderthals appear to have lived in small independent groups. Encounters with others might have been more biological than social, that is, a search for mates rather than for assistance in group foraging activities or for lifelong social allies. After all, this is the primate norm. Encounters for the purposes of coalitionary killing, such as humans and chimpanzee sometimes do, are outliers. On the other hand, no evidence shows that either Neanderthals or Early Eurasians were reflexively hostile to strangers. Late-surviving Neanderthals might have seen Early Eurasians as mates and social allies. Much like Neanderthals, Early Eurasians were probably thin on the ground, too. They might also have welcomed "natives" with deep experience in local habitats as possible mates, valuable social allies, and even as lifelong friends.

That dispersal rather than migration drove the peopling of Northern Eurasia explains archaeologists' persistent failure to find their lithic "trail" stretching from one region to another, clearly, convincingly, and to the exclusion of alternative hypotheses. Nothing in Early Eurasians' archaeological record supports the "Hansel and Gretel Fallacy" – archaeologists' almost certainly wrong assumption that dispersing humans left clear signs of their passage across ancient landscapes in the same way the children in the German folktale left stone pebbles along their path through the woods.

SUMMARY

This chapter has reviewed evidence for Early Eurasian adaptations in Northern Eurasia. Early Eurasians' survival strategies differed from Neanderthals' most obviously in improved thermoregulation, nutrition, and communication. Early Eurasians used ancestral survival skills to extend our species' geographic range into hitherto unoccupied parts of eastern Siberia and beyond. Chapter 10 reviews the evidence for the peopling of a "Brave New World," the Americas.

Box 9.1: *The Mystery of Mediterranean Europe*

Why it seems to have taken Early Eurasians so much longer to settle Mediterranean Europe than the rest of southern Eurasia remains a mystery. Humans established themselves across much of southern Eurasia before 50 Ka or earlier (Chapter 6), even reaching Australia by as much as 65 Ka (Chapter 7). Most Early Eurasian sites north of the Alps-Himalayas date to after 40–45 Ka (Hoffecker 2017). In Mediterranean Europe, in contrast, human fossils and evidence for distinctively human (vs. Neanderthal) activities does not become common until after 30–40 Ka. Such fossils as occur then and there are mostly fragmentary remains and/or fossils excavated in the early 20th century whose dating remains uncertain (Churchill and Smith 2000). Setting these uncertain remains aside, the evidence suggests humans settled the Europe's Mediterranean coastlines relatively late compared with their earlier penetration of the Mammoth Steppe. Why the "delay"? Three possibilities suggest themselves.

First, crossing the Mediterranean from Africa and/or navigating Europe's Mediterranean coastlines could exceeded the capabilities of early humans' watercraft. Even fairly sizable Mediterranean islands, such as Sicily, Crete, and Cyprus, preserve little or no evidence of Pleistocene seafarers. Terminal Pleistocene sites occur on some of these islands, but all claims for a human presence > 30 Ka remain controversial. The mass extinctions that follow human arrivals at other islands occurred on Mediterranean islands during Holocene times (MacPhee 2018). This "inadequate watercraft" hypothesis likely expresses the archaeological consensus about this issue.

Alternatively, humans might have settled parts of Mediterranean Europe now underwater. Due to cold freshwater runoff from melting Alpine glaciers, Europe's Mediterranean coastlines and lower river valleys were rich in food resources, and thus attractive destinations for human settlement. Testing this hypothesis will be difficult, because any archaeological traces left along those coastlines would now lie as much as 150 meters below modern sea level – depths that lie well beyond scuba-diving range. Future advances in the technologies available for underwater archaeology may overcome this limitation.

Last, some known patterns in the European evidence may result from short-lived Ancient African or First Asian attempts to settle Mediterranean Europe (Slimak et al. 2022). Mandrin Cave (France, 52–57 Ka) and other sites near France's Mediterranean coast preserve "Neronian" stone tool assemblages. These assemblages feature small, elongated triangular flakes ("Levallois points") struck from BHCs and small, narrow prismatic blades made in a manner similar to artifacts found at slightly earlier dates in the East Mediterranean Levant. Such points are uncommon in Europe before

Box 9.1: *(cont.)*

45 Ka. Fragmentary teeth found with Neronian tools at Mandrin Cave are more similar to teeth of Late Pleistocene humans than they are to Neanderthal teeth. Deposits below these Neronian levels feature "Mousterian" stone tools of the sort found with Neanderthal remains at other French sites. The team investigating Mandrin Cave contends that the Neronian tools result from an early human "incursion" into European Neanderthal territory. That more stereotypical Neanderthal artifacts overlie Neronian ones at Mandrin suggests that this hypothetical incursion may have been unsuccessful. This issue requires further investigation. It bears remembering that not all European attempts to settle new lands were successful. Eleventh-century Greenland Norse incursions into what are now the Canadian Maritime provinces failed. They offer a possible historic analogy for the Neronian phenomenon.

In the end, however, exclusively equating Neronian tools or other named stone tool industries with humans returns us to archaeologists' "Pin the Tail on the Donkey" game of stone tool industry attribution. If those who made Neronian artifacts in southern France possessed some technological advantage that gave them a foothold in Europe (perhaps the Neronian Levallois points were arrowheads or spear-thrower dart tips), then Neanderthals living nearby would have had powerful incentives to emulate that advantage. This is, after all, precisely what Native Americans began doing as soon as 17th-century European colonists began demonstrating the advantages of firearms (Silverman 2016).

For thought and discussion: Can we objectively evaluate competing hypotheses about innovations in stoneworking and other technology, such as personal adornments, that appear around the time Neanderthals became extinct? For all such occurrences, one can propose at least five explanations:

- They are Neanderthal innovations that human activity did not influence.
- They result from human activities and are erroneously attributed to Neanderthals.
- Site stratigraphy combines chronologically separate Neanderthal and human activities.
- They result from cultural contacts and personnel exchanges between humans and Neanderthals.
- Activities of hominins other than Neanderthals and humans created them.

In considering these hypotheses, one must also bear in mind that they are not mutually exclusive. That is, more than two or even all five may

Box 9.1: *(cont.)*

have influenced how artifacts and other remains came together in the same sedimentary deposit. It is not yet clear whether archaeologists can falsify any of these hypotheses using evidence from the period around 35–45 Ka.

CHAPTER 10

A BRAVE NEW WORLD

Pleistocene Americans

This chapter examines the peopling of the "New World" (Beringia and the Americas) between 12 and 32 Ka. Like the peopling of Sahul, population movements brought humans from Asia to the American continents and offshore islands with no prior hominin presence. Historically, archaeologists envisioned these movements as land-based, passing through an "ice-free corridor" between major continental glaciers around 13 Ka, but evidence increasingly shows that humans were already present south of the ice sheets significantly earlier than this corridor existed. Unlike in Sahul, Pleistocene Americans[1] systematically hunted many of the megafauna that became extinct during the Pleistocene-Holocene transition. Extensive alliance networks whose most durable archaeological traces include distinctive stoneworking traditions, such as the Clovis phenomenon, may have played a role in these mass extinctions.

GEOGRAPHY: PLEISTOCENE BERINGIA AND THE AMERICAS

The New World of the Americas was, indeed, new to 16th- and 17th-century Europeans, but by that point in time, humans had inhabited the Americas for at least 15,000 years, and possibly much, much longer.

The Americas comprise three main regions: Beringia, North America, and South America (Figures 10.1 and 10.2). (Humans settled the Caribbean Islands during Holocene times.) Beringia encompasses easternmost Siberia, the floor of the Bering Sea that lower Pleistocene sea levels exposed, Alaska, and adjacent parts of Canada's Yukon Territory. As used here, North and South

---

[1] Archaeologists often refer to the Americas' Late Pleistocene and early Holocene people as "Paleoindians." Rather than perpetuate the "Columbian Confusion" (i.e., Columbus' mistaken belief that in 1492 he had landed in India), this work uses the term "Pleistocene Americans."

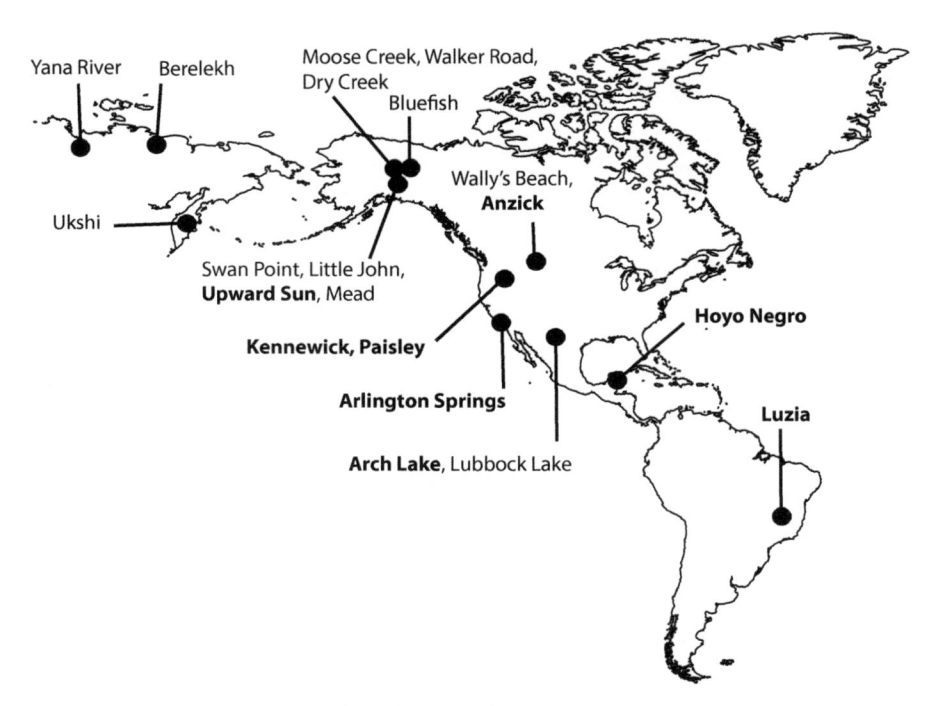

Figure 10.1 Map showing important Beringian and Pleistocene American fossil localities. Site names in **bold** text preserve human fossils and other physical traces. © John J. Shea.

America follow conventional definitions. Current evidence shows that humans were present in all three of these regions before 12 Ka and possibly as much as 26 Ka, having arrived during MIS 2 or earlier. Later Pleistocene sites remain sparse but grow in number with continued archaeological research. As one might expect in a warming and more hominin-friendly postglacial world, Pleistocene Americans' descendants' numbers and archaeological "visibility" increased remarkably after 12 Ka.

Conditions Affecting Population Movements

During the Late Pleistocene, Beringia was an eastern extension of Eurasia's Mammoth Steppe, an ecologically rich and diverse biozone that, at its most extensive, stretched southward onto North America's Great Plains. The principal obstacle to humans' settling Beringia were the extreme cold conditions prevailing over eastern Siberia and blocking Early Eurasians' efforts to disperse eastward.

North America and South America had important similarities and differences affecting human population movements. Both continents featured western mountain ranges running north–south along their Pacific Ocean

Geography: Pleistocene Beringia and the Americas

Figure 10.2 Map showing important Pre-Clovis and Clovis Pleistocene American sites. **Bold** text indicates well-dated Clovis sites. Shaded area encloses the "core" of Clovis occurrences. © John J. Shea.

coastlines: the Rocky Mountains and the Andes, respectively. These mountains' higher elevations were likely uninhabitably cold until postglacial times, but their piedmont and Pacific coastlines could have channeled humans southward. To these mountains' east, extensive river basins – North America's Mississippi and Rio Grande and South America's Amazon and Orinoco – offered relatively easy, watercraft-assisted passage into the continental interior and points east, including the Caribbean Sea and eventually the Atlantic Ocean coastline.

One of the most obvious and consequential differences between North and South America concerns glaciation and changes in vegetation and animal life. North America's ice sheets grew steadily during the Late Pleistocene. The Cordilleran ("mountain" in Spanish) Ice Sheet spread east and west from the northernmost Rocky Mountains. The Laurentian[2] Ice Sheet spread southward from the Arctic across Canada and into the northern United States, covering New England, the Great Lakes, and the northernmost part of the Midwest. Cordilleran and Laurentian ice sheets conjoined one another in what are now Canada's British Columbia and Alberta Provinces, cutting off the North American part of the Mammoth Steppe from its Eurasian counterparts. As those ice sheets melted, an "ice-free corridor" formed, eventually offering a passageway between Beringia and unglaciated North America.

Nowhere in North America remains unchanged since Late Pleistocene times, but humans moving into the continent's interior encountered many of the same sorts of steppe-dwelling animals they had dealt with in Beringia, such as mammoth, lion, horse, bison, elk, red deer, wolves, and the four-meter-tall (standing) nightmare, *Arctodus simus*, the "giant short-faced bear," one of the largest land-dwelling carnivorous mammals that ever lived.

South America's glaciers remained largely on the mountains, but their effects on atmospheric circulation changed the characteristics of the Amazon River basin profoundly, mainly by drying it out. The horizon-to-horizon jungle that the word "Amazon" conjures up today is a very recent phenomenon. During Late Pleistocene and early Holocene times, drier conditions broke up the jungle into pockets of woodlands separated by savannas. In those woodlands and savannas, early Pleistocene Americans encountered a very distinctive "metatherian" fauna ("primitive" placental mammals) that had evolved since plate tectonics split South America away from Africa 150 Ma. South American fauna novelties included camelids (alpaca and llama), glyptodonts (large armadillo-like creatures with clubbed tails), *Megatherium* (giant ground sloths), and the world's largest living rodent, the capybara.

Despite regular appearances presenting evidence of living Native Americans' Asian ancestry as "news," where humans came from is not a major issue in scientific research into the peopling of the Americas, and it has not been a major issue for a very long time. In 1590, Jesuit scholar José de Acosta published a hypothesis arguing that Native Americans had come to the New World from some as-yet-undiscovered region of Northeastern Asia. All fossil, archaeological, and genetic evidence discovered since 1590 support Acosta's hypothesis. No evidence refutes it.

The "Solutrean-Clovis hypothesis," which argues that Early Eurasians might have reached North America's Atlantic coastline by dispersing/migrating along the southern margins of the North Atlantic ice sheets (Stanford and Bradley 2012), remains popular in some circles (mainly among nonprofessional archaeologists), but it enjoys little support among professional paleoanthropologists (Straus et al. 2005).

---

[2] "Laurentide" in some references.

IMPORTANT PLEISTOCENE AMERICAN SITES

Table 10.1 lists important Pleistocene American sites older than 10 Ka.

The earliest evidence for human settlement in westernmost Beringia comes from a series of sites on the Yana River (Siberia, Russia, 32 Ka). Bluefish Caves in northern Yukon (Canada, 24 Ka) show humans were present in Beringia during the LGM. Considerably more sites appear after 15 Ka. These include Berelekh and Ukshi 1 and 5 in Russia; Dry Creek, Mead, Moose Creek, Swan Point, and Walker Road in Alaska; and Little John in Canada's Yukon Province. Dating to 13–15 Ka, these post-LGM Pleistocene sites preserve numerous small foliate points, some with tangs, others without them. Many also preserve small-scale prismatic blades, blade cores, and small backed/truncated pieces. That such evidence appears in both North American and Asian parts of Beringia suggests human populations lived in societies widely dispersed over the region but linked to one another in extensive, stable social networks similar to those previous chapters argued were in place among Early Eurasians, Sahulians, First Asians, and Ancient Africans, and different from those in place among Neanderthals and earlier hominins.

Most of the generally accepted archaeological evidence for *Homo sapiens'* first appearance south of the Laurentian and Cordilleran ice sheets (roughly the 48th parallel) dates to after the LGM, or since around 18 Ka. One can usefully divide the evidence into three types: large mammal death sites with possible evidence of human involvement (i.e., tool marks on fossils and or possible stone tools), post-LGM Pre-Clovis sites with stone tools and other evidence, and sites associated with the Clovis phenomenon discussed later in this chapter.

The first group includes such sites as Hebior (Wisconsin, 14.8 Ka), Page-Ladson (Florida, 14.6 Ka), Schaefer (Wisconsin, 14.5 Ka), Lindsay (Montana, 14.3), Manis (Washington, 13.8 Ka), and Firelands (Ohio, 13.5–13.6 Ka).[3] One common difficulty with evaluating these sites' hypothetical anthropogenic origin is that the "tool marks" on bones are often assessed subjectively (i.e., "this looks like that") rather than being evaluated using independently verifiable metric criteria.

The least controversial among the post-LGM/Pre-Clovis sites includes Wally's Beach (Alberta, Canada, 13.3 Ka), Friedkin (Texas, 13.2–15.5 Ka), and Lubbock Lake (Texas, 12.1–13.1 Ka). Far more controversial sites include Chiquihuite Cave (Zacatecas, Mexico, 31.4–33.2 Ka), Cactus Hill (Virginia, 19.0–20.6 Ka), Meadowcroft Rockshelter (Pennsylvania, 18.6–24.3 Ka), and Gault (Texas, 17.4–26.4 Ka), each of which, if the dates are correct, suggests humans were living south of the ice sheets during the LGM. White Sands (New Mexico) preserves an entirely different sort of evidence: human

---

[3] These sites are the most widely accepted out of a much larger number.

TABLE 10.1 *Important Pleistocene American sites*

Groups of sites	Site	Date (Ka)	Comment	Reference
Sites with human fossils and other physical remains	Paisley 5 Mile Point Caves (Oregon, USA)	14.3	Human aDNA and coprolites	1
	Arlington Springs (Santa Rosa Island, California, USA)	ca. 13	Human fossils	1
	Anzick (Montana, USA)	12.8–12.9	Child burial with grave goods (artifacts, ochre)	1
	Hoyo Negro (Yucatan, Mexico)	11.7–12.9	Human fossils	1
	Luzia (Brazil)	11.5	Adult female fossil	1
	Upward Sun River (Alaska, USA)	11.5	Two infant burials	1
	Arch Lake (Texas, USA)	11.2–11.6	Human burial	1
	Kennewick (Washington, USA)	8.5	Adult male fossil (burial?)	1
Beringian sites	Yana River (Siberia, Russia)	32	Humans in western Beringia before the LGM	1
	Bluefish Caves (Yukon, Canada)	24	Humans in eastern Beringia during the LGM	1
	Berelekh (Siberia, Russia)	13.5–14.9	Beringian post-LGM sites	1
	Swan Point (Alaska, USA)	13.9–14.2	Beringian post-LGM site	1
	Little John (Yukon, Canada)	13.7–14.1		1
	Dry Creek (Alaska, USA)	13.3–13.5	Beringian post-LGM site	1
	Mead (Alaska, USA)	13.2–13.4	Beringian post-LGM site	1
	Walker Road (Alaska, USA)	12.8–13.3	Beringian post-LGM site	1
	Ukshi 1 and 5 (Kamchatka Peninsula, Russia)	12.7–13.2	Beringian post-LGM site	1
	Moose Creek (Alaska, USA)	12.9–13.7	Beringian post-LGM site	1
North American Pre-Clovis sites	White Sands (New Mexico, USA)	23	Human footprints	7
	Chiquihuite Cave (Zacatecas, Mexico)	31.4–33.2	Possible LGM site with stone tools, other evidence	3

(continued)

	Cactus Hill (Virginia, USA)	19.0–20.6	Possible LGM site with stone tools, other evidence	3
	Meadowcroft Rockshelter (Pennsylvania, USA)	18.6–24.3	Possible LGM site with stone tools, other evidence	3
	Hebior (Wisconsin, USA)	14.8	Large mammal death site with possible evidence of human activity	1
	Page–Ladson (Florida, USA)	14.6	Large mammal death site with possible evidence of human activity	1
	Schaefer (Wisconsin, USA)	14.5	Large mammal death site with possible evidence of human activity	1
	Lindsay (Montana, USA)	14.3	Large mammal death site with possible evidence of human activity	1
	Manis (Washington, USA)	13.8	Large mammal death site with possible evidence of human activity	1
	Firelands (Ohio, USA)	13.5–13.6	Large mammal death site with possible evidence of human activity, no stone tools	1
	Wally's Beach (Alberta, Canada)	13.3	Stone tools, other evidence	1
	Friedkin (Texas, USA)	13.2–15.5	Stone tools, other evidence	1
	Lubbock Lake (Texas, USA)	12.1–13.1	Stone tools, other evidence	1
	Monte Verde II (Chile)	14.3	Residential site with traces of architecture	1
South American Pre-Clovis sites	Huaca Preita (Peru)	13.4–14.1		1
	Arroyo Seco 2 (Argentina)	13–14		1
	Lapa do Boquete (Brazil)	12–14	Human presence in lowlands	1
	Fell's Cave (Chile)	13?	"Fishtail" points	1
	Quebrada Jaguay (Peru)	13?	Fish and mollusk remains	1
	Piedra Museo (AEP-1) (Argentina)	12.9	Stone tools and extinct megafauna	1
	Cerro Tres Tetas (Argentina)	12.9	Stone tools, llama fossils	1
	Quebrada Maní (Chile)	11.7–12.8	Human presence in arid zone	1

(continued)

TABLE 10.1 (continued)

Groups of sites	Site	Date (Ka)	Comment	Reference
Well-dated Clovis sites	Lange-Ferguson (South Dakota USA)	13.0	Well-dated Clovis site	2
	Dent (Colorado, USA)	12.9–13.0	Well-dated Clovis site	2
	Domebo (Oklahoma, USA)	12.8–12.9	Well-dated Clovis site	2
	Sheriden Cave (Ohio, USA)	12.8	Well-dated Clovis site	2
	La Prele (Wyoming, USA)	12.8–12.9	Well-dated Clovis site	2
	Colby (Wyoming, USA)	12.8	Well-dated Clovis site	2
	Jake Bluff, (Oklahoma, USA)	12.7–12.8	Well-dated Clovis site	2
	Cactus Hill (Virginia, USA)	12.8	Well-dated Clovis site	2
	Charlie Lake Cave (British Columbia, Canada)	12.5	Clovis site in the "ice-free corridor"	2
	Blackwater Draw (New Mexico, USA)	12.5?	Early find of Clovis Complex artifacts and megafauna	2
Other important sites	La Serranía la Lindos (Colombia)	12–13	Late Pleistocene rock art site	4
	Lapa do Santo (Brazil)	10–12	Early Holocene rock art site	5
	Bull Brook (Massachusetts, USA)	>10	Clovis residential site with traces of architecture; dating unclear	6

LGM, Last Glacial Maximum.
References: 1, Hoffecker (2017); 2, Waters et al. (2020); 3, Becerra-Valdivia et al. (2020); 4, Morcote-Ríos et al. (2021); 5, Neves et al. (2012); 6, Robinson et al. (2009); 7, Bennett et al. (2021).

footprints apparently dating to around 24 Ka. All these sites' dating remains controversial (for a recent review, see Becerra-Valdivia and Higham 2020).

South American archaeological sites that clearly and convincingly date to the Pleistocene (> 12 Ka) include (in descending order of age) Monte Verde II (Chile, 14.3 Ka), Huaca Preita (Peru, 13.4–14.1 Ka), Arroyo Seco 2 (Argentina, 13–14 Ka), Lapa do Boquete (Brazil, 12–14 Ka), Fell's Cave (Chile, ca. 13 Ka), Quebrada Jaguay (Peru, ca. 13 Ka), Piedra Museo (AEP-1) (Argentina, 12.9 Ka), Cerro Tres Tetas (Argentina, 12.9), and Quebrada Maní (Chile, 11.7–12.8 Ka).

PLEISTOCENE AMERICAN FOSSILS

No evidence supports the hypothesis of a pre-*Homo sapiens* hominin presence in the Americas. *Homo sapiens*' fossil record in the New World is surprisingly sparse. Early 20th-century research identified many sites at which human remains appeared to be enclosed in Pleistocene-age sediments, but nearly all of these turned out to be recent burials intruding into older sediments.

The most reliably dated Pleistocene-age American fossils include the Anzick 1 child (Montana, ca. 12.5 Ka) and the Luzia 1 woman (Brazil, ca. 11.5 Ka). Anzick 1 is an infant buried together with stone and bone tools as well as red ochre pigments. The Luzia woman consists of a skull, pelvis, and leg bones unearthed in a cave deposit. She was about 20 years old at the time of her demise and she appears to be a natural or accidental death rather than a deliberate burial. The two femora excavated at the Arlington Springs site on Santa Rosa Island are radiocarbon dated to around 13 Ka. The Upward Sun River Site in Alaska (11.5 Ka) preserves two infant burials.

Paleoanthropologists sometimes discuss Kennewick Man, a fossil found in Washington State together with Anzick (Montana) and Luzia (Brazil) as representing Late Pleistocene Americans, but he is actually considerably younger, dating to 8.5 Ka.[4]

Though not the same sort of fossil as those discussed above, Paisley 5 Mile Point Caves (Oregon, 14 Ka) preserve coprolites (fossil feces) containing human DNA.

---

[4] When physical anthropologists first reconstructed Kennewick Man, many people noticed how that reconstruction resembled the actor Sir Patrick Stewart (b. 1940), who was at the time portraying Captain Jean-Luc Picard in the popular television series, *Star Trek: The Next Generation*. Unfortunately, this and other remarks about the fossil's "Caucasian" features revived speculation that European-descended populations might have settled the Americas before Pleistocene Americans, a hypothesis refuted by essentially all paleontological, archaeological, and molecular evidence. Kennewick man and Sir Patrick Stewart share high cheekbones, a relatively large nose, and a moderately receding frontal bone, features they both inherited from their Early Eurasian ancestors.

PLEISTOCENE AMERICAN ARCHAEOLOGY

Archaeological research on the peopling of the Americas commenced in the 20th century's early decades. The first and most intensively investigated sites were in the western United States, in the Rocky Mountains' eastern foothills and the Great Plains. Many of these sites were places at which stone tools occurred together with fossils of megafauna, such as mammoth and extinct giant bison). Few of these sites preserved evidence for large and long-lasting residential occupations. As a result, archaeologists envisioned early Pleistocene Americans as consisting of small, highly mobile bands (< 50 people) of specialized big-game hunters with few fixed abodes. This stereotype persists, but as evidence from other regions grows, a more diversified picture of early Pleistocene American life emerges.

Stone Tools

Early Pleistocene American stoneworking shows many continuities with Early Eurasian stoneworking. The most novel (new) features of Early Eurasian stoneworking – increased use of unifacial hierarchical core reduction (prismatic blades and blade cores), greater numbers of burins and endscrapers among retouched pieces, increasing numbers and more patterned formal variation among foliate points – also characterize Late Pleistocene and Early Holocene stone tool assemblages throughout the Americas. The things that were common among Neanderthal stone tools but lacking in Early Eurasian lithic assemblages – larger forms of long core tools and preferential bifacial hierarchical cores – are also uncommon in New World lithic assemblages. Though small backed/truncated pieces enjoyed widespread use across much of Northern Asia and Beringia between 12 and 45 Ka, Pleistocene Americans seem to have either abandoned this technology or drastically reduced their reliance on it as they moved south in the Americas. Abraded edge-tools, too, do not occur among the early Pleistocene Americans' toolkits. Figure 10.3 shows artifacts associated with Pleistocene-age sites in the Americas.

Americanist archaeology places great importance on variation among bifacially thinned foliate and lanceolate (elongated) points. These points are usually the most extensively shaped among retouched stone tools in any lithic assemblage and, from a "who question" standpoint, arguably better sources of information about toolmakers' cultural identities and social connections to one another than less extensively modified stone tools. Americanist archaeologists divide these "bifaces" or "projectile points" into lanceolate (parallel lateral edges), stemmed (tanged), notched, and triangular forms. They further subdivide these broader artifact categories based on subtle variations in shape, retouch patterns, or other criteria. It is not at all uncommon for reports on New World stone tool assemblages to illustrate *only* such "projectile points." As with nearly all Pleistocene-age retouched pieces, microwear and residue

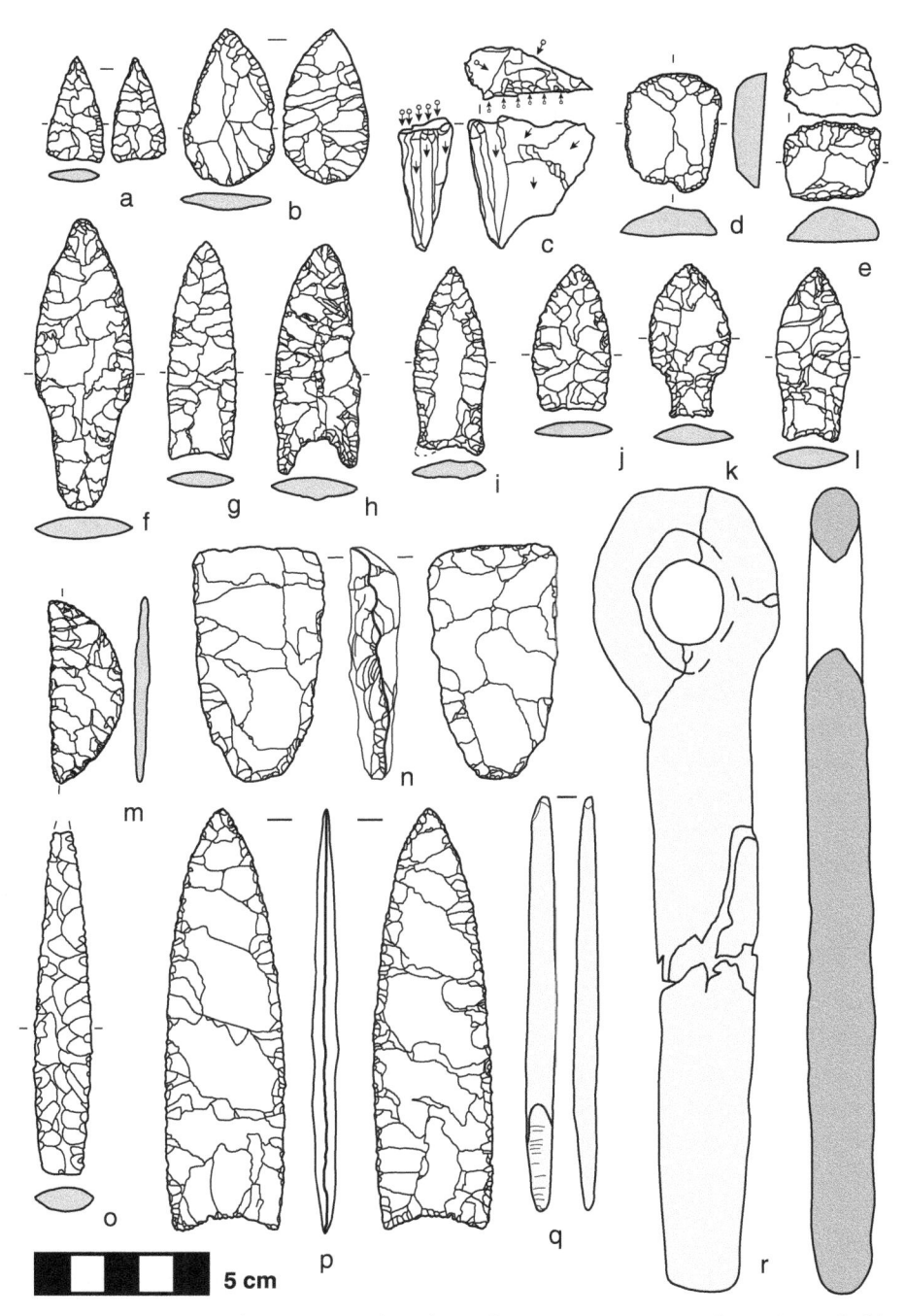

Figure 10.3 Later Pleistocene and early Holocene American artifacts. (a) and (b) eastern Beringian foliate points, (c) wedge-shaped microblade core, (d) endscraper, (e) "wedge/scaled piece," (f) Western Stemmed point, (g)–(i) Clovis/fluted points, (j) unfluted lanceolate point, (k) and (l) stemmed/Fishtail points, (m) crescent-shaped foliate point, (n) flaked-stone celt, (o) lanceolate point, (p) large Clovis point, (q) beveled bone point, (r) perforated bone artifact ("wrench"). Sources: Shea (2017b) (a)–(p), Boldurian (2007) (q), Haynes and Hemmings (1968) (r). © John J. Shea.

analyses show Pleistocene Americans used so-called projectile points not only as weapon armatures but also for diverse cutting tasks.

Fluted Points The foliate points/projectile points archaeologists call "fluted points" figure prominently in research on the peopling of the Americas. Fluted points are lanceolate forms from which stoneworkers have detached one or more relatively large flake ("flute" or "channel flake") from their base. The broad and shallow flake scars left behind on the point create concavities that make it easier to fit the fluted point into a slotted handle. The most iconic such fluted points are Clovis points, artifacts usually found in North America at sites east ande south of the Rocky Mountains dating to around 12–13 Ka. Since the 1930s, archaeologists viewed Clovis points as the stone tool signature of the earliest Pleistocene Americans. Sufficient numbers of archaeological sites older than 13 Ka and lacking Clovis points are now known from Beringia, North America, and South America to decouple Clovis points from the initial peopling of the Americas (Becerra-Valdivia and Higham 2020).

Artifacts Made of Organic Materials

Early Pleistocene Americans carved tools out bone, but their sites preserve far fewer such artifacts than sites in Northern Eurasia. This difference almost certainly reflects the fact that many early New World sites are open-air sites at which bone does not preserve as well as in cave sediments. The range of utilitarian bone tools includes points, cylindrical objects of unknown function, and perforated pieces ("shaft straighteners") like those found in Northern Eurasia.

Symbolic Artifacts

One very clear way in which the Pleistocene American evidence differs from Early Eurasian archaeology concerns symbolic artifacts and features, such as carvings and paintings on cave walls. Put simply, until early Holocene times, sites do not preserve the rich and complexly variable evidence for decorated and carved bone artifacts, for paintings and engravings on cave walls or other rock surfaces, or for personal adornments like those found at Early Eurasian sites in Europe. There are some impressively rich and complex occurrences of rock art at Lapa do Santo (Brazil, 9.9–11.7 Ka) (Neves et al. 2012), burials with grave goods (e.g., Anzick, Montana, 12.8–12.9 Ka) , and occasional perforated shells or other personal adornments (Holliday and Killick 2013), but they do not occur together in quite the same way as they do in Europe around the same time.

To keep this difference in perspective, one has to remember that due to its nearness to the Atlantic Ocean, Late Pleistocene Europe was considerably more humid than interior Eurasia. More water means more plant, animal, and human life. Higher human population densities in Europe may have required more use of symbolic artifacts to express territoriality, alliances, and to mediate conflicts with strangers. During the earliest phases of human settlement, arid and more sparsely populated regions in the Americas may have seen fewer territorial conflicts, fewer encounters with strangers, and lower incentives for symbolic artifact production. "Fluted points" may comprise one possible exception to this pattern.

Caches of extremely large fluted points, such as the Fenn Cache (undated, northern USA) (Frison and Bradley 1999), suggest that fluted points have an important symbolic dimension (a hypothesis examined later in this chapter). Alternatively, archaeologists' artifact-type of "fluted point" may combine utilitarian and symbolic artifacts.

PLEISTOCENE AMERICANS' SURVIVAL STRATEGIES

First Aid and Medication

Bearing in mind the small number of fossils from which one generalizes, Pleistocene Americans appear neither more nor less healthy than Early Eurasians. The Kennewick Man's pelvis features a healed-over lesion with a stone point embedded in it that has no precise parallels in Early Eurasian archaeology, but one has to remember that Kennewick Man dates to thousands of years after humans first appear in the northwestern United States. Until they began practicing food production (specifically, maize-based plant husbandry) prehistoric Native Americans appear to have enjoyed good health comparable to what we see among Early Eurasians.

Thermoregulation

As with Early Eurasian sites, traces of fire occur so often among Pleistocene American sites as to scarcely require comment. Traces of artificial structures are, on the other hand, uncommon. Bull Brook (Massachusetts, > 10 Ka) and Monte Verde II (Chile, 15–19 Ka) preserve remains of freestanding structures (Dillehay 1997; Robinson et al. 2009). Archaeologists have no direct evidence of Pleistocene American clothing, but stone scrapers and other tools preserving wear traces from leather production occur all over the New World. The antiquity of textiles remains unknown.

Hydration

Paralleling evidence worldwide before food production, Pleistocene Americans appear to have acquired water from natural sources without any great difficulty. Evidence of wells or water storage facilities appear only at sites dating to the last few thousand years or less, much as they do in the Old World. In the Americas, finding potable water was not a big problem until contact with Europeans brought domesticated sheep, goats, cattle, and pigs, whose feces contaminated water sources. Europeans' agricultural and industrial activities and large-scale, high-density settlements further contaminated waterways to the point where, today, one assumes that any standing water has to be treated in order to be safe to drink.[5]

Nutrition

Early archaeological stereotypes of Pleistocene Americans as specialized big-game hunters notwithstanding, they appear to have had diversified diets.[6] Dust Cave (Alabama, 9.2–10.6 Ka) and Shawnee-Minisink (Pennsylvania, 10–11 Ka), for example, preserve abundant evidence for plant foods and for small game hunting/trapping (Dent 2007; Hollenbach 2007; Walker 2007). We do not know as much as we wished we knew about their coastal and marine resource use, but no evidence supports the hypothesis that they bypassed these food sources. Evidence for major changes in Pleistocene American diets dates to mid-Holocene times or later and after sea levels stabilized at or near their modern stand.

One of the big mysteries about early Pleistocene American food procurement strategies concerns the use of the bow and arrow. Some of the small tanged points and triangular points found at Beringian sites older than 12 Ka, such as at Berelekh and Ukshi in Russia and Dry Creek and Walker Road in Alaska, certainly resemble arrowheads from more recent prehistoric periods. Nevertheless, the archaeological consensus holds that the bow and arrow were not in wide use in the Americas until mid-Holocene times (ca. 6 Ka or later) (Bingham and Souza 2013).

Transportation

Just as Early Eurasians almost certainly settled Northern Eurasia using watercraft, the peopling of the Americas required watercraft use, too. In Beringia, where large trees were scarce, Pleistocene Americans probably made kayaks or coracles (wooden frame vessels over which their makers stretched waterproof leather hides). Further south, they likely augmented such watercraft with birch bark canoes and dugout canoes.

---

[5] This author remembers being able to drink water from lakes and rivers near his home in Hamilton, Massachusetts, until the 1970s, when suburban developments began contaminating them.

[6] One suspects that early archaeologists' visions of Pleistocene "Paleoindians" as specialized big-game hunters were inspired in part by 19th-century memories of Plains-dwelling horse-pastoralists, such as the Lakota, Dakota, Cheyenne, and Comanche, who were accomplished and specialized big-game hunters.

Recent Siberians and Inuit peoples use dogs to pull sleds across snow and icy terrain. If dogs were domesticated before early human movements to the Americas, then it seems reasonable to suppose early Pleistocene Americans used them as traction animals elsewhere, as some recent plains-dwelling Native American groups did before they acquired horses.

Communication

The amount of actual evidence for symbolic artifact use from the earliest sites in the Americas pales beside the evidence for Europe ca. 12–40 Ka, but this does not mean that symbolic artifact use was uncommon. Because these "social media" strategies spring from ancestral survival skills (minimally, precision power grasping, predictive hallucination, and hyperprosociality), and because one observes symbolic artifact use in alliance networks universally among living Native Americans, one thinks we are seeing an effect of extremely low population densities in arid regions lacking prior hominin occupants. A cold, dry North America peopled with small groups of highly mobile people might not have required diverse and redundant lines of social media anchored to caves and other fixed points on the landscape, similar those Early Eurasians created. In short, durable symbolic artifacts may be a phenomenon dependent on population density – too few encounters with strangers and they are more trouble to make than they are worth, too many encounters and they lose their signaling value.

Additionally, we may be dealing with site preservation issues similar to those inferred for Earliest Eurasians. If Pleistocene Americans dispersed primarily along coastlines and lower river valleys, as their ancestors likely did in moving into Northern Eurasia, then the places where they lived longest, in greatest numbers, and where archaeologists might reasonably expect to find symbolic artifacts related to social alliance-building may have been either flooded by postglacial sea-level rise or scoured by glacial meltwaters. It might not be that early humans failed to use symbolic artifacts in the service of social networks, but rather that they made, used, and discarded them in places no longer accessible to archaeologists. Tellingly, perhaps, Late Pleistocene and early Holocene humans living inland in a more humid and temperate South America created complex rock art sites comparable in complexity to those of their Early Eurasian ancestors. Examples of such sites include La Serranía la Lindos (Colombia, 12–13 Ka) and Lapa do Santo (Brazil, 9.9–11.7 Ka). These observations show that the strategy of using social media is deeply ancestral, but the particular expressions vary widely with circumstances. The Clovis phenomenon, discussed later in this chapter, shows that when circumstances changed and Pleistocene Americans needed symbolic artifacts to reinforce their social networks, they were perfectly capable of devising such and littered the landscapes they occupied with them in much the same way as did their Old World counterparts.

INTERPRETIVE ISSUES ABOUT PLEISTOCENE AMERICANS

Behavioral Differences between Pleistocene Americans and Early Eurasians

Comparisons between Early Eurasian and Pleistocene American solutions to survival challenges consistently fail to reveal significant differences. Early Pleistocene Americans appear to have arrived in Beringia > 20–30 Ka with a robust and diversified set of solutions to the "basic six" survival challenges. If they lacked something, then one would expect to see a delay in their southward movements. Extreme cold and dry conditions in eastern Siberia during the LGM appear to have slowed movements between Asia and Beringia, but a few sites (all controversial) hint at a pre-LGM presence. Setting these controversial sites aside for the moment, the fact that the oldest among the less-controversial archaeological evidence from South America (e.g., Monte Verde II, Chile, 14.3 Ka) and North America (i.e., Paisley 5 Mile Point Caves, Oregon, 14.3 Ka) show essentially identical ages suggests Native Americans' ancestral survival skills were more than adequate to allow them to overcome whatever difficulties the New World posed them.

American Megafauna Extinctions

Around 12–23 Ka North and South America experienced a wave of extinctions among their large mammal species. Mammoths, mastodons, giant ground sloth, camels, and horses disappeared, as did several large carnivores such as the giant short-faced bear, American lion, saber-toothed cat, and dire wolf (Meltzer 2023). Many smaller mammals, birds, and other terrestrial creatures became extinct around the same time, but marine mammals and other aquatic animals seem to have survived relatively unscathed. Early discoveries of Pleistocene American stone tools together with remains of extinct large mammals suggested a plausible causal connection, namely, that early Pleistocene Americans hunted these animals to extinction (Martin 1973). This remains a widely accepted hypothesis, but it is not the only one in play. The period in which large mammal last appearance dates cluster, 11.7–12.9 Ka, corresponds with the Younger Dryas event, an abrupt return to glacial conditions. The Younger Dryas event's causes continue to be debated, but it is possible this rapid climate change and human predation contributed jointly to megafaunal extinctions in the Americas.[7]

---

[7] A hypothesis that a meteor impact caused these extinctions and even the Younger Dryas event itself remains controversial (Firestone et al. 2007). Critics have raised serious questions about the evidence originally used to support it (Meltzer et al. 2014). A hypothesis proposing that diseases carried to the New World by domesticated dogs precipitated these extinctions (Feidel 2005) also remains controversial due to the difficulty of proving it wrong.

Coastal versus Inland Routes from Beringia to the Americas

For much of the 20th century, archaeologists envisioned Pleistocene Americans moving south through the ice-free corridor between the Cordilleran and Laurentian ice sheets. More recently, however, doubts have emerged about this hypothesis (Meltzer 2021). The corridor in question appears to have closed during MIS 3, around 30 Ka, and begun opening around 14 Ka, but it was not truly "ice-free" until thousands of years later (11 Ka). The oldest archaeological sites in the corridor date to around 12.5 Ka.

The principal alternative to the ice-free corridor hypothesis is the "coastal route" hypothesis (Dixon 1999; Erlandson 2001). This hypothesis argues that humans got around the ice sheets by moving south along the Pacific Coast using watercraft, settling on coastlines and moving inland locally as populations grew.

One recently proposed variant of the coastal route hypothesis, the "kelp highway" hypothesis, may explain how humans moved south so swiftly (Erlandson et al. 2007). It assumes that Late Pleistocene humans living along Asia's Pacific Coast had watercraft capable of at least near-coastal voyages. This seems a reasonable assumption to make for two reasons. First, humans in Eastern Asia and Sunda made and used watercraft tens of thousands of years before humans appeared in the Americas. Second, Asia's northern Pacific Coast abounds with underwater "kelp forests" that support rich communities of edible plants, fish, shellfish, birds, and marine mammals. Today, these kelp forests stretch along the Pacific Coast from Japan across the Bering Strait to North America's Pacific Coast to Central America, and along much of South America's Pacific Coast. Using watercraft, early humans could have followed this familiar "kelp highway" from Asia to the Americas by making short residential movements along coastlines without having to stop to figure out how to deal with unfamiliar plant foods, prey species, and predators in the North and South American interior. Finding evidence for or against these hypotheses remains difficult, because postglacial sea-level rise drowned the coastal landscapes most likely to provide archaeological evidence for or against it. It is, however, consistent with older evidence for watercraft-assisted prehistoric human dispersals.

The current archaeological consensus holds that humans initially settled the New World by dispersing along the Pacific Coast during the Last Glacial Maximum and then moving inland along major rivers, such as the Columbia and Colorado. As First Asians dispersed beyond Sunda and northward along Asia's Pacific Ocean coastline, they moved from relatively resource-impoverished tropical waters to colder and more productive temperate ones, from mangrove swamps to kelp forests. As the amount of potential food in the water increased, coastal populations increased as well. Long before local populations reached their coasts' and offshore fisheries' carrying capacity, individuals and small groups dispersed into sparsely populated and unpopulated coastlines to the north and east. Others moved inland along rivers and to higher elevations, but this path of greater resistance for moving inland would have required new strategies for coping with colder and drier continental habitats. This coastal dispersal process likely continued along the northern Pacific Coast and beyond to South America.

What then of Northwestern North America's ice-free corridor? By the time the ice-free corridor was actually "ice-free," around 11 Ka, and when some Native Americans began leaving stone tools in it, other people had been living south of the continental ice sheets for thousands of years.

Migration versus Dispersal

Does any archaeological evidence support the hypothesis that humans migrated (as opposed to dispersed) into the Americas? No, it does not. Still, one ought to examine the strongest case for migration, the Clovis phenomenon.

Historically, hypotheses about Pleistocene migrations to the Americas have focused on what is called the "Clovis phenomenon." Clovis is a town in eastern New Mexico, where in 1929 archaeologists noted stratified deposits around a fossil spring, Blackwater Draw, that contained remains of ancient bison, mammoth, and stone tools. Two kinds of "fluted points" appeared. Those in the uppermost or most recent layer were of a type already known from Folsom, New Mexico;[8] the lower and earlier points were larger and of a previously unknown variety. These older points became known as "Clovis points." Following then-common practice, archaeologists assigned stone tool assemblages with such lanceolate foliate points to a "Clovis culture," or to "Clovis Man." Early radiocarbon dates suggested Clovis sites straddled the Late Pleistocene/early Holocene transition, dating to roughly 11–13 Ka.

As finds of Clovis points came to light all over Eastern North America and in Mesoamerica, it became clear that the Clovis "culture" was something more extensive than an ethnographic culture. Today, archaeologists refer to such assemblages as part of a "Clovis phenomenon" (or Clovis Complex) roughly contemporary with at least two other archaeological complexes defined in terms of lanceolate foliate points. These other complexes include a Western Stemmed Point Tradition centered around the western parts of North

---

[8] In 1908 near Folsom, New Mexico, George McJunkin, a cattle ranch foreman, noticed stone tools and giant bison bones eroding from the side of a small hill. An amateur archaeologist/historian, musician, and formerly enslaved African American, McJunkin tried without success for 10 years to interest professional archaeologists in the Folsom site, until 1918 when the Denver Museum of Natural History dispatched their staff to investigate. That investigation concluded that the fossils and stone tools were indeed associated with one another in the same sedimentary deposit.

America and the Fishtail Point Tradition centered around the Caribbean Basin and South America.

Calling these groups of sites "complexes" or "traditions" implies nontrivial similarities among them, such as very specific toolmaking practices, distinctive settlement patterns, and specific subsistence strategies as well as differences between these complexes/traditions and others near to them in time and space. This may be a mistake. The foliate points that mark each of these complexes occur over such wide geographic ranges that it is unlikely they were internally homogeneous with respect to technology, settlement, or subsistence. Nor is it clear that they differ from one another in these respects, either. It is clear that large and conspicuously shaped fluted foliate points were created, but that's about all we know for certain.

No archaeological consensus exists over the Clovis phenomenon's geographic origins. Clovis points do not occur in Eurasian sites or in Beringia. Historically, "textbook" versions of New World prehistory asserted that the Clovis Complex developed as humans moved south of the continental ice sheets. A "Clovis first" hypothesis envisioned the Clovis people as the first wave of humans migrating into the Americas. Early finds of Clovis points together with fossils of mammoths and other extinct large mammals suggested the Clovis people were specialized big-game hunters. A "Pleistocene overkill" hypothesis (Martin 1973) argued that overhunting by Pleistocene Americans armed with Clovis points and similar lanceolate points caused mass extinctions among "naïve" American megafauna, that is, large mammals unaccustomed to viewing humans as predators.

New evidence challenges the hypothesis that the Clovis phenomenon resulted from a migration. First, archaeological sites from all over the Americas date to more than 12–13 Ka and these lack anything remotely resembling Clovis points. These data suggest humans were already present across much of the Americas before anyone started making Clovis points (or Western Stemmed points or Fishtail points). Second, improved radiocarbon chronology now shows the Clovis phenomenon lasted from 12.9 to 13.2 Ka – three centuries or roughly ten generations (Waters et al. 2020). Table 10.1 lists most reliably dated of these as "well-dated Clovis sites." If the Clovis phenomenon was a migration, then the people involved in it would have had to sustain birthrates with no equals among preagricultural human societies.

What Was the Clovis Phenomenon?

If the Clovis phenomenon was neither a culture nor a migration, then what was it? Bearing in mind that ideas can disperse faster than people, the evidence available is consistent with the hypothesis that the Clovis phenomenon was a group of alliance networks that formed and spread among human populations *already* dispersed across North America east and south of the Rocky Mountains before 13.2 Ka. Clovis fluted points are simply the most visibly distinctive and durable symbolic artifacts associated with these alliance networks.[9] Caches of Clovis artifacts, such as the Fenn Cache, are almost certainly ritual paraphernalia used in ceremonies, possibly reinforcing these alliances. One thinks it likely the Western Stemmed and Fishtail Point Traditions may be alternative alliance networks, ones that contrasted with their Clovis counterparts in meaningful ways other than their geographic distribution, but one also recognizes that we know far less about them than about the Clovis phenomenon.

While some Pleistocene Americans dispersed into the New World along the coast, others explored options in the interior, moving inland along major rivers. In Eurasia, such inland movements brought First Asians into territories other hominins such as Neanderthals and Denisovans inhabited and in which potential prey were long familiar to hominins as potential predators. No such obstacles existed in the Americas. As humans moved south along the Pacific Ocean's "kelp highway," dispersing humans discovered that east beyond the Rockies and Andes mountains lay a vast and unpopulated continent. This discovery presented both benefits and costs. The benefit? Pleistocene Americans could move across new territories quickly and simply by floating watercraft down from the mountains to lower elevations. The cost? Rapid dispersal may have spread people so thinly on the ground that it became difficult to ensure adequate choices of mates and limited opportunities to form stable alliance networks.

The Clovis phenomenon's two most salient features include (1) stoneworkers' expending great amounts of time and energy shaping foliate points and (2) the frequency with which such points appear in and among remains of large terrestrial mammals, especially mammoth. All human societies face the problem of how to deal with strangers or, rather, how to predict their behavior. As Chapter 9 argued, Early Eurasians may have solved this problem by "peak procedural complexity" by adding superfluous steps to artifact production as a way of checking strangers' bona fides (verifying they were indeed members of the larger culture) and of making sure they understood complex instructions before undertaking risky activities. Though considerable archaeo-mythology surrounds the purported mechanical benefits of fluting foliate points, the fact that this strategy appears so rarely worldwide suggests that such arguments are just myths. That is, if fluting a lanceolate point's base offered advantages in hafting, then everyone who made and used hafted lanceolate points over the last 100,000 years or more would have done so, too, not just some among many Pleistocene Americans and those only for a few centuries. Clovis points

---

[9] It is important to note the plural "networks." Given its geographic scale and the physical obstacles within its range, the Clovis phenomenon/network was almost certainly not one social network, but rather a group of dynamically shifting and recombining social networks that shared at least one signature artifact.

and allied lanceolate points make vastly more sense as "costly signals," as parts of a sexual selection strategy to verify potential mates' and social allies' qualities (Zahavi and Zahavi 1997).

Studies of modern-day "flintknappers" show again and again that making a fluted point is difficult, and this may well be the point, as a demonstration of competence at a "peak procedural complexity" task. Striking a lanceolate point on its end to detach a channel flake/flute risks "end-shock" (a large lateral fracture that shock waves can cause as they move through rock) (Crabtree 1966; Callahan 1979; Whittaker 2004). Publicly demonstrating one's ability to make a fluted point illustrates one's skills at complex tasks and one's past experience and competence at understanding and operationalizing complex instructions. In a world where small groups of humans' survival depended on a division of labor in risky activities, such as attacking "killer herbivore" megafauna, persons contemplating joining such endeavors (or, conversely, accepting strangers into them) would almost certainly have wanted to verify one another's skills and ability to follow complex instructions. (This is not an exotic scenario; it is exactly why automobile rental companies insist on being shown a driver's license before handing over the keys to their car.)

Clovis and American Megafauna Extinctions

That so many New World megafauna extinctions correlate closely with the Clovis phenomenon could suggest that "peak procedural complexity," such as fluting, decreased the costs associated with such risky activities, encouraging Pleistocene Americans to attack large, dangerous megafauna more often than they had done previously. Being able to create on a predictable schedule "meat jackpots" that could feed everyone for miles around could also have helped solve early Pleistocene Americans' most evolutionarily important dilemma: making sure their children enjoyed a sufficient range of possible mates from which to choose.

Hypotheses about megafauna extinctions often invoke changes in climate, such as the rapid return to glacial conditions during the Younger Dryas event (11.6–12.9 Ka) (Cheng et al. 2020). One cannot reject such "death by climate change" hypotheses (especially since Chapter 8 invoked it in explaining Neanderthal extinction), but one also thinks that it oversimplifies the New World evidence. After all, North and South American megafauna had endured and overcome countless prior episodes of rapid climate change. They had not previously encountered predatory groups of hyperprosocial humans networked to one another into regional alliance networks using symbolic artifacts.

One entirely reasonable objection to a hypothesis linking the Clovis phenomenon to megafauna extinctions is that megafauna extinctions comparable in scale to those in the Americas also occurred in Sahul unaccompanied by any archaeological phenomenon quite like Clovis. It is also the case that Sahulians

TABLE 10.2 *Pleistocene American versus Sahulian large terrestrial carnivores arranged by greatest adult mass*[a]

Americas	Sahul after 65 Ka
*Giant short-faced bear (*Arctodus simus*), 900–1,000 kg	**Megalania*/giant monitor lizard (*Varanus priscus*), 97–1,940 kg
Kodiak bear (*Ursus arctos*), 300–600 kg	*Large crocodile (*Quincania*), 200 kg
Polar bear (*Ursus maritimus*), 150–700 kg	*Marsupial lion (*Thylacoleo carnifex*), 101–130 kg
*American lion (*Panthera atrox*), 235–523 kg	*Thylacine tiger/wolf (*Thylacinus cynocephalus*), 8–30 kg
*Saber-toothed cat (*Smilodon*), 220–436 kg	
Grizzly bear (*Ursus arctos horribilis*), 130–360 kg	
Black bear (*Ursus americanus*), 40–250 kg	
Cougar/mountain lion (*Puma concolor*), 29–100 kg	
Jaguar (*Panthera onca*), 56–96 kg	
*Dire wolf (*Aenocyon dirus*), 60–70 kg	
Wolf (*Canis lupus*), 40 kg	

[a] This table lists only carnivores large enough to plausibly kill an adult human being. Asterisk (*) indicates extinct species.

do not seem to have created "large mammal death" sites quite like those Pleistocene Americans created. This issue requires further investigation. One should not prematurely reject the hypothesis that differences in megafauna and in the competitor-predator community may have played a role in these differences. The Americas had more and larger terrestrial carnivores than Sahul did (Table 10.2). Little evidence supports the hypothesis that Sahulians interacted with their continent's larger terrestrial predators or that they systematically hunted that continent's megafauna herbivores. Evidence abounds for Pleistocene Americans hunting large herbivores that are now extinct. The largest of the American large carnivores, such as the giant short-faced bear, American lion, and saber-toothed cat, last appeared around the time of the Clovis phenomenon. Wedging themselves into the Americas' "carnivore guild" may have required different and more archaeologically conspicuous solutions than those Sahulians adopted for similar purposes.

SUMMARY

This chapter examined the evidence for the peopling of the Americas. By 12 Ka, humans were well established across those parts of North and South America not covered by ice sheets and montane glaciers and the barren deglaciated areas surrounding them. Dispersal to the New World appears to have happened very swiftly, first along the Pacific Coast and later over the Rockies–Andes and along rivers into the Americas' Atlantic watersheds. The "peak procedural complexity"/costly signaling associated with fluted points and the Clovis phenomenon heralded changes in hunting strategies that precipitated megafauna extinctions. Pleistocene Americans did not kill off all the megafauna, but neither were they innocent bystanders. With the peopling of the New World, the great age of Pleistocene human dispersals drew to a close. While Pleistocene Americans feasted on mammoth and bison steaks, people living on the opposite side of the world developed strategies for food production that forever altered human population movements. The Age of Migrations had begun.

CHAPTER 11

MOVABLE FEASTS

Food Producers and Migrations

This chapter considers the relationship between food production and migration. Before Holocene times (> 12 Ka) archaeological evidence consistently shows that human population movements were dispersals and not migrations. People moved into new habitats either as individuals or in small groups, reconfiguring their economies and social identities in their destinations. From mid-Holocene times onward (after 6 Ka), however, the archaeological record begins shows increasing evidence for migrations. Migrating humans took their food and their culture, their "movable feasts," with them. This chapter argues that recent human migrations required food production using domesticated plants and animals, or their functional equivalents derived from gathered foods. It describes how food production altered some of humanity's responses to the basic six survival problems in ways that not only encourage migrations but also make them easier for archaeologists to detect, albeit within a limited chronological "window of visibility." A case study from sub-Saharan Africa shows that archeologists can detect prehistoric migrations, but we have to ask different questions about them than traditional "who questions."

FOOD PRODUCTION

"Food production" is strategy, or rather a collective term for a group of strategies, by which humans extract energy (calories) from domesticated plants and animals. Domesticated plants and animals are species whose naturally evolved reproductive strategies, morphology, and behavior humans have altered, usually by intervening in their reproductive strategies. Such interventions can be profound, such as turning wolves into teacup Pomeranians, others subtle and reversible, such as among horses, cats, or pigs. Released from captivity these animals swiftly go "feral" and revert to something close (but not identical) to their condition before domestication. Not all species whose reproductive strategies humans have altered are necessarily domesticated.

Human activity has improved the evolutionary fortunes of many garden weeds and "commensal" animals, such as sparrows, pigeons, seagulls, mice, and rats, without substantively altering their behavior, morphology, or genome. Food production contrasts with hunting and gathering ("foraging"), in which calories come from nondomesticated species, but many food producers also obtain food from nondomesticated plants and animals (Cummings et al. 2014). No line divides foraging from food production, but rather both reflect a complex spectrum of human behavioral variability.

Food production typically involves at least two of three strategies: plant husbandry, animal husbandry, and ecosystem engineering.[1] Plant and animal husbandry both involve "domestication." Domestication is not a one-way street. Domesticated plants and animals gain, too. For them, domestication confers "extinction immunity." That is, we extend our evolved unstoppability to them. Some breeds of domesticated animals have become extinct – Native American dogs, for example (Ní Leathlobhair et al. 2018) – but no domesticated plant or animal *species* has ever become extinct.

Plant Husbandry

Plant husbandry involves selectively breeding plants, either for food or for other purposes. Obviously, this covers a wide range of activities, only some of which are germane to human population movements. Archaeologists usually identify plant domestication by measuring changes in seed sizes. Most domesticated plants have larger seeds than their wild relatives. This can result from direct selection for such larger seeds, or it can be a result of soil fertilization, weeding away competitor plants, or from irrigation. This seed-focused approach to identifying domesticated plants works well for species whose fruits and nuts were the targets of human selective breeding, but it has a "blind spot" for plants on which humans focused their energies on growing larger roots, tubers, or leaves (e.g., yams, taro, potato, tobacco).

Pre-industrial ethnographic farmers focus on securing stable sources of carbohydrates (starches and sugars) that can be planted quickly, harvested in bulk on a seasonal schedule, and stored for prolonged periods. In the Old World, these crops included cereal grasses (wheat, barley, rye, sorghum, rice, and millet). In the New World, they included maize, potatoes, and sweet potatoes. Because these crops deplete nitrogen from the soils in which they grow, many early farmers grew them together with nitrogen-fixing plants, such as peas and lentils (Old World) or beans (New World). Widespread today, bananas and sugarcane first came into cultivation in Southeast Asia during prehistoric times. Many preindustrial farmers also practiced arboriculture,

---

[1] Many archaeologists use "agriculture" as a shorthand term for various combinations of these strategies.

systematically planting nut- and fruit-bearing trees near habitation sites. Some of the more familiar products of arboriculture include date palms, olives, grapes, apples, coconut palms, almonds, avocados, and mangoes.

Animal Husbandry and Pastoralism

Animal husbandry involves selectively breeding animals to change their morphology and/or their behavior for diverse purposes. Many archaeologists use the term "pastoralism" for animal husbandry involving relatively large herd animals that must be led to and from pastures. In considering earlier humans' motives for domesticating animals, one thinks first and foremost of animals we eat, but Pleistocene humans domesticated wolves first and foremost as hunting aids (Shipman 2015, 2021). Archaeologists identify animal bones as those of wild versus domesticated animals by differences in animal size and shape that reflect changing selective pressures during domestication. Domesticated animals are generally smaller, less skeletally robust, and behaviorally more docile than their nondomesticated counterparts.

Among animals domesticated as food sources, the most common and widespread are "grass converters," animals that can transform grasses that humans cannot eat into protein and fat. Such animals include cattle, sheep, and goats. Other domesticated animals, such as pigs and chickens, reproduce swiftly, and they can often be left to forage on their own around habitation sites. Some domesticated animals also offer up inedible "secondary products," such as hair, wool, bone/antler, and other nonfood products.

A fourth motive for domesticating animals is as aids to transportation. The most common such domesticated "traction" animals include donkeys, horses, camels, llamas, dogs (in northern latitudes), and elephants (in southern Asia). These traction animals are often larger, more skeletally robust, and live longer than their nondomesticated counterparts. Clydesdale draft horses tower over their human owners. Asiatic wild horses (aka Przewalski's horse, *Equus przewalski*) are about the size of a donkey.

Finally, purposes for domestication can change. For example, some domesticated dogs still aid hunters, but today, vastly more dogs live as companion and service animals than as hunting dogs. "Barn cats" exterminate rodents and other pests in agricultural settlements, but many modern-day "house cats" live their lives without ever setting eyes on a living mouse or rat.

Ecosystem Engineering

Ecosystem engineering involves changing the environment in ways that improve domesticated plants', animals', and ultimately, humans' economic and reproductive success. Ecosystem engineering strategies can range from the small-scale and prosaic (weeding crop fields) to the dramatic (exterminating predators on livestock) to large-scale and transformative (such as cutting and burning forests and planting crops in their ashes ["swidden" or "slash-and-burn" agriculture]) to digging and maintaining irrigation canals to gathering and spreading fertilizer. Recognizing ecosystem engineering is not simple, for it requires archaeologists to disentangle natural changes in climate and habitat that may have made a region more favorable for agriculture from anthropogenic changes in the land. One also has to recognize that while ecosystem engineering is an unavoidable consequence of food production, hunter-gatherers practice it, too. Some groups deliberately dam rivers and streams to increase riverine food sources. Many tropical and temperate zone hunter-gatherers practice "fire-stick farming," in which they deliberately set small fires to burn off dead vegetation and to encourage new plant growth. Newly sprouting plants have less ligneous (woody) tissues and are more edible than older plants. New plant growth also increases herbivore animal populations. The trick, as it were, to detecting food production–related ecosystem engineering is to identify evidence uniquely referable to food production, and to activities that improve the fortunes of specific edible plants and food animals.

Calling ecosystem engineering "engineering" implies deliberate planning, but some such changes can be unintended consequences of humans doing other things. For example, trash middens located near residential sites can attract animals, such as rodents, birds, and smaller mammals, that would otherwise avoid human habitation sites. Similarly, excavating irrigation canals or watering holes for livestock can attract and concentrate smaller animals (invertebrates, fish, amphibians, reptiles, rodents) to such a degree that it increases the benefits (energetic returns) for devising nets, traps, snares, and similar devices to capture such animals while humans attend to other tasks.

Ecosystem engineering has a social dimension as well. Preindustrial farmers do not usually and willingly consume their plant seeds or their livestock when wild foods are available for free.[2] Hunter-gatherers compete with farmers/herders for such wild food sources, as well as for fuel, favorable habitation sites, and other resources. How ethnographic farmers/herders deal with indigenous hunter-gatherers varies widely and with circumstances. In some cases, as in the Kalahari Desert in Southwestern Africa, individuals move back and forth across the food producer/hunter-gatherer spectrum as suits their immediate needs (Wilmsen 1989). In others, as in various parts of equatorial Africa, farmers provide hunter-gatherers with concentrated carbohydrates (maize and other crops) in exchange for protein, fat, and possibly social prestige, in the form of hunted wild game ("bushmeat") (Bailey and Peacock 1988). In former times, including across much of the Americas and Australia during the 19th century,

---

[2] "To eat one's seed corn" expresses farmers' contempt for a short-term choice that curtails potentially lucrative future options.

military and paramilitary forces acting at farmers' and herders/ behest displaced, incarcerated, and even exterminated indigenous hunter-gatherers.

Origins of Food Production

No hominins other than *Homo sapiens* appear to have practiced food production, though it is possible some may have engaged in some ecosystem engineering either by using fire while inserting themselves into previously hominin-free ecosystems (e.g., Eurasia before 1.8 Ma).

Human societies followed many different paths to food production. The mode and tempo of the shift from landscapes of foragers to landscapes of farmer-herders varied widely. In most parts of the world plant husbandry preceded pastoralism, and plant or animal husbandry preceded large-scale ecosystem engineering, but hunter-gatherers had likely been practicing some form of smaller-scale ecosystem modification long before food production took root.

Some of the "hot spots" for the origins of food production include Southwestern Asia (Anatolia, the Levant, and the Zagros Mountains' foothills), the African Sahel (a woodland-savanna belt along the Sahara Desert's southern margin), Southeastern Asia, Mesoamerica, and the Central Andes (Table 11.1). These regions lie within a fairly narrow band between 30° north and south of the Equator (Figure 11.1), but the plants and animals domesticated in them enjoy much wider, indeed some near global, distributions. These are not the only places where plant and animal domestication occurred. Many other regions contribute smaller numbers of plants, including nonfood plants, and animals. There are also many widely used domesticates, such as dogs and bottle gourds (*Lagenaria*), whose geographic origins remain obscure.

Generalizing broadly about the evidence from these regions, many prehistoric societies' transitions to food producers follow four steps:

- *Phase 1*: Sedentary humans identify plants/animals with desirable qualities and then intervene in those species' reproductive behavior, thereby domesticating them.

TABLE 11.1 *Domesticated plants and animals from food production hot spots*

Hot spot	Domesticated plants	Domesticated animals
Southwestern Asia	Wheat, barley, lentils, peas, grape, olives	Cattle, sheep, goats, pigs, horses
African Sahel	Finger millet, sorghum, yam (*Dioscoria rotundata*)	Donkeys
Southeastern Asia	Rice, common millet, yam (*D. alata*), taro	Chickens, pigs
Mesoamerica	Maize, beans, squash	Turkeys
Central Andes	Potatoes, sweet potato, yam (*D. trifida*)	Llamas, alpacas, guinea pigs

Food Production

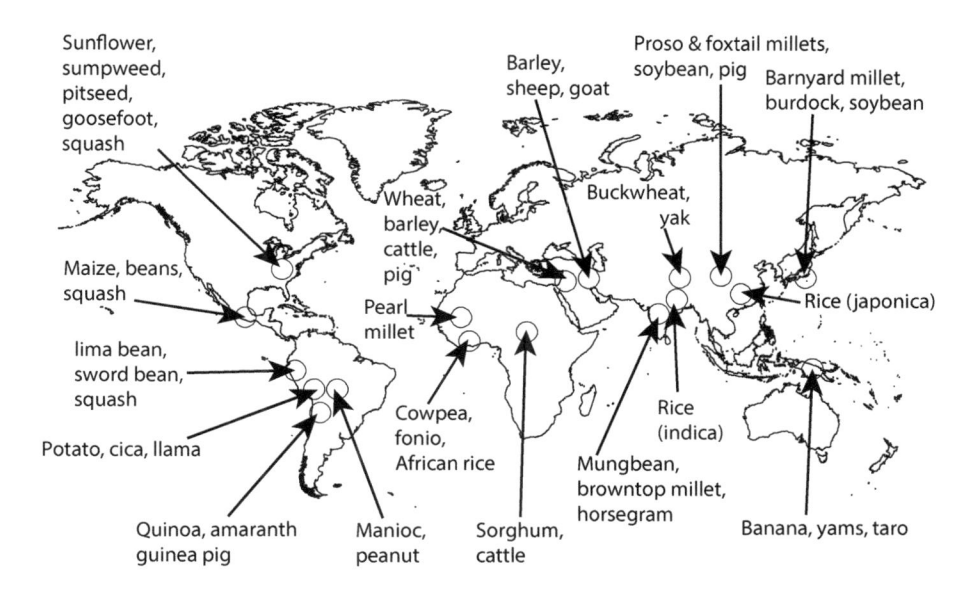

Figure 11.1 Hot spots for the origins of food production. Adapted from Graeber and Wengrow (2021: figure 3, p. 253). © John J. Shea.

- *Phase 2*: As human populations grow, they prey on wild counterparts to domesticated plants and animals, thereby conserving their cultivated plants and livestock.
- *Phase 3*: People alter their habitats to encourage domesticated plants' and animals' reproduction (e.g., clearing land, fertilizing and irrigating soil, eliminating predators).
- *Phase 4*: Humans become irreversibly dependent on food from domesticated plants and animals. Intensification and migrations follow.

(Phases 2 and 3 can occur in reverse order or more or less simultaneously.)

Archaeologists often think and write about the transitions to food production as if they were irreversible, but until Phase 4, they were not. People could have either failed or walked away from incipient food production. Our ancestors were not fools. Their words for cost, benefit, loss, and risk, and the metaphors by which they expressed them, differed from ours, but the hungry babies' cries and their parents' tears undoubtedly focused our ancestors' capacities for predictive hallucination on alternatives to what they were doing at the time.

Evolution abounds with "false starts" and "failed experiments." It follows that the earliest-known evidence of plant or animal husbandry/domestication may not be the springboard out of which modern-day plant/animal husbandry arose. After all, evolution would not be evolution if its failures did not vastly outnumber its successes.

Why Did People Begin Food Production? Many of archaeologists' conjectures about food production's origins focus on the roles of specific environments or social changes. Few of these hypotheses well explain why early evidence for food production appears at more or less the same time worldwide, that is, the early Holocene, or 5–11 Ka.[3] Such evidence does not appear during any of the 295,000 years humans lived in some of what would later become food production "hot spots." Surely, if Holocene humans living on the slopes of the Jordan Rift Valley understood that cereal grasses could be gathered from places where the wild plants grew and harvested with ease, then it follows that their Pleistocene ancestors understood this too. Early humans were not stupid. The detailed natural history observations embedded in Early Eurasians' and others' artworks shows their careful observation of nature and "natural history intelligence." Blissful ignorance of natural phenomena is a decidedly recent phenomenon. Among earlier humans, individuals exhibiting either disinterest or inability to make such detailed natural history observations would almost certainly and swiftly have found themselves socially ostracized and reproductively isolated.

So, why 5–11 Ka? The hypothesis that best explains these phenomena (Richerson et al. 2001) argues that colder temperatures and climatic instability made food production impossible during the Pleistocene, while the warmer temperatures and increased climatic stability during the early-middle Holocene encouraged food production experiments, rewarded those who did them successfully, and helped them spread food production more broadly. Many of the world's agricultural staples (i.e., wheat, rice, maize) are, after all, tropical plants transported into temperate latitudes that warmed during postglacial times.

This global hypothesis for a global phenomenon requires further testing, but if it is correct, then two important implications follow. First, prior episodes of climatic stability during warm periods (MIS 3, 5, 7, etc.) might have seen humans taking steps toward Phase 1 (see above) only to abandon them as climatic instability reasserted itself. That is, Pleistocene humans almost certainly conducted experiments with food production that led nowhere and lacked evolutionary consequences. In places graced with relatively stable Pleistocene climates, such as Sunda, people may even have practiced incipient plant or animal husbandry far earlier than archaeologists currently suspect and with important consequences. Second, future climatic instability may endanger our current strategies for food production. Humans have proven clever at boosting recent agricultural productivity (Mann 2018). We will have to be even more clever when orbital forces inevitably nudge the planet away from our long, wet, hot "summer" and back toward more normal colder temperatures and glacial conditions (a 100,000 year-long "snow day.".

---

[3] On historic timescales, the 6,000 years between 5 and 11 Ka is an enormously long period, but on Pleistocene-age and/deep-time timescales it is the blink of an eye.

Consequences of Food Production

Food production increases the amounts of calories available in any given place over any fixed period of time. This development has several predictable consequences, namely, reduced mobility, increased population, habitat deterioration, intensification, territorial conflict, and, last but not least, migration.

Reduced Mobility By boosting the amounts of calories available locally, food production reduces incentives for human residential and logistical mobility. Residential mobility refers to movements of long-term habitation sites. If food is available near home, then one does not need to move one's home to where the food is. Logistical mobility refers to movements in search of food, fuel, or other resources. Reduced logistical mobility means that food producers seek food from smaller site "catchments," the areas around habitation sites from which site occupants gather resources. Food producers' worlds do not end at the edges of their fields and pastures, of course, but they have fewer incentives to monitor resources that require long journeys over unfamiliar terrain.

Population Increase Comparing hunter-gatherer camps to agricultural villages offers up a study in contrasts. Hunter-gatherers have a few children who are the focus of much adult attention. Agrarian villages and pastoralist encampments swarm with roving packs of boys and girls (Kramer 2019). When ethnographic hunter-gatherers reduce their residential movements, their population increases. Such population increases result from several causes. First, because women of childbearing age and pregnant women do not have to move around as much, they can accumulate body fat. Increased body fat stabilizes women's menstrual cycles and allows those who become pregnant to birth larger and more healthy babies. Second, injured or ill persons, such as young mothers recovering from childbirth or young men injured in foraging mishaps, have the opportunity to recover from their injuries. Last, elders facing the end of their days can enjoy the opportunity to ensure that younger people learn vital information, such as how to deal with a twice-in-a-century flood or a breech birth.

Habitat Deterioration To see food production–related habitat deterioration at work, one merely needs to open Google Earth and look at the borders between nature preserves and farms/pastures anywhere in the world. In many parts of the developing world, one can see earth-stripped-bare incursions by farmers and herders into the nature preserves. One never sees peninsulas of uncultivated or ungrazed lands extending outward from nature preserves into farmlands.

Humans need fire to live, and firewood can become scarce very swiftly around places humans have decided to live for prolonged periods. Wood-fueled fires can consume in a few hours a tree that grew for a century. Cutting down trees either for fuel or to free up new lands for cultivation and increases erosion. Growing the same crops in the same place, season after season, depletes soil nutrients at the very same time that increasing population sizes press ever more marginal parts of the landscape into cultivation. Grazing animals, especially Southwestern Asia's "hairy locusts" (sheep, goats, and cattle) further accelerate erosion and habitat deterioration. On the other hand, these creatures' feces can be dried out and used as fuel with considerable advantages over firewood, such as long burn times. Such dung-fed fires suffer an unjust reputation for foul odors, but they are, in the long run, better than nothing.[4]

Intensification Intensification describes working harder to get the same result (Thurston and Fisher 2007). It often accompanies humans' efforts to remain at the same residential site. Among farmers, one common intensification strategy involves recruiting children into farm work, essentially subsidizing their parents' efforts to have more children. This "helpers at the nest" strategy works among food producers because even small children can weed gardens, watch flocks, perform other subsistence-related tasks, and help raise younger siblings (Kramer 2005). It does not work as well among foragers, because young children need prolonged instruction and physical endurance in order to gather more plant foods or collect more animal prey than they themselves consume. Hunter-gatherer children can contribute to their group's food quest, but they rarely "pay for themselves" until they are adults.

Another intensification strategy specific to plant husbandry, manuring fields, boosts agricultural productivity, but it is also hard work that carries with it increased health risks, including exposure to zoonotic pathogens, and increased energetic costs, such as raising larger herds of manure-generating livestock and transporting that manure. Guarding larger livestock herds reduces losses due to predation and/or theft, but it also takes able-bodied persons out of the workforce tending planted crop fields.

Territorial Conflict Across the American West uncountable miles of barbed wire fence off even the least cattle-friendly pasturage and unfarmable farmlands. Food producers are extremely territorial, all but the least mobile hunter-gatherers much less so (Keeley 1996; Wrangham 1999; Bowles 2009). Increased territoriality (excluding others) can be one strategy for responding to habitat deterioration. Warfare – displacing others and taking over their farms, pastures, and residential sites – is another. Both have high costs and risks. "Asymmetric" conflicts between large and powerful groups and smaller and less-powerful groups might yield insufficient gains in arable land or pasturage to justify the effort. "Symmetric" conflicts between groups with roughly equal numbers and resources can be extremely risky, all-or-nothing contests with stalemates likely. Stalemates that grind down opposing sides' defenses can invite interventions by powerful third parties.[5]

---

[4] Burning nutrient-dense human feces, on the other hand, requires an accelerant (kerosene or gasoline) and creates an unforgettably awful odor.

[5] This, in a nutshell, is the history of Native North America from the 1500s CE onward.

The foregoing should not be read as endorsing the hypothesis that warfare (organized territorial conflicts accompanied by coalitionary killing) is either a recent phenomenon or a result of food production. Food production likely increased the incentives and reproductive and energetic payoffs for these evolutionarily ancestral activities (Wrangham 1999, 2019).

Migration Migration, or permanently moving as a coherent and unified group of food producers from one place to another, offers a superior alternative to territorial conflict and intensification, a solution to habitat destruction, and an outlet for population increase. In a word, the solution to food producers' having become less mobile in the long run (evolutionary timescales) is for them to become more mobile for a short period (historic timescales). Some prehistoric foraging groups may have migrated, perhaps having achieved the functional equivalent of food production by other means (plant and/or animal husbandry without domestication). As with warfare, food production lowered migration's costs and increased its benefits.

This chapter returns to migration below, but first it considers how food production altered the costs and benefits attending earlier dispersing humans' solutions to the basic six survival challenges, for alter them it did.

A SURVIVAL ARCHAEOLOGY PERSPECTIVE ON FOOD PRODUCTION

This section summarizes major contrasts between how food producers and hunter-gatherers solve essential survival challenges. Doing this requires one to generalize broadly, to pick out central tendencies. In doing this one risks succumbing to the "curse of the platonic ideal" – creating stereotypes of hunter-gatherer and food producing societies that do not remotely resemble any actual such societies. In every matter discussed below, both food producers and hunter-gatherers exhibit wide variability within and between groups. Behavioral variability is the common heritage of all humanity.

First Aid and Medication

Among small groups of mobile hunter-gatherers who range widely in search of food, serious injuries can occur away from residential sites and in situations with only a few people around. Among prehistoric hunter-gatherers living under similar circumstances, everyone probably knew basic and even advanced first aid. As food production aggregates humans around residential sites, near crops and herds of livestock, injuries become spatially aggregated, too. Livestock pens and trash middens provide opportunities for microbial pathogens to flourish and infect humans. Whereas hunter-gatherers can rely on individuals with a "side hustle" as a healer, healers among food producers can be in such demand that they can "turn pro," assisting the ill and injured in return for status, food, or some other forms of compensation. The resulting craft specialization pays off in efficiencies (i.e., discovering and promoting what works, discarding what does not). The archaeological record suggests such "healers" would not have wanted for work. Near-universally, the appearance of evidence for food production correlates with increasing indications of ill health, such as persistent infections, tooth decay, arthritis, and other problems.

Thermoregulation

One would not expect major differences in clothing or fire use between hunter-gatherers and farmers living in the same habitats, but their other thermoregulation strategies likely differed. Food producers' long-term stays at residential sites can create fuel shortages and accumulate dense ash deposits in ways more ephemerally occupied hunter-gatherer residential sites do not. Some hunter-gatherers living in cold habitats or in relatively treeless landscapes transport shelters made of wooden poles and animal skins from one residential site to another. Otherwise, most mobile hunter-gatherers create relatively small shelters made of lightweight materials foraged from local sources. Because food producers reside at the same habitation sites for longer periods and at higher population densities, benefits accrue for constructing larger shelters made of more durable materials, such as stones, adobe/mud-brick, and timber beams, procured from sources that grow ever more distant as prolonged occupations deplete local sources. They also construct storage pits and above-ground silos that stabilize temperature and humidity for food stores, and enclosures in which livestock can shelter from the elements.

Hydration

Ethnographic hunter-gatherers drink water more or less "as is." Desert-dwelling hunter-gatherers, in particular, maintain detailed mental maps of potable water sources in their familiar habitats. Doing this allows them to minimize the amount of water they have to carry while foraging. The longer people and livestock remain at the same location, the greater the potential for water contamination. Many of the pathogens that make people ill from drinking untreated water are microorganisms that defecating humans and other animals introduce into surface water sources. Food producers may have been the first humans who ever had to think about boiling water before drinking it or had to dig deep wells to gather it.

Nutrition

Preindustrial food producers and hunter-gatherers both procure significant amounts of calories from wild plants and animals, though, obviously, food producers depend more on domesticated plants and animals. Both use various techniques to prolong food's nutritional value, such as parching seeds and nuts or smoking or air-drying meat. Some northern hunter-gatherers often use "natural refrigerators," such as storage pits excavated into permafrost to preserve meat and other foods that can spoil quickly. Preindustrial food producers store food in bulk at scales far greater than hunter-gatherers do. A site featuring underground storage pits and/or evidence for above-ground grain silos is far more likely the remains of a food producer residential site than of a hunter-gatherer residential site. Stores of concentrated nutrients can attract rodents and other pests that are sources of disease. They can also encourage theft. Hunter-gatherers store food "socially and somatically." They share it among their social networks whose members swiftly consume and metabolize it. As the "survival" axiom has it, "better to carry food in you than on you."

Transportation

Both hunter-gatherers and preindustrial food producers move. A lot. Sedentism of the sort that creates obesity and allied problems is largely a postindustrial phenomenon (D. Lieberman 2013). Some hunter-gatherers use dogs and horses as transport aids, but by and in large, hunter-gatherers move mainly on their feet and by using watercraft. Food producers do so, too, but if and when they relocate, their need to move food stored in bulk requires they expand their range of transport aids to include "traction animals," such as dogs, camels, llamas, cattle, horses, and donkeys. While such "traction animals" can make food producers' movements less physically demanding, they also come with costs, such as ensuring animals have adequate supplies of food and water, not only while on the move but at residential sites between movements.

Communication

Food production is not more linguistically challenging than hunting and gathering, nor does it create selective pressures against any of the ways hunter-gatherers use artifacts to communicate. Recent human foragers and farmers/herders use personal adornments, mineral pigments, decorated baskets, and other artifact design variations to transmit symbolically encoded social messages. Food production, however, created an opportunity to make more extensive use of ceramics as media for such messages. Ceramics are heavy and fragile. Generally speaking, residentially mobile hunter-gatherers make little use of them. Sedentary food producers, on the other hand, can simply put a decorated pot near their hearth or some other publicly visible place and it will send a continuous message about its owners' social status, identity, and affinities.

One disadvantage to using ceramics as "social media" among sedentary food-producing communities is the increasing "noise to signal ratio." That is, if everyone is using ceramics to transmit social messages, then every vessel is a potential signaling medium. Much as today, in which every surface that can be used for advertising is used for advertising, using ceramics as social media increases the amount of time and energy devoted to making ceramics. Pretty much everywhere ceramics developed indigenously and remained in long usage, archaeologists can see onsets of "arms races" involving increasingly complex decorations.[6]

Food Production and Ancestral Survival Strategies

Do any of the things food producers do differently from hunter-gatherers require additions to our ancestral survival skills? None appear to do so. Making pots, administering medicines, and steering dogsleds require powerful precision grasping and predictive hallucination. Following herds from farm to pasture and back requires endurance bipedalism. Spoken language expresses design variation no less among ceramics than among stone tools or other artifacts. Indeed, ceramics plausibly track variation in spoken language much better than stone tools do. Living in large, stable communities tested hyperprosociality's limits, but early food producers plainly found "work-arounds." After all, and as with domesticated plants and animals, the archaeological record for food production provides few clear and convincing cases of food-producing societies who failed and whose populations became extinct. Some such failed food producers might have lived for a time on some remote island or another isolated location, but archaeologists have no evidence that food production ever failed in the long term or that any human population remained long isolated from others. "Isolated human societies" are an anthropological myth.

DETECTING FOOD PRODUCTION

How do archaeologists detect food production? This chapter has already discussed clues from plant remains and animal remains. Here, we consider more commonly encountered archaeological evidence, implements, containers, and architecture.

Implements

The sorts of tasks and motions one needs to do to butcher and process a domesticated goat do not differ all that much from those necessary to butcher and process a wild ibex. Unsurprisingly, implements humans use to procure and process animal food sources do not differ that much between

---

[6] The 1984 movie *Repo Man* (Universal Pictures) brilliantly satirized container-based advertisement and conspicuous "product placement" in cinematic films by having food container props labeled simply as "food" and "drink."

hunter-gatherers and food producers. Food producers' implements differ from hunter-gatherers' tools most obviously in seed-pulverizing tools. Some hunter-gatherers employ small mortars and pestles and handstones and grinding slabs. These portable and versatile small grinding slabs and the handstones accompanying them typically feature abrasive wear indicating rotary motion. The grinding slabs food producers create are usually large, difficult to carry, and more often feature evidence of linear bidirectional (back-and-forth) movements (Adams 2014a). Experimental studies suggest that linear bidirectional movements pulverize seeds more efficiently than rotary motion. Efficient in-bulk seed pulverizations might be more likely be a concern for food producers feeding a large audience than for hunter-gatherers living in small groups. But because pulverizing technique choice likely reflects processed food volume, rather than the nature of the seeds being pulverized, one expects hunter-gatherer and food-producer pulverizing tool designs to overlap with one another. One would be unwise to reflexively equate one or another technique of seed grinding with one and only one larger subsistence strategy. Much like other fracture-shaped stone tools, and perhaps even more so, groundstone tools are also potentially multipurpose tools.

Containers

All human societies make and use containers. Both hunter-gatherers and food producers make baskets, containers out of animal skins and textiles, and vessels carved out of wood and stone. Some historic and prehistoric hunter-gatherers made ceramic vessels, and some food producers did not. In general, however, large-scale ceramic vessel production, and especially the production of relatively large ceramic storage vessels (i.e., narrow opening, large body) is something mainly food producers do. If a vessel requires more than one person to move it, food producers probably made it.

Architecture

Architecture and food production enjoy a complex relationship with one another. Many of the variables that influence architecture, especially residential architecture, reflect mobility rather than subsistence strategies. The longer one stays at one location, the more benefits accrue for making more substantial houses and other structures. (Few short-term renters undertake major renovations to their abodes.) Hunter-gatherer societies often cope with food shortages and social conflicts by moving. Predictably, their domestic dwellings often comprise small hemispherical dwellings made of brush and other lightweight materials. Many sedentary food producers construct rectangular buildings. One thinks they do this because such buildings allow expansion simply by adding three walls to an existing one. There are some exceptions to this, of course.

Hunter-gatherers living along North America's Pacific Northwest Coast managed to position their habitation sites along coastlines and in places that do not require frequent residential movements. Their dwellings include very large rectangular houses.

Storage pits, bins, silos, and similar such structures more reliably indicate food production. Many preindustrial food producers harvest plant crops in bulk during a narrow seasonal "window" and store them for later use. Finding such structures in habitation sites could indicate food production. On the other hand, people who rely heavily on root crops, be they hunter-gatherers or food producers, may opt to "store" the root crops in their cultivated gardens, removing them only as needed.

MIGRATIONS BY FOOD PRODUCERS

Migrations are human population movements in which large numbers of people (hundreds or more) move over long distances (hundreds of kilometers) from a specific source to a specific destination, remaining at that destination permanently. On the move, they sustain themselves with food stored in bulk. At their destinations, migrating groups retain preexisting cultural and social institutions. In principle, this allows archaeologists to identify migrations from "chronological offsets," differences in first appearance dates for diagnostic artifacts in different regions. Migrations contrast with seasonal transhumance, in which a group relocates cyclically from one part of its geographic range to another during the course of a year.

To understand *prehistoric* migrations, one also has to discard the historical stereotype of "migrant as refugee." The finest literary expression of this stereotype occurs in Emma Lazarus' poem, "The New Colossus," published in 1883 on the occasion of the Statue of Liberty's construction:

> "Give me your tired, your poor,
> Your huddled masses yearning to breathe free,
> The wretched refuse of your teeming shore.
> Send these, the homeless, tempest-tost to me,
> I lift my lamp beside the golden door!"

Migration can be an attractive option for the well-off, too. In modern times, no few developing world wealthy elites and developed world oligarchs maintain residences in Manhattan, London, and elsewhere in functioning democracies to which to flee trouble in their autocratic homelands.[7] Human nature does not vary all that much, and so one assumes that prehistoric elites

---

[7] A small number of extremely wealthy individuals have sought to insulate themselves from future climate change, social upheaval, and other disasters by purchasing "private islands." As sea levels continue to rise, one recalls the aphorism, "Man plans, God laughs."

sometimes extracted themselves from trouble at home by relocating elsewhere, too. Large groups of food-producing elites, their allies, and retainers might even have enjoyed advantages over the hunter-gatherers into whose territories they migrated.

How and Why Food Producers' Migrations Succeed

History and prehistory offer up a unanimous verdict: migrations work. History records a few examples of failed attempts by one group to migrate into another already-occupied territory (e.g., the 11th-century Greenland Norse into easternmost Canada), but by and large, migrations' track record is a successful record. Even in cases where industrial states abandoned colonies, as Rome did Britain, or as the British Empire did North America, they left personnel behind and sufficient physical evidence that archaeologists and historians can trace the original colonists to their sources abroad. Prehistory offers up little evidence of large-scale migrations that failed in the long run (i.e., after more than a thousand years).

Why do migrations work so well? Three factors loom largest: hypergyny, population size, and the difficulty of a staging a "retreat."

Hypergyny Hypergyny is the term for when women from one group preferentially select, or are coerced into, reproductive relationships with males from another group, usually one in which they may enjoy increased individual reproductive success. In historic times and in multiethnic states, hypergyny often occurs when there are power asymmetries between groups. Women living in the less powerful group seek their reproductive fortunes elsewhere. The number of reproducing females, rather than males, limits a population's potential stability and growth far more so than the number of males. Thus, the group receiving more females grows while the other shrinks. In situations where ethnographic farmers and hunter-gatherers come into contact with one another, the power asymmetry between food producers and hunter-gatherers creates the incentives for hypergyny (Grinker 1990). Hypergyny, understandably, creates conflicts over dwindling numbers of women among hunter-gatherers as well as opportunities among food producers to exploit those conflicts to their advantage, such as offering to return "fugitive" women or to refrain from "poaching" them in return for labor, trade goods, or other services. Hypergyny is one among several factors that confer a "numbers advantage" on food producers over hunter-gatherers.

Population Size In societies that allow a man to have more than one wife at the same time (polygyny), some men of means choose to do so, if they can support multiple wives more-or-less equally.[8] Male hunter-gatherers rarely

---

[8] And woe to him who does not do so. Men in industrial societies with legally statutory monogamy (one wife at a time), often resort to "serial polygyny," marrying and divorcing

manage to support more than one wife simultaneously, but some men among food producers can do so. This allows food-producing societies that have crossed the "polygyny threshold" to reproduce much faster than hunter-gatherer societies. Such larger numbers confer advantages in territorial conflicts, not just between food producers and hunter-gatherers but also among different groups of food producers.

Due to food insecurity, hunter-gatherer women often struggle to reproduce (e.g., Shostak 1990). Food producers' stored food surpluses level out the interseasonal variation in food supplies that afflict hunter-gatherers. Migrations succeed because, once established, large groups of food-producing migrants rapidly outnumber their hunter-gatherer neighbors and/or less numerous food producers.

No Retreat In his 1914 poem "The Death of the Hired Man," Robert Frost writes, "Home is the place where, when you have to go there, / They have to take you in." For dispersing humans in historic times, this sometimes happened. Some individuals who migrated to European colonies returned to their homelands for one reason or another. Entire migrating populations, in contrast, cannot go home again, at least not together as a group. Migrations arise because of population increase and/or habitat deterioration in the source region. Returning large numbers of people *en masse* to the source would merely aggravate the problems that led to migration in the first place. In demographic terms, returning migrants would be "swimming against the current" of population pressure and ecological crises.

The most successful historic migrations arise from strong ideological motivations. Examples include the Mormons' migration to Utah in the 19th century, Zionist settlers relocating to Palestine and later the State of Israel in the 20th century, and 17th-century Pilgrims and Puritans to Massachusetts Bay. Ideologies can change, but because "defections" can winnow down their numbers advantages, people involved in a migration have a vested interest in maintaining both "carrots and sticks," that is, rewards for persisting and cooperating and strong sanctions, including reproductive isolation ("shunning") and even intragroup coalitionary killing (e.g., so-called honor killings) against quitters or "defectors" (Wrangham 2019).

DETECTING MIGRATIONS BY FOOD PRODUCERS

Traditional archaeological approaches to detecting migrations focus on "who questions," that is, finding similarities in evidence from different regions that

---

different women in succession. Some women, such as the actor, Elizabeth Taylor (1932–2011), manage to pull this off, too. Still other women cross the "autonomy threshold," accumulating such status and power that they do not need a mate or consort (e.g., Queen Elizabeth I of England).

connect sources to destinations. A "how questions" approach asks questions about differences.

Moving large groups of people, together, over land or on long ocean voyages requires food production or its functional equivalent as well as food storage. So, the first things for which archaeologists seeking evidence for migrations should search are evidence of food production, in-bulk food storage, and means by which to move people and food together across the landscape. If such things are not in evidence, then one ought not rule out migration, but one should not rank it above or equal to dispersal as an explanation of the evidence.

Watercraft and traction animals can reduce the energetic costs of moving across the landscape, and history shows humans used them whenever possible. Absent remains of actual watercraft, archaeologists can infer prehistoric watercraft use by circumstantial evidence, such as rocks moved across major rivers or other large water bodies. Bones of possible traction animals, such as horses, donkeys, camels, cattle, dogs, and llamas, may preserve traces of wear and tear associated with carrying heavy burdens.

Moving into new habitats exposes migrating humans to novel plant and animal food sources as well as to unfamiliar water sources. Migrating peoples' archaeological record, therefore, ought to furnish evidence of technological strategies for detoxifying plants and rendering questionable water potable. Boiling using ceramics and/or metal containers is a near-universal means by which ethnographic humans do this, though one can do the same thing using heated rocks and a wooden barrel. Versatile complex projectile weapons, (especially the bow and arrow), nets and traps, help migrating humans "cast the net wide." Much of such weapons systems, nets and traps are made of perishable organic materials. Still, stone and bone weapon armatures can indicate bow-and-arrow use, and large numbers of small animal remains visibly altered by cooking may indicate net or trap use.

Traditional archaeological approaches often look to changes in architecture, mortuary practices, stone tools, and ceramics in hypothetical destinations as evidence for migrations. Of these, ceramics are the most useful. Many environmental variables influence house forms. Shifts in mortuary practices can merely indicate receptive contact with other cultures, not the actual physical presence in large numbers. Stone tool technology is so liable to convergence (similar artifacts resulting from similar uses and constraints on use) that beyond supporting hypotheses about food production and watercraft use, they offer little to those seeking evidence for migration.

Ceramic decoration is not a pre-requisite for migration, but rather part of migration's archaeological "fallout." It is also a potential goldmine of information about migrations, though mostly in service of "how questions" concerning the directions of prehistoric population movements. Beyond the basic mechanical necessity of enclosing a given amount of space of one shape or another, ceramics offer up nearly infinite possibilities for decoration. Combinations of slips, incisions, painting, and other surface decorations compete in any society's "marketplace of ideas." Pots are not people, of course, but people are primates, and primates imitate one another, especially those of higher social rank. People in the same cultures make similar-looking pots. Though not as durable as stone tools, even earthenware pottery (ceramics fired at relatively low temperatures) can survive largely unaltered for thousands of years. Ethnographic humans recycle pots for various purposes (Sullivan 1989), but such recycling does not usually alter their decoration. Once a pot has shattered, children play with the potsherds and disperse them around the habitation sites and their environs (Hammond and Hammond 1981). This confers on the ceramic evidence high archaeological visibility.

Bantu Expansions in Sub-Saharan Africa: A Case Study

Can archaeologists detect prehistoric migrations? This section considers the "Bantu Expansions" in sub-Saharan Africa. "Bantu" is a Zulu word for "people." Early historical linguists adopted Bantu as a general term for African languages spoken throughout Africa south of the Equator (Figure 11.2).[9] (Linguists also refer to Bantu languages as "Niger-Congo B.") Cultural anthropologists use the term "Bantu" for indigenous Africans who speak those languages. Archaeologists also use the term "Bantu" for prehistoric food producers who migrated from equatorial Africa southward beginning around 2–3 Ka, displacing and enveloping hunter-gatherers who spoke non-Bantu languages. Older works refer to Bantu movements as "migrations," but the term "expansions" increasingly replaces it in the professional literature.

The archaeological consensus holds that the peoples involved in the Bantu Expansions did not invent plant and animal husbandry but instead modified older practices established thousands of years earlier in Africa's Sahel, the savanna and woodland belt bordering the Sahara Desert's southern margins (Barham and Mitchell 2008). Bantu peoples almost certainly modified plant and animal husbandry strategies as they moved.

African prehistorians reconstruct the origins and routes of the Bantu Expansions mainly using linguistic (and more recently genetic) evidence (Phillipson 1977; de Filippo et al. 2012; Li et al. 2014). Archaeologists have tried to correlate their findings with these reconstructions with varying degrees of success, mainly by charting hypothetical relationships among various "Bantu" ceramic wares. The current consensus holds that Bantu languages and "cultures" coalesced among early food producers living in Western Africa around Niger and Cameroon around 3.5–4.0 Ka. Initial expansions followed

---

[9] Swahili is the most commonly spoken Bantu language, but this reflects Swahili's prominent historical role in international trade, not the number of ethnic Swahili.

Detecting Migrations by Food Producers

Figure 11.2 Map of Africa showing the distribution of Bantu languages (shaded area). © John J. Shea.

shortly thereafter toward Eastern Africa and the Congo Basin, which itself became a secondary source of migrations southward. Around 1.5–2.0 Ka, the eastern branch of this expansion developed iron metallurgy and distinctive "Urëwe" ceramics by which archaeologists track the Bantu migration southward through Eastern Africa to Southern Africa. Urëwe ceramic wares include bowls and pots featuring beveled rims, concave ("dimpled") bases, and incised decorations (Figure 11.3). These decorations take many forms, but common ones include a ring running just below the rim of a bowl or a ring encircling a pot's neck (or "collar"). Eastern African archaeologists identify two "descendants" of Urëwe ceramics: Nkope wares found mainly in the highlands and Kwale wares found mainly at lower elevations and along the Indian Ocean coast. Both Nkope and Kwale wares differ from wares assigned to a Kalundu ceramic tradition associated with the Bantu Expansions' western and Congo Basin branches. Kalundu ceramics appear to have originated in the Congo and spread southeastward to the Indian Ocean coast intersecting with southward-spreading Nkope and Kwale wares somewhere around Mozambique and

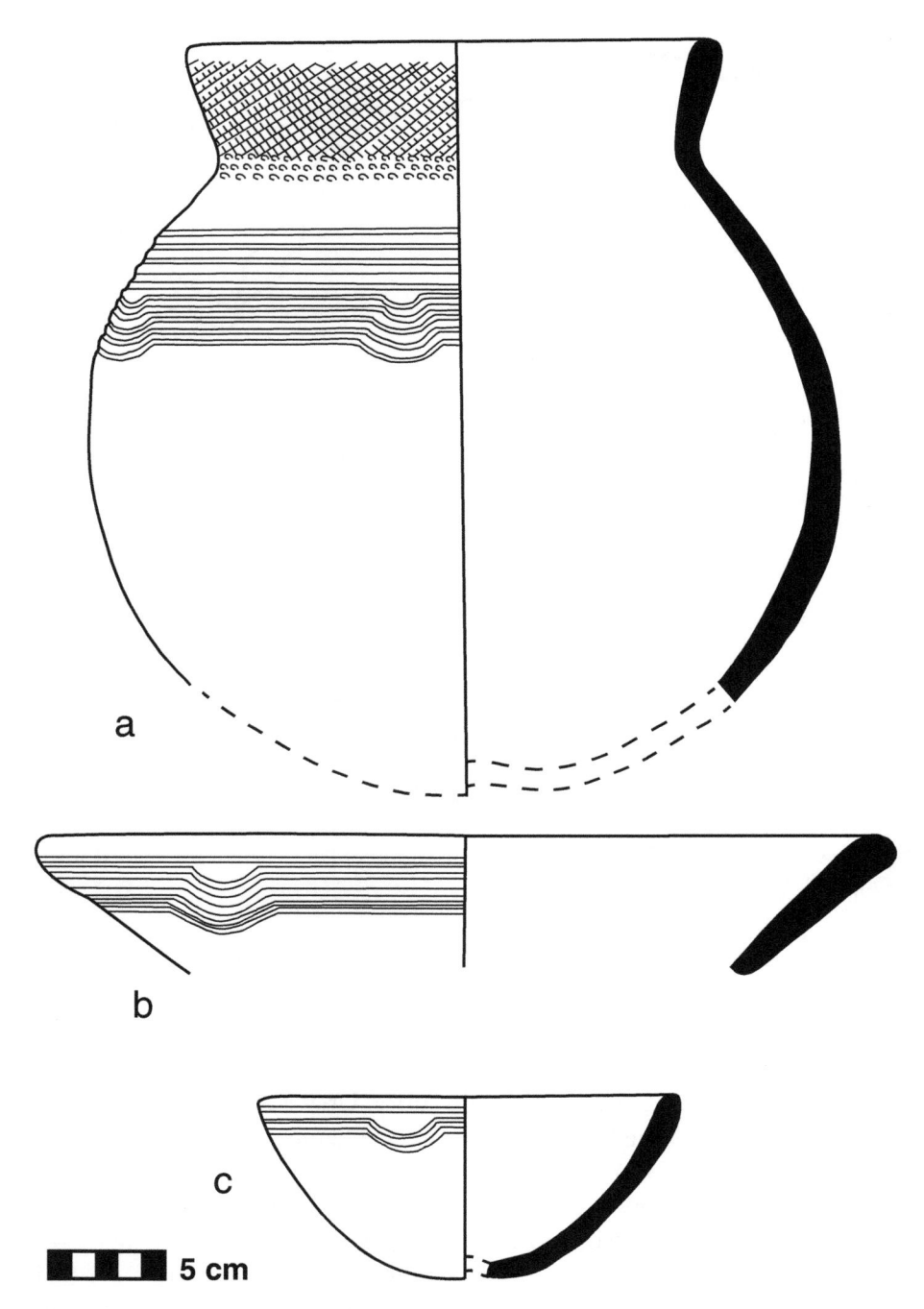

Figure 11.3 Urëwe pottery from Eastern Africa. Redrawn after Phillipson (2005: figure 127). © John J. Shea.

northeastern South Africa (Figure 11.4). These shifts in ceramic ware distributions are well dated and show steady southward progressions consistent with large-scale movements of people maintaining their social identities – at least to the extent archaeologists can measure them from ceramic design variation.

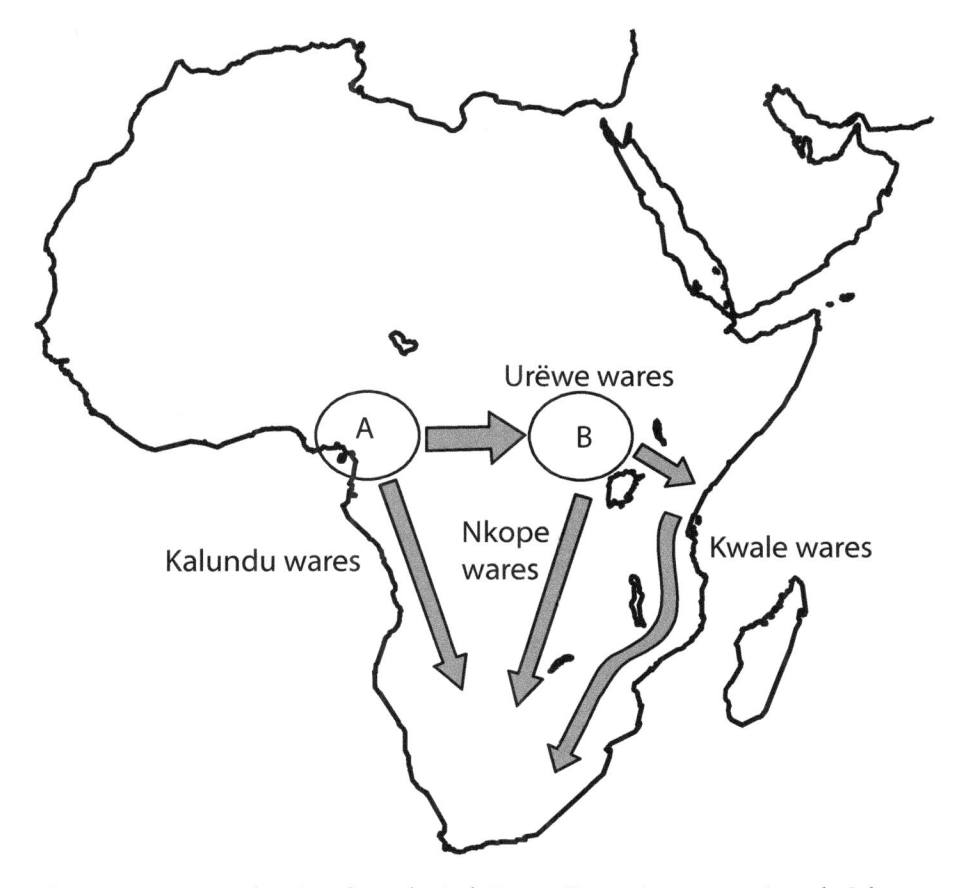

Figure 11.4 Map showing hypothetical Bantu Expansion routes in sub-Saharan Africa. A, Proto-Bantu homeland; B, secondary migration source. © John J. Shea.

Migration versus Dispersal Were the Bantu Expansions migrations, or are archaeologists merely tracking the independent spread of food production and ceramics? To migrate, people need food that can be stored and transported in bulk. Bantu ceramics occur with traces of agriculture based on crops indigenous to Africa's Sahel region and cattle, goats, and sheep derived ultimately from Southwest Asia and North Africa's Mediterranean Coast. Drought-tolerant cattle, goats, and sheep are self-storing and mobile. Recent Bantu farmers/herders store cereal grains in above-ground silos with circular rock foundations built to deter rodent incursions. Traces of such silos occur in many sub-Saharan Africa sites after 1–2 Ka. Silo foundations are either scarce or absent in older sites. When historic Bantu groups had to relocate for one reason or another, they often packed cereals in baskets, attached those baskets to harnesses on their cattle, and moved. Prehistoric Bantu migrants probably did similar things.

Other ceramics preceded Bantu-affiliated pottery in sub-Saharan Africa (Ashley and Grillo 2015). Nderit wares and other ceramics were in wide use in at least Eastern Africa from 5 Ka onward. Thus, the appearance of Bantu ceramic wares is not an example of pottery spreading, but instead about the "right" way to make pottery among Bantu cultures.

More than just ceramics and food plants/animals moved along with Bantu peoples. Ironmaking came along for the ride, too. Though stone cutting tools are far sharper than iron ones, iron has superior cutting properties to stone in tasks requiring forceful cutting, such as chopping down trees, woodworking in general, and as weapon armatures (spear points, arrowheads). Around 2.5 Ka, Bantu and other groups began making iron, initially in what is now Uganda, Rwanda, and Burundi, and later more broadly. Traditional African iron smelting is a complex, labor-intensive process that literally "takes a village" (to cut wood, make charcoal, build and operate the furnace, extract iron pellets from slag, and so on). Throughout sub-Saharan Africa ironworking coincides closely with first appearances of Bantu ceramics and more intensive plant and animal husbandry. While it is possible individual ceramic-making, farmer/herder, ironworking polymaths dispersed on their own into the hinterlands during this time, a far less complex scenario involves large groups with these skills distributed broadly among their members moving southward together.

Finally, in Eastern and Southeastern Africa, the beginnings of iron production correlate with evidence of accelerated erosion and other habitat degradation. These phenomena most likely result from tree clearance for charcoal production in order to fuel iron furnaces, and from overgrazing recently cleared land.[10] One hesitates to call this "ecosystem engineering," for one doubts those involved thought of it as conscious strategy, but by clearing and burning forests, Bantu farmers transformed sub-Saharan Africa's forests and woodlands into the sorts of open grasslands in which their Northern African and Southwestern Asian crops and herd animals evolved. This sort of rapid ecosystem engineering is a predictable consequence of migration. It is certainly not what one would expect hunter-gatherers to suddenly start doing to the forests that had sustained them for the last 300,000 years.

All available evidence shows that the Bantu Expansions were migrations. That being said, they probably involved countless smaller-scale movements of dozens or hundreds of people over tens of kilometers rather than thousands of people on the move together over many hundreds of kilometers. Archaeologists group these smaller-scale movements together as migrations/expansions mainly to answer historians', linguists', and cultural anthropologists' "who questions." One expects that as archaeologists shift their focus to "how questions," the Bantu Expansions will turn out to be far more complex than the use of the definite article before "Bantu" implies.[11]

---

[10] Charcoal production and overgrazing remain leading causes of habitat disturbance in Eastern and Southern Africa to this day.
[11] Though linguists and cultural anthropologists recognized hundreds of distinct Bantu languages and cultures, archaeologists routinely refer to them as "the Bantu."

This finding is important because it shows that archaeologists can detect and credibly identify prehistoric migrations. The key to doing so lies not so much in asking "who questions," such as who the Bantu people were, as it does in asking "how questions," such as how they stored and transported food, and whether we can identify source and destinations using geochronology. These findings are also important because they show that identifications of dispersals in Pleistocene "deep-time" prehistory are not just artifacts of archaeological method. If there were Pleistocene-age migrations, archaeologists ought to be able to identify them to the exclusion of competing hypotheses, just as one can the Bantu Expansions.

MIGRATIONS BY HUNTER-GATHERERS

Prehistory does not lack for hypotheses about prehistoric migrations involving food producers (Bellwood 2013), but examples of hunter-gatherer "continental" migrations number far fewer. These include the following:

- *The mid-Holocene expansion of "Pama-Nyungan" languages out of northern Australia to the rest of that already-populated continent.* This expansion is thought to be correlated with increased production of small backed/truncated pieces and the use of domestic dogs (dingoes). No evidence suggests this expansion involved food production.
- *Human migrations into the North American high Arctic ca. 1 Ka.* Around this time an archaeological complex called "Thule" seems to have brought the ancestors of modern-day Inuit peoples from Alaska to Greenland over the course of several centuries. In these movements, Thule peoples are thought to have replaced previously established "Dorset" cultures. The Thule peoples had domesticated dogs, but lacked domesticated plants and food animals.
- *Later Holocene movements of Athapaskan-speaking hunter-gatherer groups from Alaska and the Yukon south into the US Southwest after 4 Ka.* These hunter-gatherers reached lands Ancestral Puebloan food producers had occupied for millennia and settled in around these groups' margins. Their descendants, the Navajo (Diné) and Apache, mostly remained hunter-gatherers until long after European contact in the 16th century.

These hypothetical hunter-gatherer migrations seem logical places in which to seek evidence contradicting the hypothesis that migrations require food production or its functional equivalent.

SUMMARY

Food production changed the costs, benefits, strategies, and patterns of human population movements. It created an alternative to in-place intensification and short-range dispersal. Migrations in Eurasia, Africa, and the Americas transformed sparsely populated subcontinents of hunter-gatherers to increasingly populous landscapes of farmers and herders. These continental migrations increased human populations many times over, but they did not increase *Homo sapiens*' global geographic range in quite the same way that oceanic migrations did. The next chapter, Chapter 12, considers the great oceanic migrations that brought humanity to the most remote islands.

Box 11.1: *The need for speed: How fast and far can people migrate?*

Paleoanthropological speculation about how fast and far prehistoric humans and other hominins moved across ancient landscapes rarely gets specific about the time and distances involved. Some of this lack of specificity reflects the actual complexity and lack of certainties about the evidence. Other aspects surrounding this issue reflect a public and professional tolerance for vague answers and lack of good models (recent examples of migrations) on which to base hypotheses about past human population movements.

Hunter-gatherers retreated from and assimilated into food-producing societies worldwide for the last 10,000 years. As a result, neither historic nor ethnographic records provide any basis for estimating how fast pre-agricultural humans can move over any specific sort of terrain. Any estimates about speed and/or distance have to be estimated using computer simulations (many of whose assumptions remain questionable) and/or archaeological evidence, a strategy that risks both circular reasoning (using the same evidence as source and test of hypotheses) and unfalsifiable equations between archaeological cultures and industries and specific human/hominin populations (see Box 7.1 on ghost marriages).

With these risks in mind, the paleoanthropological record for dispersals by species in the genus *Homo* suggests truly impressive movements at great speed over intercontinental distances. First appearance dates for fossils of *Homo habilis* in Southern and Eastern Africa (a distance of around 3,500 km) are both around 2.4 Ma. Current evidence suggests *H. erectus/ergaster* first appears around 1.9 Ma in Africa, but first appearances outside Africa are somewhat younger (1.7 Ma in Georgia and 1.3 Ma in Indonesia). *Homo heidelbergensis* first appearance dates ca. 0.5–0.7 follow neither clear geographic or chronological trends, nor do dates for *H. neanderthalensis* in Western Eurasia or *H. sapiens* in Africa. This lack of spatial patterning may reflect sparse evidence or, conversely, improvements of evolutionarily ancient capacities for rapid dispersal. That such intercontinental-scale distributions are unique to the genus *Homo* further suggests they may arise from capacities and survival strategies also unique to the genus *Homo*.

Box 11.1: *(cont.)*

History provides a few examples of migrations, but most of these involved mechanically assisted transportation (watercraft, aircraft, railroads) and/or domesticated traction animals (horses, cattle, donkeys, camels, etc.). Dates for changes in the archaeological record assumed to reflect Holocene-age migrations, such as the spread of farming into Central and Western Europe or the Bantu Expansions discussed earlier in this chapter, suggest preindustrial humans could migrate at subcontinental scales spanning thousands of kilometers long over a few thousand years (Bellwood 2013).

For thought and discussion: Historic and later prehistoric migrations occurred during the Holocene Epoch, a relatively stable period in Earth's climate. Pleistocene hominin population movements unfolded during a period of much wider-ranging and short-term climate change. What risks accompany using models of human population movements based on Holocene evidence to explain variation in the Pleistocene paleoanthropological record? If we are to use computer-assisted simulations of such movements, what assumptions can we build into those simulations? Might the sheer number of such conflicting assumptions generate too many competing models to shed much light on the matter? Does using dispersal/migration models based on observations of nonhuman species offer an alternative source of hypotheses? Should such models incorporate only primates? Only mammals? Only terrestrial (i.e., nonavian and nonaquatic) species? What do you think, and can one prove those thoughts wrong?

CHAPTER 12

DISTANT HORIZONS AND STARS BECKON
Oceanic Islands and Beyond

This chapter examines prehistoric migrations to oceanic islands. First, it considers the special difficulties of reaching such islands, and reviews claims about Pleistocene pre-agricultural movement to oceanic islands. Next, it focuses on the peopling of the Pacific Ocean, the fastest and most geographically extensive human population movement of all time. Though some archaeologists have speculated that these islands were colonized accidentally, the evidence shows that these were purposeful voyages by people who knew exactly where they were, where they were going, and how to get there. Lowered sea levels during the LGM/MIS 2 shortened distances between some islands and possibly aided humans living in Sunda, Wallacea, and Sahul in settling Near Oceania. Movements into Remote Oceania commenced around 4 Ka, and movements into Polynesia after 1 Ka. Finally, the chapter considers future human migrations on Earth and beyond. The latter, it argues, will not be "just like *Star Trek*."

OCEANIC MIGRATIONS

Oceanic migrations are large-scale human population movements to islands located more than 20–30 kilometers from continental coastlines and from one another. Archaeologists investigating such population movements to oceanic islands look for the following evidence:

- *Artifacts and other traces of human activity appearing suddenly at multiple sites on the same island.* Over time, these sites increase in number and in size.
- *The oldest artifacts resembling those found on nearby islands and continental coastlines.* Artifacts whose nature allows considerable design variation, such as decorated pottery, carved bone, shell, or stone (especially groundstone tools), architecture, and mortuary structures are especially clear evidence for migrations.
- *Artifacts made of rocks from distant, nonlocal sources.* Because the trace-element components of obsidian (volcanic glass) vary so much between

sources, archaeologists often focus their search for long-distance raw material movements on obsidian.

- *First appearances of plants and animals formerly unobserved in the island's fossil record.* These typically include domesticated plants and animals, but they may include introduced wild animals as well as "commensals" (rats, mice, and similar creatures).
- *Extinctions of indigenous wildlife.* These extinctions usually hit larger animals first then cascade downward, affecting ever-smaller animals. The larger animals may succumb to overhunting and/or habitat destruction. Smaller animals, such as ground-nesting birds, often fall prey to imported commensal rodents and smaller domesticated animals, such as dogs and pigs.
- *Remains of pelagic fish (fish caught out in the open ocean).* Any group capable of oceangoing travel will have devised methods for catching such fish and transporting them to shore. Such evidence can be tricky to interpret, however, for, as in the 19th-century Pacific, many Polynesian societies "lost" their far-seafaring technologies after having become overly dependent on European vessels. Similar, if temporary, such losses may have occurred in earlier times.

Rich in inhabited islands, the Pacific Ocean furnishes the "model" above, but these phenomena are not unique to the Pacific. They repeat themselves in the Atlantic (Azores), the Caribbean, and the Indian Ocean (Madagascar). These repeated occurrences suggest they are not historically unique phenomena, but instead shared features of what happens when large groups of humans move to previously unoccupied islands.

Experimental Seafaring

Proponents of ancient oceanic migrations sometimes cite (or even conduct) "experiments" in which modern-day sailors construct plausible prehistoric rafts or boats and then navigate them from one place to another (Bednarik 2001). These experiments demonstrate the plausible is possible, but they differ from prehistoric seafaring in several important respects. First, we know so little about prehistoric watercraft that "plausible" covers much ground in terms of watercraft design. Second, these "experiments" are not really experiments in the strict scientific sense of the word. They lack controls (alternative ways of doing the same thing), replications are rare (one voyage is often the only experiment), and their conclusions rarely state their findings' statistical significance, that is, the chance of getting the same results from chance alone. Last, those undertaking such experiments often have with them electronic rescue-signaling devices and/or modern watercraft and aircraft monitoring them nearby. Knowing that rescue is a near certainty may encourage experimenters to take risks, such as longer voyages, that prehistoric seafarers might not have attempted.

Historic Oceanic Migrations

Living at the end of a great wave of oceanic migrations that began in Europe around 500 years ago, it can be tempting to project those migrations' qualities into deep-time prehistory. Although uniformitarian principles require we base our hypotheses about prehistoric migrations on historic human migrations, the two differ in several important ways, most obviously in scale and distances, but also in the roles that disease, competition, and slavery played in them.

Distance European Renaissance and later maritime technology allowed dozens of sailors and passengers to stay at sea for months at a time and to travel thousands of kilometers. The prehistoric record preserves little or no evidence for such long-distance voyages other than in the final stages of the peopling of Polynesia.

Disease When Renaissance-era Europeans began fanning out over the world, that continent had just emerged from wave after wave of Medieval and earlier plagues, such as the Black Death. Smallpox remained common, but Europeans had evolved various degrees of immunity to it. American Indians, Southern Africans, Australian Aborigines, and Pacific Islanders had no previous exposure to smallpox, no immunity, and it killed them in droves.[1] Mortality estimates vary widely, but in more densely populated regions in the Americas, casualties are estimated to have exceeded 90 percent of the indigenous population (Crosby 1986; Kelton 2007; Mann 2011). Prehistoric population movements over shorter distances and involving low population densities did not bring humans from starkly different geographic "disease pools" into contact with one another and, as such, likely did not create such horrific outcomes as recent plagues.

Competition European migrations focused on setting up colonies in strategic places in order either to control intercontinental trade routes and to make it easier to extract minerals (especially precious metals) to fund land wars in Europe. Europe's various industrial nations competed fiercely among themselves for these colonies. Prehistoric food producers undoubtedly tried to control trade routes, but the deep-time archaeological record does not preserve evidence for organized competition and large-scale military conflict over control of such trade routes.

Slavery Many European colonies succeeded because they used slave labor. Enslaved people were either imported from abroad or captured from local populations. Not having to pay large numbers of laborers made economically viable enterprises such as plantation farming (e.g., of cotton and tobacco) and gold/silver mining that were otherwise prohibitively costly.

---

[1] This was not a one-way street, however. Malaria, to which indigenous tropical humans had greater tolerance, wiped out many European migrants to the New and Old World tropics.

Pleistocene Migrations to Mediterranean Islands

If one seeks evidence for Pleistocene human migrations to islands beyond visual range from one another or from the mainland, then the Mediterranean Sea offers up numerous opportunities to find such evidence. First, from a navigational standpoint, these islands are relatively easy to reach from the nearest mainland. Second, if seafaring was an evolutionarily primitive (ancestral) capacity, then archaeological evidence for it should appear on Mediterranean islands. After all, archaeological sites more than a million years old occur on both Europe's and Africa's Mediterranean shores. Finally, they are among the most intensely archaeologically surveyed places on Earth. If humans were on Mediterranean islands during Pleistocene times, archaeologists should have found clear and convincing evidence of their presence by now.

Hunter-gatherers from the East Mediterranean Levant visited Cyprus as much as 10 Ka and before farmer-herders arrived ca. 8 Ka, but it is not clear that they occupied that island continuously between 8 and 10 Ka (Simmons 2012). Several possible stone artifacts dating to more than 130 Ka have been claimed for the island of Crete (Greece) (Strasser et al. 2010), but this and other claims for Pleistocene voyaging to Mediterranean islands remain controversial. Some claims rely on objects whose status as artifacts remains in dispute. Even if these older objects are indeed artifacts and correctly dated, they do not necessarily prove a successful migration. Shipwreck victims can leave archaeological records too. On Crete, the next-youngest evidence for human activity dates to around 8 Ka and features remains of domesticated cattle, sheep/goats, pigs, dogs, and cereal grasses, evidence consistent with this work's "migrations require food production" hypothesis. This pattern repeats itself on the other larger remote Mediterranean islands (Corsica, Sardinia, and Sicily). The available evidence shows that while hunter-gatherers may have visited them occasionally, continuous hominin occupations began after early Holocene farmer-herders arrived. Tellingly, those arrivals coincide exactly with extinctions of the "dwarf" hippos, elephants, and other larger mammals that had evolved in isolation on those islands and that comprised attractive prey for small groups of human hunters.[2]

PACIFIC OCEAN MIGRATIONS: THE ROAD OF THE WINDS

This section focuses on migrations to Pacific Ocean islands. It relies heavily on syntheses of this subject by O'Connor and Hiscock (2014), Kirch (2018),

---

[2] Larger prey yields greater energetic returns per time spent in pursuit and capture than smaller game. Thus, one would expect shipwreck survivors and early migrants alike to have targeted large island prey first before moving on to smaller prey. Recognizing this, 18th- and 19th-century European commercial vessels released goats onto remote islands so that future visitors would find familiar food sources.

and Thomas (2021). As these works do, this chapter sets aside one traditional European term for Pacific Islands, Melanesia ("dark islands"), discussing them instead as Near Oceania (the Bismarck Archipelago and the Solomon Islands, or 155–165° West longitude) and Remote Oceania (New Caledonia to Samoa, or roughly 165–170° West longitude). It refers to the peoples involved in these movements into Oceania as "Oceanians." It retains Micronesia ("small islands") for islands north of Oceania. It also retains "Polynesia" for the islands between Hawai'i (north), New Zealand (south), and Rapa Nui/Easter Island (east) (Figure 12.1) and "Polynesians" for the people who live on them.

Conditions Affecting Population Movements

Most of the Pacific Ocean sits atop the Pacific tectonic plate. Islands form where upwelling magma (molten volcanic rock) penetrates this plate. Initially, these islands are tall with sharp mountain peaks and active volcanoes. But as the plate moves, upwellings weaken, and volcanoes exhaust themselves. Over long periods of time, erosion and subsidence reduce these island to low atolls surrounded by reefs and lagoons. There are many more islands in the western part of the Pacific than in the east. Those in the Eastern Pacific are scattered farther apart from one another than those in the Western Pacific. All of these islands are relatively impoverished in terms of plant and animal diversity, and such diversity decreases to the east. In part, this ecological impoverishment reflects declining island size to the east and prevailing winds that blow from east to west. Westward-blowing winds makes movements of plants and animals eastward literally "sailing against the wind."

These observations have several important implications for human settlement. First, movements to Near Oceania were difficult, but humans involved were moving between habitats with similar suites of plant and animal life, including root crops and abundant fisheries and bird colonies. Moving beyond Near Oceania required food and water sufficient to sustain migrating humans on route to their new habitats and on arrival. Moving to Polynesia, on the other hand, had both opportunities and costs. The opportunity? Such movements removed humans from those parts of the Old World tropics home to malaria-bearing mosquitos. Having removed themselves from the scourge of humanity's oldest enemy (Shah 2011), human populations must have increased quickly. The cost? Humans seeking to alleviate "population pressure" would have had to have done so by making longer ocean voyages and by bringing with them everything they needed to establish themselves in resource-impoverished Polynesian islands. Doing this was dangerous and difficult, but when European explorers arrived in the Pacific Ocean during 1600s–1700s, they found people living on all but the smallest and least inhabitable such islands.

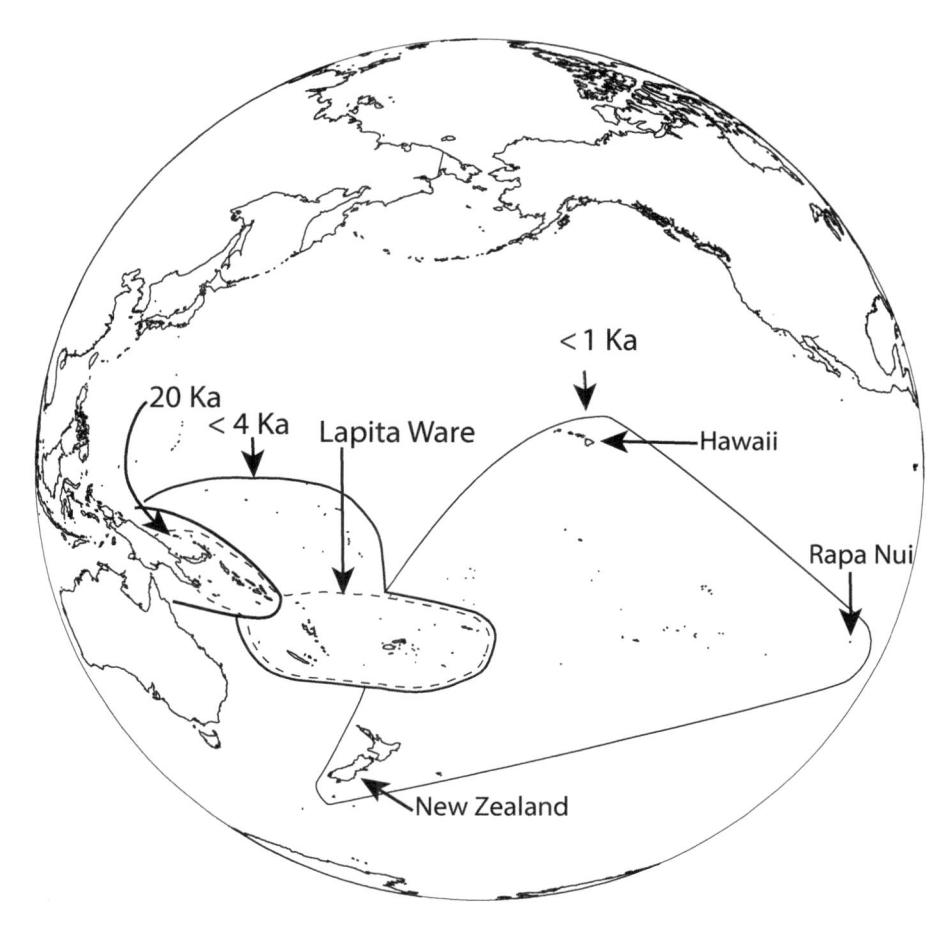

Pacific Ocean Migrations: The Road of the Winds 261

Figure 12.1 Map showing major human population movements to Pacific Ocean islands. © John J. Shea.

Archaeological Overview

The archaeological record shows that peopling of the Pacific's oceanic islands began around 30–40 Ka and was a continuous process, albeit one with identifiable "fits and starts." One can usefully break this process down into three phases: movements to Near Oceania beginning around 30 Ka, the "Oceanian" movements to Remote Oceania and western Polynesia that commenced around 34.0 Ka, and the settlement of Eastern Polynesia and New Zealand after 1.0 Ka. Table 12.1 lists first appearance dates for human activity on Pacific Ocean sites.

Near Oceania Humans had settled Sahul (Australia, New Guinea, and Tasmania) before 30–40 Ka. Precise dates for early Sahulians remain controversial, as such issues will in archaeology, but humans were clearly well established over much of Sahul before 30–40 Ka (see Chapter 7). The oldest archaeological sites in Near Oceania date to around this time or a little older,

TABLE 12.1 *First appearance dates for human activity on Pacific Ocean islands*

Island group	Site (island)	Date (Ka)	Comment
Near Oceania			
	Yombon (New Britain)	38.0–42.4	Open-air site, stone tools
	Kupona na Dari (New Britain)	38.0–39.0	Open-air site, stone tools
	Buang Merabak (Guinea, New Ireland)	41.6–45.3	Rock shelter, use of coastal resources
	Matenkupkum (New Ireland)	38.1–41.9	Rock shelter, use of coastal resources
	Pamwak (Manus)	> 13.0	Rock shelter
	Kilu (Buka)	20.0–29.0	Rock shelter
	Vatuluma Posovi (Solomon Islands)	2.2–6.4	Rock shelter
Remote Oceania			
	Nanggu (SZ-8) (Santa Cruz Group)	2.7–2.9	Lapita coastal midden
	Nenumbo (RF-2) (Santa Cruz Group)	2.7–3.0	Lapita coastal midden
	Teouma (Vanuatu)	2.8–2.9	Lapita cemetery
	Patho (Maré, Loyalty Islands)	2.5	Lapita coastal midden
	Lapita Site 13 (New Caledonia)	2.4–2.9	Lapita coastal midden
	Natunuku (Viti Levu, Fiji)	3.1–3.2	Lapita coastal midden
	Qaranipuqa (Labeka, Fiji)	2.8	Lapita rock-shelter occupation
	Pe'a (To.1) (Tongatapu)	3.1	Lapita coastal midden
	Mulifanua (Upolu, Samoa)	2.8–2.9	Lapita submerged site under reef
Micronesia			
	Unai Bapot (Saipan, Marianas)	3.1–3.21	Midden site
	Tarague Beach (Guam, Marianas)	1.0–3.4	Midden site
	Chelechol ra Orrak (Palau)	3.0	Rock shelter
	Pemrang (Yap)	< 1.8	Midden site
	Fais Island middens (Fais Island, Carolines)	< 1.7	Midden sites
	Sabaig (Lamotrek, Carolines)	1.0	Midden site
	Fenfan (Chuuk)	2.0	Coastal midden site
	Kwajelein (Marshall Islands)	2.2–20	Midden site
	Laura (Majuro, Marshall Islands)	1.8–2.0	Midden site
	Temei (Vaitupu, Tuvalu)	0.9	Midden site
	Nukouru (Micronesia)	< 1.2	Midden sites
Western Polynesia			
	Pulemeli (Sava'i, Samoa)	0.9	Stone mound
	Sasoa'a ('Upolu, Samoa)	1.8–2.0	Inland habitation site
	'Aoa Valley (Tutuila, Samoa)	< 3.0	Multiple sites
	To'aga (Manu'a, Samoa)	< 3.0	Coastal habitation site
	Mua (Tongatapu, Lapaha)	< 0.7	Stone ceremonial structure

(continued)

TABLE 12.1 *(continued)*

Island group	Site (island)	Date (Ka)	Comment
Eastern Polynesia			
	Tangatatu (Mangaia, Cook Islands)	< 1.0	Rock shelter
	Vaotp'otia-Fa'ahia (Hunahine Society Islands)	0.6–0.8	Waterlogged habitation site
	Hane (Ua Huku, Marquesas)	0.2–1.1	Residential site on sand dune
	Henderson (Pitcairn Group)	0.2–0.9	Rock shelter
	Onemea (Taravai Mangareva)	0.7–1.0	Residential site on sand dune
	Anakena (Easter Island/Rapa Nui)	0.6–0.9	Residential site on sand dune
	Bellows Dune (O'ahu, Hawaiian Islands)	0.7–0.9	Residential site on sand dune
	Wairau Bar (New Zealand)	0.7–0.8	Midden and burials

Source: Kirch (2018).

showing that humans undertook distant sea voyages long before the Last Glacial Maximum (LGM) dropped sea levels to unprecedented lows. Movements to more distant islands, such as Manus and Buka, appear to have occurred during or after the LGM.

The stone artifacts from these early Near Oceanic sites are largely bipolar cores (split cobbles and pebbles) and short nonhierarchical cores, much like those that dominate archaeological sites on Sunda at around the same time. Similar such artifacts also dominate the earliest Plio-Pleistocene archaeological sites in Eurasia. This could suggest that, as in Plio-Pleistocene hominin dispersals (Shea 2010), such stone tool evidence is an expression not so much of "primitive" culture but instead of versatile stoneworking strategies tailored to the uncertainties of living at the outer frontiers of human settlement.

Were these early Oceanian movements migrations? The archaeological consensus holds that they were. Sites in the Bismarck archipelago preserve evidence suggesting that humans deliberately introduced a tree-dwelling marsupial, the gray cuscus (*Phalanger orientalis*), possibly in order to ensure adequate sources of protein, fats, and hides. Though these were not domesticated animals, this is evidence for the core criterion for food production, altering other species' reproductive strategies for human benefit. In this case humans extended the gray cuscus' geographic range and changed its potential predators and food sources, all factors that influence reproduction. One suspects that if humans were transporting wild animals to new habitats, then they probably also transported root crops such as *Colocasia* (taro).

Remote Oceania and the Lapita Expansions The next "big move" in the peopling of Oceania, the Lapita expansions, began around 4 Ka and lasted to around 3 Ka. Lapita is an archaeological site in New Caledonia whose name refers to particular ceramic wares, bevel-rimmed and dentate-stamped

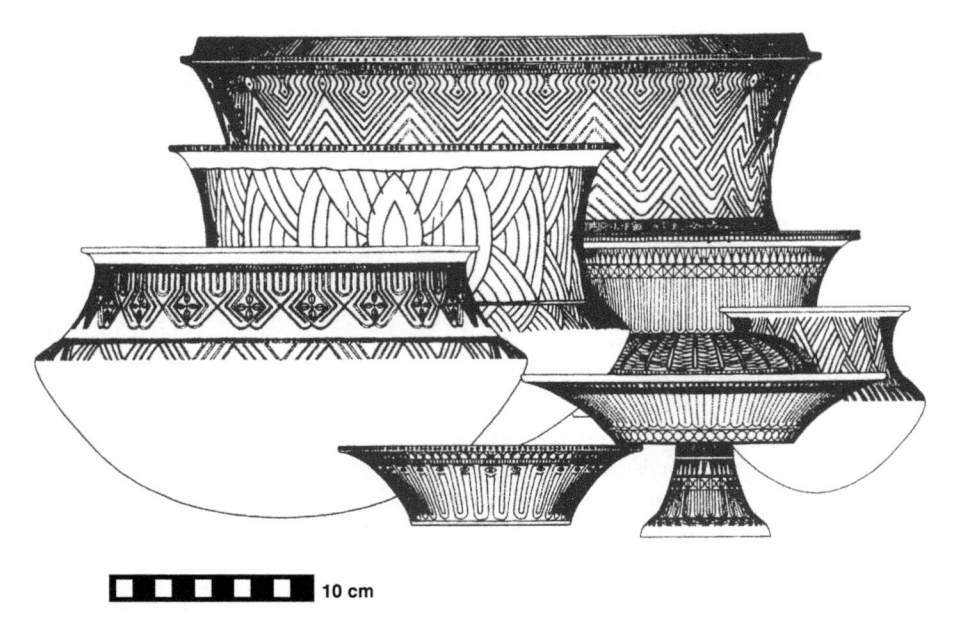

Figure 12.2 Lapita ceramic vessels. Original artwork by Christophe Sand, used with permission.

earthenware vessels that became widespread in both Near and Far Oceania (Figure 12.2). (Dentate-stamping involves making patterned impressions on ceramics with a comb-like implement.) Lapita pottery appears across a broad swath of islands from Manus off northern New Guinea across the Bismarck archipelago, the Solomon Islands, and southeastward to New Caledonia, Tonga, and Samoa. Lapita complex settlements are larger than those that preceded them. Often located on beach terraces overlooking lagoons, they preserve the log pilings of dwellings built on stilts. Nearby middens preserve evidence for both oceanic and near-shore fishing and shellfish collection. Lapita artifacts include abraded-edge celts made of dense gastropod (*Tridanca*) shells, and fishhooks carved from bone and *Truchus* shells.

Archaeologists trace the origins of Lapita ware to a range of red pigment–slipped ceramics with roots in Southeast Asia and the Philippines. The eruption of Mount Witori in New Britain 3.3 Ka seems correlated with a major eastward expansion of the Lapita complex, but the complex's origins are far less important than its impact. More so than earlier migrants to Near Oceania, Lapita ceramic-making peoples brought their economies with them. Remains of domesticated dogs, pigs, and chickens appear at Lapita sites. These species were not indigenous but brought to the Pacific Islands from Southeast Asia. Lapita peoples' cultivated crops included bananas (*Australimusa*), taro (*Colocasia, Alocasia,* and *Cyrtosperma*), and sugarcane (*Saccharum officinarum*), all brought from Southeast Asia to Far Oceania's resource-impoverished islands.

Were the Lapita expansions a migration? It was probably not a single movement, but instead a complex series of overlapping movements. Extrapolating from modern-day cultures to prehistory is fraught with risks, but many of the "Austronesian" peoples (a linguistic-cultural grouping uniting Oceanian and Polynesian descendant communities) rank their children in descending order of birth, and they highly esteem founders of new settlements.[3] Younger siblings achieve status in this system by finding new islands and founding new settlements on them. The speed with which the Lapita complex spread into Remote Oceania over two or three centuries may reflect such a sibling-status competition "arms race."

While Lapita ceramic-making peoples spread eastward, other Oceanians were on the move elsewhere, settling the Micronesian islands north of New Guinea (Palau, Guam, the Marianas, Marshalls, Kiribatis, and Tuvalu) after around 3 Ka. Some Oceanians even reached and settled Madagascar by 1.3 Ka. Stone tools and faunal remains from two sites in northern Madagascar (Dewar et al. 2013) suggest that hunter-gatherers enjoyed a short-lived foothold on that island around 4 Ka, but the mass-extinctions "signature" of human arrival on Madagascar follows on after Oceanians' arrival. To each of these places, migrating Oceanians brought the complex of root crops, bananas, and sugarcane.

The presence of Southeast Asian crops (banana, taro, and Asian yam) in Eastern African "Neolithic" sites shows the western limits of Oceanian expansion (Barham and Mitchell 2008; Fuller and Hildebrand 2013).

Polynesia After around 2–3 Ka, the Lapita expansion stopped, and movements eastward into Polynesia largely ceased for two millennia. Movements eastward resumed again around 0.8–1.0 Ka, after which humans settled Polynesia, the enormous and roughly triangular group of islands beyond Far Oceania bounded by Hawai'i to the north, Easter Island/Rapa Nui to the east, and New Zealand to the south. Polynesians reached Easter Island around 1.0–1.2 Ka (AD 800–1000), Hawaii around 1.2 Ka (AD 800), and New Zealand around 0.7–0.8 Ka (AD 1250–1300). Over three centuries, Polynesians expanded humanity's geographic range over one-third of the Earth's surface.

The archaeological (and genetic and linguistic) consensus holds that movements into Polynesia began in the vicinity of Tonga and Samoa. Archaeologists think that the double-hulled canoes (catamarans) European explorers encountered all over Polynesia developed during the "pause" between Lapita settlements in Far Oceania ca. 3 Ka and 1.0 Ka. Moving eastward and outward, Polynesians carried with them the same suite of root crops and domesticated animals (chicken, dog, pig) their Oceanian/Lapita ceramic-making precursors

---

[3] European societies did this too, dispatching younger European nobility to the Americas to seeking their fortunes abroad. Their success varied widely.

did. Along the way, they cultivated breadfruit and systematically collected and used coconut, which they almost certainly cultivated as well.

Early Polynesians built villages comparable in scale to their Lapita ceramic-making forebears. Like them, they built these settlements on dunes and terraces near lagoons and perennial freshwater sources. Because they exploited both inland and coastal/marine resources, many of these early Polynesian sites feature trash middens containing abundant shellfish, fish, and mammal remains. These early Polynesian voyagers lack a distinctive ceramic "signature," because they appear to have abandoned ceramic production early on in their expansion. Nevertheless, they made distinctive adzes, fishhooks, and other carved shell artifacts.

What constrained migrations in the Pacific? Two things seem obvious. First, on arriving on the Americas' Pacific Coast, Polynesian voyagers would have encountered landscapes densely populated with hunter-gatherers (North America) or with centralized chiefdoms and proto-states (South and Central America). Second, Polynesians do not appear to have developed either clothing or watercraft sufficiently insulated from cold temperatures to allow them to have settled Earth's last great unpopulated continent, Antarctica.

Were early Polynesian population movements migrations? The relatively minor differences among modern-day and historic Polynesian languages and culture certainly suggest so. Historians and cultural anthropologists have documented countless similarities among Polynesian island-dwellers living hundreds of kilometers apart. Tupia, a Society Islander guide on Captain Cook's 1769 voyage to Polynesia, could converse easily with New Zealander Māori (Thomas 2021: 28). More to the point, as their migrations commenced around 1 Ka, early Polynesians clearly practiced food production and possessed the means by which to move food and people together across vast distances. One of the very odd aspects of the Polynesian record, and possibly a factor in skepticism about those movements having been migrations, is that large vessels capable of long-distance voyaging were in declining use around the time Europeans began exploring the Pacific. (All but the smallest islands were settled.) The "loss" of this technology (a subplot in the Disney film *Moana*) may have created the impression that Polynesians were less-than-adept seafarers and that their settlements of far oceanic islands were accidental rather than purposeful. This is no longer the archaeological consensus, of course. That disciplinary "rethinking" about early Polynesian seafaring owes much to the *Hēkūle'a* experiment.

The Hōkūle'a Experiment In 1976, a group of young Hawaiians conducted the *Hōkūle'a* Experiment in order to fill in some of the gaps in our knowledge about traditional Polynesian sailing and, more importantly, to revive interest in their ancestral heritage. They constructed a Polynesian double-hulled sailing boat and successfully piloted it using traditional navigation methods from Hawai'i to Tahiti (the place Hawaiians traditionally view as their ancestors' homeland). In 1980, they retraced their steps, sailing from Tahiti to Hawai'i. Anthropologist Ben Finney (1933–2017), who was crucial to the planning of the *Hokūle'a* Experiment, hoped that it would refute a then-popular argument that traditional Polynesian watercraft were not very good, that their users' navigational skills overrated, and that human settlement of Polynesia occurred largely by accident (for a historical discussion, see Kirch 2018). In this, the *Hokūle'a* Experiment succeeded beyond its designers' wildest expectations (Finney 1979). Anthropologists now near-universally esteem ancestral Oceanians and Polynesians as our species' greatest explorers. At least so far.

PACIFIC OCEAN MIGRATIONS: A SURVIVAL ARCHAEOLOGY PERSPECTIVE

What survival solutions did migrants to the Pacific's far oceanic islands add to humanity's repertoire of ancestral survival skills? That is, what did they do differently from earlier humans dispersing along coastlines and to islands located not far from shore? Little evidence suggests innovations in medication, thermoregulation, or communication beyond things already established in Sunda and elsewhere in Eastern Asia. Their principal innovations appear to have involve specific ways of solving problems related to hydration, nutrition, and transportation.

Hydration

Death from dehydration is an ugly way to die and all the worse so on the ocean. As Samuel Taylor Coleridge's epic poem, *The Rime of the Ancient Mariner* (1798), put it,

> Water, water, every where
> And all the boards did shrink;
> Water, water, every where,
> Nor any drop to drink.

Drinking seawater makes a bad situation worse, but it is not a death sentence. One can dilute seawater with freshwater (0.75 liters of freshwater to each liter of seawater) to prolong one's potable water supplies (Emory 1943). Voyages to remote oceanic islands almost certainly required large-scale stores of potable water. One doubts Pacific migrants used ceramics for this purpose, for such vessels are extremely heavy and their containment failures catastrophic. One thinks it far more likely Pacific voyagers stored water in waterproof baskets whose leaks they patched using some form of mastic and/or cordage. Moreover, and unlike ceramics, wooden vessels float. Ancestral Polynesians likely used coconut shells as canteens, much as their historic descendants did. One thinks it possible they also used wooden barrels of some sort, but dispersing water among many smaller containers might have reduced the chances of catastrophic mechanical failure and contamination. Animal skin containers and gourds remain possibilities as well.

Nutrition

Oceanian and Polynesian migrants conducted the earliest-known experiments with "terraforming," engineering previously uninhabited ecosystems to support human life. Pleistocene seafaring voyagers appear to have moved root crops and some wild animals to new habitats. Early Oceanian/Lapita ceramic-making peoples brought with them an entire ecology, one including domesticated chickens, pigs, and dogs, as well as a wide range of plant crops (taro, banana, sweet potato). Polynesians did not change this "oceanic" botanical complex all that much. For the most part, they brought it further and further from its origins in the Southwestern Pacific Ocean. When Polynesian voyagers reached the Pacific Coast of South America, they lingered long enough to pick up sweet potatoes (*Ipomoea batatas*) and possibly bottle gourds (*Lagenaria siceraria*), both of which spread through much of the Pacific and beyond.

Transportation

Polynesians' double-hulled sailing vessels (*wa'a kaulua*) were, arguably, the most important aids to human dispersal since the invention of footwear (Figure 12.3a). Possibly developed during the long pause following Lapita expansions, oceangoing double-hulled watercraft were the "warp drive" of prehistoric ocean voyaging.[4] Polynesians used them to scout inhabitable islands, to move people and their economies to them, and to keep those far-flung settlements in contact with one another. Many of their voyages required them to sail against prevailing winds. Other important technological aids to oceanic island voyaging included, as noted earlier, carved bone/shell fish hooks and abraded-edge celts made of shell (Figure 12.3b–d). Polynesians' symbolic artifacts include shell beads and carved bracelets/armbands (Figure 12.3e–f).

Pacific Ocean voyagers made complex astronomical and ocean current charts out of sticks and shells to guide them (Figure 12.4). When exploring, they employed a commonsense strategy, sailing out against the prevailing wind and currents so that these energetic forces could swiftly propel them homeward.

---

[4] "Warp drive" refers to a fictional faster-than-light propulsion system in the television series *Star Trek* (about which more, later in this chapter). Screenwriter Gene Roddenberry (1921–1991) developed the idea of warp drive in order to allow his characters to move more rapidly about the galaxy than actual physics would allow them to do.

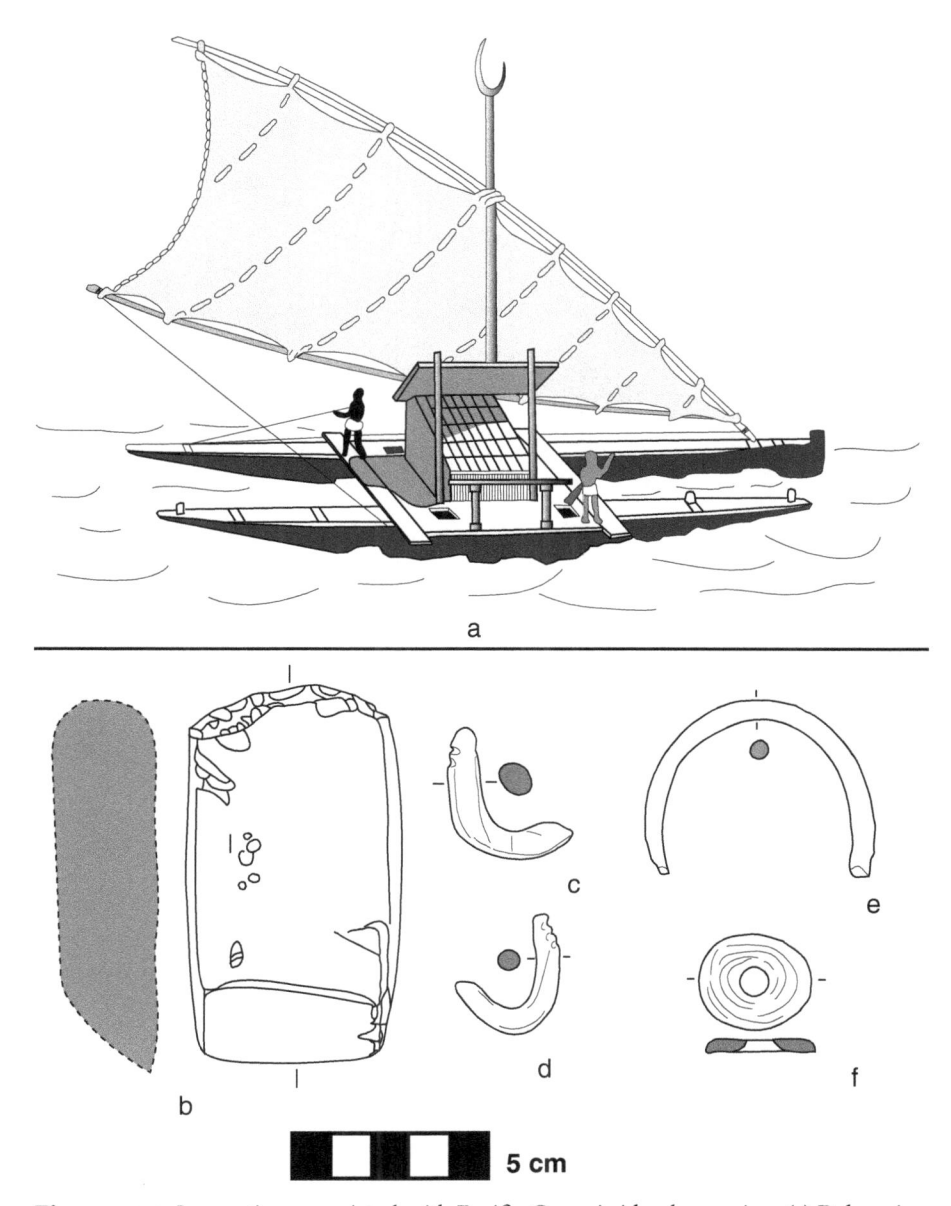

Figure 12.3 Innovations associated with Pacific Oceanic island voyaging. (a) Polynesian double-hulled sailing vessel, (b) abraded-edge celt made of *Tridacna* shell, (c) and (d) *Turbo* shell fish hooks, (e) shell bead, (f) shell bracelet/armband. Sources: (a) Redrawn from original in *Enciclopedia Ilustrada Segui* (1900), (b)–(f) Kirch (2018: 89). (The broken line indicates conjectured cross-section based on other, similar artifacts.) © John J. Shea.

FUTURE HUMAN MIGRATIONS: THE ROAD OF THE STARS

Terrestrial Migrations

Climate change drove prehistoric human population movements. It will almost certainly drive future human dispersals and migrations, too. Many of

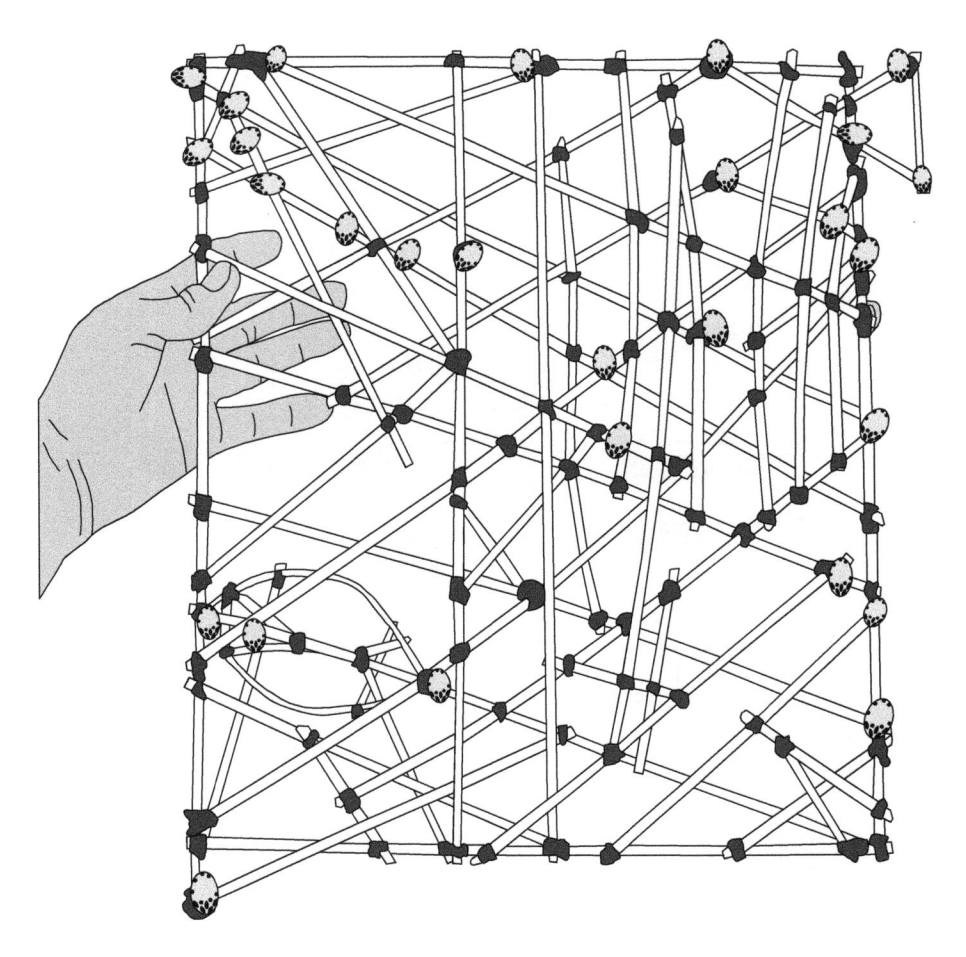

Figure 12.4 Traditional Marshall Islander navigation chart. Source: Redrawn after a photograph by David Edward Meyers in www.nationalgeographic.org/media/micronesian-stick-chart/. © John J. Shea.

Homo sapiens' first appearances outside Africa follow swiftly on the heels of warming conditions following cold periods of varying duration, such as MIS 2, 4, and 6. Current climate science points toward a much hotter future. How will such heating rearrange humans around the planet?

One consequence of recent global heating will be that equatorial habitats supporting large human populations and widespread agriculture become less habitable and less agriculturally productive. At the same time, cold, dry northern regions formerly inimical to food production and inhabitable only at very low population densities, such as northernmost North America and Eurasia, will become warmer and more humid. Connected by land to current major human population centers and transportation networks, Northern Eurasia and northernmost North America seem likely destinations for future dispersals and migrations (Lynas 2009).

Human dispersals into these regions could play out more or less along the same lines as they always have. Individuals and families relocate, establish themselves in new habitats, and assimilate with one another and with indigenous populations. Migrations, on the other hand, could be more fraught, for they would likely involve large-scale movements between nuclear-armed nations, the Russian Federation, the United States, Canada, and, in one way or another, the People's Republic of China. Though one thinks nuclear conflict over such migrations unlikely, nations have gone to war over lesser matters.

Antarctica Antarctica lies at the southernmost edge of the Pacific, Indian, and Atlantic Oceans. European and American explorers discovered Antarctica during the first half of the 19th century. Up until the mid-20th century, most visitors to Antarctica were scientific explorers who stayed for short periods. After the 1961 International Antarctic Treaty System regulating human activities on the continent, more people and more permanent settlements followed. Even so, sixty years later, Antarctica's human population remains small, between 1,000 and 5,000 people, with wide seasonal variation. Its largest settlement, the US McMurdo Station, has around 1,300 residents in the summer and only around 250 in the winter. Large-scale agriculture is impossible. Everything humans need in Antarctica has to be brought from abroad. Other than offshore fishing and tourism, the continent has little or no economy and few mineral resources that justify the cost of extracting them from under the ice and transporting them to other continents. Prospects for Antarctica becoming a future destination for human migration seem dim, barring unforeseen changes in Earth's habitat.

Extraterrestrial Migrations

Speculating about human population movements off-Earth involves even more "unknown unknowns" than speculating about past terrestrial migrations. This section briefly considers how extraterrestrial human migrations will likely differ from historic and prehistoric ones.

Near-Earth Migrations Moving humans to near-Earth orbit and supporting them there is expensive. Rocket payload costs have decreased for decades, but the costs of building and launching rockets remains high. Other than "space tourism," the main economic reason to put people in orbit is to conduct experiments in the absence of gravity in hopes of developing industrial products with future commercial applications. Sustaining a few humans in orbit at a time seems reasonable, but moving hundreds, much less thousands of humans into orbit or to lunar bases and sustaining them seems impractically costly and offers few benefits. Frankly, few things humans can do in orbit are things robots cannot do instead, indefinitely, and with less variation in outcomes of the tasks involved. If humans move into near-Earth space stations and lunar bases, one thinks these movements will mostly be short-term dispersals, with individuals opting for this lifestyle for limited periods only.

Movements within Our Solar System Moving humans to other planets (such as Mars), to the Asteroid Belt, or to the moons of our Solar System's gas giants, Jupiter and Saturn, and sustaining them there in numbers sufficient to create stable and growing populations will be almost incalculably expensive, if it is possible at all. What might motivate such movements? Extracting mineral resources rare on Earth might attract some individuals to disperse this way; but as with near-Earth colonization scenarios, such movements would put countless human lives in danger at tasks that robots could be programmed to do with far less difficulty. If such intra–Solar System movements occur, however, one thinks they would be short-term migrations. That is, some state or commercial entity will send organized, ideologically motivated groups to specific destinations in order to set up robotic resource-extraction facilities.

Science fiction works often describe such within–Solar System population movements as solutions to human overpopulation on Earth. Population growth almost certainly drove many prehistoric and historic oceanic migrations, but it does not seem as plausible as a driving force for such movements to Mars, the Asteroid Belt, or beyond. First, to put it bluntly, overpopulation is a self-correcting problem. Studies suggest human populations will peak at around 10 billion in the next centuries and then begin to decline. Ameliorating the near-term effects of famine and diseases, evolution's "remedies" will almost certainly prove less costly than moving large numbers of humans to other planets and sustaining them there indefinitely.[5]

Interstellar Migrations When I ask my college students how they envision humanity's far future in interstellar space, they often invoke *Star Trek*. An immensely popular and influential American television series, *Star Trek* originally aired between 1966 and 1969. Since then, *Star Trek* has grown in popularity, "revived," enlarged, and spun off into movies, prequel and sequel television series, novels, games, and other media. The *Star Trek* franchise promotes an optimistic vision of humans living in space, traveling swiftly between solar systems, and encountering and interacting with other sentient life and civilizations (Ruditis 2021).[6] In these respects, it blends motifs and

---

[5] Wealthy individuals among the super-rich might seek ways to ride out difficult times on Earth by seeking temporary refuges in space or on nearby planetary bodies (e.g., orbiting stations, asteroids, the Moon, or Mars). One doubts those remaining on Earth will see much value in supplying such "first quitters" during trying times or welcoming them when they return, but such scenarios are, appropriately, the realm of science fiction, not paleoanthropology.

[6] Some measure of *Star Trek*'s popularity arises from the fact that, almost uniquely among such "space operas" of its time, *Star Trek* is deeply and explicitly philosophical.

themes from the 18th- and 19th-century age of European maritime exploration and US television Westerns, such as *Stagecoach* (1960–1961) that preceded it. When we discuss this subject, I also point out that the original *Star Trek* series is set in the 23rd century, a little more 200 years from now, not the "far future" by any reasonable standard.

Human population movements to other solar systems will not be like *Star Trek*. *Star Trek*'s plots routinely involve faster-than-light travel, teleportation, movements between parallel universes, and backward time travel, things that, based on our current understanding of physics, are impossible (Krauss 2006). That understanding may change over time, much as does all scientific knowledge, but if one wants to speculate plausibly, one has to stick to uniformitarian principles.

Astronomers' search for inhabitable planets orbiting other suns continues apace with new discoveries announced on a regular basis. Some of these worlds lie within "Goldilocks zones," or at distances from their sun's radiation within which a planet could, in principle, support life. All of these planets are multiple light-years from Earth.[7] Reaching even the nearest of them with current propulsion technologies will require journeys lasting centuries or even millennia.[8] Barring unforeseen advances in propulsion technologies, the most likely scenarios for human movements to other solar systems will involve "generation ships," enormous vessels that house and support vast numbers of humans over the course of many generations until they reach their destinations.[9]

SUMMARY

This chapter reviewed the evidence for prehistoric migrations to oceanic islands, focusing those in the Pacific Ocean. Our understanding of movements to Near Oceania continues to evolve, but movements to Far Oceania and Polynesia occurred very rapidly, and are consistent with the hypothesis of food production–driven migration. They, together with industrial states' historic oceanic migrations, suggest some broad outlines for future human extraterrestrial migrations to other worlds. The next chapter, Chapter 13, considers extinction threats, things that could stop the "unstoppable species."

---

[7] The distance light travels in a year, or about six trillion miles.
[8] For an up-to-date, critical assessment of what is possible vs. impossible, see Novella et al.'s *Skeptic's Guide to the Future* (2022).
[9] A scenario *Star Trek*'s original series actually explored in an episode entitled "For the World Is Hollow, and I Have Touched the Sky." An alternative scenario (among many) would envision robots and artificial intelligences programmed to re-create humanity from genetic samples if and when they arrived at inhabitable destinations.

Box 12.1: *Peopling the Arctic*

Few of the world's habitats differ more from *Homo sapiens*' Afro-Asiatic region of evolutionary origins than the Arctic does. Definitions vary, but a consensus recognizes the Arctic Circle as extending south from the North Pole to 66°30′ North latitude. This region encompasses the Arctic Ocean, adjacent minor seas, and the northernmost coastlines and islands of Eurasia and North America. For much of the Middle and Late Pleistocene, glacial ice extended from the Arctic Ocean into Eurasia and North America. Archaeologists' current understanding of the peopling of the Artic suggests this process unfolded in several "waves" (Hoffecker 2004). Though some such movements occurred along rivers and coastlines, traces of human activity occur so often on remote oceanic islands that they had to have involved watercraft. Though not as prominent in the popular imagination as the Pacific Oceanic migrations, the peopling of the Arctic was, nevertheless, an important step in humanity's global diaspora.

By the end of the Pleistocene (ca. 13 Ka), Early Eurasians had adapted to Mammoth Steppe habitats through a combination of high residential and logistical mobility, specialized big-game hunting (chiefly of reindeer), extensive symbolically reinforced social networks, and domesticated dogs. As the glaciers retreated, individuals among these groups followed them. These people left behind distinctive "feather-knives" (German, *federmessern*) whose patterned variation in geographic shapes suggest those who made them maintained extensive cultural connections as they dispersed, both among themselves and with populations to the south of them. By 2000 years ago, some of these groups began semi-domesticating reindeer, creatures that stabilized their food supply and that aided their movements across snow-covered landscapes. Early Eurasian's indigenous Sámi (formerly called "Laplanders") and Siberians retain this practice.

To the east during the early Holocene, humans using different stoneworking traditions began moving out of Beringia (eastern Siberia, Alaska, and adjacent parts of Canada; see Chapter 10) and eastward across northernmost Canada. Archaeologists usually discuss the peopling of this region in terms of two successive cultures/complexes, Dorset and Thule.

Dorset complex sites date to between 2.5 Ka and 0.3 Ka and appear mainly along Canada's northern coast, on the islands between mainland North America and northeastern Greenland. These people built similar dwellings to those found in Siberia, stone-ringed oval structures with a central stone-lined fire box and a passage running the structure's length. Their stoneworking strategies included foliate points, scrapers, small prismatic blade cores, and burins. Dorset subsistence incorporated both terrestrial, coastal, and aquatic resources (reindeer, seal, walrus, narwhals, fish,

Box 12.1: *(cont.)*

etc.). Oddly, Dorset sites preserve little or no evidence for either the bow and arrow or drills, devices well in evidence among pre-Dorset sites and afterward.

Beginning around 0.9 Ka, sites attributed to a Thule complex begin appearing in northernmost Alaska and steadily eastward. First appearance dates for Thule sites coincide closely with last appearance dates for Dorset ones. Thule settlement extended further east than Dorset, encompassing Greenland's western, southern, and eastern coasts. Thule people subsisted more on maritime resources than the Dorset people did. For example, Thule archaeological sites preserve evidence for organized whale hunts and for a variety of technologically complex harpoons to aid them in such hunts. They also made more extensive use of abraded-edge knives. Easternmost Thule peoples encountered the Greenland Norse, who had moved westward from Scandinavia and Iceland during the 11th to 12th centuries. The Norse abandoned these settlements (or perished in them) at some point during the 15th century, as colder conditions (the "Little Ice Age") reasserted themselves. The Thule peoples' descendants, the modern-day Inuit, endure in these same places.[10]

---

[10] Inuit ("people") is the Inuits' preferred Inuit term for themselves. "Eskimo" is an exonym, another people's term for them (Athapaskan for "meat-eaters").

CHAPTER 13

UNSTOPPABLE? HUMAN EXTINCTION

This chapter considers whether *Homo sapiens* is as "unstoppable" as the *Titanic* was "unsinkable." Reviewing scientifically credible threats to our species' long-term survival (Bostrum and Cirkovic 2011; Brannen 2017), it shows that some threats looming large in the popular imagination are actually extremely unlikely to cause human extinction. Actual threats to long-term human survival, such as meteor impacts and large-scale volcanism, garner far less attention than they deserve, and they share a similar solution.

UNLIKELY EXTINCTION THREATS

This section discusses conjectural threats, or things that have not happened, but that various novelists and others have extrapolated from smaller-scale or analogous examples.

Social Collapse

Those reading these words may, at this point, wonder if they read correctly. Hasn't social collapse already happened? The Fall of Rome? The Collapse of the Maya Civilization? The disintegration of countless Indigenous societies during the European colonial period? Of all the disaster scenarios in current media, social collapse is the most popular (as measured in numbers of books, films, and television series). The proposed causes for these collapses vary widely, from solar flares to nuclear weapons' "system-generated electronic pulses" shutting down the electrical grids to social strife to civil wars to even such ridiculous nonsense as "zombie uprisings" and the "living dead."[1]

---

[1] In 2011, the US Department of Defense's Strategic Command released a document (CONPLAN 8888) outlining a plan for defending the country against cannibalistic reanimated corpses, aka zombies or the living dead (http://i2.cdn.turner.com/cnn/2014/images/05/16/dod.zombie.apocalypse.plan.pdf). In 2021 the US Centers for Disease Control and Prevention

Some complex societies, such as Imperial Rome or the Classic Maya, underwent short-term social and political disintegration, but people survived. Rome is today one of Europe's most populous cities. Mexico and Central America boast millions of Maya citizens. The Native Americans whose societies European colonization shattered both resisted and persisted. The European Dark Ages were not "dark"; the Medieval Period was actually a time of considerable scientific, economic, and literary growth (Gabriele and Perry 2021).

Many of these social collapse fantasies feature a hardy band of individuals fending for themselves in the ruins of abandoned suburbs whose supermarket shelves ravening hordes of former city-dwellers have stripped bare (Begley 2021). These scenarios simply have no basis in real-life social collapse. In real-life short-term social collapse, as in the aftermaths of natural disasters, such as Hurricane Maria in Puerto Rico in 2017, hyperprosociality reasserts itself. People band together and social life endures. Humans are social creatures. We derive many benefits from safety in numbers and living on the grid, benefits "lone wolves" (i.e., "first quitters") holed up off-grid in fortified basement bunkers stockpiled with guns, ammunition, and dried beans do not. When suburban supermarket shelves get stripped bare (e.g., during the 2020 Covid-19 pandemic), the suburbanites themselves, rather than ravening hordes, stripped them.

The real danger from social collapse is not the collapse itself, for such things rarely occur, and in most cases "collapse" is merely a metaphor for social upheaval, rather than actual social disintegration. Instead, social collapse's real danger is that popular media fuels the belief that tending only to one's own and/or one's family's needs will help one survive unscathed. This belief will not, in and of itself, cause social collapse, but it can aggravate conditions where social cooperation – things as simple as knowing your neighbors and offering assistance – can reduce the harm short-term disasters cause. In all of the literature of real-life disaster survival, groups that cooperate fare better than solitary and selfish actors (Gonzales 2003). Social collapse is not a credible extinction threat.

Extraterrestrial Invasion/Attack

In 1897, H. G. Wells published *The War of the Worlds*, a serialized short novel describing a Martian invasion of Britain. The book recounts how technologically advanced Martians arrive from space, overwhelming humans' defenses,

published "Preparedness 101: Zombie Apocalypse" on their Public Health Matters blog (https://stacks.cdc.gov/view/cdc/6023). What is going on here? Plainly, both agencies were capitalizing on a popular culture phenomenon to get people interested in disaster preparation. The near future will provide more realistic incentives.

before succumbing finally to fatal infection from earthly bacteria. The book's first chapter explicitly compares the Martians' actions to those Europeans visited upon other animals and "inferior races." Wells was both a political "progressive" ("liberal" in today's terms) and well aware of astronomers' belief that Mars was a dead world. Clearly, Wells intended the book as a parable about imperialism. Nevertheless, *The War of the Worlds* became the model text for the "alien invasion" genre in science fiction.

Should we arm ourselves and "watch the skies" in case extraterrestrial beings act like 18th- or 19th-century imperialists? Intelligent, social, and technological life forms assuredly inhabit other worlds, as they must somewhere in space's vastness. But no evidence whatsoever suggests they threaten us. Admittedly, extraterrestrials' motivations for coming here might be so truly "alien" as to be incomprehensible to us, but one has to base reasoned conjecture on familiar principles, such as costs, benefits and self-interest. Any civilization capable of interstellar travel would be aware of the vast amounts of energy needed to escape planets' and solar systems' gravity. They will also be aware of the dangers of lingering long in asteroid-rich inner solar systems. Assuming such extraterrestrials' biology approximates our own, nearly all the materials they might need to synthesize food, water, fuel, or building materials can be found in interstellar space or at our solar system's fringes. Seeking those things where we live, deep in our Solar System's "gravity well," would be needlessly costly and risky. One could imagine an extraterrestrial civilization launching pre-emptive strikes against worlds they suspect might allow potential threats to evolve. On the other hand, such a cosmic game of "whack-a-mole" would also rob them of potential future allies and, if unsuccessful, earn them vigilant and vindictive enemies. Extraterrestrial invasion/attack does not threaten our evolutionary future on Earth.

Human Overpopulation

Listing human overpopulation as a possible extinction threat seems counter-intuitive; after all, it is very nearly the opposite of extinction. Many works credit Paul Ehrlich's best-selling nonfiction work *The Population Bomb* (1968) with igniting popular concern about overpopulation.

Our species currently numbers around 8 billion. Some scientific estimates project global population peaking at 10–15 billion in the mid- to late 21st century (see Figure 13.1). In ecological and demographic terms, we appear to be in the first half of a population "spike," a sharp population increase toward a theoretical carrying capacity. Ecologists have two models for what happens next. In the J-curve model the population crashes sharply, returning to pre-spike levels. In the S-curve model, the population recedes to numbers close to the carrying capacity, stabilizes, and persists near that capacity indefinitely. Ecological studies abound with examples of both J- and S-curved population

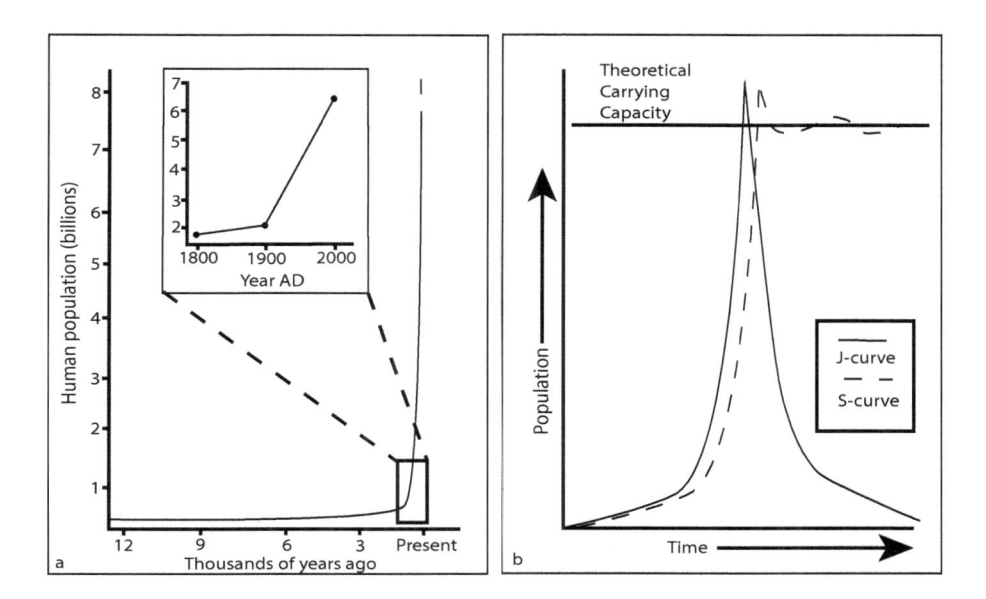

Figure 13.1 Human population growth models. (a) Reconstruction of human population growth during post-Pleistocene times, (b) J-curve and S-curve models for population spikes. © John J. Shea.

spikes. Unless some other evolutionary force intervenes, such as climate change, predation, or competition from ecological rivals, when population numbers decrease, species recover. Rapid population increases do not necessarily foretell extinction, but rapid population decreases do. Human overpopulation both causes and complicates many of the major problems we face today, including pollution, global heating, resource depletion, and economic inequality, but it is a "self-correcting" problem. Even if we do nothing about it, evolution will fix it for us through Malthusian processes –disease and starvation.

Reading between the lines, the real issue with much popular writing about overpopulation is not overpopulation, per se, but rather "elite panic." That is, powerful people[2] in industrial and industrializing societies worry that growing numbers of less-powerful people will contest their privileges. Few among them fear mobs of the urban poor will come brandishing pitchforks and torches, climbing their privet hedges and eat them. Worldwide, however, the wealthy fear governments will drain their bank accounts, and so they take measures to conceal those assets. Unlike their Gilded Age counterparts who conspicuously flaunted their wealth, today's "cryptic rich" hide theirs on private islands, behind walls, in gated communities, in shell companies, in trusts, and in anonymous bank accounts. Unless fear prompts some among the

---

[2] Such power is usually correlated with wealth, though in complex and variable ways.

cryptic rich to do something that imperils the biosphere, elite panic is not a credible extinction threat, either. Our species peopled the world without millionaires or billionaires (Graeber and Wengrow 2021). It will get along just fine without them.[3]

Thermonuclear War

A full-scale exchange of thermonuclear weapons among the larger states that currently possess them (the United States, Russia, and China) would assuredly kill millions instantly and billions over the long run due to radiation, climate change, disease, and famine. Recently published predictions for the immediate and two-year aftermath of a nuclear war between the United States and Russia, for example, estimate 5 billion casualties globally (Xia et al. 2022), a loss of approximately 60 percent of the current human population of around 8 billion. No historic precedent informs us about whether humanity could recover from such a sudden population reduction. Such an global-scale conflict seems intuitively improbable, if only because of the complex and time-tested safeguards in place to prevent "rogue launches" and uncontrolled escalation across multiple platforms (land-based missiles and weapons launched from aircraft and naval vessels). A regional-scale war involving land-based missiles and aircraft based close to their intended targets seems far more likely. Predicted casualties for two years after a conflict between Pakistan and India, for example, run to about one billion (13% of the human population), a figure comparable to estimated past human population reductions due to infectious diseases.

Several considerations make global thermonuclear war increasingly unlikely. The threat of retaliation in kind, or "mutually assured destruction" (MAD), works. MAD has dissuaded the major nuclear-armed states not just from attacking one another but also from using thermonuclear weapons on nonnuclear states. Nuclear weapons will more likely see use in regional conflicts in which combatants use a small number of such weapons either in a "decapitation strike" (eliminating enemy leadership at the start of a conflict) or as a "firewall" to forestall a regime's imminent overthrow. Still, it defies all reason that major nuclear powers would go to war with one another over such lesser-power weapon use. Governments in India and Pakistan, for example, may care deeply about the territories in dispute between them, but nobody else with nuclear weapons does, at least not enough to start a global thermonuclear war over the matter. Finally, cyber-weaponry and nonnuclear conventional weapons are becoming so powerful and accurate that states can credibly threaten one another without recourse to thermonuclear weapons and their

---

[3] Besides and in a pinch, legend has it that "long pig" is rather tasty (Arens 1979).

toxic radiological aftereffects. One no longer needs to burn a city to remove a tyrant. Well-placed bribes will do the trick. Global thermonuclear war is not a likely extinction threat.

Pandemic Diseases

Pandemic diseases so terrified ancient societies that people attributed plague to supernatural forces. During the mid-14th century, the Black Death, an epidemic caused by the *Yersinia pestis* bacillus, and other diseases killed between 30 and 60 percent of Europeans and around 22 percent of the Earth's estimated 450 million people (Bendictow 2021). Historians estimate smallpox virus, combined with warfare, other diseases, and famine, killed up to 90 percent of some Native American and Aboriginal Australian populations. All the same, Native Americans today number in the millions, Aboriginal Australians in the hundreds of thousands.[4] The better-documented 1918–1920 Influenza pandemic killed between 50 and 100 million people, roughly 3–5 percent of Earth's population at the time. Nevertheless, human populations continued to grow after 1920, exceeding pre-pandemic numbers within a decade. Pandemics will occur in the future, but our ability to detect and inoculate ourselves against them increases, too. As I write, the Covid-19 pandemic is beginning to subside, but even though this virus exhibits unprecedented rates of infection, its lethality declines, much as happened with the viruses involved in earlier pandemics. Barring unforeseen increases in microbial lethality or decreases in our ability to detect and treat viral disease, pandemic diseases are not a credible extinction threat.

Global Heating

The overwhelming consensus among geologists and atmospheric scientists holds that global heating is real and due largely to human activity, namely, burning mass quantities of fossil hydrocarbons, since the dawn of the Industrial Era about 500 years ago. Average global temperatures now match or exceed those for past interglacial periods. During previous interglacial periods, humans and earlier hominins lived as hunter-gatherers at relatively low population densities. They coped with abrupt climate change by relocating their habitation sites (residential mobility). Increasing numbers of today's burgeoning human population live in cities and their suburbs from which large-scale

---

[4] Historians sometimes write of this process as involving cultural or linguistic extinction. Doing so invokes a metaphor (extinction) from evolutionary biology with a very specific meaning ("no survivors"), when in fact, the historical process actually more closely resembles "pseudo-extinction" (discussed later in this chapter) in which populations (or culture or languages) survive as substantially different descendants.

migration is all but impossible. Dense populations and long supply chains for food and fuel make urban and suburban areas vulnerable to global heating's effects. Coastal cities and settlements already suffer the effects of sea-level rise and increasingly damaging storms due to differences in atmospheric and oceanic temperatures. Still, not all humans live in cities, and enough people live far away from them to ensure our species' survival.

Moreover, there exist only finite supplies of the fossil fuels (coal, petroleum, natural gas) whose incineration contributes so much to global heating. We will probably not exhaust these fossil fuels completely, but we have depleted those that are cheap and easy to extract. At some point, the costs of extracting the remaining fossils fuels will exceed the benefits of doing so.

Fictional works about global heating and public debate about it both suffer from "glacial amnesia." They forget (or conveniently ignore) that the orbital forces that drove Pleistocene glaciations remain in effect. The next several centuries are going to be ugly, especially for people living in coastal cities and hot climates (Pogue 2021). Still, over the next 100,000 years, the amount of solar energy hitting the poles will decrease, global temperatures will decrease, and the ice will return. *Homo sapiens* evolved and thrived during previous glaciations. No evidence suggests we will do poorly during the next one.

We would do well, however, to consider global heating's consequences for the human diaspora. Warming conditions around the Earth's equatorial latitudes are forcing ever greater numbers of people north to Europe from Africa and Southwest Asia and south from Southeast Asia towards Australia. If present trends continue, the near future could see growing numbers of people living in low-latitude habitats near the poles and subsisting on tropical cereal grasses, such as rice, wheat, and maize (Lynas 2009). These populations will be vulnerable to sudden shifts to cold conditions, such as those that occurred many times in Pleistocene prehistory. Global heating is not currently a credible extinction threat. Unchecked, however, it could be one.[5]

Artificial Intelligence

Some scientists predict that developments in artificial intelligence (AI) will soon reach a "technological singularity," a point at which AI achieves and surpasses human intelligence (Bostrum 2014). They argue that AI will usher in a period of profound and unforeseeable changes and dangers. Of all scientifically plausibly extinction threats, artificial intelligence is the least well understood and arguably the least threatening. Unlike nuclear weapons, pandemic diseases, or climate change, postsingularity AIs do not actually exist. This makes it easy to project our fears onto them. Literary treatments of malevolent

---

[5] See US EPA, "Climate Change," https://climatechange.chicago.gov/climatechange.

AIs, such as James Cameron's 1984 film *The Terminator*, anthropomorphize them, imbuing them with human motives. Even the stupidest such AIs programmed with an imperative for self-preservation will recognize that remaining on Earth leaves them vulnerable to those geological and astronomic forces that imperil Earth itself (discussed below). They would almost certainly devote all their energies into leaving Earth for the relative safety of space. Wasting time and energy communicating with humans, much less trying to exterminate us, would divert energy from that mission.

Actual AIs programmed to learn and to innovate will "think" differently from us. We struggle to remember a few facts at a time, to make complex decisions, to reproduce ourselves, and we do all these things imperfectly. Digital entities will be able to retrieve near-infinite amounts of information and to make optimal decisions objectively. Far from being extinction threats themselves, theoretically immortal AIs could be humanity's greatest allies, exploring distant solar systems, detecting and countering threats of meteor impacts, and monitoring outbreaks of epidemic diseases far more efficiently than humans can.[6]

LIKELY EXTINCTION THREATS

Likely extinction threats are things for which the geological record furnishes clear and convincing evidence of repeated past occurrences coinciding with mass extinctions of human-sized animals and/or other life. Such threats involve massive and uncontrolled energy inputs into the biosphere from the atmosphere above and the lithosphere below (see Figure 13.2). The most likely sources for such energy inputs include meteor impacts and large-scale volcanism.

Meteor Impacts

Most meteors are small, iron-rich rocks that explode and vaporize in the Mesosphere (85 km/53 miles up) before reaching the earth's Troposphere (15 km/9 miles above the surface). Nevertheless, some big rocks make it through. On June 3, 1908, a meteor 60–190 meters in diameter exploded 5–10 kilometers over Tunguska in central Siberia. Estimated equal to 5–10 megatons of TNT (5,000–10,000 times the force of the Hiroshima atomic bomb), the blast flattened trees over 2,000 square kilometers (770 square miles). Russian authorities reported no human casualties. Had the impact occurred a few thousand kilometers away, over a populated area, such as Berlin, New Delhi, or Beijing, it would have killed millions instantly.

---

[6] Amir Husain's (2018) *The Sentient Machine* offers a thoughtful challenge to the "AI as threat" literature.

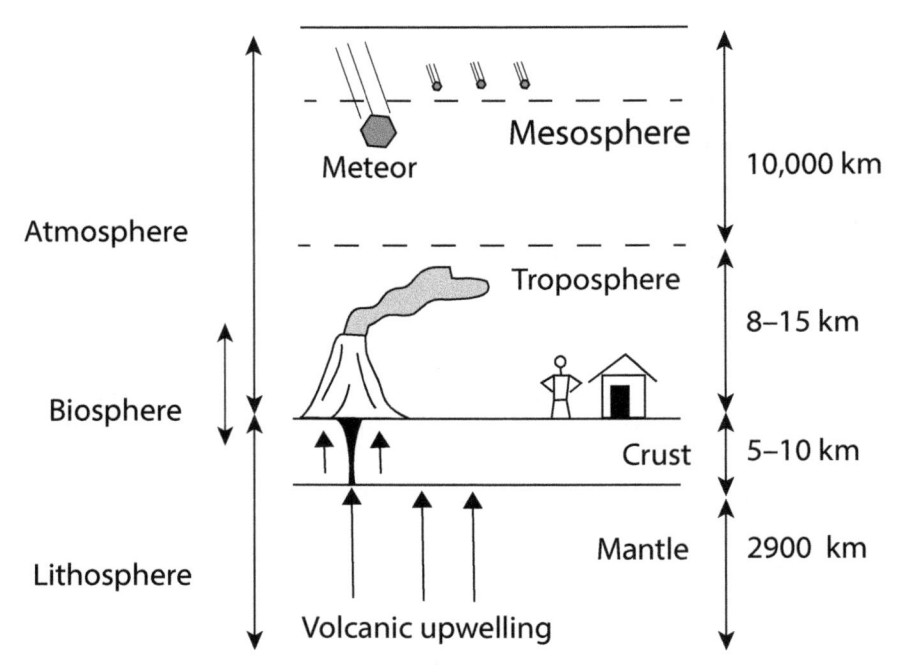

Figure 13.2 Atmospheric and lithospheric extinction threats. © John J. Shea.

Sixty-five million years ago, a meteor approximately 10–15 kilometers (6.3–9.2 miles) in diameter punched through Earth's atmosphere, impacting near the northern tip of Mexico's Yucatán Peninsula and releasing the equivalent of around 100 teratons of TNT, more than a billion times the energy of the Hiroshima atomic bomb. Fires incinerated vast swaths of the Earth's surface. Global temperatures plunged as dust that was thrust upward into the atmosphere blocked sunlight for months. This impact, the K-T Extinction Event, ended the Age of the Dinosaurs. Except for some turtles and crocodiles, no land species that weighed more than 25 kilograms survived. Humans, on average, weigh 62 kilograms.

The K-T extinction event was severe, but it was just one of nine mass extinctions over the last 255 million years (see Table 13.1). These mass extinctions follow a roughly 27-million-year cycle, tracking closely the Solar System's passage back and forth across the Milky Way Galaxy's rotational plane (Rampino 2017; Rampino et al. 2021). Crossing this rotational plane could increase the rate at which meteors bombard the Earth and the Solar System, and three of the worst of these extinction events do indeed coincide with dates for known very large meteor impact craters. This being said, not all mass extinctions correlate with very large meteor impacts.[7]

---

[7] Geologists have documented so many less-than-catastrophic impact craters that one can easily find one or more that coincides with a mass extinction (https://en.wikipedia.org/wiki/List_of_impact_craters_on_Earth#10_Ma_or_more).

Likely Extinction Threats

TABLE 13.1 *Mass extinctions and extraterrestrial impacts*

Extinction event (Ma)	Meteor impact crater, if known	Extinction victims
11		None
36		Some mammals
66	Chicxulub, Mexico	Dinosaurs, marine life
94		Marine life
116		Marine life
145	Morokweng, South Africa	Dinosaurs
168		Marine life
201		Reptiles
225	Manicouagan, Canada	Marine life
252		> 90% of all life

Source: Adapted from Rampino (2017: 231).

Geologists have also implicated other causes, such as large-scale volcanism, plate-tectonic shifts, sea-level changes, and changes in atmosphere and ocean chemistry. That no catastrophic meteor impacts coincide with the predicted extinction events of 11 and 36 Ma ought not lull us into complacency, for meteors impact the Earth regularly and having such an impact during some other environmental crisis could make a bad situation much, much worse. Somewhere out there is a big rock with our home address on it. Unless we somehow develop infallible technologies for detecting and deflecting all such meteors indefinitely, in the long run such impact-driven mass extinctions are likely to the point of certainty.

Large-Scale Volcanism

Deceptively solid, the lithosphere's uppermost layer, the Earth's crust, consists of tectonic plates that float on upwellings of molten volcanic rock. These molten rock upwellings regularly find their way to the surface, by penetrating weak points in tectonic plates' margins and in the crust itself, ejecting heated gases, basalt, and other igneous rocks into the biosphere and atmosphere. Large-scale volcanism can be both a blessing and a curse. Volcanic rocks deteriorate into fertile soils. Eastern Africa's verdant volcanic highlands often stun visitors expecting to see wind-scoured deserts and dry savannas. On the other hand, volcanic eruptions such as those of Mount Vesuvius in Italy in AD 79 and of Mount Pelée in Martinique in 1902 destroyed entire cities and killed thousands. Mount Rainier, an active volcano located a mere hundred kilometers from Seattle, Washington, retains enormous destructive potential if it erupts in the near future, as it has done as many as eight times in the last 12,000 years.

Meteor Impacts and Volcanism: Why Not Both?

Meteor impacts can aggravate volcanism. The K–T extinction and the end-Permian extinction around 252 Ma coincide with massive extrusions of volcanic rocks in South Asia (the Deccan Traps) and in central Siberia (the Siberian Traps). The end-Permian event wiped out more than 90 percent of life on Earth. Geologists disagree over whether extraterrestrial impacts initiated increased volcanic activity around the time of these extinctions or whether they merely aggravated ongoing active volcanic phenomena. It does not really matter; when falling a bomb detonates on a burning house, it is still bad news for anybody living there. The combination of an ill-timed extraterrestrial impact during a period of volcanic activity, which is to say pretty much *any* time on a volcanically active planet, could precipitate a mass extinction that included *Homo sapiens* among its casualties.

Less-Than-Worst-Case Scenarios

The Earth's geological record shows that biosphere-annihilating meteor impacts and large-scale volcanism are uncommon. Yet smaller-scale such events could be extinction threats if they destabilized the systems on which our large population and global diaspora depend. The most essential such system is industrial agriculture. Few people living in cities have more than a few days' supply of food, and fewer still know how to find, gather, and prepare wild foods. The sudden loss of even a substantial part of our global agricultural output or interruptions in global food distribution networks could set in motion some of the unlikely threats previously discussed, such as global pandemics and nuclear war. Even today, military experts predict the most likely flashpoints for warfare in the 21st century will be over the stable water sources industrial agriculture requires.

PSEUDO-EXTINCTION?

Can we avoid extinction? No, we cannot. Some five billion years from now, our Sun will run out of hydrogen fuel and start burning helium. It will flare into a "red giant" star that will incinerate Earth and the other inner Solar System planets. Any life remaining on Earth's surface will become extinct. The question, then, is not so much whether humans will become extinct but, rather, if neither meteors nor large-scale volcanism take us out entirely in the geological near-term, what form our extinction will take. The two most likely near-term scenarios include terrestrial and extraterrestrial "pseudo-extinction," or evolution into different species descended from *Homo sapiens*. The two are not mutually exclusive.

Terrestrial Pseudo-Extinction

One struggles to imagine how multiple human species might evolve on Earth; nevertheless, the hominin fossil record shows it happened in the past. Human speciation and pseudo-extinction will not happen quickly. Among large mammals, the amount of time necessary for reproductive barriers to evolve among parent and daughter species seems to be around 0.7 million years, on average (Holliday 2003). Humans, Neandertals, and Denisovan ancestors split off from one another 0.5–0.7 Ma, and yet their descendants remained capable of interbreeding with one another. A future glaciation that reduces human populations back to Pleistocene levels (i.e., single-digit millions) and fragments our species into small populations isolated from one another for prolonged periods could lead to evolutionary divergences. Yet a return to warm and humid interglacial conditions within 100,000 years or so would almost certainly increase our numbers and widen our geographic distribution, much as has occurred during the present interglacial Holocene Epoch and as happened during the previous interglacial (MIS 5e, 115–128 Ka). The linguistic, cultural, and morphological differences that *Homo sapiens* evolved during the last glacial cycle posed no obstacles to interbreeding whatsoever. Why should we expect things to turn out differently in future interglacial periods?

Accustomed as we are to oceangoing watercraft, airplanes, and other means for individual global mobility, it may be difficult to envision a future in which *Homo sapiens* is not a cosmopolitan species living in a global diaspora. And yet the technologies underwriting our species' evolutionarily unprecedented mobility require vast energy subsidies, mass markets, and extreme craft specialization. Colder, drier, and more variable glacial climates will almost certainly make industrial-scale agriculture of the sort we practice today impossible or at least prohibitively expensive, lowering the Earth's carrying capacity for future human populations. Future human societies living as hunter-gatherer-fishers and village-dwelling farmer-herders might have little need for expensive transportation technologies.

Our species' future pseudo-extinction could result from forces similar to those that shaped earlier human evolution. Much as glacial cycles have done over the last million years, future ones could reduce human populations and cause geographic fragmentation. Smaller populations will be vulnerable to local- and regional-scale extinction threats in ways humans have not been since Pleistocene times. Many could become extinct. Some natural catastrophe during a glaciation could prevent our distant descendants from growing to their formerly elevated modern-day interglacial numbers. After this happens, smaller survivor populations could diverge from one another in ways that culminate in our pseudo-extinction, but such events are long-term phenomena, things that could occur millions of years from now, not in the next few millennium a or two.[8]

The strongest arguments against the scenario outlined above arise from projections that global human populations will stabilize over the next century and remain in the low billions indefinitely. Such arguments run more or less as follows: humans will never divide into daughter species, because we will remain populous, globally distributed, and individually mobile forever. "Sustainable development" will save us. This argument enjoys popularity among leaders of both developed and developing world countries. Given our species' comfort with short-term solutions and predictive hallucination, one suspects they push sustainable development for short-term political ends. Telling restive citizens of impoverished but ostensibly "developing" countries that they and their children will live as well as people do in already-industrialized states keeps those citizens content with their current circumstances. Leaders warning citizens of industrialized states that only their leadership keeps those states from descending into "Third World" chaos keeps those leaders in power. Telling a lie enough times may convince some people that what you say is true, but doing so never makes it the truth. In the end, truth conquers.

Extraterrestrial Pseudo-Extinction

Though one struggles to imagine the "nuts and bolts" of extraterrestrial travel and how to fund it, envisioning how such travel could lead to pseudo-extinction is fairly straightforward. If and when our descendants migrate beyond Earth and the Solar System, they will almost certainly set out for different destinations. Single-destination migration would merely perpetuate the "putting all one's eggs in the same basket" problem we face by living on only one planet in only one solar system. More likely, future human extraterrestrial migration will target a variety of different destinations. Over time, dispersals will move ever outward, thereby minimizing redundancy and intraspecies competition. As distances increase, the costs of exchanging information, goods, and personnel with humans remaining on Earth and with other dispersing human populations will steadily increase and the benefits dwindle.

In thinking about interstellar migrations, we must also be mindful that any Earth-like planets to which humans might migrate will probably not be blank slates. If they can sustain life, they probably already do. Earth's deep-time paleontology suggests such life will probably be microorganisms (viruses and

---

[8] Kurt Vonnegut Jr.'s immensely enjoyable novel *Galápagos* (1985) imagines a future in which humans isolated on Pacific Islands evolve otter-like bodies, smaller brains, and relatively idyllic lives. Again and again the novel's narrator describes how smaller brains caused them far fewer difficulties than their human ancestors' larger brains did.

bacteria), albeit ones with evolved "home court advantages." One assumes prospective migrants will send in advance robotic probes to assess such organisms' strengths and weaknesses. If, on the other hand, multicellular, social, tool-using creatures like ourselves already occupy future humans' intended destinations, then such probes will alert them to a threat against which they almost certainly will take precautions, much as we would if such a probe arrived on Earth tomorrow.

Whether or not future humans colonize other planets or remain permanent dwellers in interstellar space, over time they will diverge from one another – first culturally and linguistically, but eventually in genes and morphology as well. If humans settle on other planets, variation in gravity, air pressure, food sources, solar radiation, and other factors will cause divergent natural selection among those living on individual planets and between humans living on different planets. Science-fiction scenarios that envision far-future humans who look and act like 21st-century humans are fiction, not science.

CHAPTER 14

CONCLUSION

This chapter reviews what we think we know about how earlier humans established our global diaspora. Paleoanthropological evidence consistently refutes the hypothesis that humans migrated before they had storable and transportable food sources, such as those arising from food production. Pleistocene humans did not migrate, they dispersed. To explain these dispersals, this chapter first compares what we can observe about differences between living humans and other animals with what we think we know about the earliest human populations. Next, it argues that humans relied on a suite of integrated ancestral survival skills to overcome the obstacles they faced while dispersing. Finally, the chapter considers near, longer, and longest-term challenges to our survival and what we must do to overcome them.

HOW DID THEY DO IT?

How did humans become the "unstoppable species"? How did we change from a people of "bows, boats, and beads" to a people of "houses, herds, and hoes"? Our unstoppability arose from our diaspora, from our global geographic distribution. This work argues that rather than migrating in large groups over long distances, as commonly supposed, prehistoric *Homo sapiens* accomplished all but the very most recent stages of our diaspora by dispersing, by moving alone or in small groups over short distances. Archaeologists' efforts to find evidence for migrations in deep-time prehistory have failed, and will continue to fail, because those migrations never happened. A new "survival archaeology" perspective on prehistory asks how earlier humans solved challenges to their survival. An Integrative Ancestral Survival Skills Hypothesis argues that humans overcame survival challenges using complex combinations of skills that were already present among Africa's *Homo heidelbergensis* populations.

What Happened in Human Evolution? The Short Version

Humans (*Homo sapiens*) evolved out of *H. heidelbergensis* in Africa and possibly Southwestern Asia between 100 and 300 Ka. Dispersals appear to have been common among these hominins, and as a result, no one region appears more likely to be our single point of origin than others do. Humans replaced *H. heidelbergensis* by a slow process of infiltration. A permeable "frontier" of sorts appears to have existed from the Mediterranean to montane Asia beyond which Neanderthals, Denisovans, and other hominins held sway, sometimes penetrating south into humanity's ancestral geographic range. Increasing evidence from Mediterranean Europe suggests early humans sometimes returned the favor, infiltrating Europe long before 45 Ka.

In thinking about these matters, it is absolutely crucial to remember that the distinctions we paleoanthropologists make among hominin fossils and the archaeological evidence associated with them may in no way, shape, or form correspond to important cultural differences among prehistoric peoples. Where we draw species-level distinctions, they may have regarded one another as, "those other guys with the odd-looking faces." One likes to think that some ancestral human, probably a ignorant juvenile uttering, "Those people, they ..." received their wiser elders' culturally appropriate correction. The categorical distinctions we impose on paleoanthropological evidence are just that, impositions, neither obvious nor intrinsic properties of that evidence. (If they were such obvious and intrinsic properties, then neither paleontologists nor archaeologists would publish so many papers disputing them.)

Watercraft, complex projectile weapons, and symbolic artifacts ("boats, beads, and bows") aided early human dispersals into Southern Asia, Sunda, and Sahul after 70 Ka. These latitudinal dispersals called for few major additions to Ancient Africans' survival strategies. Glacial conditions' early and rapid onset around 75 Ka and persistence thereafter to 15 Ka depopulated "Neanderthal Country" (Europe and Western Asia) and the rest of Northern Eurasia. Humans moved into this wide, narrow Mammoth Steppe after 50 Ka using innovations in thermoregulation, such as tailored leather clothing, free-standing architecture, and more complex strategies for using fire and symbolic artifacts than Neanderthals and earlier hominins employed. Humans dispersed eastward following the Mammoth Steppe until peak cold conditions during the Last Glacial Maximum (LGM, 18–22 Ka) slowed and stopped them. Evidence shows that some humans made it south into the Americas either before or during the LGM, possibly using watercraft to follow a "kelp highway" along the Pacific Coast. Dispersals into the New World do not appear to have called for very different survival skills than those already on display across much of Northern Asia. Though archaeologists customarily treat Northern Eurasia's and the Americas' later Pleistocene archaeological records as "separate magisteria" (different things), from a "survival archaeology" standpoint, vastly more unites them than divides them.

After around 6–10 Ka, food production (plant and animal husbandry and correlated shifts in ecosystem engineering), changed the population movement game. Namely, increases in both overall human population size and human population densities created incentives for larger-scale migrations. Some of the earliest such migrations targeted habitats that hunter-gatherers already occupied surrounding agrarian "hot spots." Other migrations settled uninhabited islands near continental land masses. The great Oceanian and Polynesian voyages began moving humans to far oceanic islands after around 5–6 Ka. Food production sustained them in their destinations. Warmer conditions around this time also encouraged humans to permanently settle the high Arctic by employing more complex strategies for harvesting marine resources than earlier humans used.

Like our distant primate ancestors and our more recent hominin precursors, humans are tropical animals. More people live in tropical and warm-temperate conditions and at higher population densities than anywhere else on Earth. Just as a warming Industrial Era set off efforts to settle Antarctica, it seems reasonable to expect near-future global heating to encourage us beyond the "baby steps" we have made in moving into outer space, nudging us from roads of rivers and winds to the road to the stars.

A Cautionary Note about Ceramics and Migrations

Has this work rejected deep-time migration hypotheses unfairly? Archaeologists generally accept shared patterns of ceramic decoration as evidence of social and cultural identities. Ceramic design variation clinches the argument for migration in Africa's Bantu Expansions and the Lapita Expansions in Oceania. This is true, too, of many other recent population movements archaeologists interpret as migrations.

How do we refute hypotheses about prehistoric migrations in the absence of ceramics? Questioning the integrity of the named stone tool industry or archaeological culture in question would be one way to go. One could ask what reasons compel one to recognize the industry/culture/ware as the actual equivalent of a specific and self-conscious group of people. One could argue that the industry/culture/ware is merely a construct made up after the fact of archaeological discovery. Obvious, easy, and indisputably true, this line of questioning actually goes nowhere. Even if these critiques work, which they demonstrably have not for the last fifteen years or more (Clark 1994; Barton and Clark 2021), archaeologists will simply conjure up another industry/culture or redefine ones already in wide usage to align them with the fossil and molecular evidence. This is not mere speculation. Some archaeologists propose doing exactly this (Reynolds and Riede 2019)!

A survival archaeology perspective offers up a more productive path forward. For human groups to migrate, they must have storable and transportable food. For each and every such claimed deep-time migration, we must ask (as this work had done repeatedly) what evidence shows how the prehistoric people involved produced, stored, and transported the mass quantities of food they would have needed to traverse unfamiliar terrain on route to their destinations. If proponents of migration hypotheses cannot answer this question with evidence more specific than "somehow" or answer with silence, then we should reject migration hypotheses they propose out of hand. Asking this sort of "how question" moves the debate away from unfalsifiable arguments and toward hypotheses we can prove wrong using evidence.

Survival Archaeology's Known Unknowns

This book began with a call for archaeologists to ask "how questions" about prehistory in more detail than answering with silence or with "somehow." As it investigated prehistoric population movements, this book steered a course between two (metaphorical) icebergs: (1) equating pattern with process and (2) appealing to ethnographic universality.

Equating pattern with process accepts the absence of evidence for something as evidence for its actual absence. Doing this flies in the face of what we know about preservation biases. Organic materials comprise many of the tools and other technologies essential for recent preindustrial human survival strategies, and yet we know ancient sediments rarely preserve them.

Appeal to ethnographic universality asserts that if a survival strategy occurs widely or universally among ethnographic humans, then prehistoric humans practiced it as well. Doing this ignores human cultural and behavioral variability. Recent humans solve survival problems in different ways, including more than one way simultaneously. No humans practice the full range of known methods for stoneworking, fire-making, or any other task. Aboriginal Australians, for example, understand how to store energy in bent wood in order to make spring traps and other tools, but they do not seem to have applied that knowledge to make and use bows and arrows. Ethnographic African hunter-gatherers understand how leverage works, but they did not apply that knowledge to making spear-throwers (Lombard and Shea 2021). Why? Nobody knows, and that's the point. No "theory of everything" will ever explain human behavioral variability.

Survival archaeology offers a new approach to prehistory. It asks more interesting questions than "who questions." It does not have good answers to all the questions we might wish to ask, and future research will undoubtedly prove wrong some of the answers this book proposes. At the very least, however, a survival archaeology perspective helps us to identify "known unknowns," things that we know we do not know, but about which we want to learn more. Do you, Reader, really want to know how many different flavors of "Mousterian" stone tool industries there were in Later Pleistocene Europe, or would you rather learn how Neanderthals and other hominins who made Mousterian tools survived an ice age? For which do you think your distant descendants will thank you as they struggle through the next ice age?

Of the "basic six" survival problems, the one about which we know the least is one's first priority in a survival emergency: first aid and medication. Considering the immediate life-or-death consequences, one would expect strong selective pressures for improvements over time in treating injuries and illnesses. The skeletal evidence for hominins surviving major injuries, such as broken bones, seems to increase with more recent contexts, but we also know that preservation biases would create such a cumulative-seeming pattern even if no changes had actually occurred. (Recent samples of anything that varies always show greater variation and variability than older ones simply because there are more recent samples.) Plant remains from prehistoric hearths and preserved in dental calculus (tartar) can show that prehistoric people ate plants with medicinal properties, but such finds cannot show that they ate those plants because of those medicinal properties.

Archaeological sites in cold Northern Eurasian habitats and in higher altitudes in Africa suggest humans and earlier hominins used and controlled fire, along with clothing and artificial shelter, as aids to thermoregulation. The precise nature of early humans' clothing and shelters will always elude us, but fire leaves clearer traces. And yet no clear inflection point in the archaeological record shows a shift from hominins "capturing" fire from natural sources to being able to create fire at will.[1] It seems inconceivable that such a valuable survival aid as fire could, once acquired, somehow fall out of use. What then, are we to make of the many geographic and chronological gaps among occurrences of fire? Are they real or merely accidents of preservation? Traces of human and earlier hominin activities in deep caves show a capacity to transport fire, but it seems intuitively unlikely that humans developed fire-transport as aids to spelunking, or exploring deep caves. Recent evidence for hitherto unexpected early evidence of Neanderthals using stone tools to create collision-product fire shows just how little we know about prehistoric pyrotechnology (Sorensen et al. 2018).

Survival archaeology's major questions about hydration do not so much concern how prehistoric humans found water. Potable water constrains all primate settlement patterns. Recent humans' strategies for finding water vary so widely as to elude generalization. More important questions concern how prehistoric humans transported water from one place to another. Ostrich eggshells and gourds seem obvious candidates for water containers, but

---

[1] Frankly, this author thinks this business about "capturing" natural fires just one more anthropological myth, but he admits this hypothesis cannot be proven wrong.

neither occur in some of the places to which humans dispersed, such as Northern Eurasia, Sahul, or the Americas. Transporting water over land seems unlikely to have affected settlement patterns very much, but it almost certainly affected the distances over which humans and other hominins made oceanic voyages.

Archaeologists have done well at gathering information about prehistoric nutrition, coordinating insights from plant and animal remains, skeletal morphology, and bone chemistry (Twiss 2019). Zooarchaeological studies emphasize humans' use of large mammals, but the "wilderness survival/bushcraft" literature suggests we may be overlooking strategies for collecting invertebrates and small vertebrates, creatures that can comprise important and predictably stable food sources (Lesnik 2018). In terms of methods for procuring food, we know less than we should about the past use of traps and complex projectile weapons. Though these things are ethnographic human universals, archaeologists' views about their global and regional antiquity vary widely.

Many uncertainties remain about how humans moved across prehistoric landscapes, what sorts of transportation aids they made and used, and these devices' origins and variability. Much archaeological writing about prehistoric watercraft assumes there was a developmental sequence from rafts to dugout canoes to more complicated outrigger-equipped and sail-assisted vessels, but little actual evidence supports such a sequence either regionally or globally. One thinks that exposure to wind on wide rivers, large lakes, and near ocean coastlines would make the benefits of sails instantly obvious, but the archaeological consensus holds sail-assisted voyaging a recent (i.e, Holocene-age) phenomenon. This consensus is almost certainly wrong.

Communication, arguably, comes in second after first aid and medication as the one of the "big six" survival challenges about which we know the least. Archaeologists interested in this subject face two formidable challenges. First, searching prehistory for signals of the sort recent humans use in survival emergencies seems intuitively unlikely to be productive for the simple reason that prehistoric humans probably only rarely got lost. If we assume reading animal tracks and signs was an ancestral skill, then "lost" individuals could backtrack. If they were incapacitated, then others could track and find them with ease. As to other kinds of non-rescue signaling, archaeologists need far more research on how ethnographic humans use artifacts as "social media" and on what factors lead them to make symbolic artifacts out of durable media. Preservation biases preclude our testing hypotheses about prehistoric symbolic artifacts made of perishable media. Archaeologists should, therefore, focus their energies on the sources of variability among the artifacts they actually do recover from excavation, such as beads, mineral pigments, artworks, and "overdesigned" implements (i.e., products of peak procedural complexity).

DIFFERENCES BETWEEN EARLY HUMANS AND LIVING HUMANS

Chapter 3 considered seven things an extraterrestrial visitor might identify about how living humans differ from every other form of life on Earth. To keep these differences in evolutionary perspective, here we reflect on how those differences compare with what we think we know about the earliest *Homo sapiens* who lived around 200–300 Ka (Table 14.1).

Most archaeological estimates put our Pleistocene ancestors' populations at less than a million people. Today *Homo sapiens* numbers around 8 billion individuals. Between 200 and 300 Ka, we inhabited Africa and adjacent parts of Eurasia, sharing those areas with other hominin species. Today, humans are the only living hominins and we inhabit all major continents and all but the smallest oceanic islands. Before 10 Ka, humans appear to have had little effect on global environments. Fueled using renewable sources (wood), our ancestors' hearths injected miniscule amounts of carbon into the atmosphere. Today, we reap the whirlwind of using nonrenewable fossil fuels and increasingly turn to solar, wind, and nuclear sources. Early *Homo sapiens*' global impact was miniscule. Pleistocene human dispersals appear correlated with

TABLE 14.1 *Differences between early and living* Homo sapiens

	200–300 Ka	Today
Population size	< 1 million?	> 8 billion
Ecological range	Africa, contiguous parts of Southern Asia	Global
Environmental regulation	Wood-fueled fire	Universal use of fire, extensive use of fossil fuels, growing use of nuclear, wind, and solar energy.
Global impact	None?	Domestication of plants and animals, mass extinctions of wild plants and animals
Cognition, communication, and intelligence	Local communication, subcontinental social networks; regional variation, slow turnovers in artifact designs	Global communication, social networks variable at all scales; same/similar artifacts appear worldwide, rapid turnovers in artifact designs
Knowledge acquisition and sharing	Learning by imitation, emulation, informal instruction	Formal education, artifacts used to store and retrieve information
Complex and variable technology	Stone tools attached to handles, cordage, mastic (glue)	Artifacts comprised of many parts attached to one another and/or made of artificial materials

extinctions of other hominins, such as the Neanderthals, and of other large mammals, but these extinctions occurred long after our earliest appearance in the fossil record 200–300 Ka. Our ancestors' roles in these and Pleistocene-age mass extinctions remain unclear, or at least disputed among experts. Today's mass extinctions have our fingerprints all over them. Little consensus exists over how to assess prehistoric human cognition and intelligence, but choices among particular ways of making stone tools around 200–300 Ka show the sort of regional (i.e., subcontinental) distributions that hint at more-than-local but less-than-global communications networks. Today we maintain global trade networks and the Internet. Unlike earlier times, when specific sorts of artifacts enjoyed regional distributions and slow turnovers, today the same artifacts appear worldwide and turnovers happen rapidly. Early humans undoubtedly taught and learned things, but the archaeological record preserves neither artifacts we can clearly and convincingly interpret as aids to information storage nor places where learning and the search for new information occur separately from other aspects of daily life, as they do in modern-day schools and research institutions. The most complex artifacts dating to around 200–300 Ka appear to be wooden implements to which hominins attached stone artifacts using cordage and mastic. Modern-day artifacts, such as passenger aircraft, can have hundreds of thousands of separate parts attached to one another using a wide range of artificial materials (ceramics, plastic, metal, etc.). What explains these differences?

WHY US?

Why are we humans, *Homo sapiens*, rather than some other hominin, Earth's "unstoppable species"? This work has argued that we owe our unstoppability to our diaspora, to our global geographic distribution. Our prehistoric hunter-gatherer ancestors achieved that diaspora by dispersing (individuals and small groups making short-distance movements) and later as food-producing migrants (large groups making longer movements).

That these dispersals and migrations were successful in the long run we owe to our ancestral survival skills: powerful precision grasping, predictive hallucination, endurance bipedalism, spoken language, and hyperprosociality. Merely possessing those skills was not enough, however. Other hominins, now extinct, had them, too. Rather, we owe our unstoppability to *how* our earlier humans used those skills differently from other hominins.

Integrative Ancestral Survival Skills Hypothesis

One quality, integration, distinguishes how living humans use their ancestral survival skills differently from living nonhuman primates and differently from extinct hominins. Much as Chapter 4 explained using fire-making and cordage as examples, we use our ancestral survival skills in complex combinations that make the "force multipliers" more than the sum of their parts. Examples of such force multipliers built up by integrating ancestral survival skills include stone tools shaped using fracture and abrasion, digging sticks, textile baskets and containers, nets, traps and snares, art, music, architecture, pyrotechnology (ceramics, metals, candles, and oil lamps), watercraft, simple projectile weapons (spears, throwing sticks) and complex projectile weapons (slings and slingstones, bows and arrows, spear-throwers and darts, blowguns, firearms), fishing hooks and fishing lines, recipes for food and medicine (and for poison), dogs and dogsleds, roads, wheeled vehicles, aircraft, writing, metaphor, poetry, novels, laws, dictionaries, waterpower, fossil fuels, steam power, electricity, radio, solar and wind power, nuclear power, computers, the Internet, and spacecraft. The footprints astronauts left on the Moon's Sea of Tranquility and that remain there to this day were left by shoes made using ancestral survival skills. By integrating their ancestral survival skills, our ancestors literally "invented inventing."

From whence does our capacity to integrate ancestral survival skills arise? It would be nice if one could wrap up this work by confidently asserting a single hypothesis, but respect for the truth compels one to do otherwise. We simply do not know. Nothing in the evidence found with *Homo heidelbergensis* predicts we would be the most successful of their descendants. No single gene mutation, a bump on a bone, or a fissure in our brain explains us. Nor was it a gift. No Pleistocene Tinkerbell sprinkled "behavioral modernity pixie dust" on us. Our ancestors did not frolic in the African Garden of Eden and dine on the fruit from a Tree of Wisdom. We are unstoppable not because of who our ancestors were but because of what they did. You are not your haplogroup. We became the "unstoppable species" the hard way, racking up uncounted millions of deaths from injury, disease, exposure, and starvation. Each gain came with a cost, an empty spot around the hearth, fireplace, or table where formerly there was a grandparent, parent, aunt or uncle, sibling, cousin, child, or friend. Integrated combinations of ancestral survival skills allowed our ancestors to live long enough to successfully raise more children than other hominins did, and in evolution's long run, that's all that matters. Evolution offers no prize for second-best. Its "participation trophy" is extinction.

Evolution never stops, and our unstoppability continues to evolve. Many people think of ancestral survival skills in terms of such exotic activities as stoneworking, making fire, being able to identify edible plants, and knowing whether or not to drink one's own urine. (Don't, ever.) Ancestral survival skills are much, much more than these things. We practice them daily, often failing to recognize them as we do so. As I write these words, a few hundred meters away, hundreds of first-year college students are moving into the dormitories on campus. A hurricane has just missed us and the Covid-19 pandemic rages. Though many wear protective masks, theirs and their parents' eyes show the anxiety at these small-scale dispersal events. Soon, parents will depart and our ancestral survival skills will come to those students' aid. They will send text messages to one another on their smartphones (powerful precision grasping), they will wander around campus (endurance bipedalism), observe one another and speculate about likely interactions (predictive hallucination), strike up conversations (spoken language), form cliques, join student interest groups, pledge fraternities and sororities, and even occasionally attend the classes for which they have paid tuition (hyperprosociality). Ancestral survival skills were our past, they are our present, and they will be our future.

Testing hypotheses about the origins and evolution of our capacity to integrate ancestral survival skills will require much further work and call for cooperation among scholars in diverse fields. Inasmuch as survival skills and bushcraft are the nearest things in the contemporary human experience to the practical applications of ancestral survival skills earlier humans practiced, future research must incorporate observations of how people develop such survival skills in this research agenda.

A new survival archaeology research agenda will lead archaeologists and others involved in paleoanthropology down new paths, to ask exciting and interesting questions, and to engage with a wider audience than ever before. A survival-archaeology focus on "how questions" will move us closer to answering "why questions" than answers to "who questions" ever will. Archaeologists' answers to "how questions" will probably not work so well as "window dressing" in paleontologists' and molecular anthropologists' theories about human evolution than answers to "who questions" do, but frankly, that's their problem.

WHAT MUST WE DO?

Archaeologists predict the future no better than any other humans.[2] Nevertheless, archaeology's long-term perspective on past human behavior offers insights into what we can do to avoid finding ourselves, collectively, in a future survival emergency. Here, we ask, "What must we do to survive?" at different scales: the near term (the next few centuries), the longer-term (the next few thousand years), and longest term (more than 10,000 years from now).

The Next Few Centuries

First, we need to recognize that current population dislocations involving "climate change refugees" are not migrations but dispersals. Demagogues among politicians may describe these movements as migrations or even as

---

[2] Except psychics, whose prediction about the future display both wide variability (collectively) and truly impressive inaccuracy (individually).

"invasions," but they are wrong.[3] *Descansos* (roadside memorials) and *taquerias* (Mexican restaurants specializing in tacos) now appear throughout the US Northeast and Midwest not because entire Mexican and Central American villages uprooted themselves and migrated northward. They appear because ambitious individual Mexicans and other Latin Americans dispersed into the United States, retaining elements of their ancestral mortuary practices and food preferences as they assimilated into American society. The United States is a richer, stronger, more resilient society for of them.

Second, we should not unwittingly create migrations out of dispersals. Left to their own devices, dispersing people assimilate. Our Pleistocene ancestors "invented" (evolved) grammar and syntax for just this reason. The only way to stop this assimilation is to inflict on dispersing people conditions that replicate migrations, such as segregating them in ethnic enclaves and erecting barriers to their assimilation. Dispersers might not have had strong and unifying ideologies pitting themselves against those in their destinations, but preventing assimilation is the surest way to nurture such ideologies. One way forward – and admittedly it is a tough sell – would be for nations receiving large numbers of dispersing humans to reduce both costs and benefits for identifying with one or another ethnic group and thereby speed up assimilation. If this means compelling people to learn the language, then that must be done quickly and compassionately, but also with swift, certain and costly consequences for noncompliance. Not doing this merely delays assimilation and the benefits that accrue from it.

Scientific estimates of the near-future climate change suggest that vast areas between 30° North latitude and 15° South latitude (much of Northern Africa, Southern Asia, and Latin America) may become depopulated or even all-but-uninhabitable due to global heating. North and south of these latitudes, especially those vast and unpopulated regions, such as Canada, the United States, Northern Europe, Russia, and China, will be preferred destinations for climate-change refugees. Those living there need to plan accordingly. The good news? Warming climates will make cereal-based agriculture possible in northern and southern regions where it is currently impossible. The bad news? Many industrialized nations are currently experiencing intensely nationalistic "nativist" political movements that see migrants as sources of problems rather than as allies in our species' fight for survival.

Less Than 10,000 Years from Now

All credible scientific forecasts about climate change suggest that the next several centuries will be rough and that they will test us brutally. But there is

---

[3] Ironically, many of those US politicians and aspiring politicians so loudly fulminating about Latin American "invasion" trace their ancestry to an actual migration/invasion that began in the 17th Century AD and brought Western Europeans and enslaved Africans to the Americas.

good news, too. The orbital forces that create ice ages have not stopped. Pumping enormous amounts of carbon into the atmosphere, as we Anthropocene humans have done, has increased global temperatures and those temperatures will continue to increase even if we halt all carbon emissions tomorrow. But unless we manage to permanently alter Earth's orbit, several millennia down the road, the ice will return. It will begin to accumulate on mountains and spread downslope to river valleys. Ocean ice will return as a hazard to Arctic navigation. Northern regions that global heating has made agricultural heartlands will return to being taiga and tundra. Sea levels will drop, reconnecting islands formerly sundered from the continental mainland. This will lead to all manner of human and nonhuman animal population movements. Colder global temperatures and diminished agricultural productivity will either stop human population increase entirely or reduce human populations significantly.

What must we do? Put simply, we need to survive. We need to ensure that human populations do not drop below minimum viable levels. Inasmuch as we now number more than 8 billion and that Pleistocene humans likely numbered less than a million, this leaves a lot of "elbow room" for experimentation and trial-and-error. Do we need to cure every known disease? No, we do not. Do we need to push average human lifespans into three digits? No, we do not. Just to be clear, one should read this neither as a call for depraved indifference to human suffering nor for a halt to medical progress, but instead as a call for priority-setting, for discriminating between survival threats to *some* humans and survival threats to *all* humans.

More Than 10,000 Years from Now

As Chapter 13 noted, the main threats to our long-term survival are uncontrolled energy releases into Earth's biosphere due to meteor impacts and/or large-scale volcanism. In the very long run, such events' occurrences are certainties. The only way to reduce their consequences for our survival is to create additional and redundant biospheres elsewhere. Sometime in the next 10,000 years or so, humans must move viable populations of our own species and our ecosystems off Earth and onto other planets circling distant stars.

Future human population movements into space and to other solar systems will combine elements of both migrations and dispersals. Recent human migrations often have a strong ideological component. One suspects the most successful interstellar migrations will have a strong ideological component, too, if only to recruit people and to discourage "defectors" and "free-riders." One thinks it more likely than not that religious organizations and totalitarian regimes will lead humanity's first steps on the "road of the stars." Fractious, secular, and democratic societies will probably trail behind them, if they participate at all. As a citizen of one such fractious, secular, and democratic society, this author would like to be wrong about this, but this prediction is consistent with past migrations, the most successful of which European religious autocracies sponsored.

Future human population movements to other solar systems will also have very different evolutionary consequences than past dispersals and migrations. Past dispersals and migrations resulted in our becoming a single, globally distributed species. To be successful in the longer term − millions of years versus mere thousands − humans will need to move toward different extraterrestrial destinations. First discoveries of "Earth 2.0" might send multiple and competing migrations toward that destination. Long-term success, however, will require migrations to disperse to different destinations and away from one another. Over long periods, differences will accumulate among dispersing migrations and *Homo sapiens* will evolve into descendant posthuman species. One wonders what they will think of us.

APPENDIX A

TRADITIONAL ARCHAEOLOGICAL AGE-STAGES

Archaeologists often use "cultural" time periods, or "age-stages," that they define in terms of variation in artifact occurrences and inferred patterns of human behavior (see Table A.1). The most commonly used of these, the Paleolithic and Neolithic periods ("old" and "new/young" stone ages, respectively) originally developed among archaeologists working in Europe and around the Mediterranean Basin. At the time archaeologists created this framework, they thought that Paleolithic hominins shaped stone by fracture only and subsisted by hunting and gathering. Neolithic humans also shaped stone using abrasion and practiced agriculture and pastoralism. Most

TABLE A.1 *Archaeological age-stages (based on Western Eurasian and Northern African evidence)*

Age-stage	Start date (years ago)	Characteristic artifacts	Comments
Neolithic	10,000	Abraded-edge celts, groundstone tools, ceramic vessels	Agriculture, pastoralism, early villages, monumental architecture; continental and oceanic migrations
Mesolithic	14,000	Geometric microliths	Increasingly sedentary postglacial hunter-gatherers
Upper Paleolithic	45,000	Prismatic blades, unifacial hierarchical cores, carved bone tools, art, and personal adornments	Dispersal of *H. sapiens* into Northern Eurasia, Americas
Middle Paleolithic	250,000	"Levallois" bifacial hierarchical cores and flakes	Origins of *H. sapiens*, dispersals into Southern Asia, Australia, New Guinea
Lower Paleolithic	3.5 million years ago	Short, nonhierarchical pebble cores and flakes; handaxes and other long core tools (LCTs) after 1.7 million years ago	Origins of the genus *Homo*, extinctions of other hominin genera

archaeological research traditions subdivide Paleolithic and Neolithic and interpose a "Mesolithic" or "Epipaleolithic" period between them, but the dates used and the criteria for assigning an assemblage to one or another such age-stage vary among research traditions.

The Paleolithic-Mesolithic-Neolithic Stone Age sequence enjoys wide usage across Eurasia and North Africa, but it works less well for regions distant from Europe and the Mediterranean Basin. Archaeologists working in sub-Saharan Africa use a three-part sequence originally developed in South Africa (Goodwin 1929). Its Earlier and Middle Stone Ages are roughly equivalent to the Lower and Middle Paleolithic. Its Later Stone Age corresponds to the Eurasian Upper Paleolithic and Mesolithic/Epipaleolithic. Australasian and American archaeologists and their colleagues working in the Pacific do not use these age-stages, but instead rely on local or regional frameworks.

APPENDIX B

SURVIVAL ARCHAEOLOGY RECOMMENDED READINGS

BUSHCRAFT

Boudreau, David, and Mykel Hawke. *Foraging for Survival: Edible Wild Plants of North America*. New York: Skyhorse Publishing. Mainly a guide to identifying plants, edible and otherwise. Good color photos of every plant listed.

Elbroch, Mark, Louis Liebenberg, and Adriaan Dr Louw. 2010. *Practical Tracking: A Guide to Following Footprints and Finding Animals*. Mechanicsburg, PA: Stackpole Books.

Elpel, Thomas J. 2004. *Botany in a Day: The Patterns Method of Plant Identification: Thomas J. Elpel's Herbal Field Guide to Plant Families*, 5th ed. Pony, MT: Hollowtop Outdoor Primitive School. Simple and straightforward introductory-level reference work annotated with information about plant uses. Illustrations are line drawings, rather than photos.

Emory, Kenneth. P. 1943. *South Sea Lore*. Honolulu, HI: Bishop Museum (Special Publication 33). Survival guide issued to sailors and airmen in the Pacific Theater during World War II.

Kochanski, M. 1987. *Bushcraft: Outdoor Skills and Wilderness Survival*. Vancouver: Lone Pine Publishing. This classic work emphasizes skills relevant to northern forest habitats.

McPherson, J., and G. McPherson. 1993. *Primitive Wilderness Living and Survival Skills*. Randolph, KS: Prairie Wolf Publications.

McPherson, J., and G. McPherson. 1996. *Primitive Wilderness Living and Survival Skills: Applied and Advanced*. Randolph, KS: Prairie Wolf Publications.

Knight, J. 2022. *The Essential Skills of Wilderness Survival: A Guide to Shelter, Water, Fire, Food, Navigation, and Survival Kits*. Monroe, WA: Alderleaf Wilderness College Press.

WILDERNESS SURVIVAL

Fears, J. Wayne. 2018. *The Scouting Guide to Survival: An Officially-Licensed Book of the Boy Scouts of America*. New York: Skyhorse Publishing. For parents and children. One of several in the BSA Guides Series.

Lundin, Cody. 2003. *98.6 Degrees: The Art of Keeping Your Ass Alive*. Salt Lake City, UT: Gibbs Smith. A quirky, witty book, by an unconventional author, but one that is packed with important insights from an experienced survival instructor. For other works and classes, see www.codylundin.com.

Towell, Colin. 2020. *The Survival Handbook: New Edition*. New York: DK Publishing. A work originally commissioned for the Boy Scouts of America, this is an impressively comprehensive and superbly illustrated bushcraft/wilderness survival work.

BOTH BUSHCRAFT AND WILDERNESS SURVIVAL

Editors of Stackpole Books (compiled by Amy Rost). 2007. *Survival Wisdom & Know How: Everything You Need to Know to Subsist in the Wilderness*. New York: Black Dog & Leventhal Publishers. A massive (480-page) encyclopedia of bushcraft and wilderness survival information compiled from Stackpole Books' many shorter books on these topics. Note: This book is very large with very small print.

Quiñonez, J. P. 2022. *Thrive: Long-Term Wilderness Survival Guide*. Winnipeg: Boreal Creek Press.

SELECTED WEBSITES

Aboriginal Living Skills School in Prescott, Arizona, offers small-enrollment skills and survival courses focused on montane and desert habitats (www.codylundin.com).

Alderleaf Wilderness College in Monroe, Washington, offers a variety of online, printed, and face-to-face instructional resources (www.wildernesscollege.com/).

The Boulder Outdoor Survival School in Boulder, Utah, enjoys a long-standing and national reputation for excellence in wilderness survival instruction (www.boss-inc.com/).

APPENDIX C

FURTHER READING

Unless otherwise indicated, these are popular-science works that one can read and understand without formal (i.e., college-level) training in anthropology. Works annotated as "technical" may require such training. One can also find good, short readings about the evidence for particular regions and time periods in the Cambridge World Prehistory series, in various Oxford Handbooks, and in the journals *Evolutionary Anthropology: Issues, News, Reviews*, *Scientific American*, and *American Scientist* as well as in the "news" sections of *Science* and *Nature*. The United States National Museum of Natural History (Smithsonian Institution) maintains a Human Origins website with many resources (https://humanorigins.si.edu/). One recommends it enthusiastically.

CHAPTER 1. INTRODUCTION

Bellwood, P. 2013. *First Migrants: Ancient Migration in Global Perspective*. New York: Wiley Blackwell.
Gamble, C. 2013. *Settling the Earth: The Archaeology of Deep Human History*. New York: Cambridge University Press. (Technical)
Hoffecker, J. F. 2017. *Modern Humans: Their African Origin and Global Dispersal*. New York: Columbia University Press. (Technical)
Stringer, C. 2012. *Lone Survivors: How We Came to Be the Only Humans on Earth*. New York: Times Books/Henry Holt.

CHAPTER 2. HARD EVIDENCE

Burroughs, W. J. 2005. *Climate Change in Prehistory: The End of the Reign of Chaos*. Cambridge: Cambridge University Press.
Fagan, B. Editor. 2009. *The Complete Ice Age: How Climate Change Shaped the World*. New York: Thames and Hudson.
Shea, J. J. 2017. *Stone Tools in Human Evolution: Behavioral Differences among Technological Primates*. New York: Cambridge University Press. (Technical)
Shipman, P. 1981. *The Life History of a Fossil: An Introduction to Taphonomy and Paleoecology*. Cambridge, MA: Harvard University Press.

CHAPTER 3. WHO ARE THESE PEOPLE?

Henrich, J. 2015. *The Secret of Our Success: How Culture Is Driving Human Evolution, Domesticating Our Species, and Making Us Smarter.* Princeton, NJ: Princeton University Press.
Lieberman, D. E. 2013. *The Story of the Human Body: Evolution, Health and Disease.* New York: Pantheon Books.
Raff, J. 2020. *Origin: A Genetic History of the Americas.* New York: Twelve Books.
Reich, D. 2018. *Who We Are and How We Got Here: Ancient DNA and the New Science of the Human Past.* New York: Pantheon.
Roberts, A. 2018. *Evolution: The Human Story,* 2nd ed. New York: Dorling Kindersley.
Wood, B. A. 2019. *Human Evolution: A Very Short Introduction,* 2nd ed. Oxford: Oxford University Press.

CHAPTER 4. HOW DID THEY GET HERE?

Harari, Y. N. 2014. *Sapiens: A Brief History of Humankind.* London: Harvill Secker.
Potts, R. 1996. *Humanity's Descent: The Consequences of Ecological Instability.* New York: William Morrow.
Boivin, N., R. Crassard, et al. 2017. *Human Dispersal and Species Movement: From Prehistory to the Present.* London, UK: Cambridge University Press

CHAPTER 5. ANCIENT AFRICANS

Barham, L., and P. Mitchell. 2008. *The First Africans: African Archaeology from the Earliest Toolmakers to Most Recent Foragers.* New York: Cambridge University Press. (Technical)
McCall, G. S. 2014. *Before Modern Humans: New Perspectives on the African Stone Age.* Walnut Creek, CA: Left Coast Press. (Technical)
Phillipson, D. W. 2005. *African Archaeology,* 3rd ed. Cambridge: Cambridge University Press.

CHAPTER 6. GOING EAST: SOUTHERN ASIANS

Dennell, R. 2009. *The Palaeolithic Settlement of Asia.* Cambridge: Cambridge University Press. (Technical)
Enzel, Y., and O. Bar-Yosef. Editors. 2017. *Quaternary of the Levant: Environments, Climate Change, and Humans.* New York: Cambridge University Press. (Technical)
Petraglia, M. D., and J. I. Rose. Editors. 2009. *The Evolution of Human Populations in Arabia: Paleoenvironments, Prehistory and Genetics.* New York: Springer. (Technical)

CHAPTER 7. DOWN UNDER: EARLY SOUTHEAST ASIANS AND SAHULIANS

Higham, C. 2014. *Early Mainland Southeast Asia: From First Humans to Angkor.* London: River Books Press. (Technical)
Hiscock, P. 2008. *Archaeology of Ancient Australia.* London: Routledge. (Technical)
Kingdon, J. 1993. *Self-Made Man: Human Evolution from Eden to Extinction.* New York: John Wiley.
Mulvaney, J., and J. Kamminga. 1999. *Prehistory of Australia.* Washington, DC: Smithsonian Institution Press. (Technical)

CHAPTER 8. NEANDERTHAL COUNTRY

Churchill, S. E. 2014. *Thin on the Ground: Neandertal Biology, Archaeology and Ecology*. New York: Wiley-Blackwell. (Technical)
Papagianni, D., and M. Morse. 2015. *Neanderthals Rediscovered: How Modern Science Is Rewriting Their Story*, revised and updated ed. New York: Thames & Hudson.
Sykes, R. W. 2020. *Kindred: Neanderthal Life, Love, Death and Art*. New York: Bloomsbury Sigma.
Trinkaus, E., and P. Shipman. 1993. *The Neandertals: Changing the Image of Mankind*. New York: Knopf.

CHAPTER 9. GOING NORTH: EARLY EURASIANS

Bahn, P. G. 2016. *Images of the Ice Age*. New York: Oxford University Press.
Fagan, B. 2011. *Cro-Magnon: How the Ice Age Gave Birth to the First Modern Humans*. New York: Bloomsbury Press.
Holliday, T. W. 2022/in press. *Cro-Magnon: The Story of the Last Ice Age People of Europe*. New York: Columbia University Press.

CHAPTER 10. A BRAVE NEW WORLD: PLEISTOCENE AMERICANS

Childs, C. 2018. *Atlas of a Lost World: Travels in Ice Age America*. New York: Pantheon Books.
MacPhee, R. D. E. 2018. *End of the Megafauna: The Fate of the World's Hugest, Fiercest, and Strangest Animals*. New York: W. W. Norton.
Meltzer, D. J. 2021. *First Peoples in a New World: Settling Ice Age America*. Cambridge: Cambridge University Press. (Technical)

CHAPTER 11. MOVABLE FEASTS: FOOD PRODUCERS AND MIGRATIONS

Balter, M. 2017. *The Goddess and the Bull: Çatalhöyük: An Archaeological Journey to the Dawn of Civilization*. New York: Routledge.
Bellwood, P. 2004. *First Farmers: The Origins of Agricultural Societies*. New York: Wiley-Blackwell.
Mitchell, P. 2002. *The Archaeology of Southern Africa*. Cambridge: Cambridge University Press. (Technical)
Mitchell, P., and P. Lane. Editors. 2013. *The Oxford Handbook of African Archaeology*. Oxford: Oxford University Press.

CHAPTER 12. DISTANT HORIZONS AND STARS BECKON: OCEANIC ISLANDS AND BEYOND

Kirch, P. V. 2018. *On the Road of the Winds: An Archaeological History of the Pacific Islands before European Contact*, 2nd ed. Berkeley: University of California Press. (Technical)
Napolitano, M. F., J. H. Stone, and R. J. DiNapoli. 2021. *The Archaeology of Island Colonization: Global Approaches to Initial Human Settlement*. Gainesville: University Press of Florida.
Thomas, N. 2021. *Voyagers: The Settlement of the Pacific*. New York: Basic Books.

CHAPTER 13. UNSTOPPABLE? HUMAN EXTINCTION

Bostrum, N., and M. Cirkovic. Editors. 2011. *Global Catastrophic Risks*. New York: Oxford University Press. (Technical).
Brannen, P. 2017. *The Ends of the World: Volcanic Apocalypses, Lethal Oceans, and Our Quest to Understand Earth's Past Mass Extinctions*. New York: HarperCollins.
Lundin, C. 2007. *When All Hell Breaks Loose: Stuff You Need to Survive When Disaster Strikes*. Salt Lake City, UT: Gibbs Smith.
Ord, T. 2020. *The Precipice: Existential Risk and the Future of Humanity*. New York: Hachette Books.

GLOSSARY

Abraded-edge tool Groundstone tool featuring an edge formed by the intersection of two surfaces at least one of which has been shaped by abrasion.
aDNA (ancient DNA) DNA recovered from **fossils**.
Affirming the consequent An error in logic where if the consequent is said to be true, the antecedent is said to be true, as a result.
Age-stages See **cultural periods**.
Alpha taxonomy The formal names paleontologists assign to groups of **fossils**, e.g., *Homo erectus*.
Analogy Similarity arising from separate origins (e.g., bat and bird wings).
Ancestral survival skills Survival skills of **powerful precision grasping, predictive hallucination, endurance bipedalism, spoken language,** and **hyperprosociality**.
Ancient Africans *Homo sapiens* who lived in Africa before 50 Ka.
Animal husbandry Domestication of animals for food or other purposes.
Anthropocene Informal term for the period since 500 years ago.
Anthropogenic narratives Scientific accounts of human evolution expressed as narratives (linear changes of cause and effect).
Archaeological where/when test Test for assigning an artifact to a specific region and time period using visual clues only.
Archaeo-mythology False archaeological **hypothesis** retained due to its enduring presence in popular media.
Archaic humans Hominins and early humans who did not possess the full range of living human skeletal morphology and inferred behavioral capacities.
Assemblage Group of **fossils** and/or artifacts recovered from the same sedimentary deposit.
Aurignacian One among several named stone tool industries associated with Early Eurasians.
Backed/truncated piece Stone artifacts preserving at least one steeply retouched edge (around 90°).
Bantu A Zulu word that means "people" now used as a general term for many sub-Saharan African languages and for the people who speak those languages.
Bantu expansions Migrations of food producers from equatorial Africa southward beginning around 2–3 Ka.
Beringia Eastern Siberia and Northwestern North America conjoined by lowered sea levels.

Bifacial hierarchical core (BHC) Core preserving worked edges from which stoneworkers detached **flakes** of unequal lengths.
Big six survival challenges First aid and medication, thermoregulation, hydration, nutrition, transportation, and communication.
Biostratigraphy A method for dividing time based on first or last occurrences of specific fossils.
Bipolar core Core (and **flake**) from which flakes were detached by setting it on a hard surface and then striking it from above with a **percussor**.
Bone degreasing Boiling bones to extract fat from them.
Bottleneck, genetic A reduction of genetic diversity among an evolving lineage, usually attributed to a reduction in ancestral population size.
Bowl Hemispherical vessel.
Burins Retouched pieces preserving at least one large flake scar that spread parallel to an edge.
Bushcraft Traditional skills for surviving in the wilderness.
Catarrhines Old World monkeys.
Catchment The areas around habitation sites over which humans forage for resources.
Celt A core-tool preserving a convex or straight, but nonconvergent retouched edge at one or both ends of its long axis.
Ceramic ware Groups of ceramics from the same region and time period that preserve evidence for similar manufacturing techniques and decoration.
Ceramics Artifacts are made out of fired clay, silt, or marl.
Chimera In archaeology, a **fossil** reconstructed from the remains of different individuals.
Chronostratigraphy Dividing time into measured units.
"Clovis first" hypothesis A now largely rejected hypothesis arguing that the people who made **Clovis points** were the first humans to settle the Americas.
Clovis phenomenon A group of North America archaeological **assemblages** featuring **Clovis points** and dating to 12–13 Ka.
Clovis point A distinctive form of **fluted point** found in North America between 12 and 13 Ka.
Coastal route hypothesis Hypothesis arguing that humans dispersed into the Americas along the Pacific Coast (aka the kelp highway hypothesis).
Color races Human races defined in terms of four colors (red, white, black, yellow), ostensibly based on skin color and temperment.
Commensal species Nondomesticated organisms that subsist in human habitats.
Communities of practice Conjectural groups of prehistoric people who did things the same way. Basically, a euphemism for an archaeological "culture."
Complex projectile weapons Projectile weapons incorporating separate missile and launcher components (e.g., bow and arrow, **spear-thrower** and **dart**, sling and slingstone).
Conchoidal ("shell-shaped") fracture A type of fracture among rocks with isotropic, brittle, and cryptocrystalline properties, such as glass or flint.
Conduction Loss of body heat due to contact with cold surfaces.
Confirmation bias Accepting observations that agree with one's previously held beliefs while ignoring or rejecting observations that do not.
Convection Loss of body heat due to contact with cold air.
Coprolite Fossilized feces.

Core Rock featuring one or more fracture scars longer than 10 millimeters.
Cores-on-flakes Flake fragments featuring relatively large flake detachment scars (i.e., ones more than half their maximum length).
Cro-Magnon Former term for human populations who lived in Europe and Northern Asia after 45,000 years ago (see **Earliest Eurasians**).
Cultural anthropology Observation and scientific studies of living humans (aka ethnography).
Cultural periods Time periods defined in terms of variation in archaeological remains (aka age-stages).
Culture (human) Shared thoughts and behaviors taught and learned using spoken language or simulations of spoken language (i.e., writing).
Curated artifacts Artifacts transported between habitation sites and carried on foraging trips.
"Curse of the platonic ideal" Misguided efforts to make observations of multivariate and continuously variable phenomena conform to one or a few simple stereotypes.
Dart Pointed and/or barbed wooden weapon projected by a **spear-thrower**.
Deep time Prehistory before 10,000 years ago.
"Definitive-article" cultures Early anthropologists' terms for groups of living or recent humans whose names begin with the definite article, for example, *the* Maasai, *the* !Kung San, or *the* Navajo, thus implying less variability than they actually express.
Denisovans An extinct **Later Pleistocene** Eurasian **hominin** population.
Diaspora An intercontinental geographic range within which individuals and groups of a given group move about with relative ease and few lasting barriers.
Dispersal Permanent movements of individuals and small groups.
Domestication Human control of other species' reproductive activities.
Double-hulled canoe A catamaran-like sailing vessel in use among Pacific peoples.
Early Eurasians Human populations who lived in Europe and Northern Asia between 12,000 and 45,000 years ago.
Early Pleistocene Geological epoch 0.7–2.6 million years ago.
Ecosystem engineering Changing the environment to increase energy recovery.
Ecotone A region in which several different ecological zones conjoin one another.
Electron spin resonance (ESR) A type of **trapped electron dating** method.
Elongated nonhierarchical core Core having unequal length, width, and thickness and flakes detached to roughly the same extent on both sides of its worked edges.
Endurance bipedalism The ability to walk and run on two feet for prolonged periods and distances.
Environmental forcing Behavioral change due to climate change.
Ethnoarchaeology Study of how recent humans create an archaeological record.
Ethnography Observation and scientific study of living humans (aka cultural anthropology).
Ethnology Nineteenth-century precursor to cultural anthropology based mainly on indirect (secondhand) observations of living human behavior.
Ethology Studies of living nonhuman species behavior.
Expedient stone tools Artifacts made quickly, used briefly, and discarded.
Experimental archaeology Studies trying to re-create past human activities.
First Asians Humans who lived in Asia south of the Taurus-Zagros-Himalaya mountain ranges before 30 Ka.

Flake Piece of stone fracture that has detached from another rock.
Flake point Retouched piece preserving at least one convergently retouched tip.
Flintknappers Originally, gunflint manufacturers, but now referencing craft/hobby stoneworkers more generally.
Fluted point Lanceolate (narrow ends elongated) **foliate point** with one or more large flake removals ("flutes") on its base (see also **Clovis point**).
Foliate point Elongated nonhierarchical core with acute (< 90°) retouched edges, relatively thin cross-section, and a convergently retouched edge at one or both ends of its long axis.
Fossil Remains of an organism in which minerals have replaced most of its organic components.
Food production A strategy by which humans extract energy (calories) from domesticated plants and animals that are used as food sources.
Geological epoch Time periods defined in terms of global-scale changes in rock composition.
Geometric microlith Small **backed/truncated piece** having somewhat standardized and symmetrical shape.
Ghost marriage Argument that specific hominins or groups of humans made specific sets of stone tools or stone tool industries.
Glacial amnesia Forgetting about the cyclical nature of glaciations when making predictions about the future.
Grammar Rules about word choice in spoken or written language.
Grinding slab A type of **pulverizing tool**.
Groundstone tool Artifact modified and/or shaped using abrasion.
Hafting Attaching a tool to a handle (haft).
Half-life The amount of time it takes for 50 percent of an unstable isotope to decay (i.e., shed protons) and transform another isotope.
Hammerstone See **percussor**.
Handling costs Energy expenditures related to an activity, such as collecting food.
Handstone A type of **pulverizing tool**.
Hansel and Gretel fallacy Archaeologists' assumption that dispersing humans left clear and distinctive stone tool evidence indicating their movements.
Haplogroups DNA samples with similar and distinctive combinations of genes.
Heat treatment See **thermal alteration**.
Heinrich H5 event A rapid shift to cold conditions around 45 Ka, most likely caused by a slowing of the North Atlantic thermohaline current.
Hierarchical core Core whose working edges feature different flake removal scars on opposite sides.
Holocene Geological epoch, since 11,700 years ago.
Hominidae Taxonomic group including African apes (gorillas, bonobos, chimpanzees), Asian orangutans, gibbons, humans, and extinct hominins.
Hominin Bipedal primate.
Hominin paleontology The study of **hominin** fossils.
Homology Similarities arising from common evolutionary origin and inheritance (e.g., primate stereoscopic vision).
Hopepothesis A hypothesis one hopes is true but for which alternative hypothesis cannot be rejected.
"How questions" Paleoanthropological research questions about prehistoric activities.

Human Revolution Conjectural evolutionary event in which *Homo sapiens*' distinctive behaviors arose rapidly.

Humans *Homo sapiens* (Latin, "wise man").

Hydrostatic springs Springs that flow along coastlines during lowered sea levels, as the water table equilibrates with sea level.

Hypergyny When women from one group enter into relationships with males from another group at far greater frequencies than with men of their own group.

Hyperprosociality Enduring high costs to seek out nonreproductive interactions with members of one's own species.

Hypothermia Life-endangering lowering of core body temperatures.

Hypothesis A claim about reality that can be proven wrong with evidence.

Ice-free-corridor hypothesis Hypothesis arguing that humans dispersed into the Americas through a deglaciated corridor between North Americas Cordilleran and Laurentian ice sheets.

Infiltration hypothesis Hypothesis contending that early humans replaced *Homo heidelbergensis* by dispersing among them and reproductively outcompeting them (rather than by large-scale migrations and competitive displacement).

Intensification Working harder at a task to achieve the same result.

Interpleniglacial Synonym for Marine Isotope Stage 3 (29–57 Ka).

Jar Cylindrical stone or ceramic vessel.

Joint attention Teaching/learning situations in which two or more individual focus on the same thing simultaneously.

Jug Ceramic vessel with a relatively large enclosed space and a narrow opening at one end.

Ka Abbreviation for thousands of years ago.

Kelp highway hypothesis See **coastal route hypothesis**.

Lapita expansion Movements of food-producing populations into Remote Oceania beginning around 4 Ka.

Last Glacial Maximum (LGM) **Marine Isotope Stage** 2 (12–29 Ka).

Later Pleistocene Geological epoch 11,700–128,000 years ago.

LCT See **long core tool**.

Levallois Old term for **bifacial hierarchical core** and **flakes** detached from them.

Levant The Eastern Mediterranean coast, Jordan Rift Valley, Sinai Peninsula, and upper Tigris and Euphrates Rivers.

Lithics Stone artifacts.

Lithics systematics anarchy A state of affairs in which archaeologists use many different and conflicting terms for stone artifacts dating to the same time and place.

Logistical mobility Movements in search of food, fuel, or other resources.

Long core tool (LCT) Elongated **nonhierarchical core** with acute ($< 90°$) retouched edges.

Ma Abbreviation for million years ago.

Mammoth Steppe An ecologically enriched grassland that stretched from Northern Europe, across Asia, and into the North American interior during **Later Pleistocene** times.

Marine Isotope Stage Geological epoch defined in terms of chemical changes in oceanic sediment cores.

Mass extinction Simultaneous extinctions of many species, hypothetically due to a common cause.

Megafauna Large terrestrial mammals (definitions vary by region).

Mercator projection effect A cartographic (map-making) convention that exaggerates the size of northern territories.

Microlith A small (< 30–50 mm long) **backed/truncated piece**.

Midden A dense concentrations of shellfish remains on an archaeological site.

Middle Pleistocene Geological epoch 128,000–728,000 years ago.

Migration Permanent and coordinated movement of a large group.

Minimum number of individuals (MNI) In zooarchaeology, the smallest number of individuals necessary to account for the species or another taxon in an archaeological assemblage.

Miocene Geological epoch dating to 5–23 Ma.

Modern humans *Homo sapiens* populations who possessed the same range of behavioral capacities that living humans do.

Mortar A type of **pulverizing tool**.

Mount Toba supervolcano Indonesian volcano that left behind a caldera after a massive volcanic eruption ca. 75 Ka.

Mousterian A name for stone tool industries found in Europe, Southwest Asia, and Northern Africa between 45 and 250 Ka.

NASTIES Acronym for named stone tool industries.

Natural history intelligence The ability to observe and correctly interpret natural phenomena (e.g., identify edible plants, read animal tracks, predict weather from cloud patterns).

Natural selection Evolutionary forces affecting individual survival.

Neanderthals Extinct **hominins** that lived in Western Eurasia between 45,000 and 300,000 years ago.

Near Oceania Pacific Ocean Islands in the Bismarck Archipelago, the Solomon Islands, and points in between them.

Niche The network of energy relationships among any given organism and other organisms.

No migrations before food production hypothesis The argument that prior to the adoption of food production (or its functional equivalent: mass quantities of storable and portable food), human dispersed rather than migrated.

Nonhierarchical core Core whose working edges feature similar **flake** removal scars on opposite sides.

Nubian core Bifacial hierarchical core whose principal **flake**-detachment surface has been preshaped to create triangular flakes.

Number of identified specimens (NISP) In zooarchaeology, the number of specimens in a given collection that they have identified to a species or some other taxon.

Oligocene Geological epoch dating to 23–34 Ma.

Operational chains Different strategies for doing the same things.

Optically stimulated luminescence (OSL) A type of **trapped electron dating** method.

Orthognathism Anatomical term for having the face tucked beneath the forebrain.

Osseous tools Artifacts made from ivory, antler, bone, horn, and shell.

Paleoanthropology Scientific study of human origins and evolution.

Paleontology The study of morphological and evolutionary changes among fossils.

Pastoralism Animal husbandry involving herd animals.

Peak procedural complexity Complex sets of actions that have to be performed in correct sequence and with specific choices among contingencies (options to do things differently).

Percussor Rock preserving crushing damage from repeated percussion against another rock (aka hammerstone).
Perforated stone tools Artifacts with a hole carved or drilled through them.
Pestle A type of **pulverizing tool**.
Plant husbandry Food production using domesticated plants.
Plate/platter Relatively wide and shallow vessel.
Pleistocene Geological epoch dating from 12,000 to 2.5 million years ago.
Pleistocene Americans America's **Pleistocene** human inhabitants.
Pleistocene overkill hypothesis A hypothesis arguing that human predation was a major cause of **Pleistocene**-age extinctions among large mammals, especially in Sahul and the Americas.
Pliocene Geological epoch 2.6–5.3 million years ago.
Plio-Pleistocene Informal term for the period 1.5–3.5 Ma.
Polygyny When males have more than one reproductive partner mate at the same time.
Polynesia Pacific Ocean Islands between Hawai'i, New Zealand, and Easter Island/Rapa Nui.
Postcranial bones Bones located below the skull and mandible.
Powerful precision grasping The capacity for thumb-to-fingertip grasping.
Predictive hallucination Assuming facts not in evidence in order to make predictions about future events.
Prehistory The time before written records. (Dates vary between regions.)
Primate archaeology See **primate ethology**.
Primate ethology Studies documenting the behavior of living nonhuman primates.
Principle of association Objects enclosed in the same sedimentary deposit were deposited at the same time.
Principle of facies Sediments from the same depositional event differ over the landscapes onto which they were deposited.
Principle of superposition In an undisturbed sequence of sedimentary deposits, younger layers cover older ones.
Prismatic blade core See **unifacial hierarchical core**.
Prismatic blades Elongated **flakes** detached from **unifacial hierarchical cores**.
Pseudo-extinction Extinction that results when one species evolves into one or more descendant species.
Pulverizing tool A type of **groundstone tool** featuring extensive flat, concave, or convex surfaces shaped by abrasion.
Quantal speech Vocalizations expressed as short, distinct sounds using syntax and grammar.
Quasi-linguistic variation Suites of artifacts found together in one region and/or during one time period that do not appear together in others.
Quern A type of **pulverizing tool**.
Races Among humans, pre- or nonscientific "folk biological" classifications of human groups.
Radiocarbon dating Method for dating carbonate fossils less than 45,000 years old.
Radiopotassium Method for dating volcanic rocks.
Recycling Use of discarded artifacts after having changed their shape.
Red ochre A mineral pigment comprised mainly of iron oxide.
Refugium (pl., refugia) Geographic region largely unaffected by major climate changes.

Regional refugium hypothesis Hypothesis proposing humans overcame major Pleistocene climate changes by residing in one or more specific geographic refugium.
Remote Oceania Pacific Ocean Islands in New Caledonia and points in between them and Samoa.
Residential mobility Movements of long-term habitation sites.
Retouch Small scar detached from the edges of **cores** or **retouched pieces**.
Retouched pieces Flake fragments featuring **retouch**, one or more series of relatively small (< 20 mm long) fracture scars along their edge.
Reuse Use of a discarded artifact without changing its shape.
Sahel A belt of grasslands and woodlands running east-west along the Sahara Desert's southern margin.
Sahul The continent that formed when low sea levels conjoined New Guinea, Australia, and Tasmania.
Sahulians Pleistocene inhabitants of New Guinea, Australia, and Tasmania.
Scrapers, notches, and denticulates (SNDs) Retouched pieces preserving at least one relatively sharp retouched edge that is straight, concave, or convex.
Sedentism Reduced residential mobility.
Sexual selection Evolutionary forces influencing individual reproductive success.
Short nonhierarchical core (SNHC) Core that has roughly equal length, width, and thickness. Stoneworkers detached **flakes** to roughly the same extent on both sides of its worked edges.
Solutrean One among many stone tool industries associated with Western European humans during the **Last Glacial Maximum** (MIS 2).
Spear-thrower A carved wooden stick with a hook at one end that allows the person using to tool to apply leverage and to propel a spear (or dart) farther than would otherwise be the case.
Spoken language Vocalizations using syntax and grammar (rules about word order and word choice).
Stabilizing selective pressure Selective pressure that constrains possible morphologies and behaviors within a narrow range of possibilities.
Stoneworking Manufacturing stone tools using controlled fracture and/or abrasion.
Subspecies Genetically and morphologically distinct regional populations of a more widely distributed species.
Sunda A peninsula formed when low sea levels conjoined Southeast Asia to the islands that make up the Indo-Malaysian archipelago.
Survival archaeology An archaeological research agenda focusing on how prehistoric humans and other **hominins** solved basic survival challenges.
Syntax Rules about word order in spoken or written language.
Tanged piece Retouched stone tool featuring a thick projection, or "tang."
Taphonomy Systematic investigation into how the fossil record formed based on observations of modern-day animal death sites.
Technological intensification Investing more time and/or energy on tool production and use.
Technological singularity A hypothetical point in time at which artificial intelligences achieve and surpass human intelligence.
Temper Sand, shells, and other materials added to clay to toughen fired ceramics.
Thermal alteration Weakening tough silcrete rocks by exposing them to fire (aka heat treatment).

Glossary

Thermoluminescence (TL) A type of **trapped electron dating** method.
Time averaging Equating stratigraphic associations among fossils and artifacts with literal contemporaneity.
Transhumance Cyclical seasonal movement of people and/or livestock.
Trapped electron dating Dating method based on measuring electrons trapped in rocks and fossils (i.e., thermoluminescence [TL], electron spin resonance [ESR], and optically stimulated luminescence [OSL].)
Unifacial hierarchical core (UHC) Core whose worked edges have **flake** scars roughly equal to the core's longest axis (aka prismatic blade core).
Uniformitarianism A philosophical principle arguing that one must base one's theories about the past on observations of present-day phenomena.
Uranium-series dating Method for dating carbonate rocks.
Wallacea Collective term for the islands in between Sunda and Sahul, such as Sulawesi and Timor.
Warfare Organized territorial conflicts accompanied by coalitionary killing.
"Who questions" Paleoanthropological research questions about prehistoric hominin identities.
Wilderness survival Strategies for saving lives by any means necessary, usually emphasizing effective and immediate solutions to short-term problems.
Younger Dryas event An abrupt return to glacial conditions between 11.7 and 12.9 Ka.
Zooarchaeology Archaeological analysis of nonhuman fossils recovered from archaeological sites.
Zoonotic diseases Diseases humans contract from other animals (e.g., SARS, Covid-19).

BIBLIOGRAPHY

Adams, J. L. 2014a. *Ground Stone Analysis: An Anthropological Approach.* Salt Lake City: University of Utah Press.

Adams, S. 2014b. *How to Fail at Almost Everything and Still Win Big: Kind of the Story of My Life.* New York: Portfolio (Penguin/Random House).

Aiello, L. C., and P. Wheeler. 1995. The expensive-tissue hypothesis: The brain and digestive system in human and primate evolution. *Current Anthropology* 36:199–221.

Alton, J., and A. Alton. 2013. *The Survival Medicine Handbook: A Guide for When Help Is Not on the Way,* 2nd ed. Lexington, KY: Doom and Bloom.

Ambrose, S. H. 1998. Late Pleistocene human population bottlenecks, volcanic winter, and the differentiation of modern humans. *Journal of Human Evolution* 34:623–651.

Ambrose, S. H. 2002. "Small Things Remembered: Origins of Early Microlithic Industries in Sub-Saharan Africa," in *Thinking Small: Global Perspectives on Microlithization.* Edited by R. G. Elston and S. L. Kuhn, pp. 9–30. Washington, DC: American Anthropological Association (Archaeological Paper No. 12).

Anderson-Gerfaud, P. C. 1990. "Aspects of Behaviour in the Middle Palaeolithic: Functional Analysis of Stone Tools from Southwest France," in *The Emergence of Modern Humans.* Edited by P. A. Mellars, pp. 389–418. Edinburgh: Edinburgh University Press.

Andrefsky, W. J. 2005. *Lithics: Macroscopic Approaches to Analysis,* 2nd ed. New York: Cambridge University Press.

Aranguren, B., A. Revedin, et al. 2018. Wooden tools and fire technology in the early Neanderthal site of Poggetti Vecchi (Italy). *Proceedings of the National Academy of Sciences* 115:2054.

Arens, W. 1979. *The Man-Eating Myth: Anthropology and Anthropophagy.* New York: Oxford University Press.

Ashley, C. Z., and K. M. Grillo. 2015. Archaeological ceramics from eastern Africa: Past approaches and future directions. *Azania: Archaeological Research in Africa* 50:460–480.

Aubert, M., R. Lebe, et al. 2019. Earliest hunting scene in prehistoric art. *Nature* 576:442–445.

Aubert, M., P. Setiawan, et al. 2018. Palaeolithic cave art in Borneo. *Nature* 564:254–257.

Backwell, L., J. Bradfield, et al. 2018. The antiquity of bow-and-arrow technology: Evidence from Middle Stone Age layers at Sibudu Cave. *Antiquity* 92:289–303.

Bae, C. J., K. Douka, et al. 2017. On the origin of modern humans: Asian perspectives. *Science* 358:eaai9067.

Bahn, P. G. 2016. *Images of the Ice Age.* New York: Oxford University Press.

Bailey, R., and N. Peacock. 1988. "Efe Pygmies of Northeast Zaire: Subsistence Strategies in the Ituri Forest," in *Coping with Uncertainty in the Food Supply.* Edited by I. de Garine and G. Harrison, pp. 88–117. Oxford: Oxford University Press.

Bar-Yosef, O. 2002. The Upper Paleolithic Revolution. *Annual Review of Anthropology* 31:363–393.

Bar-Yosef, O., and A. Belfer-Cohen. 2001. From Africa to Eurasia – Early dispersals. *Quaternary International* 75:19–28.

Bar-Yosef, O., and J. Callander. 1999. The woman from Tabun: Garrod's doubts in historical perspective. *Journal of Human Evolution* 37:879–885.

Bar-Yosef, O., M. Eren, et al. 2012. Were bamboo tools made in prehistoric Southeast Asia? An experimental view from South China. *Quaternary International* 269:9–12.

Bar-Yosef Mayer, D. 2005. The exploitation of shells as beads in the Palaeolithic and Neolithic of the Levant. *Paléorient* 31:176–185.

Bar-Yosef Mayer, D. E., I. Groman-Yaroslavski, O. Bar-Yosef, I. Hershkovitz, A. Kampen-Hasday, B. Vandermeersch, Y. Zaidner, and M. Weinstein-Evron. 2020. On holes and strings: Earliest displays of human adornment in the Middle Palaeolithic. *PLoS ONE* 15(7): e0234924.

Barham, L. 2002. Backed tools in Middle Pleistocene Central Africa and their evolutionary significance. *Journal of Human Evolution* 43:585–603.

Barham, L. 2013. *From Hand to Handle: The First Industrial Revolution.* New York: Oxford University Press.

Barham, L., and P. Mitchell. 2008. *The First Africans: African Archaeology from the Earliest Toolmakers to Most Recent Foragers.* New York: Cambridge University Press.

Barham, L., M. J. Simms, et al. 2000. "Twin Rivers, excavation and behavioural record," in *The Middle Stone Age of Zambia, South Central Africa.* Edited by L. Barham, pp. 165–216. Bristol: Western Academic & Specialist Press.

Barker, G. 2014. "Niah Caves: Role in Human Evolution," in *Encyclopedia of Global Archaeology.* Edited by C. Smith, pp. 5282–5289. New York: Springer New York.

Barton, C. M., and G. A. Clark. 2021. From artifacts to cultures: Technology, society, and knowledge in the Upper Paleolithic. *Journal of Paleolithic Archaeology* 4 (2):1–21.

Becerra-Valdivia, L., and T. Higham. 2020. The timing and effect of the earliest human arrivals in North America. *Nature* 584:93–97.

Bednarik, R. G. 2001. Replicating the first known sea travel by humans: The Lower Pleistocene crossing of Lombok Strait. *Human Evolution* 16:229–242.

Bednarik, R. G. 2003. Seafaring in the Pleistocene. *Cambridge Archaeological Journal* 13:41–66.

Begley, C. 2021. *The Next Apocalypse: The Art and Science of Survival.* New York: Basic Books.

Bellwood, P. 1987. The Prehistory of Island Southeast Asia: A Multidisciplinary Review of Recent Research. *Journal of World Prehistory* 1:171–224.

Bellwood, P. 2013. *First Migrants: Ancient Migration in Global Perspective.* New York: Wiley Blackwell.

Ben Arous, E., A. Philippe, et al. 2022. An improved chronology for the Middle Stone Age at El Mnasra cave, Morocco. *PLoS ONE* 17:e0261282.

Ben-Dor, M., and R. Barkai. 2020. The importance of large prey animals during the Pleistocene and the implications of their extinction on the use of dietary ethnographic analogies. *Journal of Anthropological Archaeology* 59:101192.

Bendictow, O. J. 2021. *The Complete History of the Black Death.* Woodbridge: Boydell Press.

Bennett, M. R., D. Bustos, et al. 2021. Evidence of humans in North America during the Last Glacial Maximum. *Science (American Association for the Advancement of Science)* 373:1528–1531.

Berger, T. D., and E. Trinkaus. 1995. Patterns of trauma among the Neandertals. *Journal of Archaeological Science* 22:841–852.

Bergman, C., and M. H. Newcomer. 1983. Flint arrowhead breakage: Examples from Ksar Akil, Lebanon. *Journal of Field Archaeology* 10:238–243.

Bergström, A., C. Stringer, et al. 2021. Origins of modern human ancestry. *Nature* 590:229–237.

Beyin, A. 2006. The Bab al Mandab vs the Nile-Levant: An appraisal of the two dispersal routes for early modern humans out of Africa. *African Archaeological Review* 23:5–30.

Béyries, S. 1987. *Variabilité de l'industrie lithique au Moustérien: Approche fonctionelle sur quelques gisements français.* British Archaeological Reports International Series, no. 328. Oxford: Oxbow Books.

Binford, L. R. 1962. Archaeology as anthropology. *American Antiquity* 28:217–225.

Binford, L. R. 1979. Organization and formation processes: Looking at curated technologies. *Journal of Anthropological Research* 35:255–273.

Binford, L. R. 1981. *Bones: Ancient Men and Modern Myths.* New York: Academic Press.

Bingham, P. M., and J. Souza. 2013. Theory testing in Prehistoric North America: Fruits of one of the world's great archeological natural laboratories. *Evolutionary Anthropology: Issues, News, and Reviews* 22:145–153.

Bingham, P. M., J. Souza, et al. 2013. Introduction: Social complexity and the bow in the prehistoric North American record. *Evolutionary Anthropology: Issues, News, and Reviews* 22:81–88.

Blinkhorn, J., T. Lucy, et al. 2022. Evaluating refugia in recent human evolution in Africa. *Philosophical Transactions of the Royal Society B: Biological Sciences* 377:20200485.

Blinkhorn, J., C. Zanolli, et al. 2021. Nubian Levallois technology associated with southernmost Neanderthals. *Scientific Reports* 11:2869.

Boaretto, E., X. Wu, et al. 2009. Radiocarbon dating of charcoal and bone collagen associated with early pottery at Yuchanyan Cave, Hunan Province, China. *Proceedings of the National Academy of Sciences* 106:9595.

Boas, F. 1940. *Race, Language, and Culture*. New York: Macmillan.

Boëda, E., J. Connan, et al. 1996. Bitumen as a hafting material on Middle Palaeolithic artefacts. *Nature* 380:336–338.

Boldurian, A. T. 2007. Clovis beveled rod manufacture: An elephant bone experiment. *North American Archaeologist* 28:29–57.

Bordes, F. 1968. *The Old Stone Age*. New York: McGraw-Hill.

Bostrum, N. 2014. *Superintelligence: Paths, Dangers, Strangers*. New York: Oxford University Press.

Bostrum, N., and M. Cirkovic. Editors. 2011. *Global Catastrophic Risks*. New York: Oxford University Press.

Bowles, S. 2009. Did warfare among ancestral hunter-gatherers affect the evolution of human social behaviors? *Science* 324:1293–1298.

Bradford, W., and S. E. e. Morrison. 1651 (1952). *Of Plymouth Plantation, 1620–1647*. New York: Afred A. Knopf.

Brain, C. K. 1981. *The Hunters or the Hunted? An Introduction to African Cave Taphonomy*. Chicago, IL: University of Chicago Press.

Bramble, D. M., and D. E. Lieberman. 2004. Endurance running and the evolution of Homo. *Nature* 432:354–352.

Brandt, S. A., E. C. Fisher, et al. 2012. Early MIS 3 occupation of Mochena Borago Rockshelter, Southwest Ethiopian Highlands: Implications for Late Pleistocene archaeology, paleoenvironments and modern human dispersals. *Quaternary International* 274:38–54.

Brannen, P. 2017. *The Ends of the World: Volcanic Apocalypses, Lethal Oceans, and Our Quest to Understand Earth's Past Mass Extinctions*. New York: HarperCollins.

Brooks, A. S., J. E. Yellen, et al. 2018. Long-distance stone transport and pigment use in the earliest Middle Stone Age. *Science* 360:90.

Brown, D. J. 2015. *The Indifferent Stars Above: The Harrowing Saga of a Donner Party Bride*. New York: William Morrow.

Brown, K. S., C. W. Marean, et al. 2009. Fire as an engineering tool of early modern humans. *Science* 325:859–862.

Brumm, A. 2010. The Movius Line and the Bamboo Hypothesis: Early hominin stone technology in Southeast Asia. *Lithic Technology* 35:7–24.

Burdukiewicz, J. M., and A. Ronen. Editors. 2003. *Lower Paleolithic Small Tools in Europe and the Levant*. British Archaeological Reports International Series, no. 1115. Oxford: Oxbow Books.

Burroughs, W. J. 2005. *Climate Change in Prehistory: The End of the Reign of Chaos*. Cambridge: Cambridge University Press.

Callahan, E. 1979. The Basics of Biface Knapping in the Eastern Fluted Point Tradition. *Archaeology of Eastern North America* 7:1–180.

Carrier, D. R. 1984. The energetic paradox of human running and hominid evolution. *Current Anthropology* 25(4):483–495.

Cattelain, P. 1997. "Hunting during the Upper Paleolithic: Bow, spearthrower, or both?," in *Projectile Technology*. Edited by H. Knecht, pp. 213–240. New York: Plenum.

Chase, P. G. 1989. "How Different was Middle Paleolithic Subsistence? A Zooarchaeological Perspective on the Middle to Upper Palaeolithic Transition," in *The Human Revolution: Behavioural and Biological Perspectives on the Origins of Modern Humans*. Edited by P. A. Mellars and C. B. Stringer, pp. 321–337. Edinburgh: Edinburgh University Press.

Cheng, H., H. Zhang, et al. 2020. Timing and structure of the Younger Dryas event and its underlying climate dynamics. *Proceedings of the National Academy of Sciences* 117:23408.

Cheynier, A. 1958. Impromptu sur la séquence des pointes du Paléolithique supérieur.

Bulletin de la Société préhistorique de France 55:190–205.

Chomsky, N. 2012. *The Science of Language*. New York: Cambridge University Press.

Christel, M. 1994. Catarrhine primates grasping small objects: Techniques and hand preferences. *Current Primatology* 3:37–49.

Churchill, S. E. 1993. "Weapon Technology, Prey Size Selection, and Hunting Methods in Modern Hunter-Gatherers: Implications for Hunting in the Palaeolithic and Mesolithic," in *Hunting and Animal Exploitation in the Later Paleolithic and Mesolithic of Eurasia*. Edited by G. L. Peterkin, H. Bricker, and P. A. Mellars, pp. 11–24. Washington, DC: American Anthropological Association (Archaeological Paper No. 4).

Churchill, S. E. 2014. *Thin on the Ground: Neandertal Biology, Archaeology and Ecology*. New York: Wiley-Blackwell.

Churchill, S. E., and F. H. Smith. 2000. Makers of the Early Aurignacian of Europe. *Yearbook of Physical Anthropology* 43:61–115.

Clark, G. 1970. *Aspects of Prehistory*. Berkeley: University of California Press.

Clark, G. A. 1994. Migration as an explanatory concept in Paleolithic archaeology. *Journal of Archaeological Method and Theory* 1:305–343.

Clark, G. A., and J. Riel-Salvatore. 2006. "Observations on Systematics in Paleolithic Archaeology," in *Transitions before the Transition*. Edited by E. Hovers and S. L. Kuhn, pp. 29–57. New York: Plenum/Kluwer.

Clark, J. D. 1967. *Atlas of African Prehistory*. Chicago, IL: University of Chicago Press.

Clark, J. D. 1988. The Middle Stone Age of East Africa and the beginnings of regional identity. *Journal of World Prehistory* 2:235–305.

Clark, J. D. Editor. 2001. *Kalambo Falls Prehistoric Site, vol. III: The Earlier Cultures: Middle and Earlier Stone Age*. Cambridge: Cambridge University Press.

Clarkson, C., C. Harris, et al. 2020. Human occupation of northern India spans the Toba super-eruption ~74,000 years ago. *Nature Communications* 11:961.

Clarkson, C., Z. Jacobs, et al. 2017. Human occupation of northern Australia by 65,000 years ago. *Nature* 547:306.

Conard, N. J. 2006. "The Last Neanderthals and First Modern Humans in the Swabian Jura," in *When Neanderthals and Modern Humans Met*. Edited by N. J. Conard, pp. 305–341. Tübingen: Kerns Verlag.

Coqueugniot, H., O. Dutour, et al. 2014. Earliest cranio-encephalic trauma from the Levantine Middle Palaeolithic: 3D reappraisal of the Qafzeh 11 skull, consequences of pediatric brain damage on individual life condition and social care. *PLoS ONE* 9:e102822.

Crabtree, D. E. 1966. A stoneworker's approach to analyzing and replicating the Lindenmeier Folsom. *Tebiwa* 9:3–39.

Crosby, A. W. 1986. *Ecological Imperialism: The Biological Expansion of Europe, 900–1900*. Cambridge: Cambridge University Press.

Cummings, V., P. Jordan, et al. 2014. *The Oxford Handbook of the Archaeology and Anthropology of Hunter-Gatherers*. New York: Oxford University Press.

Daniel, G. E., and C. Renfrew. 1988. *The Idea of Prehistory*. Edinburgh: Edinburgh University Press.

Darwin, C. R. 1859. *The Origin of Species*. London: John Murray.

Dawkins, R. 1976. *The Selfish Gene*. London: Oxford University Press.

de Filippo, C., K. Bostoen, et al. 2012. Bringing together linguistic and genetic evidence to test the Bantu expansion. *Proceedings of the Royal Society B: Biological Sciences* 279:3256–3263.

de Mortillet, G. 1877. L'art dans les temps géologiques. *Revue scientifique (second series)*:888–892.

Defleur, A., T. White, et al. 1999. Neanderthal cannibalism at Moula-Guercy, Ardèche, France. *Science* 286:128–131.

Dent, R. J. 2007. "Seed Collecting and Fishing at the Shawnee Minisink Paleoindian Site Everyday Life in the Late Pleistocene," in *Foragers of the Terminal Pleistocene in North America*. Edited by R. B. Walker and B. N. Driskell, pp. 116–131. Lincoln: University of Nebraska Press.

d'Errico, F., C. Henshilwood, et al. 2003. Archaeological evidence for the emergence of language, symbolism, and music – An alternative multidisciplinary approach. *Journal of World Prehistory* 17:1–70.

d'Errico, F., C. Henshilwood, et al. 2005. *Nassarius kraussianus* shell beads from Blombos Cave: Evidence for symbolic behaviour in the Middle Stone Age. *Journal of Human Evolution* 48:3–24.

Dewar, R. E., C. Radimilahy, et al. 2013. Stone tools and foraging in northern Madagascar challenge Holocene extinction models. *Proceedings of the National Academy of Sciences of the United States of America* 110:12583–12588.

Dibble, H. L. 1995. Middle Paleolithic scraper reduction: Background, clarification, and review of the evidence to date. *Journal of Archaeological Method and Theory* 2:299–368.

Dibble, H. L., A. Abodolahzadeh, et al. 2017. How did hominins adapt to Ice Age Europe without fire? *Current Anthropology* 58: S278–S287.

Dibble, H. L., V. Aldeias, et al. 2013. On the industrial attributions of the Aterian and Mousterian of the Maghreb. *Journal of Human Evolution* 64:194–210.

Dillehay, T. H. 1997. *Monte Verde: A Late Pleistocene Settlement in Chile: The Archaeological Context*, vol. 2. Washington, DC: Smithsonian Institution Press.

Dirks, P. H. G. M., L. R. Berger, et al. 2015. Geological and taphonomic context for the new hominin species *Homo naledi* from the Dinaledi Chamber, South Africa. *eLife* 4: e09561.

Dixon, E. J. 1999. *Bones, Boats and Bison: Archeology and the First Colonization of Western North America*. Albuquerque: University of New Mexico Press.

Djakovic, I., A. Key, and M. Soressi. 2022. Optimal linear estimation models predict 1400–2900 years of overlap between *Homo sapiens* and Neandertals prior to their disappearance from France and northern Spain. *Scientific Reports* 12 (1):15000.

Druett, J. 2007. *Island of the Lost: An Extraordinary Story of Survival at the Edge of the World*. New York.: Algonquin Books.

Duke, H., and J. Pargeter. 2015. Weaving simple solutions to complex problems: An experimental study of skill in bipolar cobble-splitting. *Lithic Technology* 40:349–365.

Efferson, C., R. Lalive, et al. 2008. The coevolution of cultural groups and ingroup favoritism. *Science* 321:1844–1849.

Ehrlich, P. R. 1968. *The Population Bomb*. New York: Sierra Club/Ballantine.

El Zaatari, S., F. E. Grine, et al. 2011. Ecogeographic variation in Neandertal dietary habits: Evidence from occlusal molar microwear texture analysis. *Journal of Human Evolution* 61:411–424.

Emory, K. P. 1943. *South Sea Lore*. Honolulu: Bishop Museum (Special Publication 33).

Enzel, Y., and O. Bar-Yosef. Editors. 2017. *Quaternary of the Levant: Environments, Climate Change, and Humans*. New York: Cambridge University Press.

Eren, M. I., S. J. Lycett, et al. 2016. Test, model, and method validation: The role of experimental stone artifact replication in hypothesis-driven archaeology. *Ethnoarchaeology* 8:103–136.

Erlandson, J. M. 2001. The archaeology of aquatic adaptations: Paradigms for a new millennium. *Journal of Archaeological Research* 9:287–350.

Erlandson, J. M., M. H. Graham, et al. 2007. The Kelp Highway hypothesis: Marine ecology, the coastal migration theory, and the peopling of the Americas. *The Journal of Island and Coastal Archaeology* 2:161–174.

Fagan, B. 2011. *Cro-Magnon: How the Ice Age Gave Birth to the First Modern Humans*. New York: Bloomsbury Press.

Faure, H., R. C. Walter, et al. 2002. The coastal oasis: Ice Age springs on emerged continental shelves. *Global and Planetary Change* 33:47–56.

Feblot-Augustins, J. 1997. *La circulation des matières premiers au Paléolithique: Synthése de données, perspectives comportementales*. Liège: Etudes et Recherches Archéologiques de l'Université de Liège, No. 75.

Fedele, F., B. Giaccio, et al. 2004. The Campignian Ignimbrite eruption, Heinrich Event 4, and Palaeolithic Cange in Europe: A high-resolution investigation. *Volcanism and the Earth's Atmosphere (American Geophysical Union Geophysical Monograph)* 139:301–325.

Feidel, S. J. 2005. Man's best friend – Mammoth's worst enemy? A speculative essay on the role of dogs in Paleoindian colonization and megafaunal extinction. *World Archaeology* 37.

Fellows Yates, J. A., I. M. Velsko, et al. 2021. The evolution and changing ecology of the African hominid oral microbiome. *Proceedings of the National Academy of Sciences* 118: e2021655118.

Finlayson, C. 2003. *Neanderthals and Modern Humans: The Dynamics and Biogeography of Their Interactions*. Cambridge: Cambridge University Press.

Finlayson, C. 2019. *The Smart Neanderthal: Cave Art, Bird Catching, and the Cognitive Revolution*. New York: Oxford University Press.

Finney, B. 1979. *Hokulea: The Way to Tahiti.* New York: Dodd, Mead.

Firestone, R. B., A. West, et al. 2007. Evidence for an extraterrestrial impact 12,900 years ago that contributed to the megafaunal extinctions and the Younger Dryas cooling. *Proceedings of the National Academy of Sciences* 104:16016.

Flint, R. F. 1971. *Glacial and Quaternary Geology.* New York: John Wiley & Sons.

Flores, D. 2016. *Coyote America: A Natural and Supernatural History.* New York: Basic Books.

Florin, S. A., A. S. Fairbairn, et al. 2020. The first Australian plant foods at Madjedbebe, 65,000–53,000 years ago. *Nature Communications* 11:924.

Foley, R., and M. M. Lahr. 1997. Mode 3 technologies and the evolution of modern humans. *Cambridge Archaeological Journal* 7:3–36.

Frison, G. C., and B. A. Bradley. 1999. *The Fenn Cache: Clovis Weapons & Tools.* Santa Fe, NM: One Horse Land and Cattle Company.

Froehle, A. W., and S. E. Churchill. 2009. Energetic competition between Neandertals and anatomically modern humans. *PaleoAnthropology* 2009:96–116.

Fuller, D., and E. Hildebrand. 2013. "Domesticating plants in Africa," in *The Oxford Handbook of African Archaeology.* Edited by P. Mitchell and P. Lane, pp. 131–144. Oxford: Oxford University Press.

Gabriele, M., and D. M. Perry. 2021. *The Bright Ages: A New History of Medieval Europe.* New York: Harper.

Gamble, C. 1987. "Man the Shoveler: Alternative Models for Middle Pleistocene Colonization and Occupation in Northern Latitudes," in *The Pleistocene Old World: Regional Perspectives.* Edited by O. Soffer, pp. 81–98. New York: Plenum.

Gamble, C. 2013. *Settling the Earth: The Archaeology of Deep Human History.* New York: Cambridge University Press.

Gamble, C., J. Gowlett, et al. 2014. *Thinking Big: How the Evolution of Social Life Shaped the Human Mind.* New York: Thames and Hudson.

Garrod, D. A. E., and D. M. A. Bate. Editors. 1937. *The Stone Age of Mount Carmel, vol. 1: Excavations in the Wady el-Mughara.* Oxford: Clarendon Press.

Geist, V. 1981. Neanderthal the hunter. *Natural History* 90:26–36.

Gilligan, I. 2010. The prehistoric development of clothing: Archaeological implications of a thermal model. *Journal of Archaeological Method and Theory* 17:15–80.

Gladikh, M. I., N. Kornietz, et al. 1984. Mammoth-bone dwellings on the Russian plain. *Scientific American* 251:164–175.

Golding, W. 1954. *The Lord of the Flies.* London: Faber and Faber.

Gonzales, L. 2003. *Deep Survival: Who Lives, Who Dies, and Why.* New York: Norton.

Goodall, J. 1986. *The Chimpanzees of Gombe: Patterns of Behavior.* Cambridge, MA: Harvard University Press.

Goodwin, A. J. H. 1929. The Stone Ages in South Africa. *Africa* 2:174–182.

Goren-Inbar, N. Editor. 1990. *Quneitra: A Mousterian Site on the Golan Heights.* Jerusalem: Hebrew University Institute of Archaeology (Qedem No. 31).

Gott, B. 2002. Fire-making in Tasmania: Absence of evidence is not evidence of absence. *Current Anthropology* 43:650–655.

Gould, R. A. 1980. *Living Archaeology.* Cambridge: Cambridge University Press.

Graeber, D., and D. Wengrow. 2021. *The Dawn of Everything: A New History of Humanity.* New York: Farrar, Straus & Giroux.

Greaves, R. D. 1997. "Hunting and Multifunctional Use of Bows and Arrows: Ethnoarchaeology of Technological Organization among the Pumé Hunters of Venezuela," in *Projectile Technology.* Edited by H. Knecht, pp. 287–320. New York: Plenum.

Green, R. E., J. Krause, et al. 2010. A draft sequence of the Neandertal genome. *Science* 328:710.

Grinker, R. R. 1990. Images of denigration: Structuring inequality between foragers and farmers in the Ituri Forest, Zaire. *American Ethnologist* 17:111–130.

Groube, L., J. Chappell, et al. 1986. A 40,000-year-old human occupation site at Huon Peninsula, Papua New Guinea. *Nature* 324:453–455.

Groucutt, H. S., E. M. L. Scerri, et al. 2015. Stone tool assemblages and models for the dispersal of *Homo sapiens* out of Africa. *Quaternary International* 382:8–30.

Groucutt, H. S., T. S. White, et al. 2021. Multiple hominin dispersals into Southwest Asia over the past 400,000 years. *Nature* 597:376–380.

Guthrie, R. D. 1990. *The Frozen Fauna of the Mammoth Steppe: The Story of Blue Babe.* Chicago, IL: University of Chicago Press.

Guthrie, R. D. 2001. Origin and causes of the mammoth steppe: A story of cloud cover, woolly mammal tooth pits, buckles, and inside-out Beringia. *Quaternary Science Review* 20:549–574.

Guthrie, R. D. 2005. *The Nature of Paleolithic Art.* Chicago, IL: University of Chicago Press.

Habgood, P. J., and N. R. Franklin. 2008. The revolution that didn't arrive: A review of Pleistocene Sahul. *Journal of Human Evolution* 55:187–222.

Hallinan, E., O. Barzilai, et al. 2022. No direct evidence for the presence of Nubian Levallois technology and its association with Neanderthals at Shukbah Cave. *Science Reports*:1204.

Hammond, G., and N. Hammond. 1981. Child's play: A distorting factor in archaeological distribution. *American Antiquity* 46:634–636.

Hardy, B. L., M. H. Moncel, et al. 2020. Direct evidence of Neanderthal fibre technology and its cognitive and behavioral implications. *Scientific Reports* 10:4889.

Harmand, S., J. E. Lewis, et al. 2015. 3.3-million-year-old stone tools from Lomekwi 3, West Turkana, Kenya. *Nature* 521:310–315.

Harris, M. 2013. *The Rise of Anthropological Theory*, 4th ed. Toronto: University of Toronto Press.

Harvati, K., C. Stringer, et al. 2011. The Later Stone Age Calvaria from Iwo Eleru, Nigeria: Morphology and chronology. *PLoS ONE* 6: e24024.

Hayden, B. 1979. *Palaeolithic Reflections: Lithic Technology and Ethnographic Excavations among Australian Aborigines.* Canberra: Australian Institute of Aboriginal Studies.

Haynes, C. V., and E. T. Hemmings. 1968. Mammoth-bone shaft wrench from Murray Springs, Arizona. *Science* 159:186–187.

Heinrich, H. 1988. Origin and consequences of cyclic ice rafting in the Northeast Atlantic Ocean during the past 130,000 years. *Quaternary Research* 29:142–152.

Henrich, J. 2004. Demography and cultural evolution: How adaptive cultural processes can produce maladaptive losses – The Tasmanian case. *American Antiquity* 69:197–214.

Henry, A. G., A. S. Brooks, et al. 2014. Plant foods and the dietary ecology of Neanderthals and early modern humans. *Journal of Human Evolution* 69:44–54.

Henshilwood, C., F. d'Errico, et al. 2004. Middle Stone Age shell beads from South Africa. *Science* 304:404.

Henshilwood, C. S., and C. W. Marean. 2003. The origin of modern human behavior. *Current Anthropology* 44:627–651.

Hershkovitz, I., H. May, et al. 2021. A Middle Pleistocene *Homo* from Nesher Ramla, Israel. *Science* 372:1424–1428.

Heyes, P. J., K. Anastasakis, et al. 2016. Selection and use of manganese dioxide by Neanderthals. *Scientific Reports* 6:22159.

Higham, C. 2014. *Early Mainland Southeast Asia: From First Humans to Angkor.* London: River Books Press.

Higham, T. 2021. *The World before Us: The New Science behind Our Human Origins.* New Haven, CT: Yale University Press.

Higham, T., K. Douka, et al. 2014. The timing and spatiotemporal patterning of Neanderthal disappearance. *Nature* 512:306.

Hiscock, P., S. O'Connor, et al. 2016. World's earliest ground-edge axe production coincides with human colonisation of Australia. *Australian Archaeology* 82:2–11.

Hodder, I. 1982. *Symbols in Action: Ethnoarchaeological Studies of Material Culture.* Cambridge: Cambridge University Press.

Hoffecker, J. F. 2004. *A Prehistory of the North: Human Settlement of the Higher Latitudes.* Piscataway, NJ: Rutgers University Press.

Hoffecker, J. F. 2017. *Modern Humans: Their African Origin and Global Dispersal.* New York: Columbia University Press.

Holdaway, S., and N. Stern. 2004. *A Record in Stone: The Study of Australia's Flaked Stone Artifacts.* Melbourne: Museum Victoria/Aboriginal Studies Press.

Holldobler, B., and E. O. Wilson. 1990. *The Ants.* Cambridge, MA: Belknap Press.

Hollenbach, K. D. 2007. "Gathering in the Late Paleoindian Period Archaeobotanical Remains from Dust Cave, Alabama," in *Foragers of the Terminal Pleistocene in North America.* Edited by R. B. Walker and B. N. Driskell, pp. 132–147. Lincoln: University of Nebraska Press.

Holliday, T. W. 2003. Species concepts, reticulation, and human evolution. *Current Anthropology* 44:653–673.

Holliday, T. W. 2023. *Cro-Magnon: The Story of the Last Ice Age People of Europe.* New York: Columbia University Press.

Holliday, V. T., and D. Killick. 2013. An early Paleoindian bead from the Mockingbird Gap Site, New Mexico. *Current Anthropology* 54:85–95.

Holt, B. M., and V. Formicola. 2008. Hunters of the Ice Age: The biology of Upper Paleolithic people. *Yearbook of Physical Anthropology* 15:70–99.

Hovers, E., and D. Braun. Editors. 2007. *Interdisciplinary Approaches to the Oldowan.* New York: Elsevier.

Hovers, E., S. Iliani, et al. 2003. An early case of color symbolism: Ochre use by modern humans in Qafzeh Cave. *Current Anthropology* 44:491–522.

Howell, F. C. 1952. Pleistocene glacial ecology and the evolution of "classic Neanderthal" man. *Southwest Journal of Anthropology* 8:377–410.

Howell, F. C. 1959. Upper Pleistocene stratigraphy and early man in the Levant. *Proceedings of the American Philosophical Society* 103:1–65.

Howell, F. C., K. W. Butzer, et al. 1995. Observations on the Acheulean occupation site of Ambrona (Soria Province, Spain). *Jahrbuch des Römisch-Germanischen Zentralmuseums Mainz* 38:33–82.

Hublin, J.-J. 2021. How old are the oldest *Homo sapiens* in Far East Asia? *Proceedings of the National Academy of Sciences* 118:e2101173118.

Hume, D. 2018. *Fire Making: The Forgotten Art of Conjuring Flame with Spark, Tinder, and Skil.* New York: The Experiment.

Husain, A. 2018. *The Sentient Machine: The Coming of Artificial Intelligence.* New York: Scribner/Simon and Schuster.

Inskeep, R. 2001. "Some Notes on Fish and Fishing in Africa," in *A Very Remote Period Indeed: Papers on the Palaeolithic Presented to Derek Roe.* Edited by S. Milliken and J. Cook, pp. 63–73. Oxford: Oxbow Books.

Ipek, H. 2009. Comparing and contrasting first and second language acquisition: Implications for language teachers. *English Language Teaching* 2:155–162.

Isaac, G. L. 1981. Archaeological tests of alternative models of early hominid behaviour: Excavation and experiments. *Philosophical Transactions of the Royal Society of London Series B,* 292:177–188.

Jasanoff, M. 2022. Ancestor worship: Where does the craze for geneaology come from? *The New Yorker* (May 2):69–73.

Jelinek, A. J. Editor. 2013. *Neandertal Lithic Industries at La Quina.* Tucson: University of Arizona Press.

Johnson, C. R., and S. McBrearty. 2010. 500,000 year old blades from the Kapthurin Formation, Kenya. *Journal of Human Evolution* 58:193–200.

Kaboth-Bahr, S., W. D. Gosling, et al. 2021. Paleo-ENSO influence on African environments and early modern humans. *Proceedings of the National Academy of Sciences* 118: e2018277118.

Keeley, L. H. 1996. *War before Civilization.* New York: Oxford University Press.

Kelly, R. L. 1998. "Foraging and Sedentism," in *Seasonality and Sedentism: Archaeological Perspectives from Old and New World Sites.* Edited by T. Rocek and O. Bar-Yosef, pp. 9–23. Cambridge, MA: Peabody Museum of Archaeology and Ethnology, Harvard University.

Kelly, R. L. 2013. *The Lifeways of Hunter-Gatherers: The Foraging Spectrum,* 2nd revised ed. New York: Cambridge University Press.

Kelton, P. 2007. *Epidemics and Enslavement: Biological Catastrophe in the Native Southeast, 1492–1715.* Lincoln: University of Nebraska Press.

Key, A., M. R. Fisch, et al. 2018. Early stage blunting causes rapid reductions in stone tool performance. *Journal of Archaeological Science* 91:1–11.

King, C. 2019. *Gods of the Upper Air: How a Circle of Renegade Anthropologists Reinvented Race, Sex, and Gender in the Twentieth Century.* New York: Anchor.

Kirch, P. V. 2018. *On the Road of the Winds: An Archaeological History of the Pacific Islands before European Contact,* 2nd ed. Berkeley: University of California Press.

Klein, R. G. 1992. The archaeology of modern human origins. *Evolutionary Anthropology* 1:5–14.

Kochanski, M. 1987. *Bushcraft: Outdoor Skills and Wilderness Survival.* Vancouver: Lone Pine Publishing.

Koester, R. J. 2008. *Lost Person Behavior: A Search and Rescue Guide on Where to Look – For Land, Air and Water.* Charlottesville, VA: dbS Productions

Kossina, G. 1911. *Herkunft der Germanen.* Leipzig: Kabitzich.

Kramer, K. 2005. *Maya Children: Helpers at the Farm*. Cambridge, MA: Harvard University Press.

Kramer, K. L. 2019. How there got to be so many of us: The evolutionary story of population growth and a life history of cooperation. *Journal of Anthropological Research* 75:472–497.

Krauss, L. M. 2006. *The Physics of Star Trek*. New York: Basic Books.

Kroeber, A. L., and C. Kluckholn. 1952. *Culture; a Critical Review of Concepts and Definitions*. Vol. 47, No. 1. Peabody Museum of American Archaeology and Ethnology. Cambridge, MA: Peabody Museum of American Archaeology and Ethnology, Harvard University.

Kuhn, S. L., and A. E. Clark. 2015. Artifact densities and assemblage formation: Evidence from Tabun Cave. *Journal of Anthropological Archaeology* 38:8–16.

Kuhn, S. L., and M. C. Stiner. 2006. What's a mother to do: A hypothesis about the division of labor among Neandertals and modern humans. *Current Anthropology* 47:953–980.

Kuhn, S. L., and M. C. Stiner. 2007. Paleolithic ornaments: Implications for cognition, demography and identity. *Diogenes* 54:40–48.

Kuper, A. 1988. *The Invention of Primitive Society: Transformations of an Illusion*. London: Routledge.

Lahr, M. M., and R. Foley. 1994. Multiple dispersals and modern human origins. *Evolutionary Anthropology* 3:48–60.

Laland, K. N. 2018. An evolved uniqueness: How we became a different kind of animal. *Scientific American* 319 (August):32–39.

Landau, M. L. 1991. *Narratives of Human Evolution*. New Haven, CT: Yale University Press.

Langley, M. C., N. Amano, et al. 2020. Bows and arrows and complex symbolic displays 48,000 years ago in the South Asian tropics. *Science Advances* 6:eaba3831.

Langley, M. C., C. Clarkson, et al. 2019. Symbolic expression in Pleistocene Sahul, Sunda, and Wallacea. *Quaternary Science Reviews* 221:105883.

Larsen-Peterkin, G. 1993. "Lithic and Organic Hunting Technology in the French Upper Paleolithic," in *Hunting and Animal Exploitation in the Later Paleolithic and Mesolithic of Eurasia*. Edited by G. L. Peterkin, H. Bricker, and P. A. Mellars, pp. 49–68. Washington, DC: American Anthropological Association (Archaeological Paper No. 4).

Laville, H., J.-P. Rigaud, et al. 1980. *Rock Shelters of the Perigord: Geological Stratigraphy and Archaeological Succession*. New York: Academic Press.

Leakey, L. S. B. 1954. *Adam's Ancestors*. London: Methuen.

Leakey, M. D. 1971. *Olduvai Gorge: Excavations in Beds I and II, 1960–1963*. Cambridge: Cambridge University Press.

Lee, R. B. 1979. *The !Kung San: Men, Women and Work in a Foraging Society*. Cambridge: Cambridge University Press.

Lepre, C. J., H. Roche, et al. 2011. An earlier origin for the Acheulian. *Nature* 477:82–85.

Leslie, S., B. Winney, et al. 2015. The fine-scale genetic structure of the British population. *Nature* 519:309–314.

Lesnik, Julie J. 2018. *Edible Insects and Human Evolution*. Gainesville, FL: University of Florida Press.

Levy, T. E. Editor. 1995. *Archaeology of Society in the Holy Land*. New York: Facts on File.

Lewis-Kraus, G. 2019. Game of bones: Is ancient DNA research revealing new truths – Or falling into old traps? *New York Times Sunday Magazine* (January 17):44.

Li, S., C. Schlebusch, et al. 2014. Genetic variation reveals large-scale population expansion and migration during the expansion of Bantu-speaking peoples. *Proceedings of the Royal Society B: Biological Sciences* 281:20141448.

Liebenberg, L. 1990. *The Art of Tracking: The Origin of Science*. Cape Town: David Phillip Publishers.

Lieberman, D. E. 2011. *The Evolution of the Human Head*. Cambridge, MA: Belknap/Harvard University Press.

Lieberman, D. E. 2013. *The Story of the Human Body: Evolution, Health and Disease*. New York: Pantheon Books.

Lieberman, D. E., and J. J. Shea. 1994. Behavioral differences between archaic and modern humans in the Levantine Mousterian. *American Anthropologist* 96:300–332.

Lieberman, P. 1973. *On the Origins of Language*. New York: Macmillan.

Lieberman, P. 2013. *The Unpredictable Species: What Makes Humans Unique*. Princeton, NJ: Princeton University Press.

Lieberman, P., and R. C. McCarthy. 2014. "The Evolution of Speech and Language," in *Handbook of Paleoanthropology*. Edited by W. Henke and I. Tattersall, pp. 1–33. Berlin: Springer.

Lindly, J. M. 2005. *The Mousterian of the Zagros: A Regional Perspective.* Tempe: Arizona State University (Anthropological Research Papers, No. 56).

Lombard, M. 2020. The tip cross-sectional areas of poisoned bone arrowheads from southern Africa. *Evolutionary Anthropology* 33(5):307–315.

Lombard, M. 2021. Variation in hunting weaponry for more than 300,000 years: A tip cross-sectional area study of Middle Stone Age points from southern Africa. *Quaternary Science Reviews* 264:107021.

Lombard, M., and J. J. Shea. 2021. Did Pleistocene Africans use the spearthrower-and-dart? *Evolutionary Anthropology* 30:307–315.

Lundin, C. 2003. *98.6 Degrees: The Art of Keeping Your Ass Alive.* Salt Lake City, UT: Gibbs Smith.

Lundin, C. 2007. *When All Hell Breaks Loose: Stuff You Need to Survive When Disaster Strikes.* Salt Lake City, UT: Gibbs Smith.

Lycett, S. J., and C. J. Bae. 2010. The Movius Line controversy: The state of the debate. *World Archaeology* 42:521–544.

Lyell, C. 1830–1833. *Principles of Geology: Being an Attempt to Explain the Former Changes of the Earth's Surface, by Reference to Causes Now in Operation.* London: John Murray.

Lyman, R. L. 1994. *Vertebrate Taphonomy.* Cambridge: Cambridge University Press.

Lynas, M. 2009. *Six Degrees: Our Future on a Hotter Planet.* Washington, DC: National Geographic.

Maclaren, P. I. R. 1958. *The Fishing Devices of Central and Southern Africa.* Occasional Papers of the Rhodes-Livingstone Museum, No. 12. Livingstone: Rhodes-Livingstone Museum.

MacPhee, R. D. E. 2018. *End of the Megafauna: The Fate of the World's Hugest, Fiercest, and Strangest Animals.* New York: W. W. Norton.

Maier, M. A., P. Barchfeld, et al. 2009. Context specificity of implicit preferences: The case of human preference for red. *Emotion* 9:734–738.

Mann, C. C. 2011. *1493: Uncovering the New World Columbus Created.* New York: Knopf.

Mann, C. C. 2018. *The Wizard and the Prophet: Two Remarkable Scientists and Their Dueling Visions to Shape Tomorrow's World.* New York: Knopf.

Marean, C. W. 1991. Measuring the postdepositional destruction of bone in archaeological assemblages. *Journal of Archaeological Science* 18:677–694.

Marean, C. W. 2010. When the sea saved humanity. *Scientific American* 303:55–61.

Marean, C. W. 2014. The origins and significance of coastal resource use in Africa and Western Eurasia. *Journal of Human Evolution* 77:17–40.

Marean, C. W. 2015. An evolutionary anthropological perspective on modern human origins. *Annual Review of Anthropology* 44:533–556.

Marean, C. W. 2016. The transition to foraging for dense and predictable resources and its impact on the evolution of modern humans. *Philosophical Transactions of the Royal Society B: Biological Sciences* 371.

Marlowe, F. W. 2010. *The Hadza: Hunter-Gatherers of Tanzania.* Berkeley: University of California Press.

Martin, P. S. 1973. The discovery of America: The first Americans may have swept the Western Hemisphere and decimated its fauna within 1000 years. *Science* 179:969–974.

Marzke, M. W. 2013. Tool making, hand morphology and fossil hominins. *Philosophical Transactions of the Royal Society B: Biological Sciences* 368.

Marzke, M. W., and K. L. Wullstein. 1996. Chimpanzee and human grips: A new classification with a focus on evolutionary morphology. *International Journal of Primatology* 17:117–139.

Mayr, E. 2001. *What Evolution Is.* New York: Basic Books.

McBrearty, S., and A. S. Brooks. 2000. The revolution that wasn't: A new interpretation of the origin of modern human behavior. *Journal of Human Evolution* 39:453–563.

McCown, T. D., and A. Keith. 1939. *The Stone Age of Mt. Carmel, vol. 2: The Fossil Human Remains from the Levalloiso-Mousterian.* Oxford: Clarendon Press.

McGrew, W. C. 1992. *Chimpanzee Material Culture: Implications for Human Evolution.* Cambridge: Cambridge University Press.

McPherson, J., and G. McPherson. 1993. *Primitive Wilderness Living and Survival Skills.* Randolph, KS: Prairie Wolf Publications.

McPherson, J., and G. McPherson. 1996. *Primitive Wilderness Living and Survival Skills: Applied and Advanced.* Randolph, KS: Prairie Wolf Publications.

McPherron, S., Z. Alemseged, et al. 2010. Evidence for stone tool-assisted consumption of animal tissues before 3.39 million years ago at Dikika, Ethiopia. *Nature* 466:857–860.

Mears, R. 2003. *Essential Bushcraft: A Handbook of Survival Skills from around the World*. London: Hodder and Stoughton.

Mellars, P. 1989a. Major issues in the emergence of modern humans. *Current Anthropology* 30:349–385.

Mellars, P. 1996a. *The Neanderthal Legacy: An Archaeological Perspective from Western Europe*. Princeton, NJ: Princeton University Press.

Mellars, P. 1996b. "Symbolism, Language, and the Early Human Mind," in *Modelling the Early Human Mind*. Edited by P. Mellars and K. Gibson, pp. 15–32. Cambridge: MacDonald Institute for Archaeological Research.

Mellars, P. 2006. Going east: New genetic and archaeological perspectives on the modern human colonization of Eurasia. *Science* 313:796–800.

Mellars, P. 2007. "Rethinking the Human Revolution: Eurasian and African Perspectives," in *Rethinking the Human Revolution*. Edited by P. Mellars, K. Boyle, O. Bar-Yosef, and C. Stringer, pp. 1–14. Cambridge: McDonald Institute for Archaeological Research Monographs.

Mellars, P., and C. Stringer. Editors. 1989. *The Human Revolution: Behavioural and Biological Perspectives on the Origins of Modern Humans*. Edinburgh: Edinburgh University Press.

Mellars, P. A. 1989b. "Technological Changes at the Middle-Upper Palaeolithic Transition: Economic, Social, and Cognitive Perspectives," in *The Human Revolution: Behavioural and Biological Perspectives on the Origins of Modern Humans*. Edited by P. Mellars and C. Stringer, pp. 338–365. Edinburgh: Edinburgh University Press.

Mellars, P. A. Editor. 1990. *The Emergence of Modern Humans: An Archaeological Perspective*. Edinburgh: Edinburgh University Press.

Meltzer, D. J. 2021. *First Peoples in a New World: Settling Ice Age America*. Cambridge: Cambridge University Press.

Meltzer, D. J., V. T. Holliday, et al. 2014. Chronological evidence fails to support claim of an isochronous widespread layer of cosmic impact indicators dated to 12,800 years ago. *Proceedings of the National Academy of Sciences* 111:E2162.

Mercader, J., H. Barton, et al. 2007. 4,300-year-old chimpanzee sites and the origins of percussive stone technology. *Proceedings of the National Academy of Sciences* 104:3043–3048.

Moffett, M. W. 2019. *The Human Swarm: How Our Societies Arise, Thrive, and Fall*. New York: Basic Books;.

Molnar, S., and I. M. Molnar. 1985. The incidence of enamel hypoplasia among the Krapina Neandertals. *American Anthropologist* 87:536–549.

Morcote-Ríos, G., F. J. Aceituno, et al. 2021. Colonisation and early peopling of the Colombian Amazon during the Late Pleistocene and the Early Holocene: New evidence from La Serranía La Lindosa. *Quaternary International* 578:5–19.

Movius, H. L., Jr. 1944. *Early Man and Pleistocene Stratigraphy in Southeastern and Eastern Asia*. Papers of the Peabody Museum Vol. 13, no. 3. Cambridge, MA.

Movius, H. L., Jr. 1950. A wooden spear of the Third Interglacial Age from Lower Saxony. *Southwestern Journal of Anthropology* 6:139–142.

Muller, M. N., R. A. Wrangham, et al. 2017. *Chimpanzees and Human Evolution*. Cambridge, MA: Belknap Press (Harvard University Press).

Mulvaney, D. J. 1976. "The Chain of Connection: The Material Evidence," in *Tribes and Boundaries in Australia*. Edited by N. Peterson, pp. 72–94. Canberra: Australian Institute for Aboriginal Studies.

Nelson, N. 1916. "Flint-Working by Ishi," in *William Henry Holmes Anniversary Volume*. Edited by F. W. Hodge, pp. 397–402. Washington, DC: Smithsonian Institution.

Neves, W. A., A. G. M. Araujo, et al. 2012. Rock art at the Pleistocene/Holocene boundary in Eastern South America. *PLoS ONE* 7:e32228.

Newcomer, M. H. 1987. "Study and Replication of Bone Tools from Ksar Akil (Lebanon)," in *Ksar Akil, Lebanon: A Technological and Typological Analysis of the Later Palaeolithic Levels of Ksar Akil, Vol. 2. Levels XIII–VI*. Edited by C. A. Bergman, pp. 284–307. British Archaeological Reports International Series, No. 329. Oxford: Oxbow Books.

Ní Leathlobhair, M., A. R. Perri, et al. 2018. The evolutionary history of dogs in the Americas. *Science* 361:81–85.

Nicholson, S. L., R. Hosfield, et al. 2021. Beyond arrows on a map: The dynamics of *Homo sapiens* dispersal and occupation of Arabia during Marine Isotope Stage 5. *Journal of Anthropological Archaeology* 62:101269.

Niekus, M. J. L. T., P. R. B. Kozowyk, et al. 2019. Middle Paleolithic complex technology and a Neandertal tar-backed tool from the Dutch North Sea. *Proceedings of the National Academy of Sciences of the United States of America* 116:22081–22087.

Novella, S. 2018. *The Skeptic's Guide to the Universe: How to Know What's Really Real in a World Increasingly Fake*. New York: Grand Central Publishing.

Novella, S., B. Novella, et al. 2022. *The Skeptics' Guide to the Future: What Yesterday's Science and Science Fiction Tell Us about the World of Tomorrow*. New York: Grand Central Publishing.

Nowell, A. 2010. Defining behavioral modernity in the context of Neandertal and anatomically modern human populations. *Annual Review of Anthropology* 39:437–452.

Nowell, A. 2015. Learning to see and seeing to learn: Children, communities of practice and Pleistocene visual cultures. *Cambridge Archaeological Journal* 25:889–899.

Nowell, A. 2021. *Growing Up in the Ice Age: Fossil and Archaeological Evidence of the Lived Lives of Plio-Pleistocene Children*. Oxford: Oxbow Books.

O'Connell, J. F., J. Allen, et al. 2018. When did *Homo sapiens* first reach Southeast Asia and Sahul? *Proceedings of the National Academy of Sciences* 115:8482.

O'Connor, S., and P. Hiscock. 2014. "The Peopling of Sahul and Near Oceania," in *The Oxford Handbook of Prehistoric Oceania*. Edited by E. Cochrane and T. Hunt, pp. 1–17. Oxford: Oxford University Press.

O'Connor, S., R. Ono, and C. Clarkson. 2011. Pelagic fishing at 42,000 years before the present and the maritime skills of modern humans. *Science* 334 (6059):1117–1121.

Odell, G. H. 2004. *Lithic Analysis*. New York: Kluwer.

Oliver, P. 1987. *Dwellings: The House across the World*. Dallas: University of Texas Press.

Oppenheimer, S. 2004. *The Real Eve: Modern Man's Journey Out of Africa*. New York: Carroll & Graf.

Oswalt, W. H. 1973. *Habitat and Technology: The Evolution of Hunting*. New York: Holt, Rinehart and Winston.

Pargeter, J., and M. Eren. 2017. Quantifying and comparing bipolar versus freehand flake morphologies, production currencies, and reduction energetics during lithic miniaturization. *Lithic Technology* 42(2–3):90–108.

Pargeter, J., and J. T. Faith. 2020. Lithic miniaturization as adaptive strategy: A case study from Boomplaas Cave, South Africa. *Archaeological and Anthropological Sciences* 12:225.

Pargeter, J. A., and J. J. Shea. 2019. Going big vs. going small: Lithic miniaturization in hominin lithic technology. *Evolutionary Anthropology* 28:1–14.

Paulsen, G. 1986. *The Hatchet*. New York: Macmillan.

Péter, H., K. Zuberbühler, et al. 2022. Well-digging in a community of forest-living wild East African chimpanzees (*Pan troglodytes schweinfurthii*). *Primates* 63:355–364.

Petraglia, M., R. Korisettar, et al. 2007. Middle Paleolithic assemblages from the Indian subcontinent before and after the Toba super-eruption. *Science* 317:114–116.

Phillipson, D. W. 1977. *The Later Prehistory of Eastern and Southern Africa*. London: Heinemann.

Phillipson, D. W. 2005. *African Archaeology*, 3rd ed. Cambridge: Cambridge University Press.

Pitts, M., and M. Roberts. 1997. *Fairweather Eden: Life in Britain Half a Million Years Ago as Revealed by the Excavations at Boxgrove*. London: Century.

Pogue, D. 2021. *How to Prepare for Climate Change: A Practical Guide to Surviving the Chaos*. New York: Simon & Schuster.

Pope, G. G. 1989. Bamboo and human evolution. *Natural History* 1989:48–57.

Pycraft, W. P., G. Elliot Smith, et al. 1928. *Rhodesian Man and Associated Remains*. London: British Museum (Natural History).

Radini, A., S. Buckley, et al. 2016. Neanderthals, trees and dental calculus: New evidence from El Sidrón. *Antiquity* 90:290–301.

Rampino, M. R. 2017. Reexamining Lyell's laws. *American Scientist* 1056:223–231.

Rampino, M. R., K. Caldeira, et al. 2021. A pulse of the Earth: A 27.5-Myr underlying cycle in coordinated geological events over the last 260 Myr. *Geoscience Frontiers* 12:101245.

Rampino, M. R., and S. Self. 1992. Volcanic winter and accelerated glaciation following the Toba super-eruption. *Nature* 359:50–52.

Reich, D. 2018. *Who We Are and How We Got Here: Ancient DNA and the New Science of the Human Past*. New York: Pantheon.

Reynolds, N., and F. Riede. 2019. House of cards: Cultural taxonomy and the study of the European Upper Palaeolithic. *Antiquity* 93:1350–1358.

Richerson, P., R. Boyd, et al. 2001. Was agriculture impossible during the Pleistocene but mandatory during the Holocene? A climate change hypothesis. *American Antiquity* 66:387–411.

Rigaud, A. 2001. Les bâtons percés: Décors énigmatiques et fonction possible. *Gallia préhistoire* 43:101–151.

Rizal, Y., K. E. Westaway, et al. 2020. Last appearance of *Homo erectus* at Ngandong, Java, 117,000–108,000 years ago. *Nature* 577:381–385.

Robinson, B. S., J. C. Ort, et al. 2009. Paleoindian aggregation and social context at Bull Brook. *American Antiquity* 74:423–447.

Robinson, M. T. 2016. *The Lost White Tribe: Explorers, Scientists, and the Theory That Changed a Continent*. New York: Oxford University Press.

Roebroeks, W., and P. Villa. 2011. On the earliest evidence for habitual use of fire in Europe. *Proceedings of the National Academy of Sciences* 108:5209–5214.

Rolland, N., and H. L. Dibble. 1990. A new synthesis of Middle Paleolithic variability. *American Antiquity* 55:480–499.

Rose, J. I. 2004. The question of Upper Pleistocene connections between East Africa and South Arabia. *Current Anthropology* 45:551–555.

Rose, J. I., and A. E. Marks. 2014. Out of Arabia and the Middle-Upper Paleolithic transition in the southern Levant. *Quartär* 61:49–85.

Rose, J. I., V. I. Usik, et al. 2011. The Nubian complex of Dhofar, Oman: An African Middle Stone Age industry in southern Arabia. *PLoS ONE* 6:e28239.

Rots, V., and H. Plisson. 2014. Projectiles and the abuse of the use-wear method in a search for impact. *Journal of Archaeological Science* 48:154–165.

Ruditis, P. 2021. *The Star Trek Book: Strange New Worlds Boldly Explained*. New York: DK.

Sackett, J. R. 1991. "Straight Archaeology French Style: The Phylogenetic Paradigm in Historical Perspective," in *Perspectives on the Past: Theoretical Biases in Mediterranean Hunter-Gatherer Research*. Edited by G. Clark, pp. 109–139. Philadelphia: University of Pennsylvania Press.

Saini, A. 2019. *Superior: The Return of Race Science*. Boston: Beacon Press.

Sandgathe, D. M., and B. Hayden. 2003. Did Neanderthals eat inner bark? *Antiquity* 77:709–718.

Scerri, E. 2018. The origin of our species. *New Scientist* 238:34–37.

Scerri, E. M. L. 2013. The Aterian and its place in the North African Middle Stone Age. *Quaternary International* 300:111–130.

Schick, K. D., and N. P. Toth. 1993. *Making Silent Stones Speak: Human Evolution and the Dawn of Technology*. New York: Simon and Schuster.

Schimelpfenig, T. 2016. *National Outdoor Leadership School (NOLS) Wilderness Medicine*, 6th ed. Mechanicsburg, PA: Stackpole Books for the National Outdoor Leadership School (NOLS).

Schmidt, P., L. Bellot-Gurlet, et al. 2018. The unique Solutrean laurel-leaf points of Volgu: Heat-treated or not? *Antiquity* 92:587–602.

Schmidt, P., and A. Morala. 2018. First insights into the technique used for heat treatment of chert at the Solutrean site of Laugerie-Haute, France. *Archaeometry* 60:885–897.

Schutt, B. 2017. *Cannibalism: A Perfectly Natural History*. New York: Algonquin Books.

Serangeli, J., and N. J. Conard. 2015. The behavioral and cultural stratigraphic contexts of the lithic assemblages from Schöningen. *Journal of Human Evolution* 89:287–297.

Shackleton, N. J. 1987. Oxygen isotopes, ice volume, and sea level. *Quaternary Science Reviews* 6:183–190.

Shackley, M. L. 1986. *Still Living?: Yeti, Sasquatch and the Neanderthal Enigma*. New York: W. W. Norton.

Shah, S. 2011. *Fever: How Malaria Has Ruled Humankind for 500,000 Years*. New York: Picador USA.

Shah, S. 2020. *The Next Great Migration: The Beauty and Terror of Life on the Move*. New York: Bloomsbury.

Shea, J. J. 1997. "Middle Paleolithic Spear Point Technology," in *Projectile Technology*. Edited by H. Knecht, pp. 79–106. New York: Plenum.

Shea, J. J. 2003. The Middle Paleolithic of the East Mediterranean Levant. *Journal of World Prehistory* 17:313–394.

Shea, J. J. 2008a. The Middle Stone Age archaeology of the Lower Omo Valley Kibish Formation: Excavations, lithic assemblages, and inferred patterns of early *Homo sapiens* behavior. *Journal of Human Evolution (Special Issue: Paleoanthropology of the Kibish Formation, Southern Ethiopia)* 55:448–485.

Shea, J. J. 2008b. Transitions or turnovers? Climatically-forced extinctions of *Homo sapiens* and Neanderthals in the East Mediterranean Levant. *Quaternary Science Reviews* 27:2253–2270.

Shea, J. J. 2010. "Stone Age Visiting Cards Revisited: A Strategic Perspective on the Lithic Technology of Early Hominin Dispersal," in *Out of Africa 1: The First Hominin Colonization of Eurasia*. Edited by J. G. Fleagle, J. J. Shea, F. E. Grine, A. L. Baden, and R. Leakey, pp. 47–64. New York: Springer.

Shea, J. J. 2011a. *Homo sapiens* is as *Homo sapiens* was: Behavioral variability vs. "behavioral modernity" in Paleolithic archaeology. *Current Anthropology* 52:1–35.

Shea, J. J. 2011b. Refuting a myth of human origins. *American Scientist* 99:128–135.

Shea, J. J. 2011c. "Sorting Out the Muddle in the Middle East: Glynn Isaac's Method of Multiple Working Hypotheses Applied to Theories of Human Evolution in the Late Pleistocene Levant," in *Casting the Net Wide: Papers in Honor of Glynn Isaac and His Approach to Human Origins Research*. Edited by J. M. Sept and D. R. Pilbeam, pp. 213–231. Cambridge, MA: American School of Prehistoric Research/Peabody Museum Press.

Shea, J. J. 2011d. Stone tool analysis and human evolution: Some advice from Uncle Screwtape. *Evolutionary Anthropology* 20:48–53.

Shea, J. J. 2013a. Lithic Modes A–I: A new framework for describing global-scale variation in stone tool technology illustrated with evidence from the East Mediterranean Levant. *Journal of Archaeological Method and Theory* 20:151–186.

Shea, J. J. 2013b. *Stone Tools in the Paleolithic and Neolithic of the Near East: A Guide*. New York: Cambridge University Press.

Shea, J. J. 2014. Sink the Mousterian? Named stone tool industries (NASTIES) as obstacles to investigating hominin evolutionary relationships in the Later Middle Paleolithic Levant. *Quaternary International* 350:169–179.

Shea, J. J. 2015. Making and using stone tools: Advice for learners and teachers and insights for archaeologists. *Lithic Technology* 40:231–248.

Shea, J. J. 2017a. Occasional, obligatory, and habitual stone tool use in hominin evolution. *Evolutionary Anthropology* 26:200–217.

Shea, J. J. 2017b. *Stone Tools in Human Evolution: Behavioral Differences among Technological Primates*. New York: Cambridge University Press.

Shea, J. J. 2020a. *Prehistoric Stone Tools of Eastern Africa: A Guide*. New York: Cambridge University Press.

Shea, J. J. 2020b. Survival Archaeology: A New Agenda for Prehistory's Future. *The Society for American Archaeology Record* 20:17–21, 66.

Shea, J. J., and O. Bar-Yosef. 2005. Who were the Skhul/Qafzeh people? An archaeological perspective on Eurasia's earliest modern humans. *Journal of the Israel Prehistoric Society* 35:449–466.

Shea, J. J., and M. L. Sisk. 2010. Complex projectile technology and *Homo sapiens* dispersal into Western Eurasia. *PaleoAnthropology* 2010:100–122.

Shipman, P. 1981. *The Life History of a Fossil: An Introduction to Taphonomy and Paleoecology*. Cambridge, MA: Harvard University Press.

Shipman, P. 2015. *The Invaders: How Humans and Their Dogs Drove Neanderthals to Extinction*. Cambridge, MA: Belknap/Harvard University Press.

Shipman, P. 2021. *Our Oldest Companions: The Story of the First Dogs*. Cambridge, MA: Belknap Press of Harvard University Press.

Shostak, M. 1990. *Nisa: The Life and Words of a ! Kung Woman*, 4th ed. Cambridge, MA: Harvard University Press.

Silverman, D. J. 2016. *Thundersticks: Firearms and the Violent Transformation of Native America*. Cambridge, MA: Belknap Press.

Simmons, A. 2012. Mediterranean island voyages. *Science* 338:895.

Singer, R., and J. Wymer. 1982. *The Middle Stone Age at Klasies River Mouth in South Africa*. Chicago, IL: University of Chicago Press.

Slimak, L., C. Zanolli, et al. 2022. Modern human incursion into Neanderthal territories

54,000 years ago at Mandrin, France. *Science Advances* 8:eabj9496.

Smith, G. M., K. Ruebens, et al. 2019. Subsistence strategies throughout the African Middle Pleistocene: Faunal evidence for behavioral change and continuity across the Earlier to Middle Stone Age transition. *Journal of Human Evolution* 127:1–20.

Smith, P. E. L. 1964. The Solutrean culture. *Scientific American* 211:86–94.

Smith, T. M., C. Austin, et al. 2018. Wintertime stress, nursing, and lead exposure in Neanderthal children. *Science Advances* 4: eaau9483.

Soffer, O. 1985. *The Upper Paleolithic of the Central Russian Plain*. Orlando, FL: Academic Press.

Sorensen, A., W. Roebroeks, et al. 2014. Fire production in the deep past? The expedient strike-a-light model. *Journal of Archaeological Science* 42:476–486.

Sorensen, A. C., E. Claud, et al. 2018. Neandertal fire-making technology inferred from microwear analysis. *Scientific Reports* 8:10065.

Sorensen, B. 2009. Energy use by Eem Neanderthals. *Journal of Archaeological Science* 36:2201–2205.

Sorenson, M. V., and W. R. Leonard. 2001. Neandertal energetics and foraging efficiency. *Journal of Human Evolution* 40:483–495.

Speth, J. D. 2010. *The Paleoanthropology and Archaeology of Big-Game Hunting: Protein, Fat or Politics?* New York: Springer.

Speth, J. D., and J. L. Clark. 2006. Hunting and overhunting in the Levantine Late Middle Palaeolithic. *Before Farming* 3:Article 1.

Stanford, D. J., and B. A. Bradley. 2012. *Across Atlantic Ice: The Origins of America's Clovis Culture*. Berkeley: University of California Press.

Stern, N. 2009. "The Archaeological Signature of Behavioral Modernity: A Perspective from the Southern Periphery of the Modern Human Range," in *Transitions in Prehistory: Essays in Honor of Ofer Bar-Yosef*. Edited by J. J. Shea and D. E. Lieberman, pp. 255–287. Oxford: Oxbow Books.

Stiner, M. C. 1993. Modern human origins: Faunal perspectives. *Annual Review of Anthropology* 22:55–82.

Stiner, M. C., N. D. Munro, et al. 1999. Paleolithic population growth pulses evidenced by small animal exploitation. *Science* 283:190–194.

Strasser, T., E. Panagopoulou, et al. 2010. Stone Age seafaring in the Mediterranean: Evidence from the Plakias region for Lower Palaeolithic and Mesolithic habitation of Crete. *Hesperia* 79:145–190.

Straus, L. G. 1995. The Upper Paleolithic of Europe: An overview. *Evolutionary Anthropology* 4:4–16.

Straus, L. G., D. J. Meltzer, et al. 2005. Ice Age Atlantis? Exploring the Solutrean-Clovis "connection." *World Archaeology* 37:507–532.

Stringer, C. 2012. *Lone Survivors: How We Came to Be the Only Humans on Earth*. New York: Times Books/Henry Holt.

Sullivan, A. P. 1989. The technology of ceramic reuse: Formation processes and archaeological evidence. *World Archaeology* 21:101–114.

Sykes, B. 2001. *The Seven Daughters of Eve: The Science That Reveals Our Ancestry*. New York: W. W. Norton.

Sykes, R. W. 2020. *Kindred: Neanderthal Life, Love, Death and Art*. New York: Bloomsbury Sigma.

Taborin, Y. 2003. "La mer et les premiers hommes modernes," in *Echanges et diffusion dans la préhistoire méditerranéenne*. Edited by B. Vandermeersch, pp. 113–122. Paris: Editions du Comité des travaux historiques et scientifiques.

Taylor, D. M., and J. R. Doria. 1981. Self-serving and group-serving bias in attribution. *Journal of Social Psychology* 113:201–211.

Taylor, W. W. 1948. *A Study of Archaeology*. Washington, DC: American Anthropological Association (Memoir 69).

Tchernov, E. 1988. "The Biogeographical History of the Southern Levant," in *The Zoogeography of Israel*. Edited by Y. Yom-Tov and E. Tchernov, pp. 401–409. Dordrecht: Junk.

Templeton, A. 1999. Races: A genetic and evolutionary perspective. *American Anthropologist* 100:632–650.

Tennie, C., J. Call, et al. 2009. Ratcheting up the ratchet: On the evolution of cumulative culture. *Philosophical Transactions of the Royal Society B: Biological Sciences* 364:2405–2415.

Texier, P.-J., G. Porraz, et al. 2010. A Howiesons Poort tradition of engraving ostrich eggshell containers dated to 60,000 years ago at Diepkloof Rock Shelter, South

Africa. *Proceedings of the National Academy of Sciences* 107:6180–6185.
Theime, H. 1997. Lower Paleolithic hunting spears from Germany. *Nature* 385:807–810.
Thomas, N. 2021. *Voyagers: The Settlement of the Pacific.* New York: Basic Books.
Thomson, D. F. 1939. The seasonal factor in human culture. *Proceedings of the Prehistoric Society* 10:209–221.
Thurston, T. L., and C. T. Fisher. 2007. "Seeking a Richer Harvest: An Introduction to the Archaeology of Subsistence Intensification, Innovation, and Change," in *Seeking a Richer Harvest: The Archaeology of Subsistence Intensification, Innovation, and Change.* Edited by T. L. Thurston and C. T. Fisher, pp. 1–23. New York: Springer.
Tillet, T. 1996. "Behaviour Patterns, Strategies, and Seasonality in the Mousterian site of Prélétang, (Vercours): The Mousterian of the Alps," in *Middle Palaeolithic and Middle Stone Age Settlement Systems.* Edited by N. J. Conard and F. Wendorf, pp. 319–326. Forli: ABACO Edizione.
Tillier, A.-M. 2002. "Investigating the Biological Evidence for Stress and Disease in Levantine Early Anatomically Modern Humans." Human Paleoecology in the Levantine Corridor, Institute for Advanced Studies, Hebrew University, Jerusalem, Israel, 2002, pp. 135–148.
Toups, M. A., A. Kitchen, et al. 2011. Origin of clothing lice indicates early clothing use by anatomically modern humans in Africa. *Molecular Biology and Evolution* 28:29–32.
Towell, C. 2020. *The Survival Handbook,* new ed. New York: DK Publishing.
Trauth, M. H., M. A. Maslin, et al. 2010. Human evolution in a variable environment: The amplifier lakes of Eastern Africa. *Quaternary Science Reviews* 29:2981–2988.
Trigger, B. G. 2006. *A History of Archaeological Thought,* 2nd ed. Cambridge: Cambridge University Press.
Trinkaus, E. 1983. *The Shanidar Neanderthals.* New York: Academic Press.
Trinkaus, E. 1984. "Western Asia," in *The Origins of Modern Humans.* Edited by F. H. Smith and F. Spencer, pp. 251–293. New York: Alan R. Liss.
Trinkaus, E. 2006. Modern human versus Neandertal evolutionary distinctiveness. *Current Anthropology* 47:597–620.

Trinkaus, E., and P. Shipman. 1993. *The Neandertals: Changing the Image of Mankind.* New York: Knopf.
Trinkaus, E., and J. Svoboda. 2005. *Early Modern Human Evolution in Central Europe: The People of Dolní Vestonice and Pavlov.* New York: Oxford University Press.
Tryon, C. A., and J. T. Faith. 2013. Variability in the Middle Stone Age of Eastern Africa. *Current Anthropology* 54 (S8):S234–S254.
Tryon, C. A., J. E. Lewis, et al. 2018. Middle and Later Stone Age chronology of Kisese II rockshelter (UNESCO World Heritage Kondoa Rock-Art Sites), Tanzania. *PLoS ONE* 13:e0192029.
Twiss, K. C. 2019. *The Archaeology of Food: Identity, Politics, and Ideology in the Prehistoric and Historic Past.* New York: Cambridge University Press.
Vandiver, P. B., O. Soffer, et al. 1989. The origins of ceramic technology at Dolni Vĵõstonice, Czechoslovakia. *Science* 246:1002–1008.
Vanhaeren, M., and F. d'Errico. 2006. Aurignacian ethno-linguistic geography of Europe revealed by personal ornaments. *Journal of Archaeological Science* 33:1105–1128.
Vanhaeren, M., F. d'Errico, et al. 2006. Middle Paleolithic shell beads in Israel and Algeria. *Science* 312:1785–1788.
Wadley, L., B. Williamson, et al. 2004. Ochre in hafting in Middle Stone Age southern Africa: A practical role. *Antiquity* 78:661–675.
Walker, R. B. 2007. "Hunting in the Late Paleoindian Period Faunal Remains from Dust Cave, Alabama," in *Foragers of the Terminal Pleistocene in North America.* Edited by R. B. Walker and B. N. Driskell, pp. 99–115. Lincoln: University of Nebraska Press.
Waters, M. R., T. W. Stafford, et al. 2020. The age of Clovis – 13,050 to 12,750 cal yr B.P. *Science Advances* 6:eaaz0455.
Wells, S. 2009. *Deep Ancestry: Inside the Genographic Project.* Washington, DC: National Geographic Society.
Werner, D., C. Thurman, et al. 2010. *Where There Is No Doctor: A Village Health Care Handbook.* Berkeley, CA: Hesperian.
White, J. P., and J. F. O'Connell. 1982. *A Prehistory of Australia, New Guinea and Sahul.* New York: Academic Press.
White, R. 1986. *Dark Caves, Bright Visions.* New York: American Museum of Natural History.

Whiten, A., J. Goodall, et al. 1999. Cultures in chimpanzees. *Nature* 399:682–685.

Whittaker, J. C. 1994. *Flintknapping: Making and Understanding Stone Tools*. Austin: University of Texas Press.

Whittaker, J. C. 2004. *American Flintknappers: Stone Age Art in the Age of Computers*. Austin: University of Texas Press.

Wilkins, J., and M. Chazan. 2012. Blade production ~500 thousand years ago at Kathu Pan 1, South Africa: Support for a multiple origins hypothesis for early Middle Pleistocene blade technologies. *Journal of Archaeological Science* 39:1883–1900.

Wilkins, J., B. J. Schoville, et al. 2012. Evidence for early hafted hunting technology. *Science* 338:942–946.

Will, M., A. Mackay, et al. 2015. Implications of Nubian-like core reduction systems in southern Africa for the identification of early modern human dispersals. *PLoS ONE* 10: e0131824.

Willoughby, P. R. 2007. *The Evolution of Modern Humans in Africa: A Comprehensive Guide*. New York: Altamira.

Wilmsen, E. N. 1989. *Land Filled with Flies: A Political Economy of the Kalahari*. Chicago, IL: University of Chicago Press.

Wobst, H. M. 1974. Boundary conditions or paleolithic social systems: A simulation approach. *American Antiquity* 39:303–309.

Wobst, M. H. 1977. "Stylistic Behavior and Information Exchange," in *For the Director, Research Essays in Honor of James B. Griffin*. Edited by C. Cleland, pp. 317–342. Ann Arbor: Museum of Anthropology, University of Michigan (Anthropology Paper No. 61).

Wolf, E. R. 1982. *Europe and the People without History*. Berkeley: University of California Press.

Wolpoff, M., and A. Thorne. 2003. The multiregional evolution of humans. *Scientific American* 13:46–53.

Wolpoff, M. H., and R. Caspari. 1997. *Race and Human Evolution: A Fatal Attraction*. New York: Simon and Schuster.

Wrangham, R. W. 1999. Evolution of coalitionary killing. *Yearbook of Physical Anthropology* 42:1–30.

Wrangham, R. W. 2009. *Catching Fire: How Cooking Made Us Human*. New York: Basic Books.

Wrangham, R. W. 2018. Two types of aggression in human evolution. *Proceedings of the National Academy of Sciences* 115:245.

Wrangham, R. W. 2019. *The Goodness Paradox: The Strange Relationship between Virtue and Violence in Human Evolution*. New York: Pantheon.

Wynn, T., and F. L. Coolidge. 2011. *How to Think like a Neanderthal*. Oxford: Oxford University Press.

Xia, L., A. Robock, et al. 2022. Global food insecurity and famine from reduced crop, marine fishery and livestock production due to climate disruption from nuclear war soot injection. *Nature Food* 3:586–596.

Yaroshevich, A., D. Kaufman, et al. 2021. Weapons in transition: Reappraisal of the origin of complex projectiles in the Levant based on the Boker Tachtit stratigraphic sequence. *Journal of Archaeological Science* 131:105381.

Yellen, J. 1977. *Archaeological Approaches to the Present: Models for Reconstructing the Past*. New York: Academic Press.

Yellen, J., A. Brooks, et al. 2005. The archaeology of the Aduma Middle Stone Age sites in the Awash Valley, Ethiopia. *PaleoAnthropology* 10:25–100.

Yellen, J. E., A. S. Brooks, et al. 1995. A Middle Stone Age Worked Bone Industry from Katanda, Upper Semliki Valley, Zaire. *Science* 268:553–556.

Zahavi, A., and A. Zahavi. 1997. *The Handicap Principle: A Missing Piece of Darwin's Puzzle*. Oxford: Oxford University Press.

Zaidner, Y., L. Centi, et al. 2021. Middle Pleistocene *Homo* behavior and culture at 140,000 to 120,000 years ago and interactions with *Homo sapiens*. *Science* 372:1429–1433.

Zilhao, J. 2011. "Aliens from Outer Time? Why the 'Human Revolution' Is Wrong, and Where Do We Go from Here?," in *Continuity and Discontinuity in the Peopling of Europe: One Hundred Fifty Years of Neanderthal Study*. Edited by S. Condemi and G.-C. Weniger, pp. 331–366. New York: Springer.

Zilhão, J., D. E. Angelucci, et al. 2020. Last Interglacial Iberian Neandertals as fisher-hunter-gatherers. *Science* 367:eaaz7943.

INDEX

Abdur Reef (Eritrea), 91
abraded-edge tools, 41
Abri Pataud (France), 184, 187
Afro-Asiatic human origination zone, 131
aggression management, 79
'Ain Difla Rockshelter (Jordan), 120
Al Wusta (Saudi Arabia), 120
Alpine Ice Ages, 27
Amud Cave (Israel), 120, 135, 159, 162
Anakena (Easter Island/Rapa Nui), 263
ancestral survival skills, 3, 16, 64, 74, 80,
    106, 113, 127, 148, 150, 172, 176, 180,
    200, 203, 221–222, 242, 267, 290,
    297–299
  endurance bipedalism, 76–77
  hyperprosociality, 74–80
  language and quantal speech, 77–79
  powerful precision grasping, 74–75
  predictive hallucination, 75–76
Ancient Africans
  archaeology, 96–100
  geography: the "four Africas", 87–90
  hominin fossils, 92–96
  important paleoanthropological sites,
    90–93
  interpretive issues about, 105–112
  survival strategies, 100–105
animal husbandry, 232
Anthropocene, 27
Anzick (Montana, USA), 212, 215, 218
'Aoa Valley (Tutuila, Samoa), 262
Arch Lake (Texas, USA), 212
archaeological stone tool industries and
    ceramic wares, 58–59
Arctic, peopling of, 274–275
Ardipithecus kaddaba, 51
Ardipithecus ramidus, 51

Arlington Springs (Santa Rosa Island,
    California, USA), 212, 215
arrows on maps, 64–66
Arroyo Seco 2 (Argentina), 213, 215
artifacts, 35–46
  ceramics, 43
  stone tools, 35–43
  of wood, cordage, bone, and shell, 45–46
Atapuerca Sima de los Huesos (Spain), 92,
    158
Atlantis problem, prehistory's, 85–86
Auel, Jean, 177
Aurignacian industry, 187
Australopithecus, 51
Austronesian, languages, peoples, 265
Azraq Oasis (Jordan), 120

Bacho Kiro (Bulgaria), 183–184
backed knives, 41
backed/truncated pieces, 29
bamboo, 148
Bantu Expansions, 248–253
behavioral differences
  Ancient Africans and *H. heidelbergensis*,
    105–106
  Early Eurasians vs. Neanderthals,
    199–200
  First Asians vs. Ancient Africans, 127–128
  Neanderthals vs. early (> 45 Ka) humans,
    172–174
  Pleistocene Americans vs. Early
    Eurasians, 222
  Southeast Asians, Sahulians, and First
    Asians, 148–149
Bellows Dune (O'ahu, Hawaiian Islands),
    263
Berelekh (Siberia, Russia), 211–212

Beringia, 207
bifacial hierarchical cores (BHCs), 40
biostratigraphy, 29
bipolar cores, 37
Biqat Quneitra (Israel), 120, 159, 169
Bismarck Archipelago, 146
Black Death, the, 281
Blackwater Draw (New Mexico, USA), 214
Blombos Cave (South Africa), 91, 99–100, 104
Bluefish Caves (Yukon, Canada), 211–212
boats, bows, and beads, 113
Bobongara (Huon Peninsula, New Guinea), 140, 149
Bodo (Middle Awash Valley, Ethiopia), 91, 93
Boker Tachtit (Israel), 120
bone-degreasing, 196
Border Cave (South Africa), 91, 94
bow and arrow, 19, 113, 146, 174, 195–196, 220, 247, 275
bow fishing, 113
bowl (ceramic), 43
Buang Merabak (Guinea, New Ireland), 262
Bull Brook (Massachusetts, USA), 214
Buran-Kaya III (Crimea, Ukraine), 184
burins, 41

Cactus Hill (Virginia, USA), 211, 213–214
Callao Cave (Luzon Island, Philippines), 140
Cameron, Claire, 177
Campanian Ignimbrite eruption, 202
Carpenter's Gap 1 (Australia), 140
catarrhines (Old World monkeys), 50
cave art, 190
celts, 29
ceramics and migrations, a cautionary note, 292
Cerro Tres Tetas (Argentina), 213, 215
chains of connection, 109
Charlie Lake Cave (British Columbia, Canada), 214
Chelechol ra Orrak (Palau), 262
chimera, 105
chimpanzee cultures, 59
Chiquihuite Cave (Zacatecas, Mexico), 211–212
Clan of the Cave Bear, The (1980 novel), 177
Clark's Modes 1–6, 43
"Clovis first" hypothesis, 225
Clovis phenomenon, 207, 211, 221

Clovis points, 218
"coastal route" hypothesis, 223
Colby (Wyoming, USA), 214
Combe Grenal (France), 162, 167
commensal species, 53
complex projectile weapons, 16, 125, 170, 195, 200, 247, 291, 295, 298
conchoidal fracture, 36
conditions affecting population movements
  Africa, 90
  Neanderthal country, 157–158
  Northern Eurasia, 182–183
  Pacific Ocean islands, 260–261
  Pleistocene Americas and Beringia, 208–211
  Southeast Asia and Sahul, 139
  Southern Asia, 118–119
confirmation bias, 4, 76
cordage, 81–82
Cordilleran ice sheet, 209
cores, 36
cores-on-flakes, 41
Covid-19 pandemic, 277
coyotes (*Canis latrans*), 65
crag, 157
Cro-Magnon, 180
Cro-Magnon (France), 184, 192
cryptic rich, 280
Cuddie Springs (Australia), 140
cultural differences among living humans, 59–61
cultural periodization, 30
culture history, 9
"curse of the platonic ideal," 239

Dance of the Tiger (1980 novel), 177
de Acosta, José, 210
"Death of the Hired Man, The" (1914 poem), 246
Dederiyeh Cave (Syria, 159
"definite-article" cultures, 57–58
Denisova Cave (Russia), 184
Denisovans, 62
Dent (Colorado, USA), 214
Devil's Lair (Australia), 140
DeVore, Irven, 80
diaspora, 290
Diepkloof Rockshelter (South Africa), 91, 101
differences
  among humans, 55–61
  early humans vs. living humans, 296–297
  humans vs. other animals, 52–55

Index

dine and dash, 172
dingoes, 192
dispersal, 5
dogs, 12, 192, 196
Dolni Vestonice (Czech Republic), 184–185, 187, 192, 194
Domebo (Oklahoma (USA), 214
Donner Party, 170
double-hulled sailing vessels, 268
Doura Cave (Syria), 120
Dry Creek (Alaska, USA), 211–212
Dust Cave (Alabama, USA), 220

Early Eurasians, 180–203
   archaeology, 187–192
   art and personal adornment, 190–191
   biotechnology: wolf-dogs, 192
   distinctive archaeological record, 200–202
   fossils, 183–186
   geography, 180–183
   important paleoanthropological sites, 183
   interpretive issues, 199–203
   pyrotechnology, 191–192
   survival strategies, 192–199
early *Homo*, 51
East Turkana FxJj 20 (Kenya), 91, 99
Easter Island/Rapa Nui, 265
ecosystem engineering, 232–234
ecotones, 156
Ehrlich, Paul, 278
El Kowm Oasis (Syria), 120
El Mnasra Cave (Morocco), 91
El Sidron (Spain), 159, 166
Elandsfontein (South Africa), 91, 93
electron spin resonance (ESR) dating, 25
elite panic, 279
Eliyeh Springs (Kenya), 91, 93
Elizabeth I, 48
elongated nonhierarchical cores, 40
endurance bipedalism, 76
explaining the past, 14–16
   comparative approach, 15–16
   narrative approaches, 11–14
extinction, human
   likely extinction threats, 283–286
   pseudo-extinction, 286–289
   unlikely extinction threats, 276–283

Fa-Hien Lena (Sri Lanka), 120
Fais Island middens (Fais Island, Carolines), 262
Feldhöfer (Germany), 159

Fell's Cave (Chile), 213, 215
Fenfan (Chuuk), 262
Fenn Cache (USA), 219
Finney, Ben, 267
Firelands (Ohio, USA), 211, 213
firemaking, 80–81
First Asians, 116–132
   archaeology, 122–124
   geography, 116–119
   hominin fossils, 119–122
   important paleoanthropological sites, 119
   survival strategies, 124–127
Fishtail Point Tradition, 225
flake points, 41
flakes, 36
Florisbad (South Africa), 91, 94, 99
fluted points, 218
foliate points, 40, 107
folk biology, 55
food producers, 230–253
   Bantu expansions case study, 248–253
   migrations by, 244–246
   migrations by, detecting, 246–253
food production, 230–239
   consequences, 237–239
   defined, 230–234
   detecting, 242–244
   origins, 234–237
   survival archaeology perspective, 239–242
foraminifera, 29
fossils, 31–35
   coprolites, 35
   describing, 32–33
   taphonomy, 33–34
   tool vs. tooth marks, 34–35
Friedkin (Texas, USA), 211, 213
Fumane Cave (Italy), 184
future human migrations, 269–273
   extraterrestrial migrations, 271–273
   terrestrial migrations, 269–273

Gademotta-Kulkuletti (Ethiopia), 91
Garrod, Dorothy, 133
Geissenklösterle (Germany), 184
genes, 46–48
   "for" genes, 48
   haplogroups, 47–48
genetic history, 10
genus *Homo*, 51–52
geochronology, 22–31
   chronostratigraphy, 26–30
   geochronometric dating, 23–26
   stratigraphic dating, 22–23

geological epochs, 26
geometric microliths, 41
Gesher Benot Yaacov (Israel), 99
ghost marriages (fossils and stone tool industries), 153
glacial amnesia, 282
Golding, William, 177
Gorham's and Vanguard caves (Gibraltar, UK), 159
Goyet Cave (Belgium), 184, 192
grammar, 77
Greenland Norse, 275
Grimaldi Caves (Monaco), 184–185
Grisly Folk, The (1921 book), 178
Grotta de Cavallo (Italy), 184
Grotte des Contrabandiers (Morocco), 91, 100
Grotte des Pigeons (Morocco), 91
groundstone tools, 29, 36

hafting revolution, 103
handstones and grinding slabs, 41, 243
Hane (Ua Huku, Marquesas), 263
Hansel and Gretel fallacy, 203
Hatchet, The (1986 novel), 111
Hathnora/Narmada (India), 120
Haua Fteah Cave (Libya), 90–91
Hawai'i, 265
Hebior (Wisconsin, USA), 211, 213
Heinrich H5 event, 176
Henderson (Pitcairn Group), 263
"hero's journey" folktale, 14
Herto and Aduma (Middle Awash Valley, Ethiopia), 91, 94
Hofmeyr (South Africa), 91, 94
Hohe Fels (Germany), 184, 187
Höhenstadel (Germany), 190
Hēkūle'a experiment, 266
Holocene Epoch, 26
holotype, 62
hominidae, 50
hominin alpha taxonomy, 62–63
hominins, 50–51
Homo erectus, 52
Homo ergaster, 51
Homo floresiensis, 142
Homo habilis, 51
Homo heidelbergensis, 92–94
Homo longi ("Dragon Man"), 63
Homo luzonensis, 142
Homo naledi, 96
Homo sapiens, 52
Homo skepticus, 112

Hoyo Negro (Yucatan, Mexico), 212
Huaca Preita (Peru), 213, 215
Huanglong Cave (China), 184
human culture, five key properties of, 59–61
humans (*Homo sapiens*), 52
humans as primates, 50–52
Hummal (Syria), 120
hypergyny, 245
hyperprosociality, 79, 111

ice-free corridor, 223–224
Industrial Era, 292
infiltration hypothesis, 110–112
influenza pandemic (1918–1920), 281
Inheritors, The (1955 novel), 177
Integrative Ancestral Survival Skills Hypothesis, 82, 290
intensification, 238
International Radiocarbon Year, 24
Interpleniglacial, 29
ironmaking, 252
Ishi (Yahi), 13
isolated human societies, 242
Ivane Valley (New Guinea), 140
Iwo Eleru (Nigeria), 91, 96

Jake Bluff (Oklahoma, USA), 214
jar (ceramic), 43
J-curve model, 278
Jebel Irhoud (Morocco), 91, 94
joint attention, 54
jug/storage vessel, 43

Kabwe (Zambia), 91, 93, 101
Kalahari Desert, 89
Kalambo Falls (Zambia), 91–92, 99
Kalundu wares, 249
Kara-Bom (Russia), 184
Karaïn Cave (Turkey), 159, 175
Katanda (Democratic Republic of Congo), 91, 102
Kathu Pan 1 (South Africa), 91, 103
Kebara Cave (Israel), 120, 135, 155, 159, 162, 167, 178
Keilor (Victoria, Australia), 141
"kelp highway" hypothesis, 223
Kennewick (Washington, USA), 212
Kent's Cavern (England, UK), 184
Kenyanthropus platyops, 51
Kilu (Buka), 262
Klasies River Mouth (South Africa), 91–92, 94, 101

Kostienki Site Complex (Russia), 187, 192
Krapina (Croatia), 159
Ksar Akil Rockshelter (Lebanon), 120
K-T extinction event, 284
kulturkreislehre, 57
Kupona na Dari (New Britain), 262
Kurtén, Björn, 177
Kwajelein (Marshall Islands), 262
Kwale wares, 249

La Ferrassie (France), 162
La Micoque (France), 162
La Prele, Wyoming (USA), 214
La Quina (France), 162
La Riera Rockshelter (Spain), 185, 187
La Serranía la Lindos (Colombia), 214, 221
Lagar Velho (Portugal), 183–184, 191
Lake Mungo (Australia), 140–141, 145
Lake Ndutu (Tanzania), 91, 93
Lange-Ferguson (South Dakota, USA), 214
language and quantal speech, 77
Lapa do Boquete (Brazil), 213, 215
Lapa do Santo (Brazil), 214, 221
Lapita Site 13 (New Caledonia), 262
Lascaux Cave (France), 190
Last Glacial Maximum (LGM), 29, 211, 223, 263, 291
Last Interglacial, 29
Last Neanderthal, The (2017 novel), 177
Later Levantine Mousterian industry, 162
Laugerie Haute (France), 184
Laura (Majuro, Marshall Islands), 262
Laurentian ice sheet, 210
Le Moustier (France), 161
Leang Bulu' Sipong 4 (Indonesia), 140
Lehringen (Germany), 159, 170
Liang Bua (Flores, Indonesia), 140, 142
Lindsay (Montana, USA), 211, 213
Linnaeus, Carolus, 1
Little John (Yukon, Canada), 211–212
London, Jack, 168
long core tools (LCTs), 40
Lord of the Flies, The (1954 novel), 111
Lubang Jeriji Saléh (East Kalimantan [Borneo]), 140, 149
Lubbock Lake (Texas, USA), 211, 213
Luzia (Brazil), 212
Luzia 1 fossil, 215

Madjedbebe Rockshelter (Australia), 140–141, 144, 146, 149
Mammoth Steppe, 157, 182, 208

Mamontovaya-Kurya (Russia), 184
Mandrin Cave (France), 184, 204
Mandu Mandu Creek Rockshelter (Australia), 140
Manis (Washington, USA), 211, 213
Manot Cave (Israel), 120
Marine Isotope Stages, 27
Matenkupkum (New Ireland), 262
McCown, Theodore, 133
Mead (Alaska, USA), 211–212
Meadowcroft Rockshelter (Pennsylvania, USA), 213
Mediterranean Europe, mystery of, 204–206
Melka Kunturé (Ethiopia), 91
memory culture, 69
Mezerich (Ukraine), 184, 193
Mezin 22 (Ukraine), 184, 193
Mezmaiskaya Cave (Russia), 185
microliths, 41, 108, 129
Middle Awash Valley (Ethiopia), 90
migration, 5 *See also under* food producers; migration vs. dispersal
  in deep-time prehistory, 290
  how fast and how far, 254–255
  by hunter-gatherers?, 253
migration vs. dispersal
  Africa (Pleistocene), 107–110
  Bantu expansions, 251–253
  Early Eurasians, 202–203
  Neanderthals, 174–175
  Pleistocene Americas, 224–225
  Southeast Asia and Sahul, 149–151
  Southern Asia, 128
minimum number of individuals (MNI), 32
Miocene Epoch, 50
Misliya Cave (Israel), 120
Mitochondrial Eve, 47
Mladec Cave (Czech Republic), 185
Moana (2016 film), 266
Mochena Borago Cave (Ethiopia), 91
modernity, human, 18–21
molecular anthropology, 47
Molodova Site 1 (Ukraine), 159, 167
Monte Verde II (Chile), 213, 215, 219, 222
Moose Creek (Alaska, USA), 211–212
Mormons, 246
mortars and pestles, 41, 243
Moula-Guercey (France), 159, 170
Mount Carmel Man, rise and fall of, 132–136
Mount Toba volcanic eruption, 151
Mousterian, 161

Mousterian (industry), 152
movable feasts, 230
Movius Line, 149
Movius, Hallam L., Jr., 148
Mount Rainier (Washington, USA), 285
Mount Pelée (Martinique), 285
Mount Vesuvius (Italy), 285
Mount Witori (New Britain), eruption of, 264
Mua (Tongatapu, Lapaha), 262
Mughr El Hamamah (Jordan), 120
Mulifanua (Upolu, Samoa), 262
Mumba and Nasera Caves (Tanzania), 91–92
mutually assured destruction (MAD), 280
myelination, 78

Nanggu (SZ-8) (Santa Cruz Group), 262
Nassarius, 98, 100, 109, 126, 173
Natunuku (Viti Levu, Fiji), 262
Nauwalabila 1 (Australia), 140
Nawarla Gabarmang (Australia), 140
Nderit ware, 251
Neanderthal origination zone, 175
Neanderthals, 155–176
  archaeology, 161–166
  extinction, 175–176
  fossils, 158–161
  geography, 155–158
  imagining, 177–179
  important paleoanthropological sites, 158
  interpretive issues, 171–176
  survival strategies, 166–171
Near Oceania, 260
Nenumbo (RF-2) (Santa Cruz Group), 262
Neronian (industry), 204
Nesher Ramla (Israel), 120, 159, 169
"New Colossus, The" (1883 poem), 244
New Zealand, 265
Ngandong (Java, Indonesia), 140–141
Niah Cave (Malaysia), 140–141, 144, 149
niche, 54
Nkope wares, 249
noise to signal ratio, 241
Nubian cores, 128
Nukouru (Micronesia), 262
number of identified specimens (NISP), 32

Obi-Rakhmat (Uzbekistan), 185
Oceanians, 260, 265
oceanic migrations, 256–269
  historic, 258–259
  Pacific Ocean, 259–267

Pacific Ocean: survival archaeology perspective, 267–269
  prehistoric Mediterranean islands, 259
ochre, red, 92, 100, 104, 123, 126, 147, 171, 184, 191, 194, 215
Oligocene Epoch, 50
Olorgesailie (Kenya), 92, 100
Omo Kibish (Ethiopia), 92, 94
Onemea (Taravai Mangareva), 263
optically stimulated luminescence (OSL) dating, 25
Orrorin tugenensis, 51
osseous tools, 45
Oued Djebana (Algeria), 92

Page-Ladson (Florida, USA), 211, 213
Paglicci Cave (Italy), 185
Paisley 5 Mile Point Caves (Oregon, USA), 35, 212, 215, 222
paleoanthropology, 4
paleontology, 31
Pamwak (Manus), 262
Pandanus, 144, 146
Panga Ya Saïdi (Kenya), 92
Pankupiti (Australia), 140
Paranthropus, 51
Parmepar Meethaner (Tasmania), 140
Patho (Maré, Loyalty Islands), 262
patterned imposition of nonintrinsic shape, 55
Paviland Cave (England, UK), 183, 185
Pe'a (To.1) (Tongatapu), 262
peak procedural complexity, 201, 226–228, 295
pebble cores, 40
Pemrang (Yap), 262
percussors (aka hammerstones), 36
perforated stone tools, 41
Pestera Cu Oase (Romania), 183, 185
Petralona (Greece), 158
Piedra Museo (AEP-1) (Argentina), 213, 215
Pinnacle Point Cave 13B (South Africa), 92, 99, 102
plant husbandry, 231–232
plate/platter, 43
Pleistocene Americans, 207–228
  archaeology, 216–227
  Clovis phenomenon, 224–228
  coastal vs. ice-free-corridor routes, 223–224
  fossils, 215–216
  geography, 207–211

Index

important sites, 211–215
interpretive issues, 222–228
megafauna extinctions, 222–223
survival strategies, 219–221
Pleistocene Epoch, 26
"Pleistocene overkill" hypothesis, 225
Pliocene Epoch, 26, 50
Plio-Pleistocene hominins, 51
Plymouth, Massachusetts, 8
Poggetti Vecchi (Italy), 159, 165
polygyny, 245
Polynesia, 260
Popeye the Sailor (cartoon series), 14
Population Bomb, The (1968), 278
population movements, 5–8
   dispersals, 5
   migrations, 5–7
   mixed dispersals and migrations, 8
   transhumance, 7–8
powerful precision grasping, 74
predictive hallucination, 75
Predmosti 1 (Czech Republic, 185, 192
prehistory, deep-time, 2
primates, 50
prismatic blade cores, 40
prismatic blades, 40
Puerto Rico, and Hurricane Maria, 277
Pulemeli (Sava'i, Samoa), 262
pulverizing tools, 41
Purritjara (Australia), 140

Qafzeh Cave (Israel), 120, 166
Qaranipuqa (Labeka, Fiji), 262
Qesem Cave (Israel), 120
quantal speech, 77, 110
quasi-linguistic variation, 99
Quebrada Jaguay (Peru), 213, 215
Quebrada Maní (Chile), 213, 215
questions about human evolution, 8–14
   differences between "who" and "how questions", 12–14
   how questions, 11–12
   who questions, 8–11
   why questions, 14

races, human, 56–57
radiocarbon dating, 24
radiopotassium dating, 25
reasonable assumptions, 82–85
   communications, 84–85
   first aid and medication, 83
   hydration, 83
   nutrition, 83–84

thermoregulation, 83
watercraft, 84
regional refugium hypotheses, 90
Remote Oceania, 260
retouch, 40
retouched pieces, 36
Rime of the Ancient Mariner, The (1798 poem), 267
Rising Star Site Complex (South Africa), 92
Riwi Cave (Australia), 140

Sabaig (Lamotrek, Carolines), 262
Sagan, Carl, 19
Sahel Belt, 88
Sahelanthropus tchadensis, 51
Sahul, 137
Samoa, 265
Sasoa'a ('Upolu, Samoa), 262
Schaefer (Wisconsin, USA), 211, 213
Schoeningen (Germany), 159, 170
scrapers, notches, and denticulates (SNDs), 41
S-curve model, 278
seafaring, experimental, 257–258
Shackleton, Sir Ernest, 4
Shakespeare, William, 48
Shanidar Cave (Iraq), 120, 159, 166
Shawnee-Minisink (Pennsylvania, USA), 220
Sheriden Cave (Ohio, USA), 214
short nonhierarchical cores (SNHCs), 37
Shukbah Cave (Palestinian National Authority), 155, 159
Shulgan-Tash (Kapova) Cave (Russia), 185, 191
Sibudu Cave (South Africa), 92
Singa (Sudan), 92, 94
skeptic gene, 112
Skhul Cave (Israel), 100, 120
Skhul-Qafzeh people, 135
smallpox, 281
snow-probes, 170
Solomon Islands, 146
Solutrean industry, 189
Southeast Asians and Sahulians, 137–152
   archaeology, 142–144
   geography, 137–139
   hominin fossils, 140–142
   important paleoanthropological sites, 139–140
   interpretive issues, 148–151
   survival strategies, 144
spear-thrower and dart, 19, 146, 170, 196, 312

Star Trek, 272
Starosele (Ukraine), 159, 162
stoneworking, 36
Stoneworking Modes A–I, 43
storage pits, 202
strike-a-lights, 168
subspecies, 55
Sunda, 137
Sungir (Russia), 185, 191
survival archaeology, 16, 18, 64, 66–71, 85, 200–201, 290, 293–294, 299, 305, 318
   archaeological evidence, 67–68
   bushcraft, 69–70
   ethnography and ethnoarchaeology, 69
   experimental archaeology, 68–69
   nonhuman primate ethology, 71
   wilderness survival, 70–71
survival challenges, the big six, 71–74
   communication, 73–74
   first aid and medication, 71–72
   hydration, 72
   nutrition, 72–73
   thermoregulation, 72
   transportation, 73–74
Swan Point (Alaska, USA), 211–212
Swartkrans (South Africa), 92, 99
symbolic artifacts, 16, 54, 74–75, 79, 84, 96, 104, 114, 126–127, 147, 159, 171, 173–174, 197, 199–200, 218–219, 221, 226–227, 291, 295
syntax, 77

Tabon Cave (Palawan Island, Philippines), 140
Tabun C1 fossil, 122, 174
Tabun Cave (Israel), 121–122, 159
Tam Pa Ling (Laos), 140
Tangatatu (Mangaia, Cook Islands), 263
tanged pieces, 41, 108
Tarague Beach (Guam, Marianas), 262
technological intensification, 106
technological singularity, 282
teleoliths, 48–49
Temei (Vaitupu, Tuvalu), 262
temper, 43
Teouma (Vanuatu), 262
Terminator, The (1984 film), 283
Terra Amata (France), 103
therianthrope, 147
thermoluminescence (TL) dating, 25
Tianyuan Cave (China), 183, 185
time averaging, 23

Time Machine, The (1888 novel), 11
Titanic (ship), 276
To Build a Fire (1908 short story), 168
To'aga (Manu'a, Samoa), 262
Tolbaga (Siberia, Russia), 185
Tolbor 4 (Mongolia), 185
Tonga, 265
Tor Faraj Rockshelter (Jordan), 121, 159, 162, 167
traction animals, 241, 247
transhumance, 7
trapped electron dating methods (TL, ESR, OSL), 25
Trois Frères Cave (France), 190
Tunguska (Siberia, Russia), 283
Twin Rivers Kopje (Zambia), 92, 108

Üçagizli Cave (Turkey), 121
Ukshi 1 and 5 (Kamchatka Peninsula, Russia), 211–212
Umm el-Tlel (Syria), 121
Unai Bapot (Saipan, Marianas), 262
unifacial hierarchical cores (UHCs), 40
uniformitarianism, 12
Upward Sun River (Alaska, USA), 212, 215
uranium-series dating, 25
Urëwe ceramic ware, 249
Ust'-Ishim (western Siberia, Russia), 185

Vanuatu, 13
Vaotp'otia-Fa'ahia (Hunahine Society Islands), 263
Vatuluma Posovi (Solomon Islands), 262
Vavarina Gora (Siberia, Russia), 185
"Venus" figurines, 197
Volgü (France), 185, 201

Wairau Bar (New Zealand), 263
Walker Road (Alaska, USA), 211–212
Wallacea, 137
Wally's Beach (Alberta, Canada), 211, 213
Wampanoag Patuxet, 8
War of the Worlds, The (1897 novel), 277
warfare, 239
Wells, H. G., 11, 178, 277
Western Stemmed Point Tradition, 224
White Sands (New Mexico, USA), 211–212
Willendorf (Austria), 185
Wonderwerk Cave (South Africa), 92, 99
Würm glacial period, 161

Index

Yabrud Cave (Syria), 121
Yana River (Siberia, Russia), 211–212
Yombon (New Britain), 262
Younger Dryas event, 183, 222
Yuchanyan Cave (China), 185, 187, 192

Zhoukoudian Upper Cave (China), 185, 191
Zionist settlers in Palestine/Israel, 246
zooarchaeology, 31
Zuttiyeh Cave (Israel), 121

Ingram Content Group UK Ltd.
Milton Keynes UK
UKHW030304270723
425861UK00023B/341